Computer Science Handbook

Volume II

Computer Science Handbook
Volume II

Edited by **Tom Halt**

CLANRYE INTERNATIONAL

New Jersey

Published by Clanrye International,
55 Van Reypen Street,
Jersey City, NJ 07306, USA
www.clanryeinternational.com

Computer Science Handbook: Volume II
Edited by Tom Halt

International Standard Book Number: 978-1-63240-112-0 (Hardback)

Contents

Preface

Computer Science is a field that focuses on the study of the applications, principles, and technologies of computing and consequently computers. It involves the study of data and data structures and the algorithms to process these structures, computer-related topics such as artificial intelligence, numerical analysis, operations research, principles of computer architecture - hardware and software, as well as language design, structure, and translation techniques. Computer science is a field that provides a foundation of knowledge for those with career goals in a variety of computer-related and computing professions. It has various subfields that can be divided into a plethora of theoretical and practical disciplines. Computer science is also an interdisciplinary field and has strong connections to other disciplines. Many problems in business, science, health care, engineering and other arenas can be solved efficiently with computers, but finding a solution requires expertise in the field of computer science. This discipline has a wide variety of specialties. Applications of computer science include software systems, computer architecture, artificial intelligence, graphics, software engineering and computational science. This discipline draws from a common core of computer science knowledge and various specialty areas focus on particular problems. This is a field that is rapidly becoming one of fastest growing in the industry and the demand for skilled graduates is also on the rise.

I am grateful to those who put their hard work, effort and expertise into these research projects as well as those who were supportive in this endeavor.

Editor

An Approach to Self-Assembling Swarm Robots Using Multitree Genetic Programming

Jong-Hyun Lee,[1] **Chang Wook Ahn,**[1] **and Jinung An**[2]

[1] *Department of Computer Engineering, Sungkyunkwan University (SKKU), Suwon 440-746, Republic of Korea*
[2] *Robot Research Division, Daegu Gyeongbuk Institute of Science & Technology (DGIST), Daegu 711-873, Republic of Korea*

Correspondence should be addressed to Chang Wook Ahn; cwan@skku.edu

Academic Editors: S.-S. Liaw, S. H. Rubin, and R. Valencia-Garcia

In recent days, self-assembling swarm robots have been studied by a number of researchers due to their advantages such as high efficiency, stability, and scalability. However, there are still critical issues in applying them to practical problems in the real world. The main objective of this study is to develop a novel self-assembling swarm robot algorithm that overcomes the limitations of existing approaches. To this end, multitree genetic programming is newly designed to efficiently discover a set of patterns necessary to carry out the mission of the self-assembling swarm robots. The obtained patterns are then incorporated into their corresponding robot modules. The computational experiments prove the effectiveness of the proposed approach.

1. Introduction

When robots try to successfully complete their mission in various environments, it is necessary to retain high autonomy and intelligence like humans. Robots should employ precise sensors and complex controllers and mount high performance processors in order to attain complete autonomy and intelligence. However, these enhanced devices bring forth the extremely expensive cost in constructing an autonomous robot system. Furthermore, the efficiency of the autonomous robot system dramatically decreases as the working space enlarges [1].

There is a well-known approach to solving the previously mentioned problems, which utilizes numerous robots by adopting swarm intelligence. Swarm intelligence makes a swarm of robots perform their tasks in collaboration with themselves. It denotes that the swarm robots can have a lot of advantages: stability, scalability, robustness, efficiency, and so on. Swarm robotics is a field of research on the swarm of robots, which is working in conjunction with the nature-inspired algorithms (i.e., swarm intelligence). The swarm robotics aims to develop an all-round autonomous machine in various practical areas such as industry, agriculture, fishery,

military, and medical. In recent years, many studies have been carried out on the construction, exploration, national defense, and security fields. In fact, most of the real-world autonomous problems include complex situations and broad working space. Thus, the swarm robotics can be applied to a lot of areas in the sense of improving efficiency on the cost of installation and maintenance [2].

Nevertheless, the swarm robotics still has some problems when applying to practical applications due to the hurdles of the current technologies in constructing the promising self-assembling swarm robots (i.e., module robots). For instance, the motors of module robots lack physical strength. The battery which is contained in the modules cannot be as small as a microsize. A lot of researchers have tried to improve the module robots in order to find a better mechanism for the system [3–5]. In this sense, this paper develops a new control mechanism for the swarm robots by using evolutionary techniques (i.e., genetic programming) as an effort to get over these limitations.

The rest of this paper is organized as follows. In Section 2, we introduce the fundamental knowledge on the self-assembling swarm robots, the oscillator that is the core controller of the system, and the genetic programming (GP). In Section 3, we present the proposed evolutionary self-assembling mechanism for the swarm robots. The experimental results are shown in Section 4. Finally, we conclude this paper in Section 5.

2. Related Work

2.1. Self-Assembling Swarm Robots. A self-assembling swarm robot system (S) consists of robot modules (Ms), which are a kind of robotic cell, denoted by $S = \{M_1, M_2, \ldots, M_N\}$, where N is the number of module robots. The self-assembling in the swarm robotics means that these module robots are able to be combined together in an efficient manner. Each module has two major types of equipments: *motion* and *connection* devices. The former such as rotation motor and joint devices offers the motion power and decides the degree of freedom (DOF) of the system. The latter such as magnet, ring, and hook devices connects the modules together. Also, each module robot requires the inclusion of auxiliary components such as battery, controller, processor, and sensors, which are necessary for the distributed control [6–9]. In principle, the system can transform its own shape into another one suitable to carry out given tasks. Therefore, it can conduct the work which cannot be carried out by a single module because all the robot modules operate in cooperation with themselves. For example, the system may be transformed into the shape of a snake to pass through a pipe. It is also possible to convert the system into the shape of a four-legged animal to walk on rugged roads or climb stairs.

2.2. Oscillator. A central pattern generator (CPG) makes the oscillators define their signal patterns. This CPG concept came from the biological understanding of the neural network in human's brain. In other words, the robots system is to a human and the CPG is to a brain. The CPG is a key element to determine the performance of a system. Thus, the main target of this study is to develop a new mechanism that plays a role of CPG by means of genetic programming (GP).

The oscillator contained in each module is the main issue in the self-assembling robot system that is to be controlled in a distributed fashion [5, 6]. This can be inspired by the observation that each gait of animals works at regular intervals to walk. In this sense, a lot of locomotive robots in recent days are based on the idea of using oscillators, and thus most of recent self-assembling robots have employed oscillators [10–15]. In general locomotive robots, each joint of the robots has its own oscillator which generates a signal for the motion of that joint.

As shown in Figure 1, the angular velocity of each module is defined by an absolute value of the oscillator. Usually, positive/negative values for the angles denote the rotation in clockwise/anticlockwise directions. The examples of the generated oscillations are given in Figure 2. The equation on the oscillator consists of mathematical operators: $\mathbb{F} = \{+, -, \times, \div, \wedge, \sqrt{}, \log, \sin(), \cos(), \ldots\}$. The nonlinear operators such as $\wedge$, $\sqrt{}$, $\log$, $\sin()$, and $\cos()$ are used to represent the repetitive motion of the gaits for locomotion, as shown in Figure 2. In the simple task as given in A of Figure 2, we

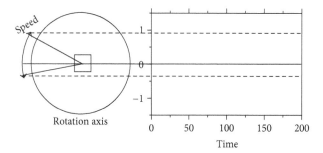

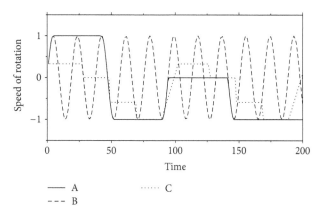

FIGURE 1: The relation between the angular velocity and the value of an oscillator.

FIGURE 2: Examples of the generated patterns of an oscillator. (A) Simple rotation: the full speed to clockwise at t [0, 50] and to anticlockwise at t [50, 100]; (B) repeating the motion of a module in a sine wave; (C) a module repeating some work.

can easily discover a pattern apt for conducting the task. Also, the regular patterns can be made the same as the walking dog (see Figure 3). When the dog walks, he repeats the movement of his legs regularly. We can find out the pattern of the movement without making too much effort. However, it is an NP problem when considering more complex tasks or a large number of modules. In other words, the defined model (i.e., pattern) is very important, but it is difficult to find the optimal model. At this point, GP can be one of the solutions to this kind of NP problem because GP is apt for generating a complex pattern of CPG. Finally, we come up with a novel tool to generate the patterns of oscillators. We are going to explain the details of the proposed approach in Section 3.

2.3. Genetic Programming. GP is a stochastic search mechanism inspired by the biological evolution (e.g., human's evolution) to discover computer programs by which user-defined tasks can be conducted [16]. In principle, GP individuals are a set of evolving computer programs that are represented by mathematical equation, context, grammar, and so on. Thus, GP can handle very complex, nonlinear problems such as symbolic regression. For instance, the symbolic regression problem is considered. The task is to find an optimal curve that covers accurately all the given data. As shown in Figure 4,

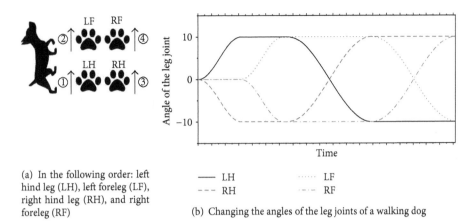

(a) In the following order: left hind leg (LH), left foreleg (LF), right hind leg (RH), and right foreleg (RF)

(b) Changing the angles of the leg joints of a walking dog

FIGURE 3: Dog walking sequence.

the GP discovers a curve that accurately fits the given data as generation passes [17]. This example has shown the outstanding regression performance of the traditional GP.

In general, GP employs a nonlinear tree structure for representing individuals. The trees consist of two types of nodes: *functional* and *terminal*. The former connects the nodes below by a computer program assigned to that node and the latter is the end point consisting of input data and random values. Meanwhile, the fitness function is a measure of how well the current program has evolved. The fitness values give feedback to GP, thereby deciding which individuals are more likely to survive. After that, GP operators (i.e., selection, crossover, and mutation) are sequentially applied. Primarily, the selection narrows down the promising region in the search space. Since a tree representation is employed in GP, the crossover and the mutation are different from those of traditional evolutionary algorithms [18]. In general, GP crossover increases the exploratory power by randomly exchanging partial subtrees of parents and GP mutation maintains the search diversity by replacing a subtree of a parent with a newly generated subtree.

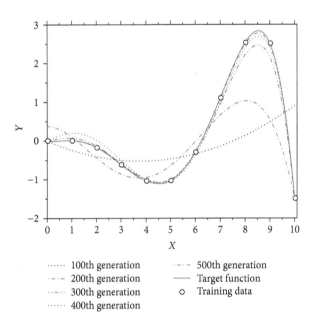

FIGURE 4: An example of symbolic regression. The error of the best individual is decreased as generation passes. The error can be calculated by summing the difference values between the actual data and the fitted data by GP.

3. Proposed GP Approach to Self-Assembling Robots

In this section, we present the proposed GP approach to the CPG for the self-assembling swarm robots. Generating the signal patterns of oscillators, which are fitted to carry out their own mission, requires very complex computation. The state of a module is influenced not only by the rotation of its adjacency modules but also by the motion of almost all modules. Existing simple solutions to these problems resort to only controlling the period and the phase of a sine wave, but they have limitations when generating more complex patterns for practical applications [4, 19]. However, the proposed GP approach is able to generate any signal pattern for each oscillator by collaboratively evolving a set of trees; thus, the self-assembling robots can precisely perform any type of action (mission). As mentioned earlier, GP has

the outstanding performance in finding out a mathematical expression on complicated patterns. Thus, the multitree GP proposed herein is apt for handling the CPG problem in the self-assembling swarm robots.

3.1. Generating Signal Patterns. In the self-assembling swarm robots, the most difficult but crucial task is to define their motion patterns since many motors are incorporated and the role of each motor is altered over time. The aim of this study is to discover an optimal pattern model by GP in order to control the motion direction of the module robots. To this end, the idea is to obtain the angular velocities of the modules from GP individuals. Note that each individual

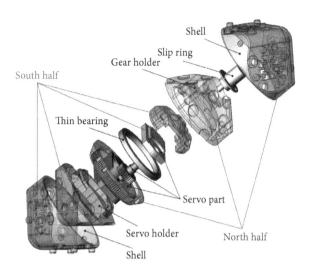

Shell
Slip ring
Gear holder
South half
Thin bearing
Servo part
Servo holder
North half
Shell

FIGURE 5: The structure of Molecube [4].

(of GP) is comprised of multiple trees that amount to the number of module robots. In other words, the ith individual consists of N trees in which N is the number of modules; $I_i = \{T_1^{(i)}, T_2^{(i)}, \ldots, T_N^{(i)}\}$. In addition, the angular velocity of the kth module at the tth time is formulated by

$$\omega_{k,i,t} = \frac{T_k^{(i)}(x_t)}{\max(T)} \times m, \tag{1}$$

where m is the maximum angular velocity. In this equation, the scaling term (i.e., m) is necessary to restrict the output value within $[-m, m]$ since the evaluation values of trees can be too high or too low. The input data x consists of the information on the states of all the modules, such as the velocity information and the conjunction information.

3.2. Module Structure.
The structure of each module is adopted from the Molecubes which are an open-source modular robotics framework [4]. As shown in Figure 5, each module robot is the same as a cube with rounded corners. It consists of two triangular pyramidal halves which are connected with their bases. Their main axes are touching each other. The halves of the cube are able to rotate around their inner motors. The module robot is equipped with an electromechanical connector at its six faces, at which other modules can be connected; thus, its degree of freedom (DOF) is three.

3.3. Process.
In general, the self-assembling robot system consists of a number of modules; $S = \{M_1, M_2, \ldots, M_N\}$ where N is the number of modules and $M_i = \{\omega_i, F_{i,1}, F_{i,2}, \ldots, F_{i,6}\}$ in which each module has one rotation axis. The angular velocity ω_i of the rotation axis corresponding to the ith module is computed from the ith tree of the best individual of GP.

Let $x_{k,i,t} = \{\omega_{k,1,t-1}, \omega_{k,2,t-1}, \ldots, \omega_{k,N,t-1}, F_{i,1}, F_{i,2}, \ldots, F_{i,6}, R\}$ be input variables for creating the ith tree in the kth

individual of GP at the tth time. Moreover, $\omega_{k,i,t-1}$ represents the angular velocity of the ith module (M_i) obtained from the kth individual at the $(t-1)$th time. The binary variable of $F_{i,j}$ (which is time invariant) denotes the information on whether the predefined jth face of M_i is connected with the face of any other module or not, and R is a random number between $[0, 1]$.

As shown in Figure 6, the sequence of the proposed system follows several steps: population initialization, fitness evaluation, preservation of the best individual, judgement on the termination criterion, and performing genetic operators: tournament selection, multitree crossover, and multitree mutation. The iteration of these procedures until satisfying the termination criteria makes the system evolve continually, thereby getting a powerful control model for the practical self-assembling robots. The detailed procedures are explained in the next section.

3.4. Representation and Evaluation.
To evaluate the individuals (i.e., trees) in GP, the functional operators in the tree are calculated along with input variables. Let $Y_i^* \in R^m$ be an optimal value with regard to the ith input, where R^m denotes an m-dimensional real space. In the proposed GP, each individual consists of N trees where N is the number of modules; $I_i = \{T_1^{(i)}, T_2^{(i)}, \ldots, T_N^{(i)}\}$. Consider a set of functions $\mathbf{f} = \{f_1, f_2, \ldots, f_N\}$ in which $f_k : T_k \rightarrow Y_k \in R^m$. Thus, the evaluation of the kth tree of individuals can be performed by $|Y_i^* - Y_i|$. Thus, the CPG problem in the self-assembling swarm robots can be formulated by

$$\arg \min \mathbf{f} = \sqrt{\frac{1}{N} \sum_{i=1}^{N} |Y_i^* - Y_i|^2}. \tag{2}$$

Note that the aim of GP is to discover an optimal set of functions $\mathbf{f}$ which mathematically models the signal patterns of the oscillators of all the modules in order to effectively carry out the given mission.

As shown in Figure 7, each individual which consists of multiple trees is evaluated by computer simulations. To do this, the value obtained from the ith tree is first converted into the angular velocity ω_i. And then, the velocity is utilized to control the ith module (M_i) of the system. The self-assembling system controlled by these angular velocities is monitored to measure their goodness in conducting the given mission. Finally, this goodness becomes the fitness value of that individual of GP. The fitness values of all individuals are evaluated by repeating this process.

The test system (i.e., simulator) is constructed by means of the Molecubes interface [4] which employs an AGEIA PhysX physics engine and an OGRE open-source graphics engine. The goal of this study is to investigate the feasibility of the self-assembling system in various applications. Thus, the achievement factor that assesses the system performance is set by the distance of migration of the whole system. Meanwhile, the functional operators used in the proposed GP are defined as $\mathbb{F} = \{+, -, \times, \div, {}^{\wedge}, \sqrt{}, \log, \sin(), \cos(), \text{AND}, \text{OR}, \text{IF-ELSE}\}$. As

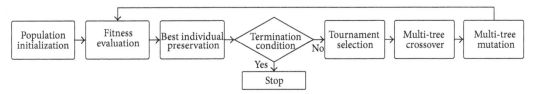

FIGURE 6: The proposed GP framework.

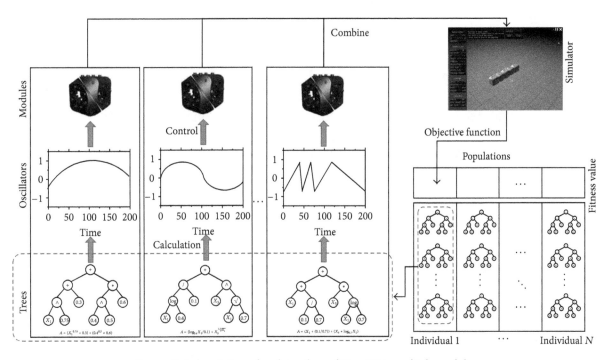

FIGURE 7: A description of applying the multitree GP to multiple modules.

the terminal set, the proposed GP employs the input variables presented in Section 3.3.

3.5. Selection.

There are many feasible selection methods for the proposed GP, such as τ-wise tournament selection, roulette-wheel selection, and elitism selection. In this study, we pick up the τ-wise tournament selection which selects τ individuals in a random manner, and then, the best individual is copied into the selection pool. This selection has a higher probability of preserving the best individual which retains the highest fitness value.

3.6. Crossover.

Conceptually, the multitree GP crossover proposed herein exchanges the randomly selected trees or the subtrees between the parents. Although there are many alternatives to realize the crossover, we implement the proposed GP crossover similar to 1-point crossover of GA in order to preserve the well-discovered motion patterns. The GP crossover conducts two sequential mechanisms: *mixing* and *swapping*. With the two parents, more specifically, the GP crossover carries out the mixing mechanism that exchanges the subtrees of their kth trees at the arbitrary point and the swapping mechanism that swaps their trees from the $(k+1)$th to the Nth positions (see Figure 8). As usual, the subtree

position for crossover is randomly chosen. For instance, consider two parent individuals as follows:

$$I_i = \left\{ T_1^{(i)}, T_2^{(i)}, \ldots, T_{k-1}^{(i)}, T_k^{(i)}, T_{k+1}^{(i)}, \ldots, T_N^{(i)} \right\}, \tag{3a}$$

$$I_j = \left\{ T_1^{(j)}, T_2^{(j)}, \ldots, T_{k-1}^{(j)}, T_k^{(j)}, T_{k+1}^{(j)}, \ldots, T_N^{(j)} \right\}. \tag{3b}$$

As a crossover result, the offspring I_i' and I_j' can be created as

$$I_i' = \left\{ T_1^{(i)}, T_2^{(i)}, \ldots, T_{k-1}^{(i)}, T_k^{(i)'}, T_{k+1}^{(j)}, \ldots, T_N^{(j)} \right\}, \tag{4a}$$

$$I_j' = \left\{ T_1^{(j)}, T_2^{(j)}, \ldots, T_{k-1}^{(j)}, T_k^{(j)'}, T_{k+1}^{(i)}, \ldots, T_N^{(i)} \right\}, \tag{4b}$$

where $T_k^{(i)'}$ and $T_k^{(j)'}$ represent the kth trees of the ith and the jth offspring after the mixing mechanism, respectively.

3.7. Mutation.

In principle, mutation randomly alters some nodes of a chosen tree. As shown in Figure 9, the proposed GP mutation consists of three mechanisms: *pruning*, *growing*, and *modifying*. In the pruning case, a subtree from an arbitrary functional node is replaced with an arbitrary leaf (i.e., terminal) node. In the growing case, an arbitrary leaf

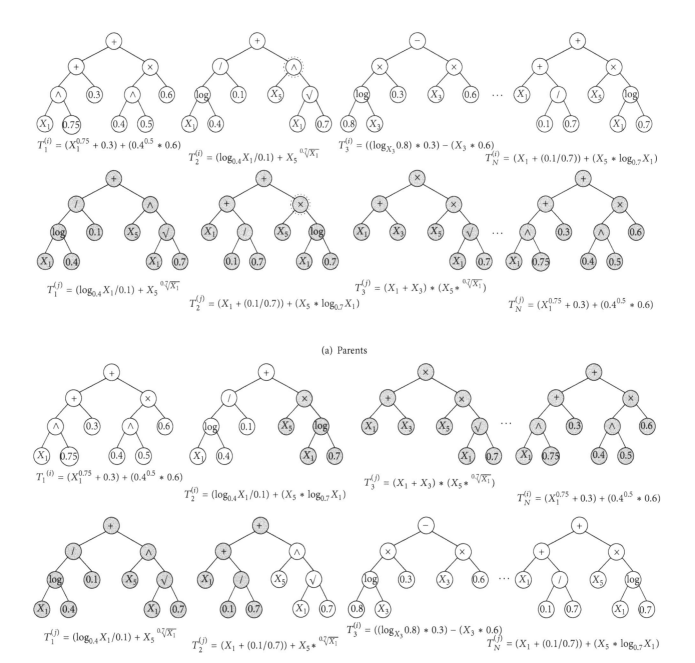

(a) Parents

(b) Offspring

FIGURE 8: An example of the proposed GP crossover.

node is replaced with a randomly created subtree. In the modifying case, an arbitrary functional node is changed by another one. For instance, an ith individual is given as

$$I_i = \left\{ T_1, T_2, \ldots, T_{m_1}, \ldots, T_{m_2}, \ldots, T_{m_n}, \ldots, T_{N-1}, T_N \right\}. \quad (5)$$

The mutation produces an offspring as follows:

$$I_i'' = \left\{ T_1, T_2, \ldots, \widehat{T}_{m_1}, \ldots, \widetilde{T}_{m_2}, \ldots, \overline{T}_{m_n}, \ldots, T_{N-1}, T_N \right\}, \quad (6)$$

where $m_1, m_2, \ldots, m_n$ are randomly chosen and $\widehat{T}, \widetilde{T}$, and $\overline{T}$ denote the results of the growing, the pruning, and the modifying mechanisms, respectively.

In the mutation process, one of these adding nodes (i.e., growing), removing nodes (i.e., pruning), and changing nodes (i.e., modifying) is settled, and then, a mutation point is chosen in a random fashion. The decided mechanism is performed at the mutation point. For instance, if the growing mechanism is conducted at a leaf node, the node type of the selected position is changed from "terminal" to "functional,"

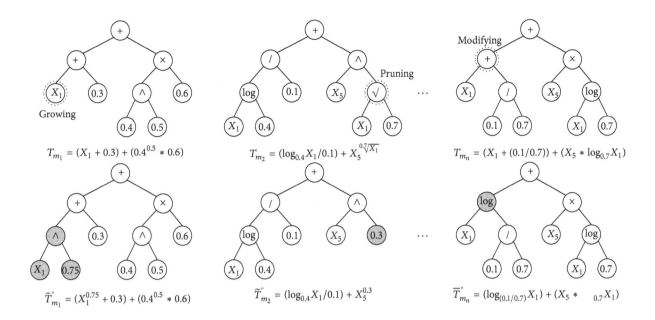

$$T_{m_1} = (X_1 + 0.3) + (0.4^{0.5} * 0.6)$$

$$T_{m_2} = (\log_{0.4} X_1/0.1) + X_5^{0.7\sqrt{X_1}}$$

$$T_{m_n} = (X_1 + (0.1/0.7)) + (X_5 * \log_{0.7} X_1)$$

$$\widehat{T}''_{m_1} = (X_1^{0.75} + 0.3) + (0.4^{0.5} * 0.6)$$

$$\widehat{T}''_{m_2} = (\log_{0.4} X_1/0.1) + X_5^{0.3}$$

$$\overline{T}''_{m_n} = (\log_{(0.1/0.7)} X_1) + (X_5 * {}_{0.7} X_1)$$

FIGURE 9: An example of the proposed GP mutation.

FIGURE 10: The initial configuration of the system.

and then, a randomly generated subtree is inserted into that position.

4. Experimental Results

The proposed approach was tested by a computational experiment in the physical environment. As mentioned earlier, the simulator was constructed on the Molecubes interface using the PhysX and OGRE engines. The goal was to move the robot system as far as possible on the ground within 200 seconds. Only focusing on the effectiveness of the proposed approach, a smaller number of robot modules were employed in this experiment. As shown in Figure 10, moreover, the initial configuration of the system was fixed by the combined five modules which are sequentially sitting on the flat ground. Assume that the gravity is the same as the earth's one and the air resistance is ignored. If a module cannot rotate on the axis due to the impediments, the module stops its rotation.

Moreover, the breakdown of the modules was not considered in this experiment.

For the parameter setting, the population size is 200, the maximum number of generations is 200, and the pairwise tournament selection is used. Moreover, the probabilities of crossover and mutation (i.e., P_c and P_m) are set to 0.8 and 0.2, respectively. These values were determined by the empirical analysis. In addition, the elitism was used to preserve the best individual discovered so far. The initial individuals were randomly generated under the depth limit of ten nodes; each tree was comprised of approximately two hundred nodes. In this experiment, five modules were deployed (i.e., $N = 5$). The functional set was defined as $\mathbb{F} = \{+, -, \times, \div, {}^\wedge, \sqrt{}, \log\}$ and the terminal set was given as $\mathbb{T} = \{\omega_{1,t}, \omega_{2,t}, \ldots, \omega_{5,t}, F_{i,1}, F_{i,2}, \ldots, F_{i,6}, R\}$ (see Section 3.3). In the case of "$\div$," the protected division was used to avoid the error when a numerator is divided by zero. When t is "zero" (i.e., the initial state), the rotation axes of all modules are at a stop; thus, we set $\omega_{k,t=0} = 0$ and $\omega_{k,t=-1} = 0$, for all k.

In Figure 11(a), the signal patterns generated on the five modules (i.e., M_1, M_2, M_3, M_4, and M_5) were obtained by the equation of each tree in the best individual at the 200th generation. Then, the self-assembling system utilized the obtained patterns. As shown in Figure 12, the proposed system could move ahead about 12 meters from the starting position during 200 seconds. In this figure, we could also find that the proposed system is evolving because its migration distance continuously increases from approximately 4 meters at the first generation to about 12 meters at the 200th generation. Note that the results in Figure 12 were averaged over ten runs in order to take into account the stochastic nature of GP.

To assure the effectiveness of the proposed GP approach, we performed a comparative experiment in which a simple

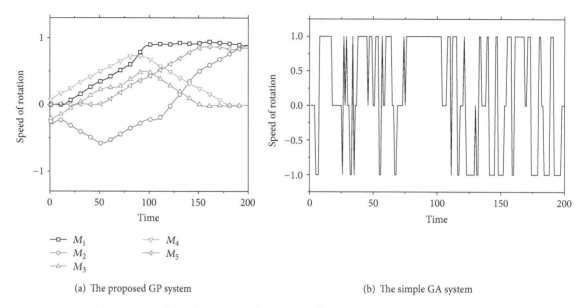

(a) The proposed GP system

(b) The simple GA system

FIGURE 11: The generated signal patterns of the oscillators by the best individual at the 200th generation.

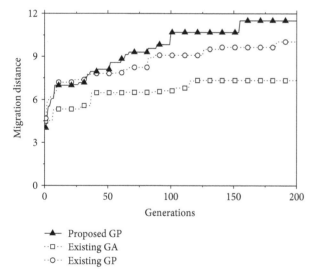

FIGURE 12: The migration distance achieved by the best individual for 200 seconds as generation progresses.

GA [18] was employed. In the GA system, each module had three states of the angular velocity: $\{-m, 0, m\}$. An individual was comprised of five chromosomes since five modules were used in this experiment. Each chromosome in the GA individual was set to 200 units, which represents the angular velocity of a module at every second. The parameter setting of GA was given as follows: the population size and the number of generations were set to 200 and 200, respectively, the pairwise tournament selection was used, and 1-point crossover and uniform mutation were applied with their probabilities of 0.7 and 0.05, respectively. They were naturally decided by the empirical observation. The elitism was employed as well. The generated signal from the best individual in the GA system is shown in Figure 11(b). In this figure, we only

plotted one signal pattern among the generated signals due to the difficulties in visualizing many overlapping signals. It was also observed that the GA system gradually improves their performance since the migration distance achieved by the GA system changes from around 4 meters at the first generation to about 7 meters at the last generation (see Figure 12). Nonetheless, this result showed that the performance of the proposed GP approach is much better than the that of GA system at all generations. While the GA system got stuck completely after the 120th generation, the proposed GP system continuously improved its performance. This implies that the proposed GP approach becomes more and more efficient as generation passes, as compared with the GA system.

For the purpose of comparison, another experiment was conducted on the existing GP approach [19]. The parameter setting used in the proposed GP approach was employed in the existing GP system. In Figure 12, it was shown that the migration distance of the existing GP system amounts to around 10 meters at the end of the generation: the proposed GP system moves faster and further than the existing GP system.

On the other hand, the movement traces in Figure 13 demonstrate that the structure of the proposed system was transformed into a suitable shape to carry out their task. For instance, the system in Figure 13(a) tried to move as far as possible by means of a structure similar to the initial one. As time goes on, the shape of the proposed system was able to be transformed into a more complex structure suitable to move faster and further than the earlier systems.

5. Conclusion

In this paper, we proposed a control algorithm for the self-assembling swarm robot system. The main idea was to generate the signal patterns of oscillators by means of

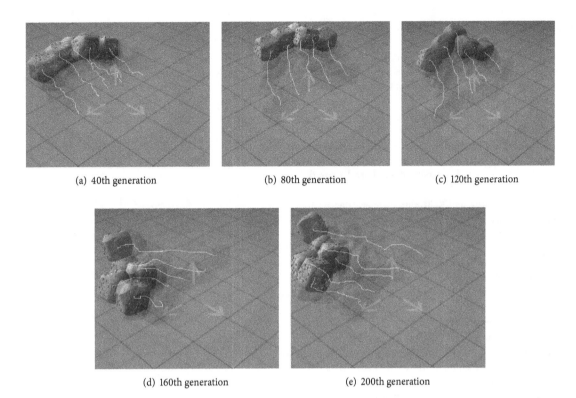

(a) 40th generation

(b) 80th generation

(c) 120th generation

(d) 160th generation

(e) 200th generation

FIGURE 13: The movement traces of the proposed system as generation passes.

GP in order to perform the locomotion of the system. To this end, new multitree GP that is apt for generating the signal patterns of robot modules for the locomotion was developed. The experimental results showed that the proposed system achieves acceptable performance due to its evolutionary nature. Moreover, the proposed GP approach outperformed the existing GA and GP methods. Although there were limitations in the experiment, such as the time-consuming simulation, a few modules, a smaller population size, and the small number of generations, the proposed system sufficiently showed great promise to design the oscillators promising for the locomotion of the self-assembling robot system.

As the future work, we are going to improve the processing speed of the proposed system to overcome the aforementioned limitations. In terms of scalability, the system can be enhanced by incorporating the domain-specific knowledge into the crossover and mutation operators. In addition, we will make progress on the research on other types of task, such as jumping, swimming, and running. It is expected that the proposed GP-based self-assembling swarm robot system provides a new gait of locomotion in carrying out their mission.

Acknowledgment

This work was supported by the DGIST R&D Program of the Ministry of Education, Science and Technology of the Republic of Korea (13-BD-01).

References

[1] E. Bonabeau, M. Dorigo, and G. Theraulaz, *Swarm Intelligence: From Natural to Artificial Systems*, Oxford University Press, New York, NY, USA, 1999.

[2] S. Garnier, J. Gautrais, and G. Theraulaz, "The biological principals of swarm intelligence," *Swarm Intelligence*, vol. 1, no. 1, pp. 3–31, 2007.

[3] K. Sims, "Evolving virtual creatures," in *Proceedings of the 21st International ACM Conference on Computer Graphics and Interactive Techniques (SIGGRAPH '94)*, pp. 15–22, 1994.

[4] A. Chen, "Modeling Molecubes with AGEIA PhysX," 2007.

[5] R. D. Beer, "Toward the evolution of dynamical neural networks for minimally cognitive behavior," in *Proceedings of the 4th International Conference on Simulation of Adaptive Behavior*, pp. 421–429, 1996.

[6] J. C. Gallagher, R. D. Beer, K. S. Espenschied, and R. D. Quinn, "Application of evolved locomotion controllers to a hexapod robot," *Robotics and Autonomous Systems*, vol. 19, no. 1, pp. 95–103, 1996.

[7] O. Michel, "Webots: professional mobile robot simulation," *Advanced Robotic Systems*, vol. 1, no. 1, pp. 39–42, 2004.

[8] E. Yoshida, S. Murata, A. Kamimura, K. Tomita, H. Kurokawa, and S. Kokaji, "Evolutionary synthesis of dynamic motion and reconfiguration process for modular robot M-TRAN," in *Proceedings of IEEE International Symposium on Computational Intelligence in Robotics and Automation*, pp. 1004–1010, 2003.

[9] M. Yim, Y. Zhang, and D. Duff, "Modular robots," *IEEE Spectrum*, vol. 39, no. 2, pp. 30–34, 2002.

[10] F. Mondada, L. M. Gambardella, D. Floreano, S. Nolfi, J.-L. Deneubourg, and M. Dorigo, "The cooperation of swarm-bots:

physical interactions in collective robotics," *IEEE Robotics and Automation Magazine*, vol. 12, no. 2, pp. 21–28, 2005.

[11] E. Tuci, R. Gross, V. Trianni, F. Mondada, M. Bonani, and M. Dorigo, "Cooperation through self-assembly in multi-robot systems," *ACM Transactions on Autonomous and Adaptive Systems*, vol. 1, no. 2, pp. 115–150, 2006.

[12] R. Fitch and D. L. Rus, "Self-reconfiguring robots in the USA," *Japanese Robotics Social Journal*, vol. 21, no. 8, pp. 4–10, 2003.

[13] E. H. Ostergaard, *Distributed control of the ATRON self-reconfigurable robot [Ph.D. thesis]*, Maersk McKinney Moller Institute for Production Technology; University of Southern Denmark, 2004.

[14] Z. Butler, K. Kotay, D. Rus, and K. Tomita, "Generic decentralized control for lattice-based self-reconfigurable robots," *International Journal of Robotics Research*, vol. 23, no. 9, pp. 919–937, 2004.

[15] S. Murata, E. Yoshida, A. Kamimura, H. Kurokawa, K. Tomita, and S. Kokaji, "M-TRAN: self-reconfigurable modular robotic system," *IEEE/ASME Transactions on Mechatronics*, vol. 7, no. 4, pp. 431–441, 2002.

[16] J. Koza and R. Poli, "Genetic programming," in *Search Methodologies*, pp. 127–164, 2005.

[17] W. Banzhaf, J. R. Koza, C. Ryan, L. Spector, and C. Jacob, *Genetic Programming—An Introduction*, Morgan Kaufmann, San Francisco, Calif, USA, 1998.

[18] D. E. Goldberg, *Genetic Algorithms in Search, Optimization, and Machine Learning*, Addison-Wesley, Reading, Mass, USA, 1989.

[19] J. H. Lee and C. W. Ahn, "Evolutionary self-assembling swarm robots using genetic programming," in *Proceedings of the SICE Annual Conference (SICE '12)*, pp. 807–811, 2012.

A Novel Complex Valued Cuckoo Search Algorithm

Yongquan Zhou[1,2] and Hongqing Zheng[1]

[1] *College of Information Science and Engineering, Guangxi University for Nationalities, Nanning 530006, China*
[2] *Guangxi Key Laboratory of Hybrid Computation and IC Design Analysis, Nanning 530006, China*

Correspondence should be addressed to Yongquan Zhou; yongquanzhou@126.com

Academic Editors: P. Agarwal, V. Bhatnagar, and Y. Zhang

To expand the information of nest individuals, the idea of complex-valued encoding is used in cuckoo search (PCS); the gene of individuals is denoted by plurality, so a diploid swarm is structured by a sequence plurality. The value of independent variables for objective function is determined by modules, and a sign of them is determined by angles. The position of nest is divided into two parts, namely, real part gene and imaginary gene. The updating relation of complex-valued swarm is presented. Six typical functions are tested. The results are compared with cuckoo search based on real-valued encoding; the usefulness of the proposed algorithm is verified.

1. Introduction

Recently, a new metaheuristic search algorithm, called Cuckoo Search (CS) [1], has been developed by Yang and Deb (2009). The algorithm is inspired by the reproduction strategy of cuckoos. Because of this method is simple, efficient and optimal random search paths, and successfully applied to practical engineering optimization problems [2]. In term of cuckoo search algorithm, there are many methods to improve its performance; some people study the parameters of cuckoo search algorithm. But these methods are using binary and decimal to encode the bird's nest, individual's information capacity is very limited.

Complex-valued encoding method is already used to express neural network weights [3] and individual genes of evolutionary algorithm [4, 5]; it uses diploid in the expression of individual genes and greatly expands the individual's information capacity. From individual coding method, this paper studies the plural coding performance improvement of cuckoo search algorithm. The value of independent variables for objective function is determined by modules, and the sign of them is determined by angles. The two variables of real and imaginary parts to represent an independent variable, thus nest groups, can enhance the information and tap the individual diversity of the population, reducing the local

convergence. We provide a new way for the Cuckoo search algorithm to solve practical problems.

2. Cuckoo Search Algorithm

2.1. Original CS. CS is a heuristic search algorithm which has been proposed recently by Yang and Deb [1]. The algorithm is inspired by the reproduction strategy of cuckoos. At the most basic level, cuckoos lay their eggs in the nests of other host birds, which may be of different species. The host bird may discover that the eggs are not its own and either destroy the egg or abandon the nest all together. This has resulted in the evolution of cuckoo eggs which mimic the eggs of local host birds. For simplicity in describing the Cuckoo Search, we now use the following three idealized rules:

(1) Each Cuckoo lays one egg, which represents a set of solution coordinates, at a time, and dumps it in a random nest.

(2) A fraction of the nests containing the best eggs, or solutions, will be carried over to the next generation.

(3) The number of nests is fixed and there is a probability that a host can discover an alien egg. If this happens,

```
Cuckoo search via Lévy flight algorithm:
Begin
            Objective function f(x), x = (x₁, x₂, ..., x_d)ᵀ
            Generate initial population of n host nests x_i (i = 1, 2, ..., n)
    While (t < Max Generation) or (stop criterion)
            Get a cuckoo randomly by Lévy flight
            Evaluate its quality/fitness F_i
                Choose a nest among n (say, j) randomly
    If (F_i > F_j),
                replace j by the new solution;
        End
            A fraction (p_a) of worse nests are abandoned and new ones are built;
            Keep the best solutions (or nests with quality solutions);
            Rank the solutions and find the current best
    End while
            Post process results and visualization
End
```

ALGORITHM 1: Pseudo code of cuckoo search via Lévy flight algorithm.

the host can either discard the egg or the nest and this results in building a new nest in a new location.

Based on these three rules, the basic steps of the Cuckoo Search (CS) can be summarized as the pseudo code shown in Algorithm 1.

When generating new solution $x^{(t+1)}$ for, say, cuckoo i, a Lévy flight is performed

$$x_i^{(t+1)} = x_i^{(t)} + \partial \oplus \text{Lévy}(\beta), \tag{1}$$

where $\partial > 0$ is the step size which should be related to the scales of the problem of interests. In most cases, we can use $\partial = 1$.

The product $\oplus$ means entry-wise walk during multiplications. Lévy flights essentially provide a random walk while their random steps are drawn from a Lévy Distribution for large steps

$$\text{Lévy} \sim u = t^{-1-\beta} \quad (0 < \beta < 2). \tag{2}$$

This has an infinite variance with an infinite mean. Here the consecutive jumps/steps of a cuckoo essentially form a random walk process which obeys a power-law step-length distribution with a heavy tail. In addition, a fraction p_a of the worst nests can be abandoned so that new nests can be built at new locations by random walks and mixing. The mixing of the eggs/solutions can be performed by random permutation according to the similarity/difference to the host eggs.

Obviously, the generation of step size s samples is not trivial using Lévy flights. A simple scheme discussed in detail by Yang can be summarized as

$$x_i^{(t+1)} = x_i^{(t)} + \partial \oplus \text{Lévy}(\beta) \sim 0.01 \frac{u}{|v|^{1/\beta}} \left(x_j^{(t)} - x_i^{(t)} \right), \tag{3}$$

where u and v are drawn from normal distributions. That is

$$u \sim N\left(0, \sigma_u^2\right), \qquad v \sim N\left(0, \sigma_v^2\right). \tag{4}$$

TABLE 1: Nest chromosome structure shown.

(R_{p1}, I_{p1})	(R_{p2}, I_{p2})	...	(R_{pM}, I_{pM})

With $\sigma_u = \{(\Gamma(1 + \beta) \sin(\pi\beta/2))/(\Gamma[(1 + \beta)/2]\beta 2^{(\beta-1)/2})\}^{1/\beta}$, $\sigma_v = 1$. Here Γ is the standard Gamma function [6].

2.2. Cuckoo Search Based on Complex-Valued Encoding. Containing the M-variable function optimization problem, with M complex, corresponding to the M complex nest location is recorded as

$$x_p = R_p + I_p j \quad p = 1, 2, ..., M. \tag{5}$$

The gene of the nest can be expressed as the diploid and is recorded as (R_p, I_p); R_p, I_p express, respectively, the real and imaginary parts of the variable in (5). So the ith nest can be expressed as shown in Table 1.

2.2.1. Initialize the Nest. Assume that the variable interval of function is $[A_L, B_L]$, $L = 1, 2, ..., M$. Of course, since the interval of the variable is open or half open, half closed, it would not affect the feasibility of the algorithm, such that only for writing convenience. Randomly generating M-modules and M-angles, the vector of the module and the angle made the following relationship:

$$\rho_L = \left[0, \frac{B_L - A_L}{2}\right], \quad \theta_L = [-2\pi, 2\pi], \quad L = 1, 2, ..., M,$$

$$R_L + jI_L = \rho_L\left(\cos\theta_L + j\sin\theta_L\right), \quad L = 1, 2, ..., M, \tag{6}$$

where M real and imaginary parts as shown in Table 2 are assigned to the Bird's Nest, resulting in an initial nest.

Complex-valued Cuckoo search via Lévy flight algorithm:

Begin

    Objective function $f(x), x = (x_1, x_2, \ldots, x_d)^T$

    Generate initial population of n plurality host nests x_i ($i = 1, 2, \ldots, n$) according to (6)

    Setting the Max Generation, and find the best modules, angles and fmin.

    While ($t <$ Max Generation) or (stop criterion)

      Keep the best module, angle for the SAN

      Get a new module and angle randomly by Lévy flight according to (7) and (8)

      Plurality nest be transformed into real nest according to (9)

      Evaluate its quality/fitness F_i

        Choose a nest among n (say, j) randomly

      If ($F_i > F_j$),

        Replace j by the new solution;

          $nest_j \leftarrow nest_i$

          $\rho_j \leftarrow \rho_i$

          $\theta_j \leftarrow \theta_i$

    End

    A fraction (p_a) of worse modules, angles are abandoned and new ones are built;

    Compare rand with p_a, obtain a new module and angle.

    Evaluate its quality/fitness F_i, and keep the best nest, module and angle

    Rank the solutions and find the current best nest, module and angle.

    End while

    Post process results and visualization

End

ALGORITHM 2: Pseudo code of the plurality cuckoo search (PCS).

2.2.2. The Method of Nest Update

(1) The method of module update is as follows:

$$\rho_i^{(t+1)} = \rho_i^{(t)} + \partial \oplus L(\lambda), \quad i = 1, 2, 3, \ldots, n, \quad (7)$$

where $\rho_i^{(t)}$ expresses the tth generation value in the ith module. The product $\oplus$ means entry-wise multiplications where $\partial > 0$ is the step size which should be related to the scales of the problem of interest. In most cases, we can use $\partial = 1$. $L(\lambda) \sim u = t^{-\lambda}$, ($1 < \lambda \leq 3$). Module vector is updated, if r and $> p_a$ then $\rho_i^{(t+1)}$ random can be changed, or not changed. The last to retain a good module vector $\rho_i^{(t+1)}$.

(2) The method of angle update is as follows:

$$\theta_i^{(t+1)} = \theta_i^{(t)} + \partial \oplus L(\lambda), \quad i = 1, 2, 3, \ldots, n, \quad (8)$$

where $\theta_i^{(t)}$ expresses the tth generation value in the ith angle. The product $\oplus$ means entry-wise multiplications, where $\partial > 0$ is the step size which should be related to the scales of the problem of interest. In most cases, we can use $\partial = 1$. $L(\lambda) \sim u = t^{-\lambda}$, ($1 < \lambda \leq 3$). Angle vector is updated, if r and $> p_a$ then $\theta_i^{(t+1)}$ random can be changed, or not changed. The last to retain a good angle vector $\theta_i^{(t+1)}$.

2.2.3. Fitness Calculation. In order to solve the fitness function, plural Bird's Nest must be changed into a real number; the real value of objective function is determined by modules,

and sign of them is determined by amplitude angle, specific practices are as follows:

$$\rho_n = \sqrt{X_{Rn}^2 + X_{In}^2}, \quad n = 1, 2, \ldots, M$$

$$RV_n = \rho_n \operatorname{sgn}\left(\sin\left(\frac{X_{In}}{\rho_n}\right)\right) + \frac{B_L + A_L}{2}, \quad n = 1, 2, \ldots, M, \quad (9)$$

where ρ_n denotes the nth dimension module, X_{Rn}, X_{In} denote the real part and imaginary part of the nth dimension; respectively, RV_n is converted real variable.

3. The Basic Steps of PCS

Based on above analysis, the basic steps of complex-valued encoding (PCS) can be summarized as the pseudo code shown in Algorithm 2.

4. Simulation Experiment

4.1. Design of Experiment. In this section, the performance of the PCS algorithm is extensively investigated by a large number of benchmark optimization problems. All computational experiments are conducted with Matlab7.0 and run on CPU T3100, 1.90 GHZ with 2 GB memory capacity.

Algorithm parameters are set as follows: because the updates of bird's nest locations are divided into two steps in the complex-valued encoding, there are two update calculations; when the two types of encoding have the same sizes

TABLE 2: Test the improved algorithm's benchmark functions.

Functions	Dim	Domain	Theoretical value
$f(x) = \sum_{i=1}^{d-1}\left[(1-x_i)^2 + 100(x_{i+1}-x_i^2)^2\right]$	10	$[-100, 100]$	0
$f(x) = \sum_{i=1}^{d} x_i^2$	15	$[5.12, 5.12]$	0
$f(x) = 10d + \sum_{i=1}^{d}\left[x_i^2 - 10\cos(2\pi x_i)\right]$	20	$[5.12, 5.12]$	0
$f(x) = -20\exp\left[-0.2\sqrt{(1/d)\sum_{i=1}^{d} x_i^2}\right] - \exp\left[(1/d)\sum_{i=1}^{d}\cos(2\pi x_i)\right] + 20 + e$	30	$[-32.768, 32.768]$	0
$f(x) = -\cos(x)\cos(y)\exp\left[-(x-\pi)^2 - (y-\pi)^2\right]$	2	$[100, 100]$	-1
$f(x) = 1 + (1/4000)\sum_{i=1}^{d} x_i^2 - \prod_{i=1}^{d}\cos(x_i/\sqrt{i})$	10	$[-600, 600]$	0

TABLE 3: The results of experiment in running 20 times.

Functions	Algorithm	Best	Worst	Mean	Variance
Rosenbrock	CS	671.2474	$4.8400e + 003$	$2.1090e + 003$	$1.0339e + 006$
	PCS	**7.9206**	**8.9835**	**8.3874**	**0.1028**
Sphere	CS	0.0648	0.1723	0.1141	0.0012
	PCS	**0**	**0.0088**	**$8.9793e - 004$**	**$4.6582e - 006$**
Rastrigin	CS	112.8084	128.5006	120.8996	20.0181
	PCS	**100**	**104.0008**	**100.8662**	**1.6589**
Ackley	CS	10.7296	13.7988	12.3351	0.5920
	PCS	**0.0052**	**13.0287**	**7.7304**	**13.5185**
Easom	CS	-1	-0.9992	-0.9998	$4.1112e - 008$
	PCS	**-1**	**-0.9998**	**-1**	**$3.1784e - 009$**
Griewank	CS	0.4814	0.9043	0.7230	0.0111
	PCS	**0**	**0.1129**	**0.0256**	**0.0017**

of population, the computational complexity of the complex-valued encoding is approximately two times the one of the real encoding. To compare with the performance of the two methods, the size of plurality population nest is half of the one of real population nest. The size of complex-valued encoding nest is 20, the size of real encoding nest is 40, and the maximum iteration times is 200, $p_a = 0.25$.

4.2. Experimental Results and Analysis. In this section, we test on six different functions to verify that the algorithm proposed in this paper is feasible and effective. 20 independent runs are made for the PCS algorithms, and the results obtained by the PCS algorithms are presented in Table 3. From Table 3 we can find that complex-valued encoding method can achieve better fitness than real number coding method. In terms of Rosenbrock function, either best fitness or average fitness, we can see that the precision of PCS is improved 10^2 and 10^3 higher than CS, respectively. As far as Sphere function are concerned, the optimal value of PCS reaches the theoretical value; the average fitness is improved 10^3 higher than CS. About Rastrigin, Ackley function, PCS average value and the optimal ratio of CS are improved, but not obvious. With respect to Easom function, the optimal value of PCS reaches the theoretical value, but CS does not. In terms of Griewank function, the optimal value of PCS can also reach the theoretical value. Figure 1 shows that this method is better than that real-coded in the convergence rate and convergence precision; this can be explained from

the average fitness evolution curves. From the average fitness figures, we can see that the change of average fitness obtained by the complex-valued encoding method is much greater than the one obtained by the real number encoding method, especially in the early evolution. Because the average fitness of the change is bigger, that individual is scattered, not concentrated in one or a few local points. In the iterative process, there is a trend that these points are close to a better location, but this is easy to make the population into the local convergence; therefore maintaining the diversity of the population is very important. Average fitness changes greatly; to some extent, the diversity of the population is better, thus not easy to fall into the local convergence.

5. Implement PCS in Determining PID Controller Parameter

In industry process, people generally implement Ziegler-Nichlos rule in determining PID controller parameters; the control effect is generally difficult to meet the requirements of the control system. In this section, we implement PCS in determining PID controller parameters and compare the results with CS and PSO results. The parameters of controller are mapped bird's nest, then optimizing them by the PCS method. In the previous work [7, 8], authors have implemented transfer function from industry

$$G(s) = \frac{2}{s^2 + 1.5s + 2} e^{-0.2s} \tag{10}$$

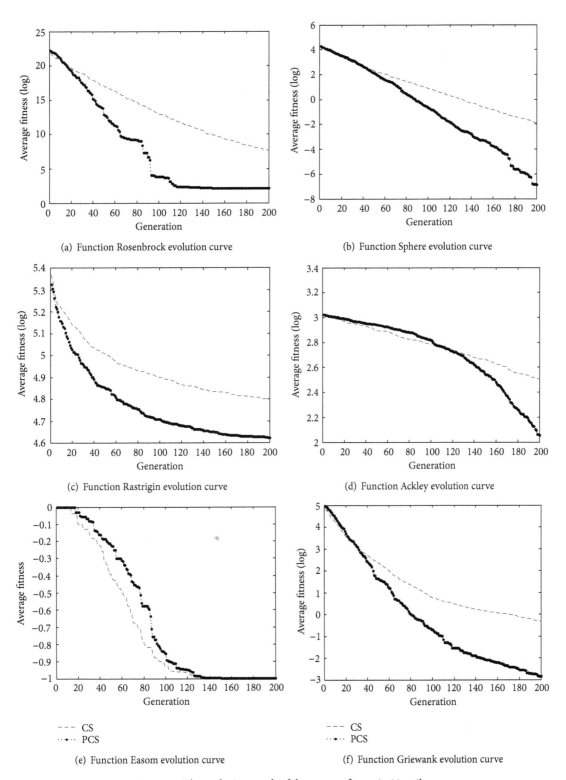

FIGURE 1: The evolution graph of the average fitness in 20 trails.

PID Controller can be described as

$$G_c(s) = k_p + \frac{k_i}{s} + k_d s. \tag{11}$$

Through adjusting the three parameters, the system satisfies the required performance indicators. The bird's nest is in the three dimensional space encoded; the parameters are set as follows: $k_p \in [0.01, 20]$, $k_i \in [0.01, 2]$, $k_d \in [0.01, 2]$.

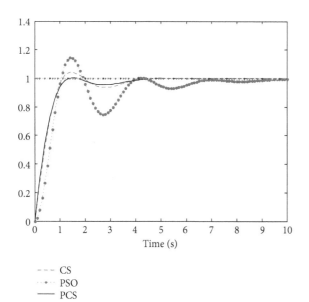

--- CS
···•··· PSO
—— PCS

FIGURE 2: The comparison of unit step response curve.

TABLE 4: PID Controller tuning parameters.

Tuning method	k_p	k_i	k_d
PSO	0.0100	2.0000	1.0518
CS	0.6491	2.0000	2.0000
PCS	0.8096	1.9738	1.9995

The number of nest is 20; the maximum iteration time; is 100. The most crucial step in applying PCS to choose the objective functions J that are used to evaluate fitness of each nest; the performance indices are defined as follow [8]:

$$J = \alpha * \int_0^\infty |e(t)|\, t d_t + \beta * ts, \qquad (12)$$

where $e(t)$ is the error signal in time domain, ts is the tuning time, α, β is weight, which is set as 0.1 and 0.9, respectively.

In the experiments, we implement PSO, CS, and PCS in determining PID controller parameters. The results obtained by the three algorithms are presented in Table 4. Figure 2 is the unit step response curve of control object.

In Figure 2, we can see that the settling time is not so different among all methods; the settling time from short to long is followed by PCS, CS, and PSO. In addition, the overshoot of the three algorithms is (in descending order): PSO, CS, and PCS.

6. Conclusions

This paper proposes Cuckoo search based on complex-valued encoding; the individual of Bird's Nest is denoted by plurality, so a diploid swarm is structured by a sequence plurality; the Bird's Nest can express the space dimension much more than the real-coded one. Compared with traditional real-coded, the Bird's Nest also has to contain more information, so that the algorithm improves the search capabilities of the

global optimum. To verify the proposed PCS algorithm, also a number of benchmark optimization problems and PID controller parameter tuning are solved using this concept and quite satisfactory results are obtained. CS is the algorithm proposed in the last two years; the theoretical analysis and other applications require further study.

Acknowledgments

This work is supported by National Science Foundation of China under Grant no. 61165015, Key Project of Guangxi Science Foundation under Grant no. 2012GXNSFDA053028, and Key Project of Guangxi High School Science Foundation under Grant no. 20121ZD008 and funded by Open Research Fund Program of Key Lab of Intelligent Perception and Image Understanding of Ministry of Education of China under Grant no. IPIU01201100.

References

[1] X. S. Yang and S. Deb, "Cuckoo search via Lévy flights," in *Proceedings of the World Congress on Nature and Biologically Inspired Computing (NABIC '09)*, pp. 210–214, IEEE, December 2009.

[2] X. S. Yang and S. Deb, "Engineering optimization by cuckoo search," *International Journal of Mathematical Modelling and Numerical Optimization*, vol. 4, pp. 330–343, 2010.

[3] D. Casasent and S. Natarajan, "A classifier neural net with complex-valued weights and square-law nonlinearities," *Neural Networks*, vol. 8, no. 6, pp. 989–998, 1995.

[4] Z. H. Zheng, Y. Zhang, and Y. H. Qiu, "Genetic algorithm based on complex-valued encoding," *Control Theory & Applications*, vol. 20, no. 1, pp. 97–100, 2003.

[5] D. B. Chen, H. J. Li, and Z. Li, "Particle swarm optimization based on complex-valued encoding and application in function optimization," *Computer and Applications*, vol. 45, no. 10, pp. 59–61, 2009.

[6] X. S. Yang and S. Deb, "Multiobjective cuckoo search for design optimization," *Computer ' Operations Research*, vol. 40, no. 6, pp. 1616–1624, 2013.

[7] X. Liu, "Improved particle swarm optimization and its application in PID parameters optimization," *Electronic Design Engineering*, vol. 19, no. 9, pp. 79–82, 2011.

[8] C. L. Zhang, J. L. Jiang, S. H. Jiang, and Q. Li, "Adaptive hybrid particle swarm optimization algorithm and application," *Application Research of Computers*, vol. 28, no. 5, pp. 1696–1698, 2011.

Dependability Modeling and Assessment in UML-Based Software Development

Simona Bernardi,[1] José Merseguer,[2] and Dorina C. Petriu[3]

[1] *Centro Universitario de la Defensa, Academia General Militar, Zaragoza, Spain*
[2] *Departamento de Informática e Ingeniería de Sistemas, Universidad de Zaragoza, 50018 Zaragoza, Spain*
[3] *Department of Systems and Computer Engineering, Carleton University, Ottawa, ON, Canada K1S 5B6*

Correspondence should be addressed to José Merseguer, jmerse@unizar.es

Academic Editors: M. Sarfraz and D. Spinellis

Assessment of software nonfunctional properties (NFP) is an important problem in software development. In the context of model-driven development, an emerging approach for the analysis of different NFPs consists of the following steps: (a) to extend the software models with annotations describing the NFP of interest; (b) to transform automatically the annotated software model to the formalism chosen for NFP analysis; (c) to analyze the formal model using existing solvers; (d) to assess the software based on the results and give feedback to designers. Such a modeling → analysis → assessment approach can be applied to any software modeling language, be it general purpose or domain specific. In this paper, we focus on UML-based development and on the dependability NFP, which encompasses reliability, availability, safety, integrity, and maintainability. The paper presents the profile used to extend UML with dependability information, the model transformation to generate a DSPN formal model, and the assessment of the system properties based on the DSPN results.

1. Introduction

Model-driven development [1] (MDD) is an evolutionary step that changes the focus of software development from code to models, with the purpose of automating the code generation from models. MDD emphasis on models facilitates also the analysis of nonfunctional properties (NFP) (such as performance, scalability, reliability, security, safety, or usability) of the software under development based on its models. These NFPs are finally responsible for the required quality of the software [2]. Among them, we address in this paper the dependability NFP. Dependability encompasses availability, reliability, safety, integrity, and maintainability as proposed in [3].

Many formalisms and tools for NFP analysis have been developed over the years. For example, queueing networks [4], stochastic Petri nets [5], stochastic process algebras [6], fault trees [7], or probabilistic timed automata [8]. One of the MDD research challenges is to bridge the gap between software models and dependability analysis models. An emerging approach for the analysis of different NFPs,

dependability included, is given in Figure 1. It consists of the following steps: (a) to extend the software models used for development with annotations describing dependability properties; (b) to transform automatically the annotated software model to the formalism chosen for dependability analysis; (c) to analyze the formal model using existing solvers; (d) to assess the software based on the results and give feedback to designers. Such a modeling → analysis → assessment approach can be applied to any software modeling language, be it general purpose such as the Unified Modelling Language [9] (UML), or domain specific such as AADL [10] or SysML [11].

In the case of UML-based software development, the extensions required for NFP-specific annotations are defined as UML profiles [9], which provide the additional advantage of being processed by standard UML tools without any change in the tool support. OMG adopted the MARTE [12] profile (see Appendix A), which extends UML for the real-time domain, including support for the specification of schedulability and performance NFPs. We use the

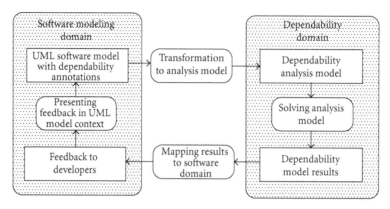

FIGURE 1: Integrating dependability modeling and analysis in a UML-based software development.

dependability modeling and analysis [13] (DAM) profile (see Appendix A) to extend the UML models with dependability concepts and then transform the extended UML model into a Deterministic and Stochastic Petri Net (DSPN) model (see Appendix B). The results of the DSPN model are converted to the software domain and are used to assess system dependability measures.

The work [14] formalized the methodology in Figure 1. In this paper, we rigorously apply this formalization, through a case study, in the context of UML-based development. Section 3 accomplishes the modeling step of the methodology. Section 4 applies the transformation step. Section 5 focusses on the analysis step. Section 6 explores the assessment step.

2. Case Study: The Voter

According to Avižienis et al. [3], the means developed to attain system dependability in the past 50 years can be grouped into four categories: fault tolerance, fault prevention, fault removal, and fault forecasting. The case we present pertains to the fault tolerance field, which aims to improve dependability by avoiding service failures in the presence of faults.

Fault tolerance [15] provides different well-known techniques mainly based on error detection and system recovery. Voting as well as software and hardware replication are the techniques we use here. Concretely, we present a voter mechanism whose purpose is to mask faults arising in computations carried out with data acquired by a *sensor*.

We are considering a *sensor* which monitors (a part of) a generic plant, such as an industrial automation system. The *sensor* periodically sends raw collected data to an *application* that carries out a heavy and critical computation with it. We replicate the computation through different nodes with the purpose of increasing the fault tolerance of the *application*. However, it can happen that one or more of the *replicas* are affected by faults, that is, they do not complete their computations as scheduled, may be due to a node failure, a memory leak or another software bug. Our system deals with this situation by implementing a voting mechanism to mask one fault, that is, the system provides results despite the presence of a fault.

Voting algorithms are often used along with recovery mechanisms, which bring back the system to a healthy state when the voting cannot be accomplished, that is, when the faults cannot be masked. For the sake of simplicity, we will not consider recovery strategies in this example.

We propose an initial UML design of the voter containing a deployment diagram and a set of state machines (UML-SMs). The design model illustrates the following:

(i) how dependability techniques can be modeled with UML behavioral diagrams and DAM annotations introduce dependability parameters;

(ii) how DAM leverages this design for dependability analysis purposes.

The deployment diagram, Figure 2(e), depicts the hardware nodes in which the identified software components (sensor, application, and replicas) execute and also the communication networks linking them. We consider a fully distributed system architecture to increase dependability. In fact, the distribution of the components is a principle in dependability modeling.

The voter exhibits a discrete behavior for which UML-SMs are well suited. According to the UML interpretation, a SM specifies the behavioral pattern for the objects populating a class, as in the case of the UML-SM for the three voting replicas(Figure 1(c)). Alternatively, a UML-SM can also specify the behavior of a software component, such as the application, voter or sensor embedded components(Figure 1(a, b, d)).

3. Dependability Modeling

UML-SMs are widely used to pragmatically model the "correct" behavior of a system, that is the behavior in absence of faults. However, dependability modeling demands to specify also the system behavior under different *fault assumptions*, and to characterize the *system failures*. Furthermore, in case of repairable systems, the *repair and reconfiguration activities* that remove basic or derived failures from the system need to be modeled. In order to define the system fault assumptions, a software engineer has to consider the following main issues:

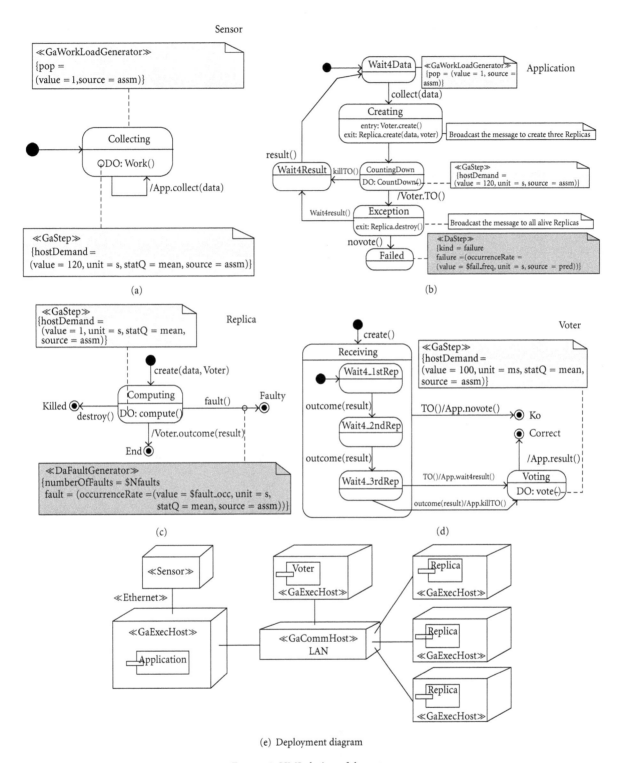

(a)

(b)

(c)

(d)

(e) Deployment diagram

FIGURE 2: UML design of the voter.

(1) which components can be affected by faults and in which states,

(2) the maximum number of faults that can concurrently affect the system components,

(3) the complete fault characterization, such as the fault occurrence rate.

Failure characterization consists in determining the failure modes and, in particular, the system failure states.

UML does not provide sufficient capabilities for a complete and rigorous modeling of all the aforementioned dependability concerns. However, the DAM profile augments a UML design with annotations that target the dependability specification. Being constructed as a specialization of MARTE, DAM ensures compatibility with the UML diagrams. The MARTE part of interest to DAM is the one devoted to quantitative analysis, also known as GQAM (see Appendix A). In fact, DAM specializes GQAM, creating a framework for the specification and analysis of dependability.

3.1. State Machines Specification. Our UML-SMs specification illustrates how the engineer can model specific dependability techniques while describing the system normal behavior. Concretely, we have leveraged the UML-SMs to propose a design for the *voting* mechanism and computation by a *replica*.

Following the UML-SM of the application in Figure 2(b), we see that it collects the data from the sensor then, it creates the voter and three replica processes (see state `Creating`) and starts a countdown. The `CountingDown` state discerns between the correct behavior of the system and masking or abnormal behaviours. It is considered that the system behaves correctly if the replicas can normally carry out their computations before the `CountDown()` completes. Then, the application eventually receives from the voter the `killTO()` event and the `result()` of the computation. The *fault masking* behavior occurs, instead when the time out expires before the voter can kill it; the application informs the voter by sending the `TO()` event. The application enters in `Exception` state, but it can still receive the `wait4result()` event and later the `result()`, which has been produced by the voter based on the `outcome()` of the remaining two no-faulty replicas. Please note in the UML-SM of the voter that if the `TO()` event is received after the outcome of the second replica, then the *voting* is still performed, so one faulty replica can be tolerated. Finally, the system abnormal behavior occurs when no vote is produced and the voter notifies it the application, which enters in Failed state.

3.2. DAM Specification. The *fault masking* specification (i.e., *voting* and *replica* computation) has been modeled by using UML-SMs, however the *fault assumptions* and the *system failures* still need to be specified. To achieve this, DAM provides a small yet sufficient set of extensions, (i.e., stereotypes and tagged values) which are `DaStep`, `DaComponent` and `DaService`.

The `DaStep` stereotype is meant to be applied to basic computational steps, which in the context of SMs are mostly states and transitions. It allows a complete specification of *failures* or *hazards* (for safety-related systems), *errors*, and *recovery actions*. In our example, we have defined a *failure state* in the application UML-SM, which corresponds to the system failure. It is worth to note that this is a simple case since, in general, a system can be subject to different failure modes and each failure is a combination of the system component failures. DAM also supports the failure specification in the general case.

The tag `failure` provides attributes to thoroughly describe a software failure, such as the failure occurrence rate (as shown in the example), but also the mean time to failure (MTTF), mean time between failures (MTBF), domain and

detectability of failure, and logical condition that leads to failure. Concerning *errors*, DAM allows one to specify the error latency and probability, while for *recovery actions* one can specify the rate, duration, distribution, and coverage factor.

`DaComponent` and `DaService`, although not illustrated in our example, are of primary importance for the dependability specification. The former describes aspects such as availability, reliability, faults, failures, or errors affecting the software components; while the latter specifies the same aspects but in the context of software services. *Repair and reconfiguration activities* are specified through the `DaRepair` and `DaRecovery` stereotypes.

Another aspect to be considered is the definition of the fault events, which can be represented as a special type of workload. The stereotype `DaFaultGenerator` provides the means to model a fault injector. In the example, we assume that only replicas can be affected by faults, so we apply this stereotype to the SM transition that leads a replica to a faulty state. The tag `NumberOfFaults` is set to an input variable, $Nfaults$, for sensitivity analysis purposes. The tag `fault` allows to completely specify the *fault assumption* within DAM, concretely its occurrence rate, latency, occurrence probability, occurrence distribution, persistency, and duration.

Finally, the definition of *dependability measures* during this stage of the design is of primary importance for the engineer to clearly specify the goals of the analysis. In this case, we have used the failure description in the `DaStep` to define the measure of interest as the inverse of Mean Time To Failure (MTTF), which represents the application failure occurrence rate. DAM allows one to specify a wide variety of measures, such as the Mean Time Between Failures or the availability.

3.3. MARTE Specification. A DAM specification is useful for addressing most of the quantitative and qualitative dependability aspects. However, for analysis purposes we may need to enhance the specification with some quantitative parameters provided by MARTE annotations. For instance, we need to indicate the population of the system and the duration of the involved activities. We use a subset of GQAM stereotypes to specify: (1) the number of objects populating a UML-SM (as `GaWorkloadGenerator` stereotype with `pop` tag), (2) the timing duration of the UML-SM activities (as `GaStep` stereotype with `hostDemand` tag), and (3) the type of DD resource for informative purposes.

In Figure 2 we defined an initial population only for the application and the sensor, while the other objects (i.e., the replicas and the voter) are dynamically created. The timing durations of the UML-SMs activities have different statistical meaning. For example, the duration of the `TimeOut` of the application is a constant value, while the duration of the `compute` activity performed by the replicas is a mean value. Concerning the type of hardware resource, we identify, through the `GaExecHost` stereotype, the processors where the UML-SM activities execute. The communication nodes are stereotyped as `GaCommHost` stereotype, see also Figure 2.

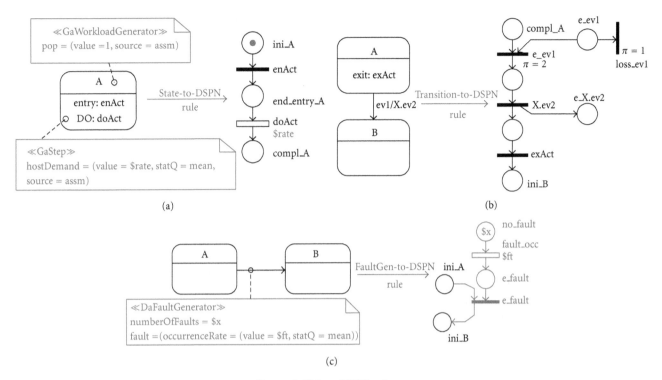

FIGURE 3: SM-to-DSPN patterns.

4. Transformation to Formal Model

The UML-DAM design of the voter specifies both the behavioral and dependability properties. The next challenge for the engineer is to analyse the system dependability before the implementation phase. The proposed approach is to transform the UML-DAM specification into a formal model appropriate for dependability analysis. In our case, DSPN (Deterministic and Stochastic Petri Net, see Appendix B) is such a formal model, which can be automatically generated from the UML-DAM design. In order to derive the DSPN model representing the whole system, we propose to start by transforming each UML-SM into a *component* DSPN following two steps.

(1) Derive the structure of a *component* DSPN from a UML-SM.

(2) Derive the fault assumptions, timing specification, and the initial marking of the DSPN from the MARTE-DAM annotations associated with the respective UML-SM.

After deriving all *component* DSPNs, they are composed according to the SMs interactions.

4.1. Deriving the DSPN's Structure. The model transformation is based on predefined patterns: for each SM model element, we derive a DSPN subnet with labeled places and transitions. The labels have a double purpose: (a) to compose the DSPN subnets by merging the places or transitions with

the same label and (b) to enable the tracing of the SM-to-DSPN mapping, an important feature needed to support the feedback of analysis results to the original SM.

In the following, we succinctly describe the transformation of the most important model elements of a SM (states, events and transitions), to allow the reader to grasp the general idea of the approach. Note that the SM-to-DSPN transformation has been completely automated (see Appendix C).

4.1.1. States. Figure 3(a) shows the transformation of a simple state with an entry action and a do-activity. The DSPN subnet contains two causally connected transitions: one immediate and one timed that model, respectively, the entry action and the do-activity. The compl_A place, when marked, represents the state reached by the SM once the do-activity has been completed.

4.1.2. Events. Events are mapped onto DSPN places, labeled as e_eventname; they represent *mailboxes* whose marking indicates the number of event occurrences of the same type.

4.1.3. Transitions. The transformation pattern of a transition *event/action* is shown in Figure 3(b). The transition fires when the *event* occurs (i.e., the DSPN place e_ev1 becomes marked), but only if the SM is in the source state of the transition (i.e., comp_A is marked), otherwise the event is lost. The consumption and the loss of an event are modeled by two immediate DSPN transitions: e_ev1 and loss_ev1, respectively, with the *event mailbox* place e_ev1 as input place. The former has greater priority ($\pi = 2$) than the latter

($\pi = 1$), so that when a conflict arises the former eventually fires. Then, the execution of the action $X.ev2$ generates an event $ev2$ for a SM named X. Finally, the exit action $exAct$ in state A is carried out and the state B represented by the place ini_B is reached.

4.2. Setting the DSPN Parameters. MARTE-DAM annotations in a SM are mainly transformed to parameters of the *component* DSPNs. In general, the tagged values specified as assumed values (*source=assm*) are mapped to DSPN input parameters, while predicted values (*source=pred*) to output dependability measures.

4.2.1. Fault Assumptions. The fault generator (*DaFaultGenerator* stereotype) is translated into a new DSPN subnet shown in Figure 3(c), which generates fault events. In the voter, the fault generator DSPN subnet generates fault events for the replicas. The *value* field of the *numberOfFaults* tagged-value is a variable that is translated to the initial marking of the DSPN subnet, which specifies the maximum number of faults that may occur in the SM. The *value* field of the *occurrenceRate* tagged-value is also a variable used to define the mean firing time parameter of the transition whose firing represents a fault occurrence.

4.2.2. Timing Specs. The *doActivities* annotated with corresponding processing demands, are translated into timed transitions, as in Figure 3(a), and the *value* field of the *hostDemand* tagged-value is mapped to the input time parameter of the corresponding DSPN transition. When the mean statistical qualifier (statQ=mean) is associated to a tagged value, the DSPN parameter represents the mean value of an exponentially distributed random variable, otherwise it models a deterministic value. In real-time system models it is useful to assume that some of the computing times are stochastic (e.g., the voting time in the voter) while others deterministic (e.g., the time-out in the application); both are naturally modeled in the DSPN formalism.

4.2.3. Initial Marking. The initial population of a SM, tagged-value *pop*, is translated into the initial marking of the corresponding *component* DSPN, as seen in Figure 3(a). In the voter, only the sensor and the application are characterized by an initial population, each represented by the initial marking of the corresponding *component* DSPNs.

5. How to Approach the Analysis

In the UML design, the software engineer specifies the output dependability measures of interest using the DAM profile. Dependability analysis consists in computing such measures by solving the DSPN model; the results will be eventually interpreted in the application domain and used for system assessment. In the voter example, the measure used to assess the fault-tolerance of the system is the failure occurrence rate of the *application*, see Figure 2(b).

The proposed analysis is carried out through the following tasks: (1) derive the dependability DSPN model of the

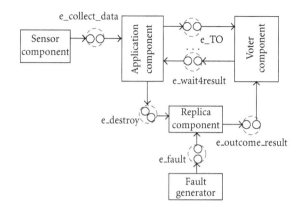

FIGURE 4: Composition of the DSPN *subnets* over interface places.

whole system, (2) define the dependability measures at DSPN level, and (3) choose and run the appropriate DSPN solver.

5.1. Derivation of the Dependability DSPN Model. The DSPN dependability model of the entire system is automatically constructed (see Appendix C) by composing the *component* DSPN subnets derived from the UML-SMs by model transformations (see Section 4). More specifically, the composition takes place by merging the interface places with matching labels that belong to different *component* DSPNs, as illustrated in Figure 4. There is a pair of interface places with matching labels e_eventname for each event generated/consumed by the SMs: one place belongs to the *component* representing the sender SM and the other to the *component* representing the receiver SM. The DSPN composition replaces the pair of interface places by a single place (bigger dotted circle).

5.2. Definition of the DSPN Dependability Measures. The DAM values, specified with the Value Specification Language [12] (VSL, see Appendix A) as predicted values (source=pred), correspond to output dependability measures to be computed by solving the DSPN model. A DSPN dependability measure is a stochastic measure defined over the set S of DSPN markings (i.e. states) reachable from the initial marking (see Appendix B). In the composed DSPN model, the state set S can be partitioned into two subsets containing the states when the system operates normally (Up) and the failure states (Down), respectively. The main concern in the definition of a DSPN dependability measure is the identification of the system failure states considering the DAM predicted values. Figure 5 (center) shows the portion of net obtained from the transformation of the UML SM on the left, according to the patterns defined in Figure 3. The red cloud contains the place corresponding to the SM state B, specified with DAM as a failure state, while the blue cloud includes the rest of the DSPN places. Observe that, in general, there can be several places in the red cloud, depending on the number of SM states specified as failure states; let's denote such a set of places as P_D. Then, the set of failure states corresponds to the set of DSPN markings Down where at least a place in P_D is marked. Conversely, the set

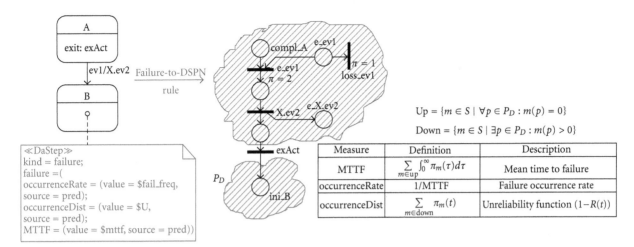

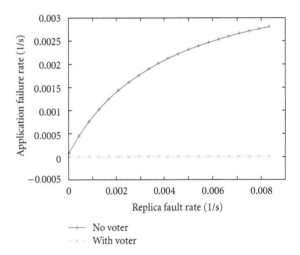

$$Up = \{m \in S \mid \forall p \in P_D : m(p) = 0\}$$

$$Down = \{m \in S \mid \exists p \in P_D : m(p) > 0\}$$

Measure	Definition	Description
MTTF	$\sum_{m \in up} \int_0^\infty \pi_m(\tau)d\tau$	Mean time to failure
occurrenceRate	$1/MTTF$	Failure occurrence rate
occurrenceDist	$\sum_{m \in down} \pi_m(t)$	Unreliability function $(1-R(t))$

FIGURE 5: Definition of DSPN dependability measures.

of operational system states corresponds to the set of DSPN markings Up where none of the places is marked.

The table in Figure 5 (bottom-right) shows the definition of some common DSPN reliability measures, that can be mapped from the homonym DAM tags attached to the state B on the left, where $\pi_m(t)$ is the probability of being in a given marking $m \in S$ at a given instant $t \geq 0$. The definition and computation of such formulas are commonly supported by DSPN tools currently available in the Petri Net community (see Appendix C) (Similar formulas apply to compute availability measures).

In the example, the measure to be predicted is the failure occurrence rate of the control *application* (see DAM annotation in the SM of the *application* in Figure 2).

5.3. Choice of the DSPN Solver. Once the dependability metrics of interest, specified in the UML design with DAM, have been mapped onto the corresponding metrics at DSPN level, we are ready to solve the composed DSPN model to get estimated values of such metrics. The choice of the appropriate DSPN solver depends mainly on two factors: (a) the characteristics of the DSPN model and (b) the dependability metric to be evaluated. Concerning the first factor, numerical methods derive a system of linear equations from the DSPN model and solve it by using either exact or approximate mathematical techniques [16]. Unfortunately, existing DSPN analytical methods suffer from the well-known state-space explosion problem. Discrete event simulation can be used as an alternative method [17].

The second factor affects the type of analysis to be used: transient versus steady state. For transient analysis, the system behavior is observed during a finite time interval, while for steady state analysis system behavior is observed for a *sufficiently large* period so that the analysis becomes time-independent. Typically, the reliability (survival) function is computed under transient state assumption while mean value metrics, such as MTTF, can be estimated in steady state.

FIGURE 6: *Application* failure rate (fail/sec.) versus the replica fault rate under one fault-assumption.

6. Analysis and Assessment Results

Let us consider the following question: could the system carry out its computations in the presence of faults due, for example, to software bugs or nodes failures? In order to answer such a question, the engineer should assess the proposed system design both with and without the fault-masking mechanism. In the first case, the UML design is as shown in Figure 2, while in the second case the voter is omitted and only one replica is created. Two different DSPN models will be derived automatically, and the failure occurrence rate will be computed for each one.

We carried out sensitivity analysis under the steady state assumption, using the simulator implemented in the GreatSPN tool (see Appendix C) to solve the two DSPN models. Two fault input parameters were considered: the replica fault rate and the maximum number of faults that may affect the replicas during the experiment.

Figures 6 and 7 show the results of the analysis, where the *application* failure rate is plotted versus the *replica* fault

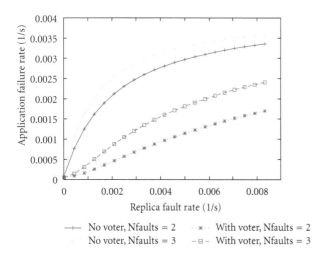

FIGURE 7: *Application* failure rate (fail/sec.) versus the replica fault rate under multiple fault-assumption.

rate. In both figures, the cases with and without the voter are represented. Figure 6 shows the measure under the *one-fault assumption*, that is, only one fault may occur during the experiment, so at most one replica is affected.

Figure 7 shows the results in the case when two or three independent faults may occur concurrently. Observe that in the first design ("with voter" case), multiple faults may affect different replicas. On the other hand in the second design ("no voter" case), where just one replica is present, considering two/three concurrent and independent faults is equivalent to assume, respectively, two/three times as much as the replica fault rate (x-axis).

As expected, the *application* failure rate increases as the number of fault occurrences grows from one to three. Moreover, when the replica fault rate grows, the probability that a replica fault affects the normal application behavior increases, and so does the application failure rate. On the other hand, when triple redundancy and voting is designed, the application is tolerant to a single replica fault, independently of the replica fault rate (Figure 6, green curve).

It is worth noting that the proposed analysis approach is flexible and powerful, especially due to the automation of the model transformation technique. The automatic derivation of DSPN models is flexible enough to easily manage different UML designs that specify different fault-tolerance solutions. Thus timely feedbacks can be provided to the software engineers when they need to assess dependability solutions for a given design.

7. Related Work

Paper [18] extensively surveys works on dependability modeling and analysis of software systems specified with UML. The survey analyses 43 papers from the literature published in the last decade on the topic. Herein, we consider the ones that mainly focus on reliability and availability analysis and propose model transformations which can be automated.

The most comprehensive approach has been proposed in [19, 20], where a UML profile for annotating software dependability properties compliant with the taxonomy and basic concepts from [3] is proposed. A model transformation process derives timed Petri net models via an intermediate model from the annotated UML models. The approach supports the specification of error propagation between components, as well as independent and dependent failures. In particular, it is possible to discriminate between normal and failure states and events, and to assign common failure mode occurrence tags to redundant structures. The main drawback of this work is the introduction of unnecessary redundant information in the UML model, as sometimes the joint use of more than one stereotype is needed.

Pai and Dugan [21] present a method to derive dynamic fault trees from UML system models. The method supports the modeling and analysis of sequence error propagations that lead to dependent failures, reconfiguration activities, and redundancies.

The papers [22–25] address specifically the reliability analysis of UML-based design. D'Ambrogio et al. [22] define a transformation of UML models into fault tree models to predict the reliability of component-based software. Cortellessa and Pompei [23] propose a UML annotation for the reliability analysis of component-based systems, within the frameworks of the SPT [26] and QoS&FT [27] profiles. The annotations defined in [23] are used by Grassi et al. [24, 25] where a model-driven transformation framework for the performance and reliability analysis of component-based systems is proposed. The method uses an intermediate model that acts as bridge between the annotated UML models and the analysis-oriented models. In particular, discrete time Markov process models can be derived for the computation of the service reliability.

Finally, the work [28] proposes a model-to-model transformation technique to support the availability evaluation of railway control systems. The availability model is a repairable fault tree that is automatically generated from the UML models (use case, component, and state machine diagrams), properly annotated with MARTE and DAM extensions.

8. Conclusion

A standard specification framework is yet needed for dependability assessment of UML-based specifications. DAM is a step toward this goal, as it is a comprehensive approach attempting to unify a great number of efforts carried out by the researchers in the last decade.

Software quality includes a number of very different NFPs (e.g., security, performance, and dependability), which are often in conflict with each other [29]. In this context, the MARTE-DAM profile is a promising common framework for the specification of different NFPs in UML-based design. We envisage that a future research goal is to devise model transformation techniques that support a comprehensive analysis in presence of conflicting NFPs (e.g., performability, vulnerability, and survivability issues), in order to provide trade-off solutions to the software engineer.

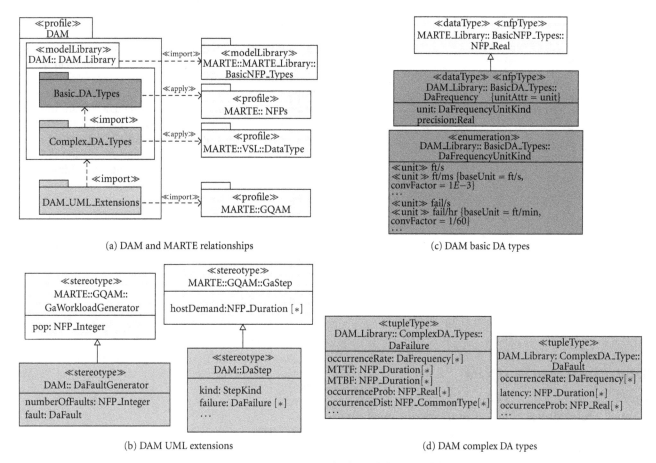

(a) DAM and MARTE relationships

(c) DAM basic DA types

(b) DAM UML extensions

(d) DAM complex DA types

FIGURE 8: UML extensions for dependability modeling.

Appendix

A. MARTE and DAM Profiles

A.1. MARTE. The "UML Profile for Modeling and Analysis of Real-Time and Embedded systems" [12] is an OMG standard profile that extends UML in a lightweight fashion (i.e. via the standard UML extension mechanism including stereotypes, tagged values, and constraints) and enables the specification of both quantitative and qualitative nonfunctional properties (NFP) in the form of annotations attached to UML model elements.

The Value Specification Language (VSL), which is a part of MARTE, provides the ability to express NFP types (defined in the so called MARTE library), values of NFP types, as well as variables, constants, and expressions. All of these are used by the modeler to assign values to tags, according to the VSL syntax (the annotations in Figure 2 show several examples). Tags of NFP types are characterized by several qualifiers: *source* defines the origin of the specification (such as required, assumed, predicted, and measured); statQ defines the type of a statistical measure (such as a maximum, minimum, or mean); *unit* indicates the measurement unit for a given NFP.

Beside VSL, another important feature of MARTE is a general analysis framework called the "General Quantitative Analysis Model" (GQAM) subprofile, which defines the foundation concepts common to different analysis domains. GQAM is specialized in MARTE to provide support for two kinds of analysis: schedulability (subprofile SAM) and performance (subprofile PAM).

A.2. DAM. The dependability analysis and modeling (DAM) profile specializes MARTE for dependability modeling and analysis, (Figure 8(a)). The entire set of DAM stereotypes, as well as the set of UML metaclasses extended by stereotypes can be found in [13]. A DAM subset supports the specification of system dependability properties at service level (e.g., a *DaService* use case) or at component level (e.g., a *DaComponent* class). Other stereotypes can be used to specify fault-tolerance redundancy structures (e.g., a *DaVariant* class). Finally, some stereotypes enable the characterization of the threats affecting the modelled system (e.g., a *DaFaultGenerator* event, a *DaStep* state) and the recovery strategies (e.g., a *DaReplacementStep* action).

According to UML, each DAM stereotype is made of a set of tags that define its attributes. For example, the *DaFaultGenerator* stereotype has *numberOfFaults* and *fault* as tags (see Figure 8(b)). The former indicates the number of concurrent faults and the latter characterizes the nature of the fault. DAM uses the MARTE library of basic NFP types

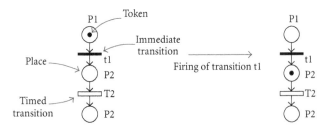

FIGURE 9: Petri net basic concepts.

C. Tool Support

The automation of the modelling → analysis → assessment chain involves different tools. For the modelling step, several tools support UML design. Concretely ArgoSPE (http://argospe.tigris.org/), which is based on ArgoUML (http://argouml.tigris.org/), translates UML state machines into DSPNs automatically. ArgoSPE produces the DSPN in the format of GreatSPN (http://www.di.unito.it/~greatspn/index.html), a tool for the analysis and simulation of DSPN. Also TimeNET (http://www.tu-ilmenau.de/sse/timenet/) is a useful tool for the analysis of DSPNs. Regarding DAM profile, currently it has been implemented as a plug-in (http://webdiis.unizar.es/GISED/?q=tool/dam-profile) for the Papyrus tool, but it has not been yet integrated with the analysis tools. MARTE has also been implemented for Papyrus and MagicDraw.

Acknowledgments

This paper has been partially supported by Fundación Aragón I+D, by Spanish Projects TIN2011-24932 and DPI2010-20413 and by a Discovery grant from the Natural Sciences and Engineering Research Council of Canada (NSERC).

for the definition of tag types and relies upon the MARTE VSL for the specification of tagged-values. It also defines new dependability specific types either as specialization of basic NFP types (e.g., the *DaFrequency* type in Figure 8(c) is a NFP real type, characterized by a fault/failure frequency unit), or as complex types, which consist of a set of basic NFP types (e.g., the *DaFault* and *DaFailure* in Figure 8(d)).

B. Introduction to Petri Nets

A Petri net (PN)—shown in Figure 9—is a bipartite graph, in which the vertices can be either transitions or places. The transitions, graphically depicted by bars, represent events that may occur in the system; the places, represented by circles, are used to model conditions. The directed arcs, shown by arrows, describe which places are pre- or postconditions for which transitions. Places may contain tokens, depicted by black dots; the (initial) distribution of tokens over the places of a PN is called (initial) marking.

The PN dynamics is governed by the transition enabling and firing rules. A transition is enabled whenever there is at least a token in each of its precondition places, and it may fires if there are not enabled transitions with higher priority. When it fires, a token is consumed from each of its precondition places and a token is produced in each of its postcondition places (see Figure 9). A reachable marking is then a marking reached through the firing of a transition sequence from the initial one. In Deterministic and Stochastic Petri Nets (DSPNs), common metrics are the probabilities associated to the reachable markings, which can be either time-dependent (transient metrics) or time-independent (steady-state metrics).

DSPNs are characterized by two types of transitions: immediate and timed. Once enabled, an immediate transition fires immediately while a timed transition has an associated firing delay, which can be a constant value (deterministic) or a mean value of the negative exponential distribution (stochastic).

Place and transition labels have been introduced to enable the net composition. In particular, the places (transitions) belonging to two different net components and having the same label are merged into a unique place (transition), where the set of its input/output arcs is the union of the sets of the input/output arcs of the merged places (transitions).

References

[1] B. Selic, "The pragmatics of model-driven development," *IEEE Software*, vol. 20, no. 5, pp. 19–25, 2003.

[2] H. Stephen Kan, *Metrics and Models in Software Quality Engineering*, Addison-Wesley Longman Publishing, Boston, Mass, USA, 1st edition, 1994.

[3] A. Avižienis, J. C. Laprie, B. Randell, and C. Landwehr, "Basic concepts and taxonomy of dependable and secure computing," *IEEE Transactions on Dependable and Secure Computing*, vol. 1, no. 1, pp. 11–33, 2004.

[4] G. Bolch, S. Greiner, H. de Meer, and K. Trivedi, *Queueing Networks and Markov Chains*, Wiley, New York, NY, USA, 1998.

[5] M. Ajmone Marsan, G. Balbo, G. Chiola, G. Conte, S. Donatelli, and G. Franceschinis, "An introduction to generalized stochastic Petri nets," *Microelectronics Reliability*, vol. 31, no. 4, pp. 699–725, 1991.

[6] H. Hermanns, U. Herzog, and J. P. Katoen, "Process algebra for performance evaluation," *Theoretical Computer Science*, vol. 274, no. 1-2, pp. 43–87, 2002.

[7] W. E. Vesely and N. H. Roberts, *Fault Tree Handbook*, U.S. Nuclear Regulatory Commission, 1987.

[8] M. Kwiatkowska, G. Norman, R. Segala, and J. Sproston, "Automatic verification of real-time systems with discrete probability distributions," *Theoretical Computer Science*, vol. 282, no. 1, pp. 101–150, 2002.

[9] Object Management Group, "Unified Modeling Language," version 2.4.1, 2011, http://www.omg.org/.

[10] Software Engineering Institute, Carnegie-Mellon, "The Architecture Analysis and Design Language (AADL): an introduction," Final report, 2006.

[11] S. Friedenthal, A. Moore, and R. Steiner, *A Practical Guide to SysML: The Systems Modeling Language*, Morgan Kaufmann, 2011.

[12] Object Management Group, "A UML Profile for MARTE: Modeling and Analysis of Real-Time Embedded systems," Document formal/2011-06-02, 2011.

[13] S. Bernardi, J. Merseguer, and D. C. Petriu, "A dependability profile within MARTE," *Software and Systems Modeling*, vol. 10, no. 3, pp. 313–336, 2011.

[14] J. Merseguer and S. Bernardi, "Dependability analysis of DES based on MARTE and UML state machines models," *Discrete Event Dynamic Systems*, vol. 22, pp. 163–178, 2012.

[15] B. Randell and J. Xu, "The evolution of the recovery block concept," in *Software Fault Tolerance*, M. R. Lyu, Ed., chapter 1, pp. 1–22, John Wiley and Sons, 1995.

[16] R. German, "New results for the analysis of deterministic and stochastic Petri nets," in *Proceedings of the IEEE International Computer Performance and Dependability Symposium (IPDS '95)*, pp. 114–123, IEEE CS Press, April 1995.

[17] C. Kelling, *Conventional and fast simulation techniques for Stochastic Petri Nets*, Technische Universität Berlin, Fachbereich 13, Informatik, Berlin, Germany, 1996.

[18] S. Bernardi, J. Merseguer, and D. C. Petriu, "Dependability modeling and analysis of software systems specified with UML," *ACM Computing Survey*. In press.

[19] A. Bondavalli, M. Dal Cin, D. Latella, I. Majzik, A. Pataricza, and G. Savoia, "Dependability analysis in the early phases of UML-based system design," *Computer Systems Science and Engineering*, vol. 16, no. 5, pp. 265–275, 2001.

[20] I. Majzik, A. Pataricza, and A. Bondavalli, "Stochastic dependability analysis of system architecture based on UML models," in *Proceedings of the Architecting Dependable Systems*, vol. 2677, pp. 219–244, Springer, 2003.

[21] G. J. Pai and J. B. Dugan, "Automatic synthesis of dynamic fault trees from UML system models," in *Proceedings of the 13th International Symposium on Software Reliability Engineering*, pp. 243–256, IEEE CS, Annapolis, Md, USA, 2002.

[22] A. D'Ambrogio, G. Iazeolla, and R. Mirandola, "A method for the prediction of software reliability," in *Proceedings of the 6th IASTED Software Engineering and Applications Conference (SEA '02)*, Cambridge, Mass, USA, November 2002.

[23] V. Cortellessa and A. Pompei, "Towards a UML profile for QoS: a contribution in the reliability domain," in *Proceedings of the 4th International Workshop on Software and Performance (WOSP '04)*, pp. 197–206, January 2004.

[24] V. Grassi, R. Mirandola, and A. Sabetta, "From to analysis a models: a kernel language for performance and reliability analysis of component-based systems," in *Proceedings of the 5th International Workshop on Software and Performance (WOSP '05)*, pp. 25–36, July 2005.

[25] V. Grassi, R. Mirandola, and A. Sabetta, "Filling the gap between design and performance/reliability models of component-based systems: a model-driven approach," *Journal of Systems and Software*, vol. 80, no. 4, pp. 528–558, 2007.

[26] SPT, "UML Profile for Schedulability, Performance and Time," Object Management Group Version 1.1, formal/05-01-02, 2005.

[27] QoS, "UML Profile for Modeling Quality of Service and Fault Tolerant Characteristics and Mechanisms," Object Management Group Version 1.0, formal/06-05-02, 2006.

[28] S. Bernardi, F. Flammini, S. Marrone, J. Merseguer, C. Papa, and V. Vittorini, "Model-driven availability evaluation of railway control systems," in *Proceedings of the 30th International Conference on Computer Safety, Reliability, and Security (SAFECOMP '11)*, F. Flammini, S. Bologna, and V. Vittorini, Eds., vol. 6894 of *Lecture Notes in Computer Science*, pp. 15–28, Springer, 2011.

[29] M. Hneif and S. P. Lee, "Using guidelines to improve quality in software nonfunctional attributes," *IEEE Software*, vol. 28, no. 6, pp. 72–77, 2011.

4

Wavelet Neural Network Using Multiple Wavelet Functions in Target Threat Assessment

Gaige Wang,[1,2] **Lihong Guo,**[1] **and Hong Duan**[3]

[1] *Changchun Institute of Optics, Fine Mechanics and Physics, Chinese Academy of Sciences, Changchun 130033, China*
[2] *Graduate School of Chinese Academy of Sciences, Beijing 100039, China*
[3] *School of Computer Science and Information Technology, Northeast Normal University, Changchun 130117, China*

Correspondence should be addressed to Lihong Guo; guolh@ciomp.ac.cn

Academic Editors: J. Bajo and Q. Zhao

Target threat assessment is a key issue in the collaborative attack. To improve the accuracy and usefulness of target threat assessment in the aerial combat, we propose a variant of wavelet neural networks, MWFWNN network, to solve threat assessment. How to select the appropriate wavelet function is difficult when constructing wavelet neural network. This paper proposes a wavelet mother function selection algorithm with minimum mean squared error and then constructs MWFWNN network using the above algorithm. Firstly, it needs to establish wavelet function library; secondly, wavelet neural network is constructed with each wavelet mother function in the library and wavelet function parameters and the network weights are updated according to the relevant modifying formula. The constructed wavelet neural network is detected with training set, and then optimal wavelet function with minimum mean squared error is chosen to build MWFWNN network. Experimental results show that the mean squared error is 1.23×10^{-3}, which is better than WNN, BP, and PSO_SVM. Target threat assessment model based on the MWFWNN has a good predictive ability, so it can quickly and accurately complete target threat assessment.

1. Introduction

With the development of science and technology, the requirement of information is increasingly improving in modern warfare. To adapt to this change, many countries have begun the research of multisensor information fusion from the 1970s. After years of research, the United States, Britain, and other military powers have developed a number of information fusion systems which can be used for combat. Target threat assessment belongs to the third level in information fusion model and is a kind of high-level information fusion. The target threat assessment is the essential basis for the allocation of force and fire in C4ISR system.

The traditional methods to solve threat assessment are Bayesian inference [1, 2], multiattribute decision-making theory [3], GSOBP [4], Elman_AdaBoost [5], analytic hierarchy process [6], Dempster-Shafer theory [7], Hypothesis-drive [8], and so forth. These methods are based on constant weight vector and must rely on expertise available, which makes these methods significantly increase subjective factor of threat assessment, and it is highly possible to evaluate inaccurate results, making the complex relationship between evaluation indicators not effectively reflected. In addition, the models created by these methods have a fatal drawback; that is, these models do not have the self-learning and adaptive capacity, so it is difficult to adapt to change as the change of the enemy air attack weapons performance and tactical means brought to the weights of each factor changes. As the neural network has many advantages, such as strong learning ability and adaptability, it is adept at working out the target threat assessment compared with the above-mentioned methods. BP is a mature and effective method, with the advantages of rigorous derivation process, solid theoretical basis, strong versatility, and clear physical concepts. Literature [7, 8] studies threat assessment using BP networks, and achieve good results. However, with the dimension of training data increasing, the convergence of BP slows down, and the network performance deteriorates; moreover, in the training process, it is easy to fall into local minimum solution. Wavelet neural network (WNN) has many advantages compared with other neural networks; for example, the parameters (hidden nodes and weight) are more easily determined than the radial basis function (RBF) neural networks; it requires smaller training amount than multilayer perceptron network; also, wavelet neural network has a fast convergence. In the same approximation quality, the wavelet neural network requires fewer nodes. For WNN, one of the biggest drawbacks is the difficulty of the choice of mother wavelet function, so this paper proposes an algorithm for selecting optimal mother wavelet function. And then, we construct the (Multiple Wavelet Function Wavelet Neural Networks) MWFWNN using the above method to select optimal mother wavelet function for threat assessment.

2. MWFWNN Network

2.1. Wavelet Theory.
Firstly proposed by Grossman and Morlet in the 1980s, wavelet theory [9] is a mathematical theory and analysis method to make up the shortages of Fourier transform. In the field of signal processing, the most widely used analysis method is the Fourier transform, but it has obvious deficiency that the Fourier transform has no distinguishable ability in the time domain, because the time information is not included in the results of Fourier transform. Wavelet is special waveform with the mean 0 and the limited length.

Wavelet function is constructed through a series of basic transformation with a mother wavelet function. Not all functions can be used as wavelet mother function if a wavelet function is to be available and then develop into a good wavelet transform function, it must satisfy many conditions. Therefore, it is difficult to find the practical wavelet function. In the practical wavelet functions, some of them do not have expressions.

Let $\varphi(t)$ be a square integrable function, that is, $\varphi(t) \in L^2(R)$. If its Fourier transform $\Psi(\omega)$ can satisfy the following compatibility condition:

$$\int_R \frac{|\Psi(\omega)|^2}{\omega} d\omega < \infty \tag{1}$$

then $\varphi(t)$ is called a basic wavelet or mother wavelet function. We make translation and scale for wavelet function, the translation factor τ, and the scale factor (also known as the expansion factor) a, so that we get function $\varphi_{a,\tau}(t)$:

$$\varphi_{a,\tau}(t) = a^{1/2}\Psi\left(\frac{t-\tau}{a}\right), \quad a > 0, \ \tau \in R. \tag{2}$$

As the translation factor τ and the scale factor a are continuous variables, their value can be positive or negative; so $\Psi_{a,\tau}(\omega)$ is called continuous wavelet function (also called the mother wavelet function).

Wavelet transform calculates the inner product between the signal $x(t)$ with mother wavelet function

$$f_x(a,\tau) = \frac{1}{\sqrt{a}} \int_{-\infty}^{\infty} x(t)\varphi^*\left(\frac{t-\tau}{a}\right) dt. \tag{3}$$

Equivalent expression in time domain is given as

$$f_x(a,\tau) = \frac{\sqrt{a}}{2\pi} \int_{-\infty}^{\infty} X(\omega)\Psi^*(a\omega)e^{j\omega\tau} d\omega, \tag{4}$$

where $a > 0$, $\tau \in R$, $X(\omega)$ and $\Psi(\omega)$ are the Fourier transform of $x(t)$ and $\varphi(t)$, respectively.

The conclusion can be drawn from (3) and (4) that is wavelet analysis can analyze the local characteristics of the signal through the mother wavelet function transformation; therefore, wavelet theory is considered to be the breakthrough for the Fourier transform, and the theory has been successfully applied to image processing, optical devices detection, and signal analysis and other fields.

2.2. Wavelet Neural Network.
Wavelet transform has time-frequency localization property and focal features and neural network (NN) has self-adaptive, fault tolerance, robustness, and strong inference ability. How to combine the advantages of wavelet transform and NN to solve practical problems has been one of the hot spots. So-called wavelet neural network (WNN) or wavelet network (WN) is a variety of two techniques and inherits the advantages of the neural network and wavelet transformation. Proposed by Q. Zhang in 1992 [10], WNN uses the wavelet function as the activation function instead of the Sigmoid activation function.

For WNN, its topology is based on BP network; the transfer function of hidden layer nodes is the mother wavelet function; and the network signal is prior to transmission while error is backpropagation in the training process. The network topology is shown in Figure 1. In Figure 1, $x_1, x_2, \ldots, x_n$ is the input vector; $y_1, y_2, \ldots, y_l$ is the predicted output; ω_{ij} and ω_{kj} are the weights connecting every layer; and h_j is mother wavelet function.

For the input signal sequence $x = (x_1, x_2, \ldots, x_n)$, the output of the hidden layer is calculated as

$$h(j) = h_j\left[\frac{\sum_{i=1}^{n}\omega_{ij}x_i - b_j}{a_j}\right], \quad j = 1, 2, \ldots, m, \tag{5}$$

where $h(j)$ is output value for the node j in the hidden layer; h_j is the mother wavelet function; ω_{ij} is weight connecting the input layer and hidden layer; b_j is the shift factor, and a_j is the stretch factor for h_j.

Currently, the choice of mother wavelet functions has not yet formed a standard theory; commonly used wavelet functions are Morlet, Haar, Daubechies (dbN), Symlet (symN), Meryer, Coiflet, Biorthogonal wavelets, and so on.

The output of the output layer is calculated as

$$y(k) = \sum_{i=1}^{m}\omega_{ik}h(i), \quad k = 1, 2, \ldots, l, \tag{6}$$

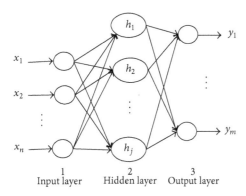

FIGURE 1: Topology of wavelet neural network.

where $h(i)$ is the output value for node i in the hidden layer; ω_{ik} is weight connecting the hidden layer and output layer; l and m are the number of nodes for output layer and the hidden layer, respectively.

For WNN, the updating weight algorithm is similar to BP network; the gradient method is used to update mother wavelet function parameters and connection weights between the layers, making the prediction output closer and closer to the desired output. The weights of WNN and the parameters of wavelet function are updated as follows.

(1) Calculating the prediction error of WNN

$$e = \sum_{k=1}^{m} yn(k) - y(k), \qquad (7)$$

where, $y(k)$ is the predicted output value, $yn(k)$ is the expected output value for the network.

(2) Updating the weights of WNN and the parameters of wavelet function according to the prediction error e

$$\omega_{n,k}^{(i+1)} = \omega_{n,k}^{(i)} + \Delta\omega_{n,k}^{(i+1)},$$
$$a_k^{(i+1)} = a_k^{(i)} + \Delta a_k^{(i+1)}, \qquad (8)$$
$$b_k^{(i+1)} = b_k^{(i)} + \Delta b_k^{(i+1)},$$

where $\Delta\omega_{n,k}^{(i+1)}$, $\Delta a_k^{(i+1)}$, and $\Delta b_k^{(i+1)}$ are calculated by the network prediction error:

$$\Delta\omega_{n,k}^{(i+1)} = -\eta \frac{\partial e}{\partial \omega_{n,k}^{(i)}},$$

$$\Delta a_k^{(i+1)} = -\eta \frac{\partial e}{\partial a_k^{(i)}}, \qquad (9)$$

$$\Delta b_k^{(i+1)} = -\eta \frac{\partial e}{\partial b_k^{(i)}},$$

where η is the learning rate.

The process of training WNN is as follows

(1) Data preprocessing: first, the original data is quantified and normalized, and then the data is divided into training set and testing set for network training and testing, respectively.

(2) Initializing WNN: connection weights ω_{ij} and ω_{jk}, translation factor b_k, and scale factor a_k are randomly initialized, and the learning rate η is set.

(3) Training network: input the training set into WNN, compute network predicted output values, and calculate the error e between output and the expected value.

(4) Updating the weights: update mother wavelet function parameters and network weights according to the prediction error e, making the predictive value of the network as close to actual values.

(5) If the results satisfy the given conditions, use the testing set to test the network, otherwise, return to Step 3.

2.3. MWFWNN. MWFWNN will be provided in this section.

2.3.1. MWFWNN Algorithm

Step 1. Initializing: initialize mother wavelet function library waveFunction = {waveFunction$_i$}, i = 1, 2, ..., K, K = ||waveFunction|| is the number of elements waveFunction included, the variance δ_i for mother wavelet functions waveFunction$_i$, and optimal wavelet function waveFunction$_{\text{best}}$ = waveFunction$_1$ and its variance δ_{best} = δ_1.

Step 2. Choosing the best mother wavelet function: for each mother wavelet function,

(i) Update the weights and parameters of wavelet function waveFunction$_i$ according to (7)–(9).

(ii) if $\delta_i < \delta_{\text{best}}$

$$\delta_{\text{best}} = \delta_i$$
$$\text{waveFunction}_{\text{best}} = \text{waveFunction}_i \qquad (10)$$

End

Step 3. Constructing MWFWNN using waveFunction$_{\text{best}}$ as mother wavelet function.

Step 4. Testing constructed MWFWNN network in Step 3 using the testing set.

Step 5. Analyzing results.

3. Target Threat Assessment Using MWFWNN

Strictly speaking, threat assessment is an NP-hard problem, belonging to the third level in the JDL information fusion model. Target threat assessment needs to consider many factors (such as geography, weather, enemy, etc.), and the relation among the various factors is not a simple linear combination and it is difficult to determine a function between the target threat value and various factors. Therefore, we must consider various factors and their relationships when studying the threat assessment. However, we consider the following six factors in general: target type, target speed, target heading angle, target height, and target distance. We will test the performance of MWFWNN using these factors in this paper.

3.1. Target Threat Assessment Factor. We mainly consider the following six key factors when studying the target threat assessment in the paper:

(1) Target Type: large targets (such as fighter-bombers), small targets (such as stealth aircraft, cruise missiles), and helicopters;

(2) Target heading angle: such as 22°, 26°, and 6°;

(3) Target speed: such as 100 m/s, 500 m/s, and 220 m/s;

(4) Target height: such as very low, low, medium, and high;

(5) Target interference: such as strong, medium, and weak;

(6) Target distance: such as 100 km, 110 km, and 220 km.

3.2. Threat Assessment Model Using MWFWNN. We design MWFWNN model according to the data characteristics. Because the data is 6-dimensional, and the output is 1-dimensional, the structure of WNN is 6-12-1. Firstly, we input six indicators that are the target type, target speed, target heading angle, target interference, target height, and the distance to the input layer. The hidden layer nodes are formed by the wavelet function, and the output layer outputs predicted target threat assessment value under the current indicators. On the basis of the above analysis, we construct the target threat assessment model based on MWFWNN with these six selected indicators, and its architecture is shown in Figure 2.

4. Model Simulation

In this section, we will test the target threat assessment model using MWFWNN proposed in Section 3.

4.1. Data Preprocessing. Part of the data used in our work is shown in Table 1. Target value is quantified using G. A. Miller's quantitative theory, which represents the degree of threat: extremely small, very small, little small, small, medium, large, little large, very large, and extremely large. The properties of the specific quantitative criteria are quantified as follows.

(1) Target Type: helicopter, large target (such as fighter-bombers), and small targets (such as stealth aircraft, cruise missiles), are quantified by 3, 5, and 8, respectively;

(2) Target interference: strong, medium, weak, and no are quantified by 8, 6, 4, and 2, respectively;

(3) Target height: very low, low, medium, and high are quantified 8, 6, 4, and 2, respectively;

(4) Target speed: 0 m/s~1800 m/s equal interval (200 m/s) is quantified by 9 to 1.

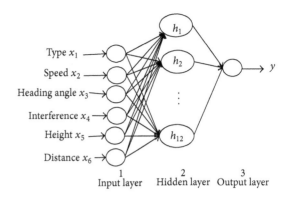

FIGURE 2: Architecture for the model of target threat assessment based on MWFWNN.

(5) Target heading angle: 0°~36° equal interval (4°) is quantified by 9 to 1.

(6) Target distance: 0 km~450 km equal interval (50 km) is quantified by 9 to 1.

(7) Determining the target output: firstly normalize the various factors from air combat situation and then put them into the WMF_WNN proposed in Section 3.2. At last, the WMF WNN outputs threatening assessment value.

After quantifying the data, we can normalize the training set and testing set using the following expression:

$$f : x \longrightarrow y = \frac{x - x_{\min}}{x_{\max} - x_{\min}}, \tag{11}$$

where $x, y \in R^n$, $x_{\min} = \min(x)$, $x_{\max} = \max(x)$. The values are converted into the range $[0, 1]$ through the normalization, that is, $x_{\max} \in [0, 1]$, $i = 1, 2, \ldots, n$.

4.2. Analysis of Simulation Results. In this paper, we implement the MWFWNN algorithm by MATLAB R2009a with the CPU Pentium (R) 4 3.06 GHz, 1 G memory (2 ∗ 512 M). The network prediction is compared with WNN, PSO_SVM and BP neural network. The results show that the proposed network is superior to the WNN, PSO_SVM and BP neural network.

4.2.1. Creating the Mother Wavelet Function Library. Because many mother wavelet functions have no specific expression, we cannot work out their derivatives. Therefore, in this work, we only use the following seven mother wavelet functions to bulid a library waveFunciton. Their expressions are as follows:

(1) Haar wavelet function:

$$\Psi(t) = \begin{cases} 1, & 0 \le t \le \frac{1}{2} \\ -1, & \frac{1}{2} \le t \le 1 \\ 0, & \text{other.} \end{cases} \tag{12}$$

TABLE 1: Part of data.

No.	Type	Velocity (m/s)	Heading angle (°)	Inference	Height	Distance (km)	Threat value
1	Large	450	8	Medium	Low	300	0.5843
2	Large	400	3	Strong	High	100	0.5707
3	Large	450	16	Medium	Low	200	0.5333
4	Large	800	4	Strong	High	100	0.6895
5	Large	800	12	Strong	Low	320	0.6896
6	Small	530	6	Strong	Medium	230	0.6056
7	Small	650	8	Strong	Medium	200	0.7425
8	Small	700	12	Strong	Low	320	0.7336
9	Small	750	15	Medium	Very low	400	0.7541
10	Small	640	18	Strong	Medium	280	0.6764
11	Helicopter	90	12	Weak	Very low	320	0.3937
12	Helicopter	110	3	No	Medium	100	0.3927
13	Helicopter	100	9	No	Medium	260	0.3351
14	Helicopter	120	15	No	Low	160	0.3586
15	Helicopter	80	6	Weak	High	180	0.3471

TABLE 2: Predicting results of different mother wavelet function.

Wavelet function	Haar	Gaussian	Morlet	Mexihat	Shannon	Meyer	GGW
MSE	2.10×10^{-2}	1.03×10^{54}	1.23×10^{-3}	1.27×10^{-3}	1.11×10^{55}	3.90×10^{57}	1.60×10^{-2}
Running time (s)	4.74	4.76	4.85	4.88	4.84	5.24	4.88

(2) Gaussian wavelet function:

$$\Psi(t) = \frac{t}{\sqrt{2\pi}} \exp\left(-\frac{t^2}{2}\right). \tag{13}$$

(3) Morlet wavelet function:

$$\Psi(t) = \cos(1.75t) \exp\left(-\frac{t^2}{2}\right). \tag{14}$$

(4) Mexican Hat (Mexihat) wavelet function:

$$c = \frac{2}{\sqrt{3}}\pi^{-1/4},$$
$$\Psi(t) = c\left(1 - t^2\right) \exp\left(-\frac{t^2}{2}\right). \tag{15}$$

(5) Shannon wavelet function:

$$\Psi(t) = \frac{\sin\pi(t - 1/2) - \sin 2\pi(t - 1/2)}{\pi(t - 1/2)}. \tag{16}$$

(6) Meyer wavelet function (approximate formula):

$$\Psi(t) = 35t^4 - 84t^5 + 70t^6 - 20t^7. \tag{17}$$

(7) Wavelet function GGW constructed by the authors:

$$\Psi(t) = \sin(3t) + \sin(0.3t) + \sin(0.03t). \tag{18}$$

We use the following parameters to initialize the network: the input layer nodes $M = 6$, the hidden layer nodes $n = 12$, the output nodes $N = 1$, and parameter learning rates $lr_1 = 0.01$ and $lr_2 = 0.001$, respectively.

We construct wavelet neural network using each wavelet function in wavelet function library and then input training set into network and train the network. The MSEs are as follows (from small to large): Morlet < Mexihat < GGW < Haar < Gaussian < Shannon < Meyer, as shown in Table 2. From Table 2, we can draw the conclusion that running time and MSE of Morlet and Mexihat are slightly different, but the MSE of Gaussian, Shannon, and Meyer is extremely great, completely divorced from reality. The results we got in this paper are consistent with the fact that most papers adopt Mexihat or Morlet as mother wavelet functions to construct wavelet neural network. So, we can use wavelet functions Morlet or Mexihat as mother wavelet function to create MWFWNN network. In this paper, we use the Morlet wavelet function as the basic mother wavelet function to construct MWFWNN.

4.2.2. Comparing with WNN and PSO_SVM, BP. Similar to MWFWNN, WNN, BP network, and support vector machine (SVM) can be used to solve the target assessment. As the choice of the support vector machine parameters c and g has no uniform standard except relying on experience; in this paper, we use particle swarm optimization (PSO) algorithm to optimize the SVM parameters c and g. Next, we use wavelet neural network, BP neural network, and PSO_SVM to solve threat assessment, and the results are compared with MWFWNN.

The structure of wavelet neural network and BP neural network is 6-12-1 according to the characteristics of the data

TABLE 3: Predicting results of BP, PSO_SVM, MWFWNN, and WNN.

Neural network	BP	PSO_SVM	MWFWNN	WNN
MSE	9.39×10^{-3}	4.80×10^{-3}	1.23×10^{-3}	4.01×10^{-3}
Running time (s)	1.86	10.6	4.88	5.10

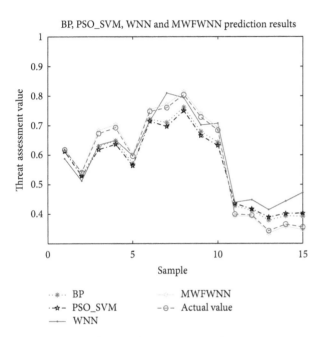

FIGURE 3: Result of target threat assessment based on WNN, BP, MWFWNN and PSO_SVM.

used. Where the WNN and other parameters are setting as shown in Section 4.2.1. PSO SVM uses LIBSVM toolbox [11] whose default is C-SVR and RBF kernel function, where $C = 1$, $\gamma = 1/n$. By default, PSO local search $c_1 = 1.5$, the global search $c_2 = 1.7$, the maximum evolution times maxgen = 200, the maximum population size sizepop = 20, the rate $k = 0.6$ between V and X ($k \in [0.1, 1.0]$, $V = kX$), SVM parameter $c \in [0.1, 100]$, and the parameter $g \in [0.01, 1000]$.

Threat assessment is predicted by the trained WNN, BP network, and PSO_SVM and their MSE are 4.01×10^{-3}, 9.39×10^{-3} and 4.80×10^{-3}, all of which are greater than MWFWNN (1.23×10^{-3}) (as shown in Table 3). For the running time, due to BP neural network calling MATLAB embedded functions, running time is least; wavelet neural networks need to call each mother wavelet function and its derivative, so it is time to consume more; MWFWNN network needs to find the optimal wavelet function from the library, so the running time is more than WNN; the PSO_SVM call PSO algorithm to optimize parameter c and g, but PSO optimization algorithm is more complex, so it implements most slowly.

Prediction error of BP, PSO_SVM, WNN, and MWFWNN is shown in Figure 3. The figure shows that, prediction errors of WNN, BP, and PSO_SVM are simlilar. The error is less than the true value at sample 1–10, while the error was significantly greater than the true value at sample 11–15. MWFWNN network error has similar trend, but the

error was significantly less than the WNN, BP network and PSO_SVM, prediction value closer to the expectations.

5. Conclusion

Based on requirements for quickly processing information in the modern information war, aiming to the characteristics of threat assessment in data fusion functional model, we adopt MWFWNN to solve the threat assessment under the comprehensive consideration of various factors which influence the threat degree. After constructing wavelet function library with 7 wavelet functions, we get the best performance wavelet function Morlet as mother wavelet function to construct MWFWNN network and its result is compared with the WNN, BP, and PSO_SVM networks. Simulation results show that, the MSE of MWFWNN is 1.23×10^{-3}, which is far better than WNN (4.01×10^{-3}), BP network (9.39×10^{-3}), and PSO_SVM (4.80×10^{-3}), achieving the desired goal. In our future work, we will further expand the scale of wavelet function library to find more suitable wavelet function to solve the threat assessment and other problems.

References

[1] F. Johansson and G. Falkman, "A Bayesian network approach to threat evaluation with application to an air defense scenario," in *Proceedings of the 11th International Conference on Information Fusion (FUSION '08)*, pp. 1–7, July 2008.

[2] J. Yang, W. Y. Gao, and J. Liu, "Threat assessment method based on Bayesian network," *Journal of PLA University of Science and Technology*, vol. 11, no. 1, pp. 43–48, 2010.

[3] J. Li and L. Han, "Threat ordering of interference targets based on uncertain multi-attribute decision-making," *Telecommunication Engineering*, vol. 49, no. 10, pp. 62–64, 2009.

[4] G. Wang, L. Guo, H. Duan, L. Liu, and H. Wang, "Target threat assessment using glowworm swarm optimization and BP neural network," *Journal of Jilin University*. In press.

[5] G. Wang, L. Guo, H. Duan, L. Liu, and H. Wang, "The model and algorithm for the target threat assessment based on Elman_AdaBoost strong predictor," *Acta Electronica Sinica*, vol. 40, no. 5, pp. 901–906, 2012.

[6] X. D. Gu, Z. X. Tong, S. J. Chai, X. W. Yuan, and Y. L. Lu, "Target threat assessment based on TOPSIS combined by IAHP and the maximal deviation," *Journal of Air Force Engineering University*, vol. 12, no. 2, pp. 27–31, 2011.

[7] K. Sycara, R. Glinton, B. Yu et al., "An integrated approach to high-level information fusion," *Information Fusion*, vol. 10, no. 1, pp. 25–50, 2009.

[8] A. Kott, R. Singh, W. M. McEneaney, and W. Milks, "Hypothesis-driven information fusion in adversarial, deceptive environments," *Information Fusion*, vol. 12, no. 2, pp. 131–144, 2011.

[9] A. Grossmann and J. Morlet, "Decomposition of Hardy functions into square integrable wavelets of constant shape," *SIAM*

Journal on Mathematical Analysis, vol. 15, no. 4, pp. 723–736, 1984.

[10] Q. Zhang and A. Benveniste, "Wavelet networks," *IEEE Transactions on Neural Networks*, vol. 3, no. 6, pp. 889–898, 1992.

[11] C. C. Chang and C. J. Lin, "LIBSVM: a library for support vector machines," *ACM Transactions on Intelligent Systems and Technology (TIST)*, vol. 2, no. 3, p. 27, 2011.

5

Discrete Particle Swarm Optimization with Scout Particles for Library Materials Acquisition

Yi-Ling Wu,[1] **Tsu-Feng Ho,**[2] **Shyong Jian Shyu,**[2] **and Bertrand M. T. Lin**[1]

[1] *Institute of Information Management, National Chiao Tung University, Hsinchu 30010, Taiwan*
[2] *Department of Computer Science and Information Engineering, Ming Chuan University, Taoyuan 33348, Taiwan*

Correspondence should be addressed to Tsu-Feng Ho; tfho@mail.mcu.edu.tw

Academic Editors: S. Balochian, V. Bhatnagar, and Y. Zhang

Materials acquisition is one of the critical challenges faced by academic libraries. This paper presents an integer programming model of the studied problem by considering how to select materials in order to maximize the average preference and the budget execution rate under some practical restrictions including departmental budget, limitation of the number of materials in each category and each language. To tackle the constrained problem, we propose a discrete particle swarm optimization (DPSO) with scout particles, where each particle, represented as a binary matrix, corresponds to a candidate solution to the problem. An initialization algorithm and a penalty function are designed to cope with the constraints, and the scout particles are employed to enhance the exploration within the solution space. To demonstrate the effectiveness and efficiency of the proposed DPSO, a series of computational experiments are designed and conducted. The results are statistically analyzed, and it is evinced that the proposed DPSO is an effective approach for the studied problem.

1. Introduction

In recent years, the price inflation of library materials, the shrinking of library budget, and the growth of electronic resources continue to challenge the acquisition librarians [1]. Complicating the effects of these challenges is the growth of scholarly and popular publications. With the great increase in publications, the librarians have not only to acquire the latest and the preferred materials within the limited budget but also to take the collection policy into consideration. Walters [2] reports that the annual inflation rate of academic books and periodicals were 1.4 and 8.5 percent. The research planning and review committee of the Association of College and Research Libraries (ACRL) [3] develops the 2010 top ten trends in academic libraries and finds that many libraries will face the budget pressure in the near future. These reaffirm the fact that the materials acquisition problem is exacerbated by the difficulty of aligning the library offerings with patron needs under the budget pressure.

Over the past few decades, researches on materials acquisition have been conducted and implemented with a number of operations research based models and approaches.

Beilby and Mott Jr. [4] develop a linear goal programming model for acquisition planning of academic libraries, and incorporate with multiple collection development goals such as acquiring an adequate number of titles (at least 7,500 but not more than 10,500 titles), not exceeding the total acquisition budget ($200,000), and/or limiting periodical expenditures to 60% of the total acquisition expenditures. Wise and Perushek [5] introduce another model that takes into account more goals, like reaching the minimum limit for each subject fund, not surpassing the maximum limit for each subject fund, and so forth. Later, Wise and Perushek [6] not only address an important claim that the suggestions of collection development librarians and faculties must be taken into consideration but also elaborate another model to reflect the opinion of librarians and faculties. Ho et al. [7] present a model that maximizes the average preference of patrons subject to both the acquisition cost and the number of materials in each category.

In most of the cases, academic libraries are positioned to acquire materials for multiple departments, for example, Science, Business, Engineering, and so forth, within the budget of each department. Goyal [8] proposes an operations research model of funds allocation to different departments of a university. The objective of this model is to maximize the total social benefits conveyed by the funds exercised for the purchase of materials among all departments, and the constraints of this model are the lower and upper limits of fund for each department and the total funds available. Arora and Klabjan [9] point out the critical concern about fairness in materials acquisition of academic libraries. They provide a model for maximizing the usage in the future time period subject to the bounds on the number of materials of each category and the lower and the upper bounds on the budgets of the library units. Existing researches on materials acquisition assume a single total budget or multiple department budgets. This study will investigate the scenario where each individual department has its own budget limit for the preferred materials that are to be acquired. This type of budget plan will introduce financial constraints that are much more complicated.

From the viewpoint of acquisition staffs, it is questionable if the patrons are satisfied with the decision outcome. Niyonsenga and Bizimana [10] indicate various factors related to the patron satisfactions with academic libraries services, such as a list of new acquisitions, lending services, serial collection. In this paper, we adopt the patron preferences of acquisitions to reflect the patron satisfactions. To allocate the budget as fairly as possible, we assume that the preferences are obtained from the patrons of all departments due to the different interests of the departments. Besides, a low budget execution rate may lead to a budget cut in the next fiscal year. Librarians sometimes are on the horns of a dilemma whether to purchase the less preferred materials or cause a low budget execution rate. Therefore, we concentrate on how to select materials to be acquired in order to maximize the average preference as well as the budget execution rate under the real-world restrictions including departmental budget and limitation of the number of materials in each category.

In the view of computational complexity, the materials acquisition problem is a generalized version of the knapsack problem which is known to be computationally intractable [11]. In other words, it is extremely time consuming and even unlikely to find an optimal solution when the problem size is large. By far, metaheuristics, such as genetic algorithm, ant colony optimization, and particle swarm optimization are successfully applied to cope with many hard optimization problems with impressive performances in obtaining solutions with in an effective and efficient way [12, 13]. This paper is devoted to tackling the studied problem by particle swarm optimization (PSO) that has earned a good reputation by the trustworthy merits including simplicity, efficiency, and effectiveness in producing quality solutions [14, 15]. Furthermore, to avoid premature convergence, we introduce a discrete particle swarm optimization with *scout particles*, introduced by Silva et al. [16], to enhance the exploration capability of the adopted swarms.

The rest of this paper is organized as follows. In Section 2, a mathematical model of the materials acquisition problem with departmental demands is proposed and followed by a greedy algorithm. Section 3 presents the fundamental concept and structure of the discrete particle swarm optimization

(DPSO). In Section 4, we depict how the proposed DPSO with scout particles is tailored for the characteristics of the studied problem. A computational study is carried out to examine the performances of the proposed solution approaches. Our experimental settings and results of DPSO are presented in Section 5. We summarize the results of this study and give some concluding remarks in Section 6.

2. Problem Statements and Greedy Algorithm

A formal specification of the materials acquisition problem is presented in this section. Then, an integer programming model is developed to formulate the problem considered in a mathematical way.

2.1. Problem Specification. Consider a set of n materials to be acquired and a set of m departments. Each material is associated with a cost c_i and a preference value p_{ij} recommended by each department j for $1 \leq i \leq n$ and $1 \leq j \leq m$. Each department owns an amount B_j of budget for $1 \leq j \leq m$. Since one material may be recommended by more than one department, the acquisition cost would be apportioned by these recommending departments in proportion to their preferences. For instance, if a material with cost 100 is acquired to meet the recommendations from two departments j and j' with preferences 0.9 and 0.6, then departments j and j' should pay 40 ($= 100 \times (0.9/(0.9 + 0.6))$) and 60 ($= 100 \times (0.6/(0.9 + 0.6))$), respectively, from their budgets B_j and $B_{j'}$. We denote the actual expense by department j for material i as e_{ij}. To meet the acquisition requirements from various departments, q written languages (e.g., English, Japanese, Chinese, etc.) and r classified categories (e.g., Art, Science, Design, etc.) are considered such that the amount of materials belongs to a certain language and a specific category may be restricted into a range. In addition, the authority would expect the remainder of budget B_j, once granted, for department j to be the less the better after allocation. We thus define the *execution rate* to be the actual expenses of all departments divided by the budget of all departments.

The decision is to determine which materials should be acquired and which departments should cover the cost associated with these materials under the constraints of departmental budgets and the limitation of the amounts in each written language and each category. The objective is to maximize the combination of the average preference and the budget execution rate.

In Table 1, we summarize the notations that will be used in the integer programming model throughout the paper.

2.2. Problem Formulation. The materials acquisition problem is mathematically formulated as the following integer programming model:

$$\text{maximize} \quad O(x) = \rho \times \left(\frac{\sum_{j=1}^{m} \left(\sum_{i=1}^{n} x_{ij} p_{ij} / \sum_{i=1}^{n} x_{ij} \right)}{m} \right)$$

$$+ (1 - \rho) \left(\frac{\sum_{i=1}^{n} \sum_{j=1}^{m} x_{ij} e_{ij}}{\sum_{j=1}^{m} B_j} \right)$$

$$(1)$$

TABLE 1: Notations.

Variable	Description
n	Number of materials
m	Number of departments
q	Number of categories
r	Number of languages
p_{ij}	Preference for material i recommended by department j, for $1 \leq i \leq n$ and $1 \leq j \leq m$
c_i	Cost of material i, for $1 \leq i \leq n$
B_j	Budget limit of department j, for $1 \leq j \leq m$
LU_l	Upper bound on the number of materials in language l, for $1 \leq l \leq r$
LL_l	Lower bound on the number of materials in language l, for $1 \leq l \leq r$
a_{il}	$a_{il} = 1$ if material i is in language q; $a_{il} = 0$ otherwise, for $1 \leq i \leq n$ and $1 \leq l \leq r$
CU_k	Upper bound on the number of materials in category k, for $1 \leq k \leq q$
CL_k	Lower bound on the number of materials in category k, for $1 \leq k \leq q$
b_{ik}	$b_{ik} = 1$ if material i belongs to category k; $b_{ik} = 0$ otherwise, for $1 \leq i \leq n$ and $1 \leq l \leq r$
x_{ij}	Decision variable: $x_{ij} = 1$ if material i is acquired for department j from which the cost will be charged; $x_{ij} = 0$ otherwise, for $1 \leq i \leq n$ and $1 \leq j \leq m$
z_i	Auxiliary variable: $z_i = 1$, if $\sum_{j=1}^{m} x_{ij} > 0$; otherwise $z_i = 0$, for $1 \leq i \leq n$ (z_i reveals whether material i is acquired or not)
e_{ij}	Actual expenses of material i by department j, for $1 \leq i \leq n$ and $1 \leq j \leq m$

subject to

$$e_{ij} \geq \left(\frac{x_{ij} p_{ij}}{\sum_{\hat{j}=1}^{m} x_{i\hat{j}} p_{i\hat{j}}} \right) \times c_i \quad \text{for } 1 \leq i \leq n, \ 1 \leq j \leq m, \tag{2}$$

$$\sum_{i=1}^{n} e_{ij} \leq B_j \quad \text{for } 1 \leq j \leq m, \tag{3}$$

$$\sum_{i=1}^{n} x_{ij} - z_i M \leq 0 \quad \text{for } 1 \leq i \leq n, \tag{4}$$

$$\sum_{i=1}^{n} x_{ij} + (1 - z_i) M > 0 \quad \text{for } 1 \leq i \leq n, \tag{5}$$

$$\sum_{i=1}^{n} z_i a_{il} \leq LU_l \quad \text{for } 1 \leq l \leq r, \tag{6}$$

$$\sum_{i=1}^{n} z_i a_{il} \geq LL_l \quad \text{for } 1 \leq l \leq r, \tag{7}$$

$$\sum_{i=1}^{n} z_i b_{ik} \leq CU_k \quad \text{for } 1 \leq k \leq q, \tag{8}$$

$$\sum_{i=1}^{n} z_i b_{ik} \geq CL_k \quad \text{for } 1 \leq k \leq q. \tag{9}$$

The objective function (1) is to maximize the weighted sum of the average preference and the budget execution rate, where ρ, $0 \leq \rho \leq 1$, is a parameter controlling the degree of importance between these two terms. The actual expense of material i apportioned by department j (e_{ij}) is given in constraints (2), where all the cost of materials will be apportioned according to the proportion of the preference (p_{ij}). Constraints (3) confine that the expense of any department j do not exceed its budget (B_j). To ease the amount computation of the acquired materials, we introduce an auxiliary variable z_i, which is 1 (0) if $\sum_{j=1}^{m} x_{ij} > 0$ (otherwise), to show whether material i is acquired or not. Using a sufficiently large positive number M, constraints (4) and (5) are deliberately designed to obtain the proper value of z_i. If $\sum_{j=1}^{m} x_{ij} \leq 0$, constraint (4) becomes irrelevant, where z_i may be either 0 or 1, but constraints (5) pledge $z_i = 0$, which indicates that material i is not acquired. On the contrary ($\sum_{j=1}^{m} x_{ij} > 0$), constraints (5) would be redundant, yet constraint (4) promises $z_i = 1$, which means that material i is acquired. If the material i is acquired ($z_i = 1$); then constraints (6) and (7) will force the number of acquired materials in each language l to be larger than or equal to the lower bounds and not to exceed the upper bounds. If material i is not acquired ($z_i = 0$), constraints (6) and (7) will assure the number of acquired materials in each language l included no material i. Constraints (11) and (12) are similarly defined to abide by the lower bound and upper bound specified on the number of materials in each category k.

2.3. *Greedy Algorithm.* A greedy solution method, denoted by Algorithm Greedy as shown in the Algorithm 1, is designed to be the comparison counterpart for other approaches. First, to decide if each material i will be acquired or not, all the materials are sorted in nonincreasing order of the ratio $(\sum_{j=1}^{m} p_{ij})/c_i$. We thus assume the materials are reindexed in accordance with this sequencing rule. The first material, the one that attains the maximum $(\sum_{j=1}^{m} p_{ij})/c_i$ ratio, will be considered if the following two conditions are satisfied: (1) the upper bound on the number of languages LU_l is not exceeded, and (2) the upper bound on the number of categories CU_k is

Algorithm Greedy:
Sort all materials in nonincreasing order of the ratio $(\sum_{j=1}^{m} p_{ij})/c_i$;
for $i := 1$ to n **do**
   while (the upper bound on the number of materials in language LU_l is not exceeded, $1 \leq l \leq r$)
      while (the upper bound on the number of materials in category CU_k is not exceeded, $1 \leq k \leq q$)
         Sort the departments that propose material i in nonincreasing order of p_{ij}
         Let $(j_1, j_2, \ldots, j_m)$ be the sorted sequence;
         for $j := 1$ to m **do**
            if (budget B_j is not exhausted)
               Set $x_{ij} = 1$
         endfor
         Calculate the residual budget of all departments j with $x_{ij} = 1$ by
         deducing the apportioned cost of material i.
      endwhile
   endwhile
endfor

ALGORITHM 1: Greedy solution method.

not exceeded. Next, to determine which departments will apportion the cost of material i, all departments are sorted in nonincreasing order of p_{ij}, and let $(j_1, j_2, \ldots, j_m)$ be the sorted list. Material i will be acquired by department j ($x_{ij} = 1$), if the budget of this department is not exceeded.

3. Related Works of PSO

This section presents an overview on particle swarm optimization and describes two widely used topologies. What follows is a review on how to handle constraints and how to avoid premature convergence.

3.1. PSO. Particle swarm optimization (PSO) [14], introduced by Kennedy (a social psychologist) and Eberhart (an electrical engineer) in 1995 as an optimization method, is inspired by the observation on behavior of flocking birds and schooling fish. With the simplicity and lessened computation loads, PSO has been widely applied to many research areas, such as clustering and classification, communication networks, and scheduling [15, 17–19].

In foraging, birds flock together and arrange themselves in specific shapes or formations by sharing their information about food sources. The movement of each particle will be influenced by the experiences of itself and the peers. In the process of optimization, each particle s of flock S is associated with a *position*, a *velocity*, and a *fitness value*. A position, which is a vector in a search space, represents a potential solution to an optimization problem; a velocity, which is a vector, represents a change in the position; a fitness value, which is computed by the objective function, indicates how well the particle solves the problem.

To find an approximate solution, each particle s determines its movement iteratively by learning from its own experience and communication with its neighbors. The mechanism of coordination is encapsulated by the *velocity control* over all particles at each iteration t of the algorithm.

For each particle s, the velocity at iteration $t + 1$ (V_s^{t+1}) is updated with (10), where P_s^t denotes the solution found by (position of) particle s at iteration t, $\overline{P}_s^t$ denotes the best solution found by particle s until iteration t, and $\widehat{P}_s^t$ denotes the best solution found by the neighbors of particle s. The *cognition learning* rate (c_1) and *social learning* rate (c_2) are introduced to control the influence of individual experience and their neighbors' experience, respectively. At the next iteration $t + 1$, the position of each particle is updated by (11). One has

$$V_s^{t+1} = V_s^t + c_1 r_1 \left(\overline{P}_s^t - P_s^t \right) + c_2 r_2 \left(\widehat{P}_s^t - P_s^t \right), \quad (10)$$

$$P_s^{t+1} = P_s^t + V_s^{t+1}. \quad (11)$$

For discrete optimization problems, Kennedy and Eberhart [20] also introduce a binary particle swarm optimization that changes the concept of velocity from adjustment of the position to the probability that determines whether a bit of a solution becomes one or zero. The velocity of each particle s at iteration t, V_s^{t+1}, is squashed in sigmoidal function as shown in (12); the position updating function is replaced by (13), where rand() is a random number drawn from the interval $[0, 1]$. One has

$$S\left(V_s^{t+1}\right) = \frac{1}{1 + e^{-(V_s^{t+1})}}, \quad (12)$$

$$P_s^{t+1} = \begin{cases} 1 & \text{if rand}() < S\left(V_s^{t+1}\right), \\ 0 & \text{otherwise}, \end{cases} \quad (13)$$

To better balance the exploration and exploitation, several variants of PSO algorithm have been proposed in the literature. A widely used method, proposed by Eberhart and Shi [21], is to introduce an *inertia weight* (w) to the velocity updating function shown in (14). The inertia weight is used to adjust the influence of the current velocity on the new velocity:

$$V_s^{t+1} = wV_s^t + c_1 r_1 \left(\overline{P}_s^t - P_s^t \right) + c_2 r_2 \left(\widehat{P}_s^t - P_s^t \right). \qquad (14)$$

3.2. Communication Topology. In the literature, several communication topologies have been extensively studied. Poli et al. [22] classify the communication structures into two categories: static topologies and dynamic topologies. Static topologies are that the number of neighbors does not change at all iterations of a run; dynamic topologies, on the other hand, are that the size of neighborhoods dynamically increases.

Local topology, global topology, and von Neumann topology are some well-known examples of static topology. As for dynamic topologies, the neighborhood size can be influenced by a dynamic hierarchy, a fitness distance ratio, or a randomized connection, just to name a few. The canonical PSO algorithm, proposed by Bratton and Kennedy [23], is equipped with global and local topologies.

A PSO with a global topology (or *gbest* topology) allows each particle to communicate with all other particles in the swarm, while a PSO with a local topology (or *lbest* topology) allows each particle to share information with only two other particles in the swarm. Therefore, a *gbest* PSO could lead to a faster convergence but might be trapped into a local optimal solution. Conversely, an *lbest* PSO could result in a slower rate of convergence but might be able to escape from a local optimal.

3.3. Constraint Handling. As reported in the literature, there are various different methods for handling constrained optimization problems. Several commonly used methods are based on penalty functions, rejection of infeasible solutions, repair algorithm, specialized operators, and behavioral memory [24–26]. In this paper, we focus on the method based on penalty function. Details concerning the penalty function for the studied problem are given in the next section.

When implementing penalty functions, the fitness evaluation for a solution is not just dependent on the objective function but incorporated the penalty function with the objective function. This method can be implemented as stationary or nonstationary. If there is an infeasible solution, the stationary penalty function simply adds a fixed penalty. Contrary to the stationary one, the nonstationary function adds a floating penalty which changes the penalty value according to the violated constrains and the iterations number. Parsopoulos and Vrahatis [25] note that the results obtained by nonstationary penalty functions are superior to the stationary one for the most of the time. A high penalty leads to a feasible solution even it is not approximate to the optimal solution, while a low penalty reduces the probability to obtain a feasible solution. Therefore, Coath and Halgamuge [24] point out that a fine-tuning of the parameters in the penalty function is necessary when using this method. The method based on the rejection of infeasible solution is to discard an infeasible solution even if it is closer to the optimal solution than some feasible ones. The repair algorithm, an

extensively employed method in genetic algorithms (GA), is equipped to fix an infeasible solution, but the cost is more computationally expensive than other methods.

3.4. Avoiding Premature Convergence. Most of the global optimization methods suffer from premature convergence. One of the most used approaches to tackle this problem is to introduce diversity to the velocity or the position of a particle. As mutation operators are to the genetic algorithm, so is introduction of diversity to PSO algorithms. The focus of this paper is to introduce the diversity by employing scout particles. The details of how the proposed DPSO algorithm circumvents premature convergence are described in Section 4.

García-Villoria and Pastor [27] introduce the concept of diversity into the velocity updating function. The proposed dynamic diversity PSO (PSO-*c3dyn*) dynamically changes the diversity coefficients of all particles through iterations. The more heterogeneity of the population will be, the less diversity will be introduced to the velocity updating function, and vice versa. Blackwell and Bentley [28] incorporate diversity into the population by preventing the homogeneous particles from clustering tightly to each other in the search space. They provide collision-avoiding swarms that reduce the attraction of the swarm center and increase the coverage of a swarm in the search space. Silva et al. [16] attempt to apply the diversity to both the velocity and the population by a predator particle and several scout particles. A predator particle is intended to balance the exploitation and exploration of the swarm, while scout particles are designed to implement different exploration strategies. The closer the predator particle will be to the best particle, the higher probability of perturbation will be.

4. DPSO with Scout Particles

This section details how to tackle the materials acquisition problem by discrete particle swarm optimization with scout particles. The representation of a particle and the initialization method for the studied problem are described in Section 4.1. Then, Section 4.2 elaborates on the details of preventing premature convergence by deploying scout particles. Section 4.3 redefines a constraints handling mechanism for solving the constrained optimization problem.

4.1. Representation and Initialization. The solution of materials acquisition problem with n materials and m departments obtained by particle s at iteration t can be represented by an $n \times m$ binary matrix, proposed by Wu et al. [29], as shown in (15). Each entry of the matrix $(P_s^t)_{ij}$ indicates whether material i is acquired by department j or not. Note that each entry of the matrix $(P_s^t)_{ij}$ corresponds to the decision variable (x_{ij}) that was mentioned in Section 2.1:

$$P_s^t = \begin{bmatrix} P_{s(11)}^t & \cdots & P_{s(1m)}^t \\ \vdots & \ddots & \vdots \\ P_{s(n1)}^t & \cdots & P_{s(nm)}^t \end{bmatrix}. \qquad (15)$$

Step 1. Compute the sum of the lower bound on the number of materials in
language l ($\sum_{l=1}^{r} LL_l$); the sum of the lower bound on the number of
materials in category k ($\sum_{k=1}^{q} CL_k$).

Step 2. **If** ($\sum_{l=1}^{r} LL_l$) < ($\sum_{k=1}^{q} CL_k$)
then randomly select a material i that is in language l,
randomly select a department j, and set $(P_s^t)_{ij} = 1$,
until all the lower bounds on the number of materials in all languages are reached.

Step 3. **If** ($\sum_{l=1}^{r} LL_l$) ≥ ($\sum_{k=1}^{q} CL_k$)
then randomly select a material i that belongs to category k,
randomly select a department j, and set $(P_s^t)_{ij} = 1$,
until all the lower bounds on the number of materials belong to all categories are reached.

ALGORITHM 2: Initialization procedure of DPSO.

The initial population is generated by setting a void velocity and randomly generated entries of matrix P_s^t for each particle s. To find feasible solutions for the initial population, an initialization procedure is designed and depicted in Algorithm 2. To determine which constraint should be satisfied first, the sum of the lower bounds on the numbers of materials in all languages $\sum_{l=1}^{r} LL_l$ and in all categories $\sum_{k=1}^{q} CL_k$ are computed. The one with less sum will be satisfied first by randomly selecting the material that belongs to language l or category k.

4.2. Constraints Handling. In the literature, repair operators and penalty functions are widely used approaches to handling constrained optimization problems. However, due to the computationally heavy load of repair operators, we focus on solely penalty functions. For each particle, the fitness value is evaluated by (16), where $O(x_{ij})$ is the objective value of the studied problem given in (1), and $H(x_{ij})$ is a penalty factor defined in (17). A feasible solution reflects its objective value as the fitness value, while an infeasible solution receives an objective value and a penalized value by (17). It can be seen from (17) that each term is associated with constrains (3), (6), (7), (8), and (9), as mentioned in Section 2.2. For instance, if a solution reports that the expense of any department j exceeds the budget B_j, addressed in constraints (3), then a positive penalty value can be subtracted from the fitness value to reflect the infeasibility. One has

$$F\left(x_{ij}\right) = O\left(x_{ij}\right) - H\left(x_{ij}\right), \qquad (16)$$

$$H\left(x_{ij}\right) = \sum_{j=1}^{m} \max\left\{0, \frac{\sum_{i=1}^{n} x_{ij} e_{ij} - B_j}{B_j}\right\}$$
$$+ \sum_{l=1}^{r} \max\left\{0, \frac{\sum_{i=1}^{n} y_i a_{il} - LU_l}{|\sum_{i=1}^{n} y_i a_{il} - LL_l|}\right\}$$
$$+ \sum_{l=1}^{r} \max\left\{0, \frac{LL_l - \sum_{i=1}^{n} y_i a_{il}}{|LU_l - \sum_{i=1}^{n} y_i a_{il}|}\right\}$$

$$+ \sum_{k=1}^{q} \max\left\{0, \frac{\sum_{i=1}^{n} y_i b_{ik} - UC_k}{|\sum_{i=1}^{n} y_i b_{ik} - CL_k|}\right\}$$
$$+ \sum_{k=1}^{q} \max\left\{0, \frac{CL_k - \sum_{i=1}^{n} y_i b_{ik}}{|CU_k - \sum_{i=1}^{n} y_i b_{ik}|}\right\}. \qquad (17)$$

4.3. Scout Particles. Premature convergence is a challenging problem faced by PSO algorithms throughout the optimization process. To avoid premature convergence in the DPSO algorithm for the studied problem, this paper employs scout particles to enhance the exploration. The concept is to send out scout particles to explore the search space and collect more extensive information of optimal solutions for other particles. If a scout particle finds a solution that is quite different from the best solution and the expected fitness value is better, the scout particle will share the information with some particles by affecting their velocities.

The DPSO procedure with scout particles is depicted in Figure 1. Firstly, in order to generate a feasible swarm, the particles are generated by the initialization procedure as mentioned in Section 4.1. Secondly, when the swarm has not yet converged, the regular particle s (P_s^t) flies through the search space by the following steps: fitness evaluation, velocity calculation, and position updating. If the swarm converges, on the other hand, scout particles $\tilde{P}_s^t$ will be generated for exploration by randomly selecting a material to be acquired by all departments until the solution meets the lower bound and the upper bound on the number of languages and categories. In this paper, the convergence of DPSO is specified by the fitness variance.

The scout particles will share the information with the peer particles subject to a probability that depends on the velocity of each particle s. The larger velocity of particle s, the higher probability of the scout particle affecting the particle s by (19), where the diversity coefficient (c_3) is a prespecified parameter and r_3 is a random number drawn from the interval $[0, 1]$. Also, if the expected fitness value of the scout particle $\tilde{P}_s^t$ is greater than the fitness of the best solution bound by particle $\bar{P}_s^t$, the particles will share

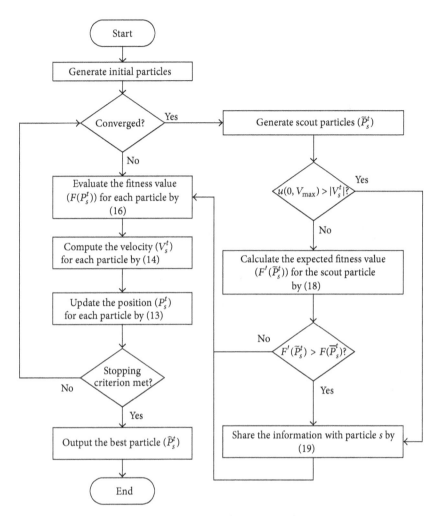

FIGURE 1: DPSO with scout particles.

information with other particles by (19). The expected fitness of the scout particle $\widetilde{P}_s^t$ is calculated by (18), where ρ is a nonnegative weight and p_i is the total preference of material i cast by all departments, $p_i = \sum_{j=1}^m p_{ij}$. One has

$$F'\left(\widetilde{P}_s^t\right) = \rho \times \frac{\sum_{i=1}^n \left(\widetilde{P}_s^t\right) p_i / \sum_{i=1}^n \left(\widetilde{P}_s^t\right)}{m}$$
$$+ (1 - \rho) \times \frac{\sum_{i=1}^n \left(\widetilde{P}_s^t\right) c_i}{\sum_{j=1}^m B_j}, \tag{18}$$

$$V_s^{t+1} = wV_s^t + c_3 r_3 \left(\widetilde{P}_s^t - P_s^t\right). \tag{19}$$

5. Computational Experiments

To manifest the effectiveness and efficiency of the proposed DPSO of materials acquisition, a series of computational experiments were designed and conducted. The experiment setting and test instances are described in Section 5.1 and the computational results and analysis are given in Section 5.2.

5.1. Test Instances and Settings. Small-size test instances and large-size test instances are exhibited in Tables 2 and 3, respectively. The number of materials n, the number of departments m, the budget limits B_j of department j, the number of languages r, the lower bound on the number of materials LL_l in language l, the upper bound on the number of materials LU_l in language l, the number of categories q, the lower bound on the number of materials CL_k in category k, the upper bound on the number of materials CU_k in category k were tabulated. The small-size test instances (Case I), determined by the combinations of n, m, r, and q, were composed of 60 (= $3 \times 5 \times 2 \times 2$) instances. The large-size test instances (Case II) were composed of 20 (= $5 \times 2 \times 2$) instances, where n was 100,000.

The default values of the parameters in both DPSO and DPSO with scout particles algorithms were set as particle size $S = 30$, number of iterations $t = 500$, inertia weight $w = 0.9$, cognition learning rate $c_1 = 2.05$, social learning rate $c_2 = 2.05$, and diversity coefficient $c_3 = 0.5$. The number of scout particles was set to one. All of the programs were implemented in C#.net and run on a PC with an Intel Core i5-2400 3.1 GHz CPU and 4 G RAM. The stopping criteria of all

TABLE 2: Small-size test instances, Case I.

n	$\{m, \{B_j\}\}$	$\{r, \{LU_l\}, \{LL_l\}\}$	$\{q, \{CU_k\}, \{CL_k\}\}$
100	$\{1, \{15000\}\}$, $\{2, \{6000, 9000\}\}$, $\{3, \{3000, 3000, 4000\}\}$, $\{4, \{3000, 3000, 4500, 4500\}\}$, $\{5, \{1500, 1500, 3000, 4500, 4500\}\}$.	$\{2, \{10, 20\}, \{5, 12\}\}$, $\{3, \{5, 10, 15\}, \{3, 3, 3\}\}$.	$\{3, \{6, 6, 12\}, \{3, 3, 6\}\}$, $\{5, \{3, 3, 6, 9, 9\}, \{3, 3, 3, 3, 3\}\}$.
200	$\{1, \{20000\}\}$, $\{2, \{8000, 12000\}\}$, $\{3, \{4000, 10000, 6000\}\}$, $\{4, \{3000, 3000, 3000, 4000, \}\}$, $\{5, \{2000, 2000, 2000, 8000, 4000, \}\}$.	$\{2, \{15, 25\}, \{5, 10, \}\}$, $\{3, \{10, 15, 15\}, \{5, 5, 5\}\}$.	$\{3, \{10, 10, 20\}, \{2, 4, 6\}\}$, $\{5, \{4, 4, 8, 12, 12\}, \{0, 0, 2, 3, 3\}\}$.
300	$\{1, \{30000\}\}$, $\{2, \{10000, 20000\}\}$, $\{3, \{6000, 6000, 18000, \}\}$, $\{4, \{6000, 6000, 9000, 9000\}\}$, $\{5, \{2000, 4000, 7000, 8000, 9000\}\}$.	$\{2, \{25, 35\}, \{10, 20\}\}$, $\{3, \{15, 15, 30\}, \{10, 10, 15\}\}$.	$\{3, \{10, 20, 30\}, \{5, 10, 10\}\}$, $\{5, \{10, 10, 10, 15, 15\}, \{5, 5, 5, 5, 5\}\}$.

TABLE 3: Large-size test instances, Case II.

$\{m, \{B_j\}\}$ (unit of B_j: 10000)	$\{r, \{LU_l\}, \{LL_l\}\}$	$\{q, \{CU_k\}, \{CL_k\}\}$
$\{5, \{80, 80, 100, 120, 120\}\}$, $\{10, \{40, 40, 40, 50, 50, 50, 50, 60, 60, 60\}\}$, $\{15, \{30, 30, 30, 30, 30, 33, 33, 33, 33, 33, 36, 36, 36, 36, 36\}\}$, $\{20, \{20, 20, 20, 20, 20, 25, 25, 25, 25, 25, 25, 25, 25, 25, 25, 30, 30, 30, 30\}\}$, $\{25, \{16, 16, 16, 16, 16, 18, 18, 18, 18, 18, 20, 20, 20, 20, 20, 22, 22, 22, 22, 22, 24, 24, 24, 24, 24\}\}$.	$\{2, \{4000, 6000\}, \{1000, 2000\}\}$, $\{3, \{3000, 3000, 4000\}, \{500, 500, 1000\}\}$.	$\{5, \{1000, 1000, 2000, 3000, 3000\}, \{200, 400, 800, 1000, 1200\}\}$, $\{10, \{600, 600, 800, 1000, 1000, 1000, 1200, 1400, 1400\}, \{100, 200, 300, 500, 500, 600, 700, 700, 800, 1000\}\}$.

test cases were defined as no improvement on the incumbent solution can be achieved within 50 consecutive iterations.

5.2. Results and Analysis. To understand the effectiveness and efficiency of the proposed DPSO, we examine the four key features, including initialization, swarm topology, constraints handling, and scout particles. The following subsections detail the results and analysis (Tables 4–7). The rows labeled "*Average*" and "*Stdev*" in each table list the average and standard deviations of improvement and execution time for several observations. The next three rows in each table report the number of observations on the results of different DPSO algorithms for the test instances, the z-score of statistical test where the null hypothesis is that the different features of DPSO algorithm have the same improvement (or execution time), and the P value which is translated from z-score. Note that the number of observations for case I (resp., II) is set as 480 (resp., 160), the combinations $8 \ (= \ 2 \times 2 \times 2)$ of features for 60 (resp., 20), for the purpose of evading the influence of other features. The significance level α is set at 0.05. Also, to facilitate a comparison of the effectiveness of the proposed DPSO algorithm across different test instances, the improvement in percentage over Algorithm Greedy, calculated as in (20), is employed instead of an absolute difference in objective value:

$$\text{improvement} = \left(\frac{\text{DPSO} - \text{greedy}}{\text{greedy}} \right) \%. \quad (20)$$

TABLE 4: Results of different initialization strategies on two test cases.

Case	Measure	Improvement		Execution time	
		Random	Greedy	Random	Greedy
I	Average	52.46%	52.11%	1.6455	1.5956
	Stdev	0.2805	0.2795	1.5258	1.3455
	Observations	480	480	480	480
	z-score	0.1942		0.5362	
	P value	0.8460		0.5918	
II	Average	71.32%	73.01%	779.9824	800.9922
	Stdev	0.3675	0.3722	318.31	324.77
	Observations	160	160	160	160
	z-score	−0.4090		−0.5843	
	P value	0.6825		0.5590	

5.2.1. Initialization. Results of different initialization strategies on the 60 small-size test instances (Case I) and 20 large-size test instances (Case II) are summarized in Table 4. The column labeled "*Random*" reports the results of DPSO algorithm that generates the initial swarms by the proposed initialization procedure in Section 4.1; the column labeled "*Greedy*" reports the results of DPSO algorithm that generates the initial swarms by both the abovementioned initialization procedure and the Algorithm Greedy in Section 2.3.

TABLE 5: Results of different swarm topologies on two test cases.

Case	Measure	Improvement		Execution time	
		Star	Ring	Star	Ring
I	Average	62.47%	42.10%	1.3193	1.9219
	Stdev	0.2244	0.2216	0.4285	1.9427
	Observations	480	480	480	480
	z-score	12.1029		−6.6364	
	P value	0.0000		0.0000	
II	Average	80.98%	63.35%	772.2568	808.7178
	Stdev	0.4147	0.2934	370.76	262.47
	Observations	160	160	160	160
	z-score	4.3889		−1.0202	
	P value	0.0000		0.3076	

TABLE 6: Results of different constraints handlings on two test cases.

Case	Measure	Improvement		Execution time	
		Accept	Reject	Accept	Reject
I	Average	52.81%	51.76%	1.6610	1.5802
	Stdev	0.2826	0.2773	1.4622	1.4135
	Observations	480	480	480	480
	z-score	0.5825		0.8703	
	P value	0.5603		0.3841	
II	Average	72.85%	71.48%	803.15	777.82
	Stdev	0.3693	0.3705	310.83	331.79
	Observations	160	160	160	160
	z-score	0.3304		0.7047	
	P value	0.7410		0.4810	

TABLE 7: Results of DPSO with and without scout particles on two test cases.

Case	Measure	Improvement		Execution time	
		Standard	Scout	Standard	Scout
I	Average	47.36%	57.21%	2.0065	1.2346
	Stdev	0.2443	0.3037	1.8070	0.7588
	Observations	480	480	480	480
	z-score	−5.5393		8.6285	
	P value	0.0000		0.0000	
II	Average	62.99%	81.34%	839.9745	741.0001
	Stdev	0.3015	0.4073	295.65	338.65
	Observations	160	160	160	160
	z-score	−4.5795		2.7849	
	P value	0.0000		0.0054	

It can be seen from Table 4 that the improvements achieved by two different initialization strategies are appealing. For case I, the improvement on the random strategy is slightly better than that on the greedy strategy (52.46% versus 52.11%); for case II, the greedy strategy performs slightly better (73.01% versus 71.32%). However, the difference in improvement between the "Random" and "Greedy" initializations for case I and case II yielded P values of 0.8460 and 0.6825 using z-test at α of 0.05. Therefore, the difference in

improvement of two initialization strategies is not statistically significant. We could thus reason that the DPSO equipped with these different initialization strategies will lead to the same significant improvement rate.

Regarding the execution time, both initialization strategies can produce solution for small test instances (Case I) in a very short time. The difference in execution time between the "Random" and "Greedy" initialization on case I and II yielded a P value of 0.5918 and 0.5590 by z-test at $\alpha = 0.05$. It reveals that the difference is not statistically significant on both cases. This phenomenon is reasonable because both of the initialization strategies enable the diversity of initial swarms before they satisfy the stopping criterion. These results suggest that DPSO can obtain good solutions with these initialization strategies.

5.2.2. Swarm Topology. Results of different swarm topologies on the 60 small-size test instances (Case I) and 20 large-size test instances (Case II) are summarized in Table 5. The columns labeled "*Star*" and "*Ring*" list the results of DPSO algorithm with star topology and ring topology.

From Table 5, the improvements of both star and ring topologies on two test cases reached a high percentage (on average 62.25%), being quite attractive. For cases I and II, the difference in execution time yielded a P value less than 0.05 (P value = 0.0000), indicating that a statistically significant difference in improvement existed. Accordingly, we would suggest that star topology (*gbest*) is an effective swarm topology to deliver solutions with satisfactory qualities.

In Table 5, the results of execution time needed by different topologies reaffirm the fact that star topology (*gbest*) seem to have a faster convergence rate than the ring topology (*lbest*). For small-size test instances (Case I), the z-test of the difference in execution time between star topology (1.31 seconds) and ring topology (1.92 seconds) yielded a P value less than 0.05, indicating that a statistically significant difference in execution time exists; for large-size test instances (Case II), even though the star topology spent less computation time, the difference in execution time between the star topology (772.26 seconds) and ring topology (808.72 seconds) yielded a P value of 0.3076 by z-test at $\alpha = 0.05$, specifying that no statistically significant difference in execution time was found. This is reasonable because of the large standard deviation in the results of case II. The result suggests that the star topology spent less computational time to obtain attractive solutions to the studied problem.

5.2.3. Constraints Handling. Results of different constraints handling mechanisms on Cases I and II are shown in Table 6. The column labeled "*Accept*" reveals the results of DPSO algorithm that accept infeasible solutions as the best solution found by particle s at iteration t ($\overline{P}_s^t$); on the other hand, the column labeled "*Reject*" reveals those reject infeasible solutions.

As can be seen from Table 6, the improvements of two different constraint handling approaches do produce good solutions. For the small-size test instances (Case I), the average improvements of the "Accept" mechanism and the

"Reject" mechanism are 52.81% and 51.76%; for the large-size test instances (Case II), the average improvements are 72.85% and 71.48%. The results show that the "Accept" mechanism reaches slightly higher improvement than the "Reject" mechanism in both cases within a longer execution time. This is reasonable because the "Accept" mechanism has more chance to explore the infeasible solution space and takes more iteration to converge. However, to have a concise comparison of "Reject" mechanism and the "Accept" mechanism, the z-test yields P values of 0.5603 and 0.7410, which indicate that there is no statistical difference. The computational results and analysis shown in Table 6 suggest that DPSO with both constraints handling mechanisms can produce quality solutions.

5.2.4. Scout Particles. Results of DPSO and DPSO with scout particles on two test instances (small size and large size) are exhibited in Table 7. The column labeled "*Scout*" displays the results of DPSO algorithm with scout particles, while the column labeled "*Standard*" displays the results of DPSO algorithm without scouts.

For the improvement, the DPSO with scouts does produce better solutions than the standard DPSO on all test instances. It can be seen from Table 7 that the DPSO with scout particles reported 57.21% improvement rate on small-size test instances and 81.34% improvement rate on large-size test instances, while the standard DPSO showed 47.36% and 62.99%. The z-test of the difference in improvement yielded a P value less than 0.05 which indicates that a statistically significant difference in execution time existed. The effectiveness of the proposed DPSO can be attributed to the scout particles that decrease the chance to be trapped in local optimal by exploring the search space. This reveals that the proposed DPSO is an effective approach to the problem.

As for the execution time, the DPSO with scouts took less computation time than the standard DPSO on all test instances as well. In Table 7, the DPSO with scout particles took 1.23 seconds for solving the small-size test instances and 741 seconds 741 for large-size test instances. On the other hand, the elapsed times of the standard DPSO are 2.01 seconds and 839.97 seconds. For each case, the z-test yields a P value below 0.05, indicating that the difference in execution times is significant. This result evinces the efficiency of the DPSO with scouts by showing that the time elapsed is smaller than the standard DPSO. This phenomenon may be due to the fact that scout particles were evaluated by the expected fitness instead of the objective function.

6. Conclusions

In this paper, we have proposed an integer programming model for the materials acquisition problem, which is to maximize both the average preference and the budget execution rate being subject to some constraints of the budget, the required number of materials in each category and language. To solve the constrained problem, we have developed a DPSO algorithm and designed an initialization strategy to generate feasible particles. We have also conducted computational

experiments of two sets test instances to demonstrate the effectiveness and efficiency of the proposed DPSO algorithm.

To better solve the studied problem, four different features of the proposed DPSO, including initialization strategies, swarm topology, constraints handling mechanism, and scout particles, are discussed. Firstly, we compare the results of employing the proposed initialization procedure, and the results of employing both the proposed Algorithm Greedy and initialization procedure. The computational results show that DPSO algorithm can obtain quality solutions with both the initialization strategies in a reasonable time. Secondly, we compare the results of performing star topology and ring topology. The results evince that star topology significantly outperforms ring topology in all test instances. Next, we compare the performances resulted from different constraint handling mechanisms. One mechanism is to accept the infeasible solutions as the best solution found by each particle, while the other is to reject the infeasible solutions as the best solution found by each particle. The computational results demonstrate that these two mechanisms reach the same performance. Lastly, we compare the results of standard DPSO and DPSO with the proposed scout particles. The results reveal that DPSO with scouts reaches higher improvement rates and takes shorter execution time. Accordingly, we would suggest that DPSO with the proposed initialization procedure, star topology, and scout particles is an effective approach to delivering attractive solutions in a reasonable time.

References

[1] J. Harrell, "Literature of acquisitions in review, 2008–9," *Library Resources and Technical Services*, vol. 56, no. 1, pp. 4–13, 2012.

[2] W. H. Walters, "Journal prices, book acquisitions, and sustainable college library collections," *College and Research Libraries*, vol. 69, no. 6, pp. 576–586, 2008.

[3] L. S. Connaway, K. Downing, Y. Du et al., "2010 top ten trends in academic libraries," *College and Research Libraries News*, vol. 71, no. 6, pp. 286–292, 2010.

[4] M. H. Beilby and T. H. Mott Jr., "Academic library acquisitions allocation based on multiple collection development goals," *Computers and Operations Research*, vol. 10, no. 4, pp. 335–343, 1983.

[5] K. Wise and D. E. Perushek, "Linear goal programming for academic library acquisitions allocations," *Library Acquisitions: Practice and Theory*, vol. 20, no. 3, pp. 311–327, 1996.

[6] K. Wise and D. E. Perushek, "Goal programming as a solution technique for the acquisitions allocation problem," *Library and Information Science Research*, vol. 22, no. 2, pp. 165–183, 2000.

[7] T.-F. Ho, S. J. Shyu, B. M. T. Lin, and Y.-L. Wu, "An evolutionary approach to library materials acquisition problems," in *Proceedings of the IEEE International Conference on Intelligent Systems (IS '10)*, pp. 450–455, London, UK, July 2010.

[8] S. K. Goyal, "Allocation of library funds to different departments of a university—an operational research approach," *College and Research Libraries*, vol. 34, pp. 219–222, 1973.

[9] A. Arora and D. Klabjan, "A model for budget allocation in multi-unit libraries," *Library Collections, Acquisition and Technical Services*, vol. 26, no. 4, pp. 423–438, 2002.

[10] T. Niyonsenga and B. Bizimana, "Measures of library use and user satisfaction with academic library services," *Library and Information Science Research*, vol. 18, no. 3, pp. 225–240, 1996.

[11] M. R. Garey and D. S. Johnson, *Computers and Intractability: A Guide to the Theory of NP-Completeness*, W.H. Freemaan and Company, New York, NY, USA, 1979.

[12] C.-J. Liao, C.-T. Tseng, and P. Luarn, "A discrete version of particle swarm optimization for flowshop scheduling problems," *Computers and Operations Research*, vol. 34, no. 10, pp. 3099–3111, 2007.

[13] T. J. Ai and V. Kachitvichyanukul, "A particle swarm optimization for the vehicle routing problem with simultaneous pickup and delivery," *Computers and Operations Research*, vol. 36, no. 5, pp. 1693–1702, 2009.

[14] J. Kennedy and R. Eberhart, "Particle swarm optimization," in *Proceedings of the IEEE International Conference on Neural Networks*, pp. 1942–1948, Perth, Australia, December 1995.

[15] R. Poli, "Analysis of the publications on the applications of particle swarm optimisation," *Journal of Artificial Evolution and Applications*, vol. 2008, Article ID 685175, 10 pages, 2008.

[16] A. Silva, A. Neves, and T. Goncalves, "An heterogeneous particle swarm optimizer with predator and scout particles," in *Autonomous and Intelligent Systems*, Lecture Notes in Computer Science, pp. 200–208, 2012.

[17] A. Hatamlou, "Black hole: a new heuristic optimization approach for data clustering," *Information Science*, vol. 222, pp. 175–184, 2013.

[18] C.-C. Chiu, M.-H. Ho, and S.-H. Liao, "PSO and APSO for optimizing coverage in indoor UWB communication system," *International Journal of RF and Microwave Computer-Aided Engineering*, vol. 23, no. 3, pp. 300–308, 2013.

[19] Y. Tian, D. Liu, D. Yuan, and K. Wang, "A discrete PSO for two-stage assembly scheduling problem," *International Journal of Advanced Manufacturing Technology*, vol. 66, no. 1-4, pp. 481–499, 2013.

[20] J. Kennedy and R. C. Eberhart, "Discrete binary version of the particle swarm algorithm," in *Proceedings of the IEEE International Conference on Systems, Man, and Cybernetics*, pp. 4104–4108, Piscataway, NJ, USA, October 1997.

[21] R. C. Eberhart and Y. Shi, "Comparing inertia weights and constriction factors in particle swarm optimization," in *Proceedings of the Congress on Evolutionary Computation (CEC '00)*, pp. 84–88, La Jolla, Calif, USA, July 2000.

[22] R. Poli, J. Kennedy, and T. Blackwell, "Particle swarm optimization: an overview," *Swarm Intelligence*, vol. 1, pp. 33–57, 2007.

[23] D. Bratton and J. Kennedy, "Defining a standard for particle swarm optimization," in *Proceedings of the IEEE Swarm Intelligence Symposium (SIS '07)*, pp. 120–127, Honolulu, Hawaii, USA, April 2007.

[24] G. Coath and S. K. Halgamuge, "A comparison of constraint-handling methods for the application of particle swarm optimization to constrained nonlinear optimization problems," in *Proceedings of the Congress on Evolutionary Computation*, pp. 2419–2425, Canberra, Australia, December 2003.

[25] K. E. Parsopoulos and M. N. Vrahatis, "Particle swarm optimization method for constrained optimization problems," in *Intelligent Technologies—Theory and Applications: New Trends in Intelligent Technologies*, vol. 76, pp. 214–220, 2002.

[26] G. T. Pulido and C. A. Coello Coello, "A constraint-handling mechanism for particle swarm optimization," in *Proceedings of the Congress on Evolutionary Computation (CEC '04)*, pp. 1396–1403, Portland, Ore, USA, June 2004.

[27] A. García-Villoria and R. Pastor, "Introducing dynamic diversity into a discrete particle swarm optimization," *Computers and Operations Research*, vol. 36, no. 3, pp. 951–966, 2009.

[28] T. M. Blackwell and P. Bentley, "Don't push me! Collision-avoiding swarms," in *Proceedings of the Congress on Evolutionary Computation*, pp. 1691–1696, Honolulu, Hawaii, USA, May 2002.

[29] Y.-L. Wu, T.-F. Ho, S. J. Shyu, and B. M. T. Lin, "Discrete particle swarm optimization for materials acquisition in multi-unit libraries," in *Proceedings of the Congress on Evolutionary Computation*, pp. 1–7, Brisbane, Australia, June 2012.

6

The Effects of Different Representations on Static Structure Analysis of Computer Malware Signatures

Ajit Narayanan,[1] **Yi Chen,**[1] **Shaoning Pang,**[2] **and Ban Tao**[3]

[1] *School of Computing and Mathematical Sciences, Auckland University of Technology, Auckland 1010, New Zealand*
[2] *Department of Computing, Unitec Institute of Technology, Auckland 1025, New Zealand*
[3] *National Institute of Information and Communications Technology, Tokyo 184-8795, Japan*

Correspondence should be addressed to Yi Chen; yixchea3@aut.ac.nz

Academic Editors: H.-l. Liu and Y. Wang

The continuous growth of malware presents a problem for internet computing due to increasingly sophisticated techniques for disguising malicious code through mutation and the time required to identify signatures for use by antiviral software systems (AVS). Malware modelling has focused primarily on semantics due to the intended actions and behaviours of viral and worm code. The aim of this paper is to evaluate a static structure approach to malware modelling using the growing malware signature databases now available. We show that, if malware signatures are represented as artificial protein sequences, it is possible to apply standard sequence alignment techniques in bioinformatics to improve accuracy of distinguishing between worm and virus signatures. Moreover, aligned signature sequences can be mined through traditional data mining techniques to extract metasignatures that help to distinguish between viral and worm signatures. All bioinformatics and data mining analysis were performed on publicly available tools and Weka.

1. Introduction

If users do not have confidence that their machines will not be attacked when connected to the internet, major areas of computing will be constrained due to fear of denial of service and massive data fraud [1]. Symantec reported over 5 billion attacks in 2011, an 81% increase over 2010 [2]. Over 400 million new malware variants were identified that year alone. From a theoretical perspective, while virus detection is undecidable [3–5], it is still not known whether there exist algorithms that will take an arbitrary program or code and decide correctly whether it contains specific forms of malware [6]. This is not just because malware is behavioural (actions performed at run time) and hence characterized semantically [7], usually in the form of execution traces [8], control flow [9], and process calculi [10]. Rather, an essential aspect of viruses and worms is obfuscation through polymorphic and metamorphic mutation [11–13], that is, the ability to replicate with modification. While polymorphic mutation (payload algorithm is kept constant, but viral code

is mutated) has led to computable detection in some cases [6, 14, 15], metamorphic mutation involves generating logically equivalent code with changes in program length and flow as well as data structures [16]. Because of increasing complexity of obfuscation as well as discovery of new types of malware (e.g., spyware, botnets), human experts are still required to implement the variety of polymorphic and metamorphic malware detection techniques currently known to exist [17–20]. This manual process leads to the use of "signatures" by antiviral software systems when scanning network packets or memory block hashes for contiguous appearance of key parts of malware code. This in turn leads to the situation where malware infections must occur first before solutions can be found and hence the threat to user confidence.

Research has continued in static structure checking algorithms [21–24] despite current emphasis on semantic-based approaches. Static structure analysis can reveal deep structural similarities between superficially dissimilar sequences irrespective of control flow. Static checkers have faced problems in identifying complex obfuscation, however [25]. We have recently demonstrated a potential breakthrough in static approaches by using the ever-expanding base of already available hexadecimal signatures [26] for polymorphic and metamorphic malware. The key was to represent these signatures under an interpretation derived from biology: amino acids forming polypeptide sequences. After signature alignment using bioinformatics sequence alignment techniques involving substitution matrices derived from the large number of biosequence databases now available, static metasignatures for distinguishing between worms and viruses were extracted with high accuracy [27, 28]. However, there are some limitations to this work.

Antiviral signatures can be calculated from a pattern of operations in the malware code or can represent the encryption algorithm used to hide the virus or worm. Signatures were originally and continue to be identified and calculated by human experts and are typically a sequence of hexadecimal numbers intended to uniquely identify viruses and worms. Automatic generation of signatures for new malware continues to be a difficult problem [29]. Such signatures can also be consistent for a "family" of viruses or worms that share parts of the code or have similar function and are essentially variants of each other. For instance, "Virus.Acad.Bursted.a" is a typical computer virus name that indicates the platform (Autocad, or "Acad"), the family (Bursted), and the variant "a". Achieving consistency of signatures for members of the same family is especially important when dealing with polymorphic (the functional parts of the code are the same but hidden differently) and metamorphic (the function remains the same, but the code is altered with every replication) malware designed to avoid such signature detection [30, 31]. Due to the security dangers inherent in making the original malware code available for public dissemination, only signatures are made publicly available.

AVS scanners use a dictionary or library of signatures in a variety of different ways. For instance, for simple polymorphic malware detection, the hexadecimal representation of a signature can be used to match against incoming network packets containing bytes also represented in hexadecimal. This allows the AVS to check for contiguous similarities between parts of the signature and packet contents. For metamorphic and more complex polymorphic malware detection, increasingly sophisticated techniques must be used that allow for contiguous parts of the signature to be detected noncontiguously across different packets [32]. Signature detection through pattern matching is usually supported by other techniques, such as stateful monitoring, to minimize false positives and false negatives [33]. Malware writers adopt a variety of sophisticated techniques for avoiding detection. By the time a new variant is identified and signatures released, the infection may already have reached epidemic proportions [34]. One of the problems in applying automatic data mining techniques to static malware code directly, even if it is available, is the variable length of the code [35], since most data mining and other machine learning techniques assume fixed length sequences with a column representing measurements of the same variable across many samples. There is surprisingly little work reporting on the application of machine learning techniques to malware signature detection, mainly due to the problem of obtaining malware source code as well as the need to deal with variable length code to identify the critical parts of the code from which to derive signatures. Also, mining the signatures directly can lead to results that are difficult to interpret, since the hexadecimal signatures cannot always be mapped back to meaningful and individual operations in the source code (op code). The variable length of the malware code, the difficulty of legally obtaining source malware code for detailed analysis, and the lack of interpretability of results if hexadecimal signatures are used and the partially sequential aspects of the data all obstruct the use of machine learning techniques, thereby limiting their use in the urgent problem of finding automatic ways of generating static signatures.

Sequence analysis is used in biology to understand the relationship between two or more sequences (multiple sequence alignment) of genetic information, such as DNA or amino acids. There are databases of genetic information which are processed by string alignment algorithms to better understand the relationship between species and also determine the location of specific genes. In particular, sequence analysis and alignment can be used to identify conserved regions or motifs (regions of similarity) in biological data that identify common genes and shared ancestry as well as common structure and function of amino acid sequences [36]. One advantageous side effect of alignment methods is that variable length biological sequences can be converted into fixed length sequences through appropriate insertion and deletion techniques. Powerful data mining algorithms that assume fixed length sequences or patterns can then be applied to identify critical features that help to determine whether a sequence is malware or not.

Sequence alignment techniques are not confined to biological sequences, however, and there have been applications of sequence alignment in linguistics [37] and marketing [38]. The first demonstration of multiple sequence alignment to malware signatures to identify motifs [39], or metasignatures, for families of computer viruses and worms demonstrated the feasibility of the approach. The signatures of 30 worms and 30 viruses were converted into amino acid residue representation using a random mapping (hex 1 became "A", hex 2 "C"..). Since there are 20 amino acid residue characters, that left four spare amino acid residues. The amino acid W was used to represent gaps in the alignment of worms and viruses separately and the amino acid Y to represent gaps in the alignment when the aligned worms and viruses were jointly aligned to produce a common fixed length set of sequences. ClustalW [40] was used as the multiple alignment tool. The advantage of alignment was that initially fixed length signatures can be expanded to find common or conserved regions across families of viruses and worms separately. The length of expansion will vary between families so that the length of the aligned signatures of worms will almost certainly be different from aligned virus signatures. These separately aligned worm and virus signatures were then multiply aligned together into fixed length (but significantly longer) sequences that were annotated with a class value ("1" for worm, "0" for virus) for supervised learning. The doubly aligned sequences were in turn converted into decimal ASCII code ("A" became 66, "C" 67 ... "Z" 90) for input to a two-layer perceptron for checking accuracy of classification. This conversion to numeric code was necessary because of the input requirements of ANNs. Comparison between the classification of nonaligned sequences and doubly aligned sequences showed improvement (80% average accuracy for unaligned, 91% average accuracy for doubly aligned), thereby demonstrating the feasibility of the approach [39].

Subsequent work [41] reported on a variation to the neural network representation of the doubly aligned sequences. Instead of using ASCII, residues were converted into numerical values for an ANN through real numbers 0.1 to 0.95 in steps of 0.05. This allowed the use of a single layer perceptron, with the ANN returning on average 72% accuracy on nonaligned sequences and 83% on average on doubly aligned sequences. These results demonstrated the sensitivity of the results to ANN architecture (one layer rather than two layers) as well as coding representations. Further work [42] showed the effects of applying different three different amino acid representation methods to virus and worm signatures. The first method was the same as originally used [39, 40], the second method reversed the order of representation, and third shifted the representation by one letter but kept the first letter constant [42] (more details below). Also, the number of signatures was doubled to 60 worm and 60 viral signatures. Accuracy figures showed significant improvement, irrespective of representation method adopted, providing evidence that applying multiple sequencing techniques to malware signatures enhanced predictive capability.

The aim of this paper is to significantly extend the work started in [42] and to explore the implications of adopting five different residue representations when forming alignments of signatures and extracting motifs. Also, it is important to know whether motifs/metasignatures reported earlier [39, 41, 42] are an accidental by-product of the representations used or evidence of a deeper and unpredicted aspect of applying biosequence techniques to artificial virus and worm signatures.

2. Representations and Methods

There are several tools for alignment and many algorithms used in the study of biosequence analysis. In general, an alignment is an adjustment of a sequence in relation to other sequences. The aim is to arrange two (pairwise alignment) or more (multiple sequence alignment) possibly variable length sequences of DNA or protein in such a way that regions of similarity across sequences (rows of a matrix) fall in the same successive columns of the matrix, where such similarity signifies functional, structural, or evolutionary commonality. Global alignment tries to align every item in every sequence and tends to work best when the sequences are of roughly similar length, such as the Needleman-Wunsch technique [43]. Local alignment, on the other hand, tries to align regions of the sequences even if the sequences are not similar overall, such as the Smith-Waterman technique [44]. ClustalW is

a global alignment tool available from the EBI [45] and is the global alignment tool used below.

Malware is a generic term given to any program or code intended to cause disruption or gain access to unauthorised information and resources. Viruses can be written in any programming language before being compiled. Viral source code signatures are provided on the internet for experimental use and viral source code as such will not be used in this paper. Instead, in line with viral signature detection, the virus signatures, expressed in hexadecimal, are used here. Signature detection is usually effective for new viruses of a known family, where code and functionality are shared and therefore there is some consistency among the signatures to allow or detection of new variants of the same family. The first part of the *virus.1C.Tanga.a* computer virus signature has the hexadecimal coding *8e5ef1aec91259d70c5e62* and the worm *Bat.Agent.bo*, the hexadecimal coding *fb56373bde3881741*. The hexadecimal code for 60 viruses belonging to 12 families and 60 worms belonging to 13 families were downloaded from VX Heavens [46] for use in the experiments below.

Five different representations of the signatures were tried for alignment purposes (Table 1). The first representation (R1) uses the same order of hexadecimal to amino acid residues. The second (R2) reverses this order and the third (R3) uses a shift of one amino acid residue after the initial residue. R4 essentially swaps the two halves of R1 and R5 reverses the two halves of R1. In previous work, gaps introduced by alignment were coded differently. Here, we use "W" to represent all gaps introduced during the first stage of alignment and "Y" to represent all gaps introduced during the second alignment stage (details below). Given that there are 18! ways to undertake the conversion from hexadecimal plus two gaps into amino acid characters, there is clearly much more work required to assess the effects of different representations. The five chosen here are pseudorandom selections, with no attempt made to ensure lack of random duplication. For instance, hex 5 is represented twice by *F* (R1 and R5). The use of these five representations results in five files, each of 120 instances. The experimental method adopted is as follows.

(a) Download 60 virus and 60 worm signatures in hexadecimal format from VX Heavens and calculate unaligned benchmarks prior to alignment as follows.

   (i) Convert the 120 hexadecimal sequences into their five different representation files using Table 1 (R1–R5), resulting in five files of artificial protein sequences (AP1–AP5).

   (ii) Convert these artificial protein sequence representation files (AP1–AP5) into their numeric versions (NR1–NR5) using Table 2 (details below).

   (iii) Input files AP1–AP5 into J48 and Naive Bayes to provide benchmarks for unaligned sequences. Input NR1–NR5 into perceptrons to provide a benchmark for unaligned sequences.

(b) Input all 60 R1 worm signatures from AP1 (but not virus signatures) into ClustalW to form an initial set

TABLE 1: Five different representations R1–R5 of malware hexadecimal signatures.

Hex	1	2	3	4	5	6	7	8	9
R1	A	C	D	E	F	G	H	I	K
R2	S	R	Q	P	N	M	L	K	I
R3	A	D	E	F	G	H	I	K	L
R4	I	K	L	M	N	P	Q	R	S
R5	K	I	H	G	F	E	D	C	A
Hex	0	a	b	c	d	e	f	—	—
R1	L	M	N	P	Q	R	S	Y	W
R2	H	G	F	E	D	C	A	Y	W
R3	M	N	P	Q	R	S	C	Y	W
R4	A	C	D	E	F	G	H	Y	W
R5	S	R	Q	P	N	M	L	Y	W

of aligned worm sequences. Code gaps as "W." Repeat for R2–R5 worm signatures. Call these sequences WAR1-WAR5 ("W" for worm, "A" for aligned using ClustalW).

(c) Input all 60 R1 virus signatures into ClustalW to form an initial set of aligned virus sequences. Code gaps as "W." Repeat for R2–R5 virus signatures. Call these sequences VAR1–VAR5 ("V" for virus, "A" for aligned using ClustalW).

(d) Recombine the two aligned sets (WAR1 worm and VAR1 virus) into one dataset (120 sequences of two different lengths) and input into ClustalW to form a second, combined set of aligned sequences, DAR1 ("D" for doubly aligned, "R1" for representation 1). Code all gaps introduced at this (double alignment) stage as "Y." Repeat for WAR2-WAR5 worm and VAR2-VAR5. This results in five doubly aligned datasets DAR1-DAR5, with each consisting of doubly aligned worm and virus signatures using the same representation.

(e) Input DAR1-DAR5 to J48 and Naive Bayes. Convert DAR1-DAR5 using Table 2 into their numeric versions (DANR1-DANR5, where "N" is numeric) and input to perceptrons. Compare the results against the benchmarks produced in (a)(iii) above.

(f) Input DAR1-DAR5 to the rule extractor PRISM to identify virus and worm motifs, or metasignatures.

Whereas previously J48 (a rule extractor with pruning) had been used [39, 41], this paper reports on the application of PRISM (a modular rule extractor [47]) to extract motifs from the signatures. J48 is now used here to provide benchmarks and comparative measures against perceptrons and Naive Bayes because of earlier confidence that J48 works effectively with doubly aligned sequences. J48 and Naive Bayes interpret the input as categorical. However, neural networks require numerical input, hence the conversion to numeric form in Table 2.

Previous work [41] had shown that a single layer perceptron was sufficient but, to take into account the arbitrary nature of the conversion of amino acid residues to numerical

values (Table 2), a hidden layer of 72 units was introduced. The hidden layer is intended to collect summed activations from the input layer irrespective of the mode of representation R1-R5 as well as deal with any aspects of nonlinearity due to numerical representation. The hypothesis is that the different representations R1-R5 would make no difference to the training and test results due to the hidden layer acting as a "buffer" between input and output layers. Previous work [41, 43] had shown that a 72 node hidden layer, in comparison to other architectures, was effective. This architecture is used for both benchmarking and comparative purposes on the double aligned sequences. The numeric conversion was used successfully previously [41, 43] and so there is confidence in its effectiveness. The same numeric conversion is used so that any differences in the results can be due only to the mode of representation R1-R5. Class information for supervised learning is attached to the end of each sample as before, with "0" denoting virus and "1" denoting worm.

Aligning the 60 viruses and 60 worms separately (steps (b) and (c) above) allows the conserved regions of viruses and worms to be independently extracted by ClustalW. ClustalW alignments are based on the frequency of residue occurrence in the 120 input sequences and default weighting parameters based on similarity and dissimilarity of sequences. Without a substitution matrix, ClustalW default parameters use gap insertion and gap extension penalties (e.g., gaps at the ends of sequences are penalised less than gaps in the middle of sequences) as well as protein weight matrices that use similarity of amino acids to each other when calculating where to insert gaps. For the experiments below, it was decided to try the Gonnet substitution matrix [46] with ClustalW. Very generally, Gonnet matrices represent evolutionary substitution information gained from pairwise analysing all protein sequences known in 1992. Current substitution matrices based on exhaustive pairwise alignment tend to focus on specific families of organisms because of the large number of protein sequences now available in public databases. Gonnet matrices have been subsequently refined to take into account growing knowledge of mutations between amino acids. Given that many worm and virus signature sequences are mutated variants of each other, it would be interesting to see how a substitution method based on evolutionary distance would handle the sequences. After the first alignment (steps (b) and (c) above), the length of the virus set alignment will be different from the length of the worm set alignment. This is because there is no guarantee that ClustalW with Gonnet will make the same number of insertions (gaps) for each set of sequences. A second and joint alignment is required to ensure that all 120 sequences are of the same length for machine learning purposes (step (d) above).

For instance, after alignment by ClustalW, we have (for the first parts of three viral signature sequences only using R1):

```
FIIDIDNGLFDSRPLEEFKGALEGEI...
GE-----SQMPSIDMPQF---PGLPS...
---------ILHSPMHQFRF-PRSQR...
        :  :*
```

TABLE 2: Conversion of the 16-amino acid alphabet to numeric form between 0 to 1 for input to perceptrons. Y and W (two extra characters) represent the gaps introduced during alignment (see main text).

A	C	D	E	F	G	H	I	K	L	M	N	P	Q	R	S	Y	W
0.1	0.15	0.2	0.25	0.3	0.35	0.4	0.45	0.5	0.55	0.6	0.65	0.7	0.75	0.8	0.85	0.9	0.95

which shows that only F is aligned across all three sequences (*) and M and Q across two sequences (:). The gaps (−) introduced at this stage are coded "W." The 60 aligned sequences for the virus set and the 60 aligned sequences for the worm set were then combined into a composite 120 sequence set for a second alignment. Gaps introduced at this stage are Y gaps. Y and W gaps have their own numeric representation (Table 2). Weka perceptrons were used to implement the neural networks, which has as many input nodes as residues in the fixed length, nonaligned and doubly aligned sequences. (Waikato Environment for Knowledge Analysis: http://www.cs.waikato.ac.nz/ml/weka/). For Weka, each residue position was given its own attribute and the class information was either "virus" or "worm." J48 and Naive Bayes within Weka were also used for all experiments in this paper. The machine learning task was therefore to determine whether using different representations at the initial stage of encoding worm and virus signatures affected the performance of the perceptrons, J48 and Naive Bayes. For reporting the test results, the following formulae are used (virus is negative; worm is positive):

$$\text{Accuracy} = \frac{\text{Number of true positives} + \text{number of true negatives}}{\text{Number of true positives} + \text{false positives} + \text{false negatives} + \text{true negatives}},$$

$$\text{Sensitivity} = \frac{\text{Number of true positives}}{\text{Number of true positives} + \text{number of false negatives}},$$

$$\text{Specificity} = \frac{\text{Number of true negatives}}{\text{Number of true negatives} + \text{number of false positives}}. \tag{1}$$

3. Experimental Results

The downloaded 60 virus and 60 worm signatures of fixed length 72 hexadecimal characters were first converted into five representation files using R1–R5 (Table 1) and input to Weka perceptrons for benchmark purposes (i.e., without alignment). Previous work had shown that a $72 \times 72 \times 1$ perceptron, with learning rate 0.1 and momentum of 0.25, was sufficient to reduce the root mean squared error to below 0.1 within 150 epochs. A severe training to test ratio of 50 : 50 was used to fully evaluate the generalizability of the three different representations using 10-fold cross-validation as well as test for possible overfitting due to the large number of hidden units. The overall accuracy result for the unaligned sequences was 0.531 (Table 1), which is not much better than tossing a coin. This confirms the problematic nature of the dataset in its raw form.

The double alignments of worm and virus signatures (steps (b), (c), and (d) above) resulted in fixed length sequences of 140, 123, 128, 133, and 109 for DAR1–DAR5, respectively. These five datasets were converted into numerical input using the coding in Table 2 and input to five perceptrons with architectures $140 \times 72 \times 1$, $123 \times 72 \times 1$, $128 \times 72 \times 1$, $133 \times 72 \times 1$, and $109 \times 72 \times 1$, respectively (step (d) above). The ANN experiment was repeated for 10-folds using the same 50% training, 50% testing regime, and learning parameters as for the benchmark results, leading to the figures displayed in Table 3. Also, DAR1–DAR5 were input to J48 and Naive Bayes in Weka using the same train-test ratios and numbers of folds. The results of the benchmarking (no alignment) and all doubly aligned analysis are provided in Table 3.

For rule extraction purposes, DAR1–DAR5 were input to PRISM (all samples used for maximum knowledge extraction) to produce the following metasignatures for each representation (where "pos" stands for position in the doubly aligned sequence):

R1: Virus signature if pos5 = A, pos20 = N, pos32 = G or A, pos33 = N or C, pos34 = N, pos60 = C. pos5 = A, pos20 = N, pos21 = D, pos28 = E, pos30 = L, pos32 = A, pos36 = P, pos53 = A.

R1: Worm signature if pos16 = G, pos37 = M, pos93 = I, pos94 = I, pos96 = A, pos100 = C or M, pos104 = D, pos149 = C. pos10 = L, pos41 = C, pos44 = I, pos45 = D or L, pos46 = R, pos51 = H, pos54 = L, pos59 = S, pos70 = G or R, pos71 = S, pos72 = L or M, pos73 = D or P.

R2: Virus signature. No rules found except involving gaps W and Y. pos4 = Q or R, pos43 = K, pos69 = F or Q, pos84 = K.

R2: Worm signature if pos5 = C, pos8 = H, pos11 = C or L, pos27 = G or N, pos28 = D or E, pos43 = A, pos45 = R, pos67 = S. pos5 = C, pos7 = P, pos27 = I, pos28 = D or G, pos29 = C, pos31 = K, pos83 = F.

R3: Virus signature if pos12 = A, post13 = A, pos65 = F.

TABLE 3: Results of 50 : 50 train-test ratio, 10-fold cross-validation on all five representations, non-aligned and aligned, using perceptrons, J48 and Naive Bayes.

	Unaligned					Aligned					Unaligned summary	Aligned summary
	R1	R2	R3	R4	R5	R1	R2	R3	R4	R5		
Perceptrons												
Accuracy	0.517	0.533	0.533	0.608	0.617	0.967	0.967	0.975	**1**	0.983	0.562	0.978
Sensitivity	0.516	0.54	0.542	0.607	0.613	0.983	0.967	0.967	**1**	0.968	0.564	0.977
Specificity	0.517	0.529	0.528	0.617	0.633	0.95	0.967	0.983	**1**	1	0.565	0.980
J48												
Accuracy	0.483	0.508	0.558	0.542	0.542	0.825	0.883	0.958	0.883	**0.975**	0.527	0.905
Sensitivity	0.483	0.508	0.554	0.541	0.541	0.783	0.871	**0.982**	0.848	0.967	0.525	0.890
Specificity	0.483	0.509	0.564	0.55	0.55	0.9	0.9	0.933	0.933	**0.983**	0.531	0.930
Naive Bayes												
Accuracy	0.425	0.475	0.533	0.542	0.542	0.975	0.967	0.992	**1**	0.983	0.503	0.983
Sensitivity	0.426	0.476	0.537	0.545	0.545	0.983	0.967	0.984	**1**	0.968	0.506	0.980
Specificity	0.424	0.474	0.53	0.5	0.5	0.967	0.967	1	1	1	0.486	0.987
Summary												
Accuracy	0.475	0.506	0.542	0.564	0.567	0.922	0.939	0.975	0.961	**0.98**	0.531	0.955
Sensitivity	0.475	0.508	0.544	0.564	0.566	0.916	0.935	**0.978**	0.949	0.968	0.531	0.949
Specificity	0.475	0.504	0.541	0.556	0.561	0.939	0.945	0.972	0.978	**0.994**	0.527	0.966

R3: Worm signature if pos11 = A, pos33 = I, pos55 = L or M, pos88 = M, pos119 = N, pos122 = A, pos124 = H or M.

R4: Virus signature if pos9 = K, pos18 = I, pos21 = K.

No rules found for virus or worm signatures except those involving W and Y.

R5: Virus signature if pos51 = E or M, pos52 = C, pos53 = P, pos54 = F, pos57 = D, pos58 = F, pos59 = D.

R5: Worm signature if pos13 = H then 1.

Converting these metasignatures back into hexadecimal patterns produces (where "." means any number of hexadecimal characters and "[ ]" gives alternatives):

R1: Virus signature if "..2..[df]..[61][b2]b..2.." "..1..b3..4.. 0..1..c..1.."; Worm signature if "..6..a..88..1..[2a]..3..2.." "..0..2..8[30]e..7..0..f..[6e]f[0a][3c].."

R2: Virus signature if "..[32]..8..[b3]..8.." Worm signature if "..6..1..[67]..[25][5c]..f..2..1.." "..e..4..9[ad]e..8..b.."

R3: Virus signature if "..11..4.."; Worm signature if "..1..7 ..[90]..0..a..1..[60].."

R4: Virus signature if "..2..1..2.."

R5: Virus signature if "..[6e]8c5..757.."; Worm signature if "..3.."

4. Discussion of Results

Table 3 indicates that the mode of representation affects both unaligned and doubly aligned sequences. The two-layer perceptron performs best on the unaligned sequences (0.562) and Naive Bayes on aligned sequences (0.983) in terms of accuracy. There are major improvements in the results for double aligned sequences, irrespective of representation. The perfect accuracy returned by perceptrons and Naive Bayes on R4 indicates that the insertion of gaps (coded as W and Y) has allowed these two techniques, which use the information present in all attributes including gaps, to distinguish between doubly aligned worm and virus signatures. That is, these two techniques found sufficient information in combinations of attributes (weighted in the case of perceptrons, frequency of occurrence in the case of Naive Bayes) to classify perfectly. J48, however, looks for minimal and selective attributes that distinguish between the two classes. Its performance across all five representations (0.905 average accuracy) is still a major improvement in comparison to unaligned performance (0.527).

Across the three machine learning algorithms, R5 was best for accuracy and specificity (0.98 and 0.994, resp.), and R3 for sensitivity (0.978). When R1 was used with 60 virus and 60 worm signatures, the metasignatures "..1..b3..4..0..1.. 1(/c)..1.." for virus and "..0..2..83(/0)e.. 7..0..f..6(/c)fa(/0)3(/c).." were reported [42]. The results above indicate that the choice of alignment method and use of substation matrix can affect the metasignatures extracted. R1 appears to be best for extracting metasignatures for both virus and worms in terms of information contained in the patterns, followed by R2 and R4 for worm metasignatures only and R5 for virus signatures only. The metasignature for virus using R5 ("..[6e]8c5..757..") in particular contains a number of contiguous hexadecimal characters (no gaps) that could be useful for future AVS to help distinguish viral malware from nonmalware.

5. Conclusions

The results indicate that aligning computer virus and worm signatures using multiple alignment techniques leads to improved classification accuracy using the techniques described in this paper. While the differences in representation are reflected to some extent in classification accuracy after alignment, there is a difference when PRISM is used, with R1 producing more informative metasignatures for both virus and worm. The method of converting malware hexadecimal signatures to residue representation has been clearly demonstrated to affect learning and the motifs extracted. More work is required to determine the tradeoff between representations and richness or usefulness of motifs extracted. Converting the hexadecimal signatures of viruses and worms to amino acids and then rational numbers between 0 to 1 has also been shown to be effective for perceptron learning. Naive Bayes for separating worm from virus signatures after alignment has also been shown to be the most accurate. However, extracting the knowledge contained in Naive Bayes is not easy and symbolic rule extraction techniques are to be preferred when trying to generate malware signatures for scanning files and network packets directly. The derivation of metasignatures provides a new way to look at viral and worm signatures at a "motif" level. These motifs represent common subpatterns among the signatures after initial alignment of virus and worm signatures separately (to allow commonalities among variants of virus and worm signatures to be formed) and then together (to allow differences between virus and worm signatures to be separated). The machine learning task was to separate worm signatures from virus signatures using their hexadecimal form and different amino acid representations, rather than distinguish malware from nonmalware. To test for malware versus nonmalware classification will require mapping the metasignatures back to malware op code, and this is not possible for the signatures used in this research. Nevertheless, we have shown how the growing databanks of malware signatures can be mined for interesting signature information, even if the relationship back to op code is lost or not available. More work is required, however, to identify the most effective alignment algorithms, substitution matrices, and representations for rich and informative metasignatures extraction.

References

[1] "World Economic ForumGlobal Risks 2012," 7th edition, 2012, http://www3.weforum.org/docs/WEF_GlobalRisks_Report_2012.pdf.

[2] Symantec, "Internet security threat report: 2011 trends," vol. 17, April 2012, http://www.symantec.com/threatreport/.

[3] F. Cohen, "Computer viruses: theory and experiments," *Computers and Security*, vol. 6, no. 1, pp. 22–35, 1987.

[4] F. Cohen, "Computational aspects of computer viruses," *Computers and Security*, vol. 8, no. 4, pp. 325–344, 1989.

[5] L. M. Adleman, "An abstract theory of computer viruses," in *Proceedings of the Advances in Cryptology (CRYPTO '88)*, pp. 354–374, Santa Barbara, Calif, USA, 1990.

[6] Z. Zuo and M. Zhou, "Some further theoretical results about computer viruses," *Computer Journal*, vol. 47, no. 6, pp. 627–633, 2004.

[7] M. Christodorescu, S. Jha, S. A. Seshia, D. Song, and R. E. Bryant, "Semantics-aware malware detection," in *Proceedings of the IEEE Symposium on Security and Privacy (IEEE S and P '05)*, pp. 32–46, May 2005.

[8] M. D. Preda, M. Christodorescu, S. Jha, and S. Debray, "A semantics-based approach to malware detection," in *Proceedings of the 34th ACM SIGPLAN-SIGACT Symposium on Principles of Programming Languages (POPL '07)*, pp. 377–388, January 2007.

[9] S. Cesare and Y. Xiang, "Classification of malware using structured control flow," in *Proceedings of the 8th Australasian Symposium on Parallel and Distributed Computing*, pp. 61–70, 2010.

[10] G. Jacob, E. Filiol, and H. Debar, "Formalization of viruses and malware through process algebras," in *Proceedings of the 5th International Conference on Availability, Reliability, and Security (ARES '10)*, pp. 597–602, February 2010.

[11] C. Collberg, C. Thomborson, and D. Low, "A taxonomy of obfuscating transformations," Tech. Rep. 148, Department of Computer Science, The University of Auckland, 1997, https://researchspace.auckland.ac.nz/bitstream/handle/2292/3491/TR148.pdf.

[12] P. Beaucamps, "Advanced metamorphic techniques in computer viruses," in *Proceedings of the International Conference on Computer, Electrical, and Systems Science, and Engineering (CESSE'07)*, p. 8, 2007.

[13] J.-M. Borello and L. Mé, "Code obfuscation techniques for metamorphic viruses," *Journal in Computer Virology*, vol. 4, no. 3, pp. 211–220, 2008.

[14] D. Spinellis, "Reliable identification of bounded-length viruses is NP-complete," *IEEE Transactions on Information Theory*, vol. 49, no. 1, pp. 280–284, 2003.

[15] G. Bonfante, M. Kaczmarek, and J.-Y. Marion, "On abstract computer virology from a recursion theoretic perspective," *Journal in Computer Virology*, vol. 1, no. 3-4, pp. 45–54, 2006.

[16] S. M. Sridhara and M. Stamp, "Metamorphic worm that carries its own morphing engine," *Journal of Computer Virology and Hacking Techniques*, vol. 9, no. 2, pp. 49–58, 2012.

[17] N. Idika and A. P. Mathur, "A survey of malware detection techniques," Tech. Rep. 286, Department of Computer Science, Purdue University, USA, http://www.serc.net/system/files/SERC-TR-286.pdf.

[18] Y. Robiah, S. Rahayu S, M. Zaki M, S. Shahrin, M. A. Faizal, and R. Marliza, "A new generic taxonomy on hybrid malware detection technique," *International Journal of Computer Science and Information Security*, vol. 5, no. 1, pp. 56–60, 2009.

[19] Y. Fukushima, A. Sakai, Y. Hori, and K. Sakurai, "A behavior based malware detection scheme for avoiding false positive," in *Proceedings of the 6th IEEE Workshop on Secure Network Protocols (NPSec '10)*, pp. 79–84, October 2010.

[20] A. A. E. Elhadi, M. A. Maarof, and A. H. Osman, "Malware detection based on hybrid signature behaviour application programming interface call graph," *American Journal of Applied Sciences*, vol. 9, no. 3, pp. 283–288, 2012.

[21] Q. Zhang and D. S. Reeves, "MetaAware: identifying metamorphic malware," in *Proceedings of the 23rd Annual Computer Security Applications Conference (ACSAC '07)*, pp. 411–420, December 2007.

[22] F. Leder, B. Steinbock, and P. Martini, "Classification and detection of metamorphic malware using value set analysis," in *Proceedings of the 4th International Conference on Malicious and Unwanted Software (MALWARE '09)*, pp. 39–46, October 2009.

[23] K. Griffin, S. Schneider, X. Hu, and T. Chiueh, "Automatic generation of string signatures for malware detection," in *Recent Advances in Intrusion Detection*, vol. 5758 of *Lecture Notes in Computer Science*, pp. 101–120, Springer, Berlin, Germany, 2009.

[24] Y. Ye, T. Li, Q. Jiang, and Y. Wang, "CIMDS: adapting post-processing techniques of associative classification for malware detection," *IEEE Transactions on Systems, Man and Cybernetics C*, vol. 40, no. 3, pp. 298–307, 2010.

[25] A. Moser, C. Kruegel, and E. Kirda, "Limits of static analysis for malware detection," in *Proceedings of the 23rd Annual Computer Security Applications Conference (ACSAC '07)*, pp. 421–430, usa, December 2007.

[26] Y. Chen, A. Narayanan, S. Pang, and B. Tao, "Malicious software detection using multiple sequence alignment and data mining," in *Proceedings of 26th IEEE International Conference on Advanced Information Networking and Applications (AINA '12)*, pp. 8–14, 2012.

[27] Y. Chen, A. Narayanan, S. Pang, and B. Tao, "Multiple sequence alignment and artificial neural networks for malicious software detection," in *Proceedings of the 8th IEEE Conference on Natural Computation (ICNC '12)*, pp. 261–265, 2012.

[28] A. Narayanan, Y. Chen, S. Pang, and B. Tao, "The effects of different representations on malware motif identification," in *Proceedings of the International Conference on Computational Intelligence and Security (CIS '12)*, pp. 86–90, 2012.

[29] Y. Tang and S. Chen, "An automated signature-based approach against polymorphic internet worms," *IEEE Transactions on Parallel and Distributed Systems*, vol. 18, no. 7, pp. 879–892, 2007.

[30] P. Szor, *The Art of Computer Virus Research and Defense*, Addison Wesley, 2005.

[31] J. Parikka, *Digital Contagions. A Media Archaeology of Computer Viruses*, Peter Lang, New York, NY, USA, 2007.

[32] B. Bayoglu and I. Sogukpinar, "Polymorphic worm detection using token-pair signatures," in *Proceedings of the 4th International Workshop on Security, Privacy and Trust in Pervasive and Ubiquitous Computing (SecPerU '08)*, pp. 7–12, July 2008.

[33] T. Chen, "Intrusion detection for viruses and worms," *IEC Annual Review of Communications*, vol. 57, 2004.

[34] J. Strickland, "Ten worst computer viruses of all time," 2011, http://computer.howstuffworks.com/worst-computer-viruses1.ht.

[35] T. Xinguang, D. Miyi, S. Chunlai, and L. Xin, "Detecting network intrusions by data mining and variable-length sequence pattern matching," *Journal of Systems Engineering and Electronics*, vol. 20, no. 2, pp. 405–411, 2009.

[36] D. M. Mount, *Bioinformatics: Sequence and Genome Analysis*, Cold Spring Harbor Laboratory Press, Cold Spring Harbor, NY, USA, 3rd edition, 2001.

[37] G. Kondrak, *Algorithms for language reconstruction [Ph.D. thesis]*, Computer Science Department, University of Toronto, Ontario, Canada, 2002, http://www.cs.ualberta.ca/~kondrak/papers/thesis.pdf.

[38] A. Prinzie and D. Van den Poel, "Incorporating sequential information into traditional classification models by using an element/position-sensitive SAM," *Decision Support Systems*, vol. 42, no. 2, pp. 508–526, 2006.

[39] Y. Chen, A. Narayanan, S. Pang, and B. Tao, "Malicious software detection using multiple sequence alignment and data mining," in *Proceedings of the IEEE International Conference on Advanced Information Networking and Applications (AINA '12)*, pp. 8–14, Fukuoka, Japan, March 2012.

[40] M. A. Larkin, G. Blackshields, N. P. Brown et al., "Clustal W and Clustal X version 2.0," *Bioinformatics*, vol. 23, no. 21, pp. 2947–2948, 2007.

[41] Y. Chen, A. Narayanan, S. Pang, and B. Tao, "Multiple sequence alignment and artificial neural networks for malicious software detection," in *Proceedings of the 8th IEEE Conference on Natural Computation (ICNC '12)*, pp. 261–265, Chonqing, China, May, 2012.

[42] A. Narayanan, Y. Chen, S. Pang, and B. Tao, "The effects of different representations on malware motif identification.," in *Proceedings of the International Conference on Computational Intelligence and Security (CIS '12)*, pp. 86–90, 2012.

[43] S. B. Needleman and C. D. Wunsch, "A general method applicable to the search for similarities in the amino acid sequence of two proteins," *Journal of Molecular Biology*, vol. 48, no. 3, pp. 443–453, 1970.

[44] T. F. Smith and M. S. Waterman, "Identification of common molecular subsequences," *Journal of Molecular Biology*, vol. 147, no. 1, pp. 195–197, 1981.

[45] "T-Coffee Multiple Sequence Alignment," http://www.ebi.ac.uk/Tools/msa/tcoffee/.

[46] "Viruses andWorms Datasets collected from VX heavens," http://www.vxheavens.com/vl.php.

[47] J. Cendrowska, "PRISM: an algorithm for inducing modular rules," *International Journal of Man-Machine Studies*, vol. 27, no. 4, pp. 349–370, 1988.

7

Is the Linear Modeling Technique Good Enough for Optimal Form Design? A Comparison of Quantitative Analysis Models

Yang-Cheng Lin,[1] Chung-Hsing Yeh,[2] Chen-Cheng Wang,[3] and Chun-Chun Wei[4]

[1] Department of Arts and Design, National Dong Hwa University, Hualien 974, Taiwan
[2] Faculty of Information Technology, Monash University, Clayton, VIC 3800, Australia
[3] Department of Computer Simulation and Design, Shih Chien University, Kaohsiung 845, Taiwan
[4] Department of Industrial Design, National Cheng Kung University, Tainan 701, Taiwan

Correspondence should be addressed to Yang-Cheng Lin, lyc0914@cm1.hinet.net

Academic Editors: P. Melin, J. Montero, and P. Whigham

How to design highly reputable and hot-selling products is an essential issue in product design. Whether consumers choose a product depends largely on their perception of the product image. A consumer-oriented design approach presented in this paper helps product designers incorporate consumers' perceptions of product forms in the design process. The consumer-oriented design approach uses quantification theory type I, grey prediction (the linear modeling technique), and neural networks (the nonlinear modeling technique) to determine the optimal form combination of product design for matching a given product image. An experimental study based on the concept of Kansei Engineering is conducted to collect numerical data for examining the relationship between consumers' perception of product image and product form elements of personal digital assistants (PDAs). The result of performance comparison shows that the QTTI model is good enough to help product designers determine the optimal form combination of product design. Although the PDA form design is used as a case study, the approach is applicable to other consumer products with various design elements and product images. The approach provides an effective mechanism for facilitating the consumer-oriented product design process.

1. Introduction

Products have been considered a symbol of occupation, personality, opinion, and other human attributes. Whether a product is successful largely depends on the final judgment of consumers [1]. Therefore, product designers need to comprehend the consumers' needs in order to design successful products (highly-reputable and hot-selling) in an intensely competitive market [2]. Moreover, a successful product should not only possess good functionalities, interface design, and operating performance, but also need to take the product image design into account to satisfy consumers' psychological requirements [3]. The external appearance of a product can represent a product image that evokes consumers' internal resonance and consuming motivation [4]. The product image engages an influential factor in

consumers' preference structure [5]. When choosing a product, consumers tend to rely on their own particular perception of the product, which is regarded as something of a black box [6]. As an ergonomic consumer-oriented methodology, Kansei Engineering is developed as integrative design strategies for affective design to satisfy consumers' psychological requirements [7–9]. The word "Kansei" indicates the consumers' psychological requirements or emotional feelings of a product. Kansei Engineering has been used to assist product designers in designing product forms that can best match specific product images [10, 11].

In this paper, we present a consumer-oriented design approach addressing for challenging issues in designing consumer products, such as personal digital assistants (PDAs). What are the key form elements for a desirable product image? How to use the adequate product form combination to enhance consumers' preference? Is there an optimal combination of product form that best matches a desirable feeling of the consumers? For example, if product designers want to design a product with "simple-to-look" appearance, are there guidelines of product form design to follow? In addition, nonlinear modeling techniques (such as the artificial intelligent system or the soft computing) are defined as "an emerging approach to reasoning and learning the human mind in an uncertainty and imprecision environment" [12, 13]. These techniques are supposed to possess humanlike expertise within a specific domain, adapt themselves and learn to do better in changing environments, and explain how they make decisions [9, 12]. Hence, are the nonlinear modeling techniques suitable for exploring the relationship between the consumers' perceptions of product images and product form elements? Or are the linear modeling techniques good enough to do so [14]? What specific technique should be used to help product designers determine the optimal form combination of product design for a particular design concept of product image? To illustrate how the approach can be used to answer these research questions, we conduct an experimental study on PDAs, using two linear modeling techniques and one nonlinear modeling technique. Two linear modeling techniques are the quantification theory type I (QTTI) [15] and the grey prediction (GP) [16], and the nonlinear modeling technique is the neural networks (NNs) [17].

The QTTI is a variant of linear multiple regression analysis and can be used to quantify the relationships between product form elements and product images [5], while the GP model can deal with incomplete information effectively and requires only four data sets or more [16]. As such, the GP can be used to predict how a particular combination of product form elements matches a product image, particularly when the information is available only for a limited number of product form elements [10]. Due to the effective learning ability, NNs have been applied successfully in a wide range of fields, using various learning algorithms [18–20]. NNs are well suited to formulate the product design process for matching the product form (the input variables) to the consumers' perceptions (the output variables), which is often a black box and cannot be precisely described [10].

In subsequent sections, we first present the quantitative analysis methods used to analyze the experimental data sets for answering the research questions. Then we conduct an experimental study on PDAs to describe how Kansei Engineering can be used to extract representative samples and product form elements as numerical data sets required for analysis. Finally, we discuss the results of applying these techniques and evaluate their performance in order to determine the better model that can be used to help product designers meet consumers' requirements for a desirable product image.

2. Methods of Quantitative Analysis

In this section, we present a brief outline of the relevant theories and algorithms, including the QTTI, the GP, and the NNs. We use these techniques to examine the relationship between product form elements and product images.

2.1. Quantification Theory Type I. The QTTI can be regarded as a method of qualitative and categorical multiple regression analysis method [15], which allows inclusion of independent variables that are categorical and qualitative in nature, such as product form elements and quantitative criterion variables within Kansei Engineering. In Kansei Engineering, product form elements are typically classified into two levels that correspond to form design element and its treatments, respectively. The QTTI consists of the followings six steps [15].

Step 1. Define the Kansei relational model associated with the Kansei measurement scores of experimental samples with respect to an image word pair.

In Kansei Engineering, the criterion variables represent the product image, and the explanatory variables represent the product form elements. The categorical multiple regression model can be defined as

$$\hat{y}_s^k = \sum_{i=1}^{E} \sum_{j=1}^{C_i} \beta_{ij} x_{ijs} + \varepsilon, \tag{1}$$

where $\hat{y}_s^k$: the predicted value of the criterion variable for the sth product sample on the kth image word; i: the index of design element, E: the number of design element; j: the index of category; C_i: the number of category of the ith design element; ε: a stochastic variable whose expectation value $E(\varepsilon) = 0$; β_{ij}: the category score of the jth style within the ith design element; x_{ijs}: the coefficient of the dummy variable that is the explanatory variable or the dummy variable representing the jth style within the ith design element using the sth experimental sample.

Step 2. Calculate the standardized regression coefficients and the standardized constant in the model. The model of categorical multiple regression analysis can be redefined as

$$\hat{y}_s^k = \sum_{i=1}^{E} \sum_{j=1}^{C_i} \beta_{ij}^* x_{ijs} + \overline{y}_s^k,$$

$$\beta_{ij}^* = \beta_{ij} - \frac{1}{n} \sum_{j=1}^{C_i} \beta_{ij} x_{ijs}, \tag{2}$$

$$\overline{y}_s^k = \frac{1}{n} \sum_{s=1}^{n} y_s^k,$$

where β_{ij}^* represents the standardized coefficient of explanatory variables and $\overline{y}_s^k$ is the standardized constant in the model.

Step 3. Determine the matrix CCR of correlation coefficient of all variables.

Step 4. Calculate the multiple correlation coefficient R that is regarded as the relational degree of external criterion variable and explanatory variables.

Step 5. Calculate the partial correlation coefficients (PCC) of design elements to clarify the relationships between product form elements and a product image.

Step 6. Determine the statistical range of a categorical variable (product form element) by the difference between the maximum value and minimum value of the category score. The range of the categorical variable indicates its contribution degree to the prediction model with respect to a given product image.

2.2. Grey Prediction. The grey system theory [16] has been developed to examine the relationship among factors in an observable system where the information available is grey, meaning uncertain and incomplete (i.e., only part of the information is known). It has been successfully used in a wide range of fields, including some recent application results [10, 21–23] highlighting its effective handling of incomplete known information for exploring unknown information. The system that can be built for answering specific research questions in product design with respect to product form and product image is grey in essence, as there is no way to identify all the product form elements that affect a particular product image perceived by consumers [10].

The GP model uses a grey differential model (GM) to generate data series from the original data series of a dynamic system. The data series generated by the GM are converted back to the original data series by a reverse procedure to predict the performance of the system. Since the generated data series are more coherent than the original, the accuracy of the modeling is enhanced. The GM has three basic operations [16]: (1) accumulated generation, (2) inverse accumulated generation, and (3) grey modeling. The accumulated generation operation (AGO) is used to build differential equations. The GM is usually represented as GM(M, N) for dealing with Mth-order differential equations with N variables. Since any higher-order differential equation can be transferred into a first-order differential equation, we use the first-order differential equation in this paper.

The GM(1, 1), a single variable and first-order grey model, is one of the most frequently used grey prediction models. Its procedure involves the following four steps.

Step 1. Denote the original sequence as

$$x^{(0)} = \left(x^{(0)}(1), x^{(0)}(2), \ldots, x^{(0)}(n) \right), \tag{3}$$

where $x^{(0)}(i)$ is the time series data at time i ($i = 1, 2, \ldots, n$).

Step 2. Generate a new sequence $x^{(1)}$ by the AGO based on the original sequence $x^{(0)}$, where

$$x^{(1)} = \left(x^{(1)}(1), x^{(1)}(2), \ldots, x^{(1)}(n) \right), \tag{4}$$

$$x^{(1)}(1) = x^{(0)}(1), \qquad x^{(1)}(k) = \sum_{i=1}^{k} x^{(0)}(i). \tag{5}$$

Step 3. Define the first-order differential equation as

$$\frac{dx^{(1)}}{dt} + ax^{(1)} = b. \tag{6}$$

Step 4. Use the least square method to solve (4) by

$$\hat{x}^{(1)}(k+1) = \left(x^{(0)}(1) - \frac{b}{a} \right) e^{-ak} + \frac{b}{a},$$

$$\hat{x}^{(0)}(k+1) = \hat{x}^{(1)}(k+1) - \hat{x}^{(1)}(k), \tag{7}$$

where

$$\hat{a} = \begin{bmatrix} a \\ b \end{bmatrix} = \left(B^T B \right)^{-1} B^T y_1,$$

$$B = \begin{bmatrix} -0.5 \left(x^{(1)}(1) + x^{(1)}(2) \right) & 1 \\ -0.5 \left(x^{(1)}(2) + x^{(1)}(3) \right) & 1 \\ \vdots & \vdots \\ -0.5 \left(x^{(1)}(n-1) + x^{(1)}(n) \right) & 1 \end{bmatrix}, \tag{8}$$

$$y_1 = \left(x^{(0)}(2), x^{(0)}(3), \ldots, x^{(0)}(n) \right)^T.$$

The $\hat{x}^{(1)}(k+1)$ is the predicted value of $x^{(1)}(k+1)$ and $\hat{x}^{(0)}(k+1)$ is the predicted value of $x^{(0)}(k+1)$ at time $k+1$. We can also use the inverse accumulated generation operation (IAGO) to obtain $\hat{x}^{(0)}(k+1)$ as

$$\hat{x}^{(0)}(k+1) = \left(x^{(0)}(1) - \frac{b}{a} \right) (1 - e^a) e^{-ak}. \tag{9}$$

The GM(1, 1) grey model can be extended to the GM(1, N) model [10, 16], first-order with N variables $(x_1^{(0)}, x_2^{(0)}, x_3^{(0)}, \ldots, x_N^{(0)})$. The differential equation can be defined as

$$\frac{dx_1^{(1)}}{dt} + ax_1^{(1)} = b_1 x_2^{(1)} + b_2 x_3^{(1)} + \cdots + b_{N-1} x_N^{(1)}$$

$$= \sum_{i=2}^{N} b_{i-1} x_i^{(1)}, \tag{10}$$

where $a, b_1, b_2, \ldots, b_{N-1}$ are unknown parameters and can be calculated by

$$\hat{a} = (a, b_1, b_2, \ldots, b_{N-1}) = \left(B^T B \right)^{-1} B^T y_N, \tag{11}$$

where

$$B = \begin{bmatrix} -0.5\left(x_1^{(1)}(1) + x_1^{(1)}(2)\right) & x_2^{(1)}(2) & \cdots x_N^{(1)}(2) \\ -0.5\left(x_1^{(1)}(2) + x_1^{(1)}(3)\right) & x_2^{(1)}(3) & \cdots x_N^{(1)}(3) \\ \vdots & \vdots & \vdots \\ -0.5\left(x_1^{(1)}(n-1) + x_1^{(1)}(n)\right) & x_2^{(1)}(n) & \cdots x_N^{(1)}(n) \end{bmatrix},$$

(12)

$$y_N = \left(x^{(0)}(2), x^{(0)}(3), x^{(0)}(4), \ldots, x^{(0)}(n)\right)^T.$$

The prediction of $x_1^{(1)}$ is defined as

$$\hat{x}_1^{(1)}(k+1) = \left(x_1^{(0)}(1) - \sum_{i=2}^{N} \frac{b_{i-1}}{a} x_i^{(1)}(k+1)\right) e^{-ak}$$

$$+ \sum_{i=2}^{N} \frac{b_{i-1}}{a} x_i^{(1)}(k+1).$$

(13)

The $\hat{x}^{(1)}(k+1)$ is the predicted value of $x^{(1)}(k+1)$ of the GM$(1, N)$ at time $k + 1$.

2.3. Neural Networks. NNs are nonlinear models and are widely used to examine the complex relationship between input variables and output variables [17]. In this paper, we use the multilayered feedforward neural networks trained with the backpropagation learning algorithm, as it is an effective and the popular supervised learning algorithm [10].

A typical three-layer network consists of an input layer, an output layer, and one hidden layer, with n, m, and p neurons, respectively (indexed by i, j, and k, resp.) [24]. The w_{ij} and w_{jk} represent the weights for the connection between neuron i ($i = 1, 2, \ldots, n$) and neuron j ($j = 1, 2, \ldots, m$), and between neuron j ($j = 1, 2, \ldots, m$) and neuron k ($k = 1, 2, \ldots, p$), respectively. In training the network, a set of input patterns or signals, $(x_1, x_2, \ldots, x_n)$ is presented to the network input layer. The network then propagates the inputs from layer to layer until the outputs are generated by the output layer. This involves the generation of the outputs (y_j) of the neurons in the hidden layer as given in (14) and the outputs (y_k) of the neurons in the output layer as given in (15).

$$y_j = f\left(\sum_{i=1}^{n} x_i w_{ij} - \theta_j\right),$$

(14)

$$y_k = f\left(\sum_{j=1}^{m} x_j w_{jk} - \theta_k\right),$$

(15)

where $f(\cdot)$ is the sigmoid activation function as given in (16), and θ_j and θ_k are threshold values:

$$f(X) = \frac{1}{1 + e^{-X}}.$$

(16)

If the outputs (y_k) generated by (15) are different from the target outputs (y_k^*), errors $(e_1, e_2, \ldots, e_p)$ are calculated

by (17) and then propagated backwards from the output layer to the input layer in order to update the weights for reducing the errors.

$$e_k = y_k^* - y_k.$$

(17)

The weights (w_{jk}) at the output neurons are updated as $w_{jk} + \Delta w_{jk}$, where Δw_{jk} is computed by (known as the delta rule)

$$\Delta w_{jk} = \alpha y_j \delta_k,$$

(18)

where α is the learning rate (usually $0 < \alpha \le 1$) and δ_k is the error gradient at neuron k, given as

$$\delta_k = y_k(1 - y_k)e_k.$$

(19)

The weights (w_{ij}) at the hidden neurons are updated as $w_{ij} + \Delta w_{ij}$, where Δw_{ij} is calculated by

$$\Delta w_{ij} = \alpha x_i \delta_j,$$

(20)

where α is the learning rate (usually $0 < \alpha \le 1$) and δ_j is the error gradient at neuron j, given as

$$\delta_j = y_j\left(1 - y_j\right) \sum_{k=1}^{p} \delta_k w_{jk}.$$

(21)

The training process is repeated until a specified error criterion is satisfied.

3. Experimental Procedures of Consumer-Oriented Design

We conduct an experimental study using the concept of Kansei Engineering in order to collect numerical data about the relationship between product form elements and a given product image of PDAs. The experimental study involves three main steps: (a) extracting representative experimental samples, (b) conducting morphological analysis of product form elements, and (c) assessing consumers' perceptions for a given product image.

3.1. Extracting Representative Experimental Samples. In the experimental study, we investigate and categorize various PDAs on the market. We first collect 88 PDAs and then classify them based on their similarity degree. To collect opinions

TABLE 1: Morphological analysis of PDA design forms.

Form element	Form type			
	Type 1	Type 2	Type 3	Type 4
Top shape (X_1)	Line (X_{11})	Chamfer (X_{12})	Fillet (X_{13})	
Bottom shape (X_2)	Fillet (X_{21})	Chamfer (X_{22})	Arc (X_{23})	
Function keys arrangement (X_3)	Line (X_{31})	Symmetry (X_{32})	Irregular (X_{33})	Grouping (X_{34})
Arrow-key style (X_4)	Cycle (X_{41})	Ellipse (X_{42})	Straight (X_{43})	
Color treatment (X_5)	Single color (X_{51})	Non-color segment (X_{52})	Color segment (X_{53})	
Outline partition style (X_6)	Normal partition (X_{61})	Fitting outline (X_{62})	Fitting surface (X_{63})	

regarding the usage, function, and form of PDAs, a focus group is formed by six subjects with at least two years' experience of using the PDA. The focus group eliminates some highly similar samples through discussions. Then the K-means cluster analysis is used to extract representative samples of PDAs. There are 30 representative PDA samples, including 24 samples as the training set and six samples as the test set for building quantitative models in Section 4.

3.2. Conducting Morphological Analysis of Product Form Elements. The product form is defined as the collection of design features that the consumers will appreciate. The morphological analysis [25], concerning the arrangement of

objects and how they conform to create a whole of Gestalt, is used to explore all possible solutions in a complex problem regarding a product form.

The morphological analysis is used to extract the product form elements of the 30 representative samples. The six subjects of the focus group are asked to decompose the PDA samples into several dominant form elements and form types according to their knowledge and experience. Table 1 shows the result of the morphological analysis, with six product design elements (i.e., top shape, bottom shape, function-keys arrangement, arrow-key style, color treatment, and outline partition style) and 19 associated product form types being identified. The form type indicates the relationship between the outline elements. For example, the "top shape (X_1)" form element has three form types, including "line (X_{11})," "chamfer (X_{12})," and "fillet (X_{13})." A number of design alternatives can be generated by various combinations of morphological elements [26].

3.3. Assessing Consumers' Perceptions of Product Images. In Kansei Engineering, image assessment experiments are usually performed to elicit the consumers' psychological feelings or perceptions about a product using the semantic differential method. Pairs of image words are often used to describe the consumers' perceptions of the product in terms of ergonomic and psychological estimation. With the identification of the form elements of the product, the relationship between the image words and the form elements can be established.

In this paper, the image word pair used for representing the product image of PDAs is Simple-Complex (S-C) about the visibility aspect, according to our previous study [27]. In Wang et al. [27], we use these 30 representative PDA samples and product images to examine whether the NN model is an effective technique and what structure is better for the product form design among 4 NN models built with different hidden layer neurons. In this study, we use the same experimental data as a basis for addressing new and significant research issues as stated in Section 1.

To obtain the assessed values for the product image of 30 representative PDA samples, a 10-point scale (1–10) of the semantic differential method is used. 52 subjects (30 males and 22 females with ages ranging from 26 to 45, mean = 35.4, SD = 4.4) are asked to assess the form (look) of PDA samples on a simplicity-complexity scale of 1 to 10, where 10 is most simple and 1 is most complex. The last column of Table 2 shows the assessed S-C value of the 30 PDA samples, including 24 samples in the training set and six samples in the test set (asterisked). For each selected PDA in Table 2, the first column shows the PDA number and Columns 2–7 show the corresponding type number for each of its six product form elements, as given in Table 1. Table 2 provides a numerical data source for building quantitative models, which can be used to develop a design support system for simulating the optimal form design process for PDAs.

4. Experimental Analysis and Results

In this section, we present the results of applying the QTTI, the GP, and the NN models in order to explore the relationship between product form elements and consumers' perceptions for a given product image, using the assessing results summarized in Tables 1 and 2.

4.1. The QTTI Analysis and Results. We use the QTTI analysis to examine the relationship between the six product form elements and the S-C product image. In this paper, six independent variables (i.e., the six product form elements) and one dependent variable (i.e., the S-C product image) are used. The result of QTTI analysis is given in Table 3. In Table 3, the partial correlation coefficients indicate the relationship between the six product form elements (X_1,

TABLE 2: Product image assessments of 30 PDA samples.

PDA no.	X_1	X_2	X_3	X_4	X_5	X_6	S-C value
1	3	1	1	3	1	1	1.67
2	3	1	1	3	1	1	2.33
3	2	2	3	3	3	2	3.33
4	1	2	2	3	1	1	3.67
5	3	3	1	2	1	1	1.67
6	2	2	1	1	1	1	8.33
7	3	3	1	3	1	3	2.33
8	3	3	2	2	1	1	2.33
9	3	3	2	2	2	1	6.33
10	3	1	3	1	2	1	3.33
11	3	3	2	2	2	1	4.67
12	1	3	1	1	1	1	1.67
13	3	3	1	1	1	1	3.33
14	2	1	1	2	3	2	2.33
15	3	1	2	1	3	3	2.33
16	3	1	3	1	3	3	4.67
17	2	3	2	1	2	1	7.33
18	1	3	2	2	2	2	8.33
19	3	3	1	2	1	1	4.67
20	3	2	4	3	1	1	1.67
21	3	1	1	2	1	1	5.67
22	2	3	1	1	1	1	1.67
23	2	2	2	1	2	1	1.33
24	3	3	4	2	3	1	4.67
25*	3	1	2	2	3	2	5.33
26*	2	2	1	2	1	1	2.33
27*	3	3	1	1	1	1	4.33
28*	3	2	2	1	1	1	5.67
29*	2	1	1	1	1	1	2.33
30*	3	3	1	3	2	2	4.33

*Mean that the 6 PDA samples are the test set for quantitative analysis models.

X_2, X_3, X_4, X_5, and X_6) and the S-C product image (Y). The highest variable of the partial correlation coefficient in the "S-C" image is the "arrow-key style" form element ($X_4 = 0.42$), meaning that "arrow-key style" primarily affects the "S-C" image of the product, followed by the "color treatment" form element ($X_5 = 0.37$) and the "top shape" form element ($X_1 = 0.26$). This implies that the product designers should focus their attention more on these most influential elements, when the objective of designing a new PDA is to achieve a desirable "S-C" image. On the contrary, the product designers can pay less attention to the less influential elements such as "bottom shape" form element ($X_2 = 0.14$), and the "function-keys arrangement" form element ($X_3 = 0.16$), as these form elements contribute relatively little to the consumers' perceptions of the "S-C" image on the PDAs.

In the last second row of Table 3, R means the correlation between the observed and predicted values of the dependent variable, and R^2 is the square of this correlation. R^2 ranges from 0 to 1. If there is no linear relation between the

TABLE 3: The result of QTTI analysis.

Form element		Form type		Category grade (form type grade)		Partial correlation coefficient
				Complex	Simple	
X_1	Top shape	X_{11}	Line		1.00	0.26
		X_{12}	Chamfer		0.54	
		X_{13}	Fillet	−0.42		
X_2	Bottom shape	X_{21}	Fillet	−0.11		0.14
		X_{22}	Chamfer		0.61	
		X_{23}	Arc	−0.19		
X_3	Function-keys arrangement	X_{31}	Line		0.01	0.16
		X_{32}	Symmetry	−0.37		
		X_{33}	Irregular		0.65	
		X_{34}	Grouping		0.48	
X_4	Arrow-key style	X_{41}	Cycle	−0.42		0.42
		X_{42}	Ellipse		1.28	
		X_{43}	Straight	−1.29		
X_5	Color treatment	X_{51}	Single color	−0.21		0.37
		X_{52}	Noncolor segment		1.35	
		X_{53}	Color segment	−1.06		
X_6	Outline partition style	X_{61}	Normal partition	−0.20		0.23
		X_{62}	Fitting outline	−0.13		
		X_{63}	Fitting surface		1.32	

Constant = 3.74, R = 0.55, R^2 = 0.31.

dependent variable (Y) and independent variables (X_1, X_2, X_3, X_4, X_5, and X_6), R^2 is 0 or very small. Otherwise, if all the values fall on the regression line, R^2 is 1. The category grade (form type grade) shown in Table 3 indicates the preference degree of the consumers' perception on each category of independent variables. If the grade is negative, the consumers' perception leans towards the "complex" image. On the contrary, the positive grade indicates that the consumers' perception favors the "simple" image. For example, the category grades of 3 selected values of "outline partition style (X_6)" in the "S-C" image are −0.20, −0.13, and 1.32, respectively. The result shows that the consumers' perception prefers the "complex" image if the "outline partition style (X_6)" is "normal partition (X_{61})" or "fitting outline (X_{62})," and favors the "simple" image while "outline partition style (X_6)" is "fitting surface (X_{63})."

As the result of the QTTI analysis, Model (22) indicates the relationship between product form elements and the S-C product image. We can use this model to input the values of six product form variables, and then output the predicted value of the S-C product image. This model can help the product designers understand consumers' perceptions to

find out the optimal combination of product form design in terms of a given product image:

$$\hat{y} = 3.74 + X_{11} + 0.54X_{12} - 0.42X_{13} - 0.11X_{21} + 0.61X_{22}$$

$$- 0.19X_{23} + 0.01X_{31} - 0.37X_{32} + 0.65X_{33} + 0.48X_{34}$$

$$- 0.42X_{41} + 1.28X_{42} - 1.29X_{43} - 0.21X_{51} + 1.35X_{52}$$

$$- 1.06X_{53} - 0.20X_{61} - 0.13X_{62} + 1.32X_{63}.$$

$$(22)$$

4.2. The GP Analysis and Results. The GP is used as a technique for determining the optimal combination of product form elements for matching a desirable product image. The 24 samples in the training set, given in Table 2, are used as the data set for building the GP model.

As a GM(1, 7), the GP model uses the six form elements as the comparison series X_i and the average S-C values as the reference series X_0. To build the GP model, we first obtain a

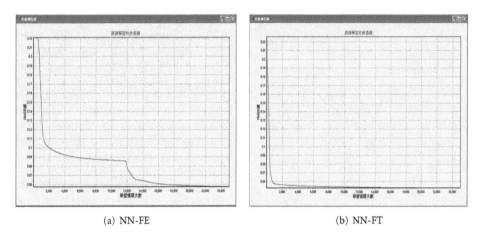

(a) NN-FE   (b) NN-FT

FIGURE 1: The convergence diagrams of NN-FE and NN-FT in the training process.

new sequence $x^{(1)}$ for each series using (3)–(5) and the AGO as

$$
\begin{pmatrix} x_0^{(1)} \\ x_1^{(1)} \\ x_2^{(1)} \\ \vdots \\ x_6^{(1)} \end{pmatrix} = \begin{pmatrix} 1.67, & 4.00, & 7.33, & \cdots & 89.66 \\ 3, & 6, & 8, & \cdots & 60 \\ 1, & 2, & 4, & \cdots & 53 \\ \cdots & \cdots & \cdots & \cdots & \cdots \\ 1, & 2, & 4, & \cdots & 33 \end{pmatrix}. \quad (23)
$$

We then apply (10)–(12) to obtain the parameters of $\hat{a}$ as

$$
\hat{a} = \begin{pmatrix} a \\ b_1 \\ b_2 \\ b_3 \\ b_4 \\ b_5 \\ b_6 \end{pmatrix} = \begin{pmatrix} 0.38 \\ -0.25 \\ -0.29 \\ -0.60 \\ 0.69 \\ 1.13 \\ -0.36 \end{pmatrix}. \quad (24)
$$

The GP model for predicting the S-C value based on the six form elements is thus built by (13) as

$$
\begin{aligned}
\hat{X}_0^{(1)}(k+1) = & \left[1.67 + 6.46 X_1^{(1)}(k+1) + 7.68 X_2^{(1)}(k+1) \right. \\
& + 15.67 X_3^{(1)}(k+1) - 17.92 X_4^{(1)}(k+1) \\
& \left. - 29.52 X_5^{(1)}(k+1) + 9.51 X_6^{(1)}(k+1) \right] e^{-0.038k} \\
& - 6.46 X_1^{(1)}(k+1) - 7.68 X_2^{(1)}(k+1) \\
& - 15.67 X_3^{(1)}(k+1) + 17.92 X_4^{(1)}(k+1) \\
& + 29.52 X_5^{(1)}(k+1) - 9.51 X_6^{(1)}(k+1).
\end{aligned} \quad (25)
$$

With the GP model in (25), product designers can input the value of the corresponding form elements, and then obtain a predicted S-C value.

4.3. The NN Analysis and Results. To examine whether the NN model is an effective technique for determining the optimal combination of product form elements for matching a desirable product image, we develop two neural network models, called NN-FE and NN-FT, respectively. The NN-FE uses all the six form elements (FE) as input variables (input neurons), while the NN-FT has 19 input neurons, which are the whole 19 form types (FT) of the six form elements identified from the experimental study. For the NN-FE model, if a PDA has a particular type of form element, the value of the corresponding input neuron is 1, 2, 3, or 4. On the other hand, for the NN-FT model, if a PDA has a particular type of form element, the value of the corresponding input neuron is 1; otherwise the value is 0. Both NN models use a widely used rule [17], (the number of input neurons + the number of output neurons)/2, for determining the number of neurons in the single hidden layer. Table 4 shows the neurons of these two NN models, including the input layer, the hidden layer, and the output layer. The learning rule used is Delta-Rule and the transfer function is Sigmoid [17] for all layers. All of input and output variables (neurons) are normalized before training. The learning rate is 0.2, and momentum is 0.5, based on our previous study [28].

The experimental samples are separated into two groups: 24 training samples and six test samples. Each model is trained ten epochs at each run. When the cumulative training epochs are over 25,000, the training process is completed. The root of mean square errors (RMSE) of the NN-FE model is 0.057, while the NN-FT model is 0.052. This result seems to suggest that the number of input neurons and hidden neurons have little influence on the training effect of NN models. However, after further examination, we find out that if more neurons are in the input or hidden layer, the faster the convergence speed becomes (as shown in Figure 1). In other words, if the input layer or hidden layer has more neurons, then the network converges faster. This result suggests that if the input variable has multiple categories (i.e., the qualitative or categorical variable, such as product form elements), the total number of categories (not the number of variables) should be used as the layer neurons.

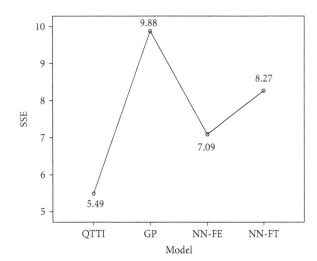

FIGURE 2: Multiple Comparisons for the SSE of four models.

TABLE 4: Neurons of two NN models.

NN-FE model	Input layer: 6 neurons, including six form elements of PDAs
	Hidden layer: 4 neurons, $(6 + 1)/2 = 3.5 \fallingdotseq 4$
	Output layer: 1 neuron for the S-C image value
NN-FT model	Input layer: 19 neurons, including 19 types of six form elements
	Hidden layer: 10 neurons, $(19 + 1)/2 = 10$
	Output layer: 1 neuron for the S-C image value

5. Performance Evaluation and Discussion

To evaluate the performance of the QTTI, GP, NN-FE, and NN-FT models developed in this paper in terms of their prediction ability in determining the optimal design combination of PDA form elements for matching a given S-C image, the six samples in the test set given in Table 2 are used.

5.1. Performance Comparison. The second row of Table 5 shows the average S-C values of the six test samples assessed by 52 subjects, which are used as a comparison base for the performance evaluation. With the six test samples as the input, Table 5 shows the corresponding S-C values predicted by using the QTTI (i.e., Model (22)), GP (i.e., Model (25)), NN-FE, and NN-FT models, respectively. To evaluate the performance of a model, the root of mean square errors (RMSE) is commonly used, given as

$$\text{RMSE} = \sqrt{\frac{\sum_{i=1}^{n}(x_i - x_0)^2}{n}}, \quad (26)$$

where X_i is the ith output value predicted by the model, and X_0 is the expected values assessed by 52 subjects in the experiment. If there is no difference or error between the predicted value and the expected value, the RMSE is 0.

The last column of Table 5 shows the RMSE of these four models in comparison with the assessed S-C values.

Table 5 shows that the lowest RMSE is the QTTI model (0.2343), followed by the NN-FE model (0.2663) and the NN-FT model (0.2875), and the RMSE of the GP model is the highest. The result indicates that the QTTI model has the highest predictive consistency (an accuracy rate of 76.57% = 1 − 0.2343) for predicting the value of the S-C image. This is in line with the result of Multiple Comparisons by one-way Analysis of Variance (one-way ANOVA), as shown in Figure 2. Figure 2 shows the mean of error sum of squares (SSE) for these four models. The lower the SSE, the higher the prediction performance. The result of performance comparison suggests that QTTI is the model to be used for matching a given set of product form elements with a specific product image.

Nevertheless, this result is not consistent with the common notion that nonlinear quantitative models or systems are more suitable to simulate human beings' thinking and generally have a better performance for predicting consumers' psychological requirements or emotional feelings, in comparison with linear quantitative models [6, 10–12, 18, 29]. In addition, the NN model usually has a better performance and an effective technique to formulate the product design process for determining the optimal combination of product form elements with respect to a desirable product image [5].

5.2. Further Evaluation. To further examine the prediction performance of the NN model, we conduct a set of analyses by using different learning rate and momentum factors for getting the better structure of the NN model. Another 3 pairs of learning rate and momentum factors are used for different conditions based on the complication of the research problem. For example, if the research issue is very simple, a large learning rate of 0.9 and momentum of 0.6 are recommended. On more complicated problems or predictive networks where output variables are continuous values rather than categories, use a smaller learning rate and momentum, such as 0.1 and 0.1 respectively. In addition, if the data are complex and very noisy, a learning rate of 0.05 and a momentum of 0.5 are used [30]. To distinguish between the NN-FE and NN-FT models using different input neurons and hidden neurons, both models are associated with the learning rate and momentum mentioned above, such as -P, -S, -C, -N, as shown in Table 6.

As described in Section 4.3, 24 training samples and six test samples are used, and the training process is not stopped until the cumulative training epochs are over 25,000. Figure 3 shows the RMSE of these eight NN models and the convergence diagrams in the training process. As shown in Figure 3, the convergence speed of NN-FT models are faster than NN-FE models. This is in line with the result of Section 4.3 that the more neurons in the input or hidden layer, the faster the convergence speed. In addition, we find the "-S" models (i.e., NN-FE-S model and NN-FT-S model, both using the large learning rate of 0.9 and momentum of 0.6 if the research issue is very simple) have larger movements as compared to other NN models, thus indicating that the essentials of consumers' perceptions are complicated, and often a block box and cannot be precisely described [10].

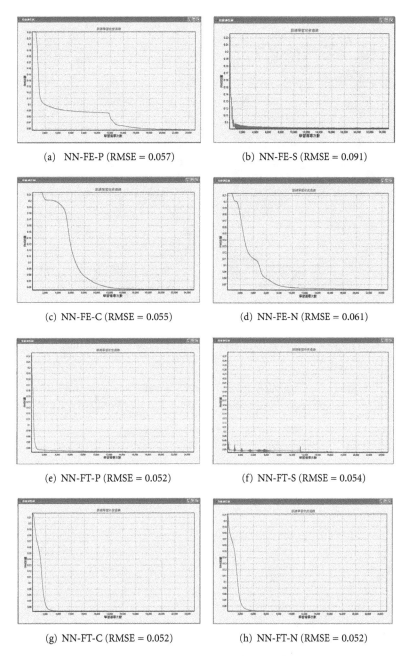

(a) NN-FE-P (RMSE = 0.057)

(b) NN-FE-S (RMSE = 0.091)

(c) NN-FE-C (RMSE = 0.055)

(d) NN-FE-N (RMSE = 0.061)

(e) NN-FT-P (RMSE = 0.052)

(f) NN-FT-S (RMSE = 0.054)

(g) NN-FT-C (RMSE = 0.052)

(h) NN-FT-N (RMSE = 0.052)

FIGURE 3: The RMSE and convergence diagrams of NN models in the training process.

With the six test samples as input, Table 7 lists the predicted S-C image values and RMSE of these eight NN models for the further test set. Table 7 shows that the lowest RMSE is the NN-FE-N model (0.2203). In addition, the average RMSE value of NN-FE (0.3033) is slightly smaller than the value of NN-FT (0.3168). This is in line with the result of Section 4.3 that the number of layer neurons (the input or hidden neurons) has little influence on the performing effect of NN models.

5.3. Discussion. From the RMSE shown in Table 7, except the NN-FE-N model (the RMSE being 0.2203), the other 7 NN models are larger than the QTTI (the RMSE being 0.2343) shown in Row 3 of Table 5. Further analysis shows

that the QTTI model is a better approach for matching a given set of product form elements with a specific product image, regardless of what learning rate and momentum factors are chosen for constructing the NN model. This result implies that the linear modeling technique is good enough to help product designers determine the optimal form combination of product design for a particular design concept of product image. Consequently, in some product design settings, applying nonlinear modeling techniques may not necessarily produce a better outcome. In some settings, the QTTI model (the linear modeling technique) can be used to better explore the relationship between the consumers' perceptions and product form elements without compromising the prediction performance.

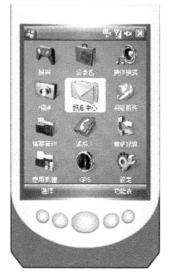

Product form: X_{11}-X_{22}-X_{31}-X_{42}-X_{52}-X_{63} Product form: X_{12}-X_{22}-X_{34}-X_{42}-X_{52}-X_{63}

(a) (b)

FIGURE 4: New PDA form designs for the desirable "simple" image.

TABLE 5: Predicted image values and RMSE of four models for the test.

PDA no.	25	26	27	28	29	30	RMSE
Subject Assessment	5.33	2.33	4.33	5.67	2.33	4.33	
QTTI	2.93	5.77	2.31	2.73	3.35	3.07	0.2343
GP	2.85	1.54	0.34	0.05	1.16	2.43	0.3143
NN-FE	5.08	6.28	3.57	4.18	5.32	8.22	0.2663
NN-FT	2.50	8.27	3.44	6.04	3.97	2.69	0.2875

TABLE 6: Neurons, learning rate, and momentum of NN models.

	Input neuron	Hidden neuron	Output neuron	Learning rate	Momentum	Note
NN-FE-P	6	4	1	0.2	0.5	According to our previous study
NN-FE-S	6	4	1	0.9	0.6	Research issue is very simple
NN-FE-C	6	4	1	0.1	0.1	Research issue is more complicated
NN-FE-N	6	4	1	0.05	0.5	Research issue is complex and very noisy
NN-FT-P	19	10	1	0.2	0.5	According to our previous study
NN-FT-S	19	10	1	0.9	0.6	Research issue is very simple
NN-FT-C	19	10	1	0.1	0.1	Research issue is more complicated
NN-FT-N	19	10	1	0.05	0.5	Research issue is complex and very noisy

TABLE 7: Predicted image values and RMSE of NN models for the test set.

PDA no.	25	26	27	28	29	30	RMSE	
NN-FE-P	5.08	6.28	3.57	4.18	5.32	8.22	0.2663	
NN-FE-S	4.43	5.04	3.53	5.20	9.23	8.76	0.3565	
NN-FE-C	1.45	2.95	3.71	9.03	9.38	6.65	0.3701	0.3033
NN-FE-N	4.63	6.04	3.26	3.67	5.25	5.41	0.2203	
NN-FT-P	2.50	8.27	3.44	6.04	3.97	2.69	0.2875	
NN-FT-S	1.58	8.27	3.41	1.46	3.38	5.07	0.3405	
NN-FT-C	2.22	8.19	3.42	7.03	3.72	3.46	0.2865	0.3168
NN-FT-N	1.49	8.39	3.40	2.08	3.83	1.66	0.3526	

TABLE 8: The design support information for product form elements of PDAs.

Form element		With "Simple" image		With "Complex" image	
X_1	Top shape	X_{11}	Line	X_{13}	Fillet
		X_{12}	Chamfer		
X_2	Bottom shape	X_{22}	Chamfer	X_{23}	Arc
				X_{21}	Fillet
X_3	Function-keys arrangement	X_{33}	Irregular	X_{32}	Symmetry
		X_{34}	Grouping		
		X_{31}	Line		
X_4	Arrow-key style	X_{42}	Ellipse	X_{43}	Straight
				X_{41}	Cycle
X_5	Color treatment	X_{52}	Noncolor segment	X_{53}	Color segment
				X_{51}	Single color
X_6	Outline partition style	X_{63}	Fitting surface	X_{61}	Normal partition
				X_{62}	Fitting outline

According to the experimental analysis and results mentioned above, model (22) can help product designers understand consumers' perceptions of product form for a given product image. This model can also be used to examine the effect of the corresponding product image for a given combination of product form elements. Consequently, the QTTI model enables us to build a PDA design support database that can be generated by inputting each of all possible combinations (972, $3 \times 3 \times 4 \times 3 \times 3 \times 3$) of product form elements to the QTTI model individually for generating the associated image values. Product designers can specify a desirable image value for a new PDA form design, and the database can then work out the optimal combination of form elements.

Table 8 shows the design support information for product designers to find out the optimal combination of product form elements in terms of a given product image. In addition, the design support database can be incorporated into a computer-aided design (CAD) system to facilitate the product form in the new PDA development process. To illustrate, we focus the attention more on the most influential elements, such as the "arrow-key style" form element (X_4) and the "color treatment" form element (X_5), for the desirable "simple" image of PDA. Figure 4 shows two new PDA form designs with the optimal combination of form elements for the desirable "simple" image.

5.4. Limitations and Further Suggestions. In this paper, we use two linear modeling techniques (i.e., quantification theory type I and grey prediction) and one nonlinear modeling technique (i.e., neural networks) to determine the optimal form combination of product design for matching a given product image. In the further studies, other quantitative analysis models should be adopted to test the prediction performance, for example, fuzzy system, genetic algorithm, rough set, multiple regression analysis, and so on. Although PDAs are chosen as the experimental product, the consumer-oriented design approach presented can be applied to other consumer products (e.g., smart phones, Tablet PC, etc.) with various design elements (e.g., color, texture, brand, etc.) and product images (e.g., classic or modern, artificial or artistic, etc.).

6. Conclusion

In this paper, we have conducted an experimental study on PDAs to demonstrate how a consumer-oriented design approach can be used to help determine the optimal form combination for matching a given product image. The consumer-oriented design based on the process of Kansei Engineering has used the QTTI model, the grey model, and the neural network model to predict the desirable simple-complex image of consumers' perception. The result of the experimental study has shown that the QTTI model has the highest predictive consistency, thus suggesting that the QTTI model is a better methodological alternative for modeling the consumers' perception of a product characterized by a given set of product form elements. Noteworthily, this result has shown that the QTTI model (the linear modeling technique) is good enough to help product designers determine the optimal form combination of product design for a particular design concept of product image. Consequently, in some product design settings, we can use the linear modeling technique to explore the relationship between the consumers' perceptions and product form elements without compromising the prediction performance. Furthermore, the consumer-oriented design approach has been built a PDA design support database, in conjunction with the computer-aided design (CAD) system, to help product designers facilitate the product form in the new PDA development process.

Acknowledgments

This research is supported in part by the National Science Council of Taiwan, Taiwan under Grant no. NSC 97-2918-I-026-001. The authors are grateful to the 58 subjects in Taiwan for their participation and assistance in the experimental study.

References

[1] S. L. Brown and K. M. Eisenhardt, "Product development: past research, present findings, and future directions," *Academy of Management Review*, vol. 20, pp. 343–378, 1995.

[2] N. Leon, "The future of computer-aided innovation," *Computers in Industry*, vol. 60, no. 8, pp. 539–550, 2009.

[3] C. Jonathan and M. V. Craig, *Creating Breakthrough Products-Innovation from Product Planning to Program Approval*, Prentice Hall, Upper Saddle River, NJ, USA, 2002.

[4] M. C. Lin, C. C. Wang, M. S. Chen, and C. A. Chang, "Using AHP and TOPSIS approaches in customer-driven product design process," *Computers in Industry*, vol. 59, no. 1, pp. 17–31, 2008.

[5] H. H. Lai, Y. C. Lin, C. H. Yeh, and C. H. Wei, "User-oriented design for the optimal combination on product design," *International Journal of Production Economics*, vol. 100, no. 2, pp. 253–267, 2006.

[6] Y. C. Lin, H. H. Lai, and C. H. Yeh, "Consumer-oriented product form design based on fuzzy logic: a case study of mobile phones," *International Journal of Industrial Ergonomics*, vol. 37, no. 6, pp. 531–543, 2007.

[7] M. Nagamachi, "Kansei engineering: a new ergonomic consumer-oriented technology for product development," *International Journal of Industrial Ergonomics*, vol. 15, no. 1, pp. 3–11, 1995.

[8] M. Nagamachi, "Kansei engineering as a powerful consumer-oriented technology for product development," *Applied Ergonomics*, vol. 33, no. 3, pp. 289–294, 2002.

[9] M. Y. Ma, C. Y. Chen, and F. G. Wu, "A design decision-making support model for customized product color combination," *Computers in Industry*, vol. 58, no. 6, pp. 504–518, 2007.

[10] H. H. Lai, Y. C. Lin, and C. H. Yeh, "Form design of product image using grey relational analysis and neural network models," *Computers and Operations Research*, vol. 32, no. 10, pp. 2689–2711, 2005.

[11] S. M. Yang, M. Nagamachi, and S. Y. Lee, "Rule-based inference model for the Kansei Engineering System," *International Journal of Industrial Ergonomics*, vol. 24, no. 5, pp. 459–471, 1999.

[12] J. S. Jang, C. T. Sun, and E. Mizutani, *Neuro-Fuzzy and Soft Computing*, Prentice-Hall, Upper Saddle River, NJ, USA, 1997.

[13] P. T. Helo, Q. L. Xu, S. J. Kyllönen, and R. J. Jiao, "Integrated Vehicle Configuration System-Connecting the domains of mass customization," *Computers in Industry*, vol. 61, no. 1, pp. 44–52, 2010.

[14] R. B. Page and A. J. Stromberg, "Linear methods for analysis and quality control of relative expression ratios from quantitative real-time polymerase chain reaction experiments," *TheScientificWorldJournal*, vol. 11, pp. 1383–1393, 2011.

[15] T. Komazawa, C. Hayashi, F. T. In: de Dombal, and F. Gremy, Eds., *A Statistical Method for Quantification of Categorical Data and Its Applications to Medical Science*, North-Holland, Amsterdam, The Netherlands, 1976.

[16] D. Ju-Long, "Control problems of grey systems," *Systems and Control Letters*, vol. 1, no. 5, pp. 288–294, 1982.

[17] M. Nelson and W. T. Illingworth, *A Practical Guide to Neural Nets*, Addison-Wesley, New York, NY, USA, 1991.

[18] S. Ishihara, K. Ishihara, M. Nagamachi, and Y. Matsubara, "An automatic builder for a Kansei Engineering expert system using self-organizing neural networks," *International Journal of Industrial Ergonomics*, vol. 15, no. 1, pp. 13–24, 1995.

[19] B. Kim, J. Lee, J. Jang, D. Han, and K. H. Kim, "Prediction on the seasonal behavior of hydrogen sulfide using a neural network model," *TheScientificWorldJournal*, vol. 11, pp. 992–1004, 2011.

[20] W. Wong, P. J. Fos, and F. E. Petry, "Combining the performance strengths of the logistic regression and neural network models: a medical outcomes approach," *TheScientificWorldJournal*, vol. 3, pp. 455–476, 2003.

[21] T. C. Chang and S. J. Lin, "Grey relation analysis of carbon dioxide emissions from industrial production and energy uses in Taiwan," *Journal of Environmental Management*, vol. 56, no. 4, pp. 247–257, 1999.

[22] F. M. Tseng, H. C. Yu, and G. H. Tzeng, "Applied hybrid grey model to forecast seasonal time series," *Technological Forecasting and Social Change*, vol. 67, no. 2-3, pp. 291–302, 2001.

[23] C. C. Hsu and C. Y. Chen, "Applications of improved grey prediction model for power demand forecasting," *Energy Conversion and Management*, vol. 44, no. 14, pp. 2241–2249, 2003.

[24] M. Negnevitsky, *Artificial Intelligence*, Addison-Wesley, New York, NY, USA, 2002.

[25] F. Zwicky, "The morphological approach to discovery, invention, research and construction, new method of though and procedure: symposium on methodologies," *Pasadena*, pp. 316–317, 1967.

[26] N. Cross, *Engineering Design Methods: Strategies for Product Design*, John Wiley and Sons, Chichester, UK, 2000.

[27] C. C. Wang, Y. C. Lin, and C. H. Yeh, "Neural networks for optimal form design of personal digital assistants," in *Proceedings of the 15th International Conference on Advances in Neuro-Information Processing (ICONIP '08)*, vol. 5506 of *Lecture Notes in Computer Science*, pp. 647–654, Auckland, New Zealand, November 2009.

[28] C. C. Wang, *Development of an integrated strategy for customer requirement oriented product design [Ph.D. dissertation]*, Department of Industrial Design, National Cheng Kung University, Tainan, Taiwan, 2008.

[29] K. Smith, M. Palaniswami, and M. Krishnamoorthy, "A hybrid neural approach to combinatorial optimization," *Computers and Operations Research*, vol. 23, no. 6, pp. 597–610, 1996.

[30] *NeuroShell 2 Tutorial*, Ward Systems Group, Frederick, Md, USA, 1993.

8

Application of Particle Swarm Optimization Algorithm in the Heating System Planning Problem

Rong-Jiang Ma,[1] Nan-Yang Yu,[1] and Jun-Yi Hu[1,2]

[1] *School of Mechanical Engineering, Southwest Jiaotong University, Chengdu 610031, China*
[2] *CSR Qishuyan Institute Co., Ltd., Changzhou 213011, China*

Correspondence should be addressed to Rong-Jiang Ma; swjtumrj@139.com

Academic Editors: P. Agarwal, S. Balochian, and Y. Zhang

Based on the life cycle cost (LCC) approach, this paper presents an integral mathematical model and particle swarm optimization (PSO) algorithm for the heating system planning (HSP) problem. The proposed mathematical model minimizes the cost of heating system as the objective for a given life cycle time. For the particularity of HSP problem, the general particle swarm optimization algorithm was improved. An actual case study was calculated to check its feasibility in practical use. The results show that the improved particle swarm optimization (IPSO) algorithm can more preferably solve the HSP problem than PSO algorithm. Moreover, the results also present the potential to provide useful information when making decisions in the practical planning process. Therefore, it is believed that if this approach is applied correctly and in combination with other elements, it can become a powerful and effective optimization tool for HSP problem.

1. Introduction

Humanity faces serious energy and environment problems at present. The environment is increasingly threatened. For instance, with the increase of greenhouse gas emissions in the atmosphere the environments have already reached concerning levels in terms of their potential to cause climate change. Air pollution, acid precipitation, and stratospheric ozone depletion are other serious environmental concerns. The severity of climate change impacts shows the increasing trend if significant action is not taken to reduce greenhouse gas emissions [1]. An important action to address energy and environmental challenges lies in the intelligent and efficient use of energy, including reducing energy waste and using low-carbon fuels.

In China, heating utilities have been developed rapidly, but the energy consumption of production and transport is still too much, which accounts for 21.5% of building energy consumption; building energy consumption accounts for 20.9% of social total energy consumption [2]. With the perfection of the systematic reform, the adjustment of energy structure in China and the requirement of environmental protection, heating energy structure had been changing, and it had been promoting the development of heating mode. It has very important significance to analyze, evaluate, and select heating mode correctly which suits its local characteristics. With the speeding up of urbanization, more and more heating systems will be built due to the importance of infrastructure in urban area. The research on optimal plan of heating system is very imperative for saving project investment, decreasing heating energy consumption, and improving enterprise benefit.

Sustainable development of heating system requires application of planning procedures, which includes optimization of both demand and supply sides of heating. Because the heat source site selection and heating pipe network optimizing plan have an important role in the HSP, there are many scholars concerning this subject and lots of optimization methods have been proposed. The methods of HSP can be classified into three separate categories [3]: planning by models, planning by analogy, and planning by inquiry. The planning by models can be based either on econometric or optimization models. Econometric models utilize mathematical or statistical methods and relay on statistical data. Optimization model allows for the identification of best possible solution—minimization or maximization of objective function, with the predefined set of constrains which describes the space of acceptable solutions. The planning by analogy utilizes the simulation of heating system. That kind of HSP is usually used for the verification of planning results which were achieved by other planning methods [4]. The planning by inquiry is used in the case when other aforementioned methods are not reliable. Good example of planning by inquiry is DELPHI method, which is based on the questioning of group of heating, ventilating, and air conditioning (HVAC) experts or municipal planners and statistical evaluation of their answers [5]. All the methods of HSP listed earlier have a limited transparency, especially for decision makers who do not have good mathematical background. Those methods do not give opportunity to create decision makers preference model or define that model a priori. Hence, many scholars have carried out extensive and deep research on optimization method of HSP. Shen and He [6] investigated optimal planning method of central heating system of water boiler and then put forward optimal planning model and solving method. According to the method, it can be determined the size, location, and so forth of regional heating plant and intermediate heat exchanger station, but there were no further discussions about how to design the pipe network. Wang et al. [7–9] investigated design method of central heating system with double "duct-station," proposing two-step optimization method, but this method was only applicable to double "duct-station" system. For solving the problem, the study in [8] used fully stratified sequence method [10–12] simultaneously taking into account only one objective function for each layer of heating source layout optimization and pipe network system. However, for HSP problem, there are kinds of complex logic even iterative relationships between/among objective functions of layers. This method usually can provide the optimal solution of each layer, but it cannot ensure that the solution of the objective function for last layer is the optimal solution of the whole system exactly. Shi and Li [13] first applied genetic algorithm (GA) for solving the heating source location problem in the study. This method described the cost of the heat source and heating substation as the function of heat load and described the cost of the heating network as the function of heat load and pipe length simply. So the calculated result by this method and actual situation often put in certain error. Shi et al. [14, 15] and Mu et al. [16] put forward the relatively consistent mathematical model for heating system optimization, based on the life cycle cost method, but formula or method for some of parameters was not given clearly and integrally in the model. It seems that limitation is inevitable in the process of the practical application of these methods. But we noticed the life cycle cost (LCC) and particle swarm optimization (PSO) algorithm in the more extensive research areas.

Life cycle cost (LCC) has been applied since the 1960s when the United States' Department of Defense stimulated the development and application of LCC to enhance its cost effectiveness. Defense systems, such as an aircraft or a special land vehicle, are ideal for LCC analyses since the Department of Defense mainly controls the entire life cycle [17]. LCC may be defined as "the cost of acquisition, ownership, and disposal of a product over a defined period of its life cycle" [18, 19]. LCC is a standard engineering economic approach used for choosing among alternative products or designs that approximately provide the same service to the customer [20]. In many cases it may not be necessary to perform a complete LCC analysis, but rather to estimate the differences between the alternatives for the major cost elements [21]. The LCC process may also provide information, for example, in the assessment of the economic viability of products and projects, in the identification of the cost drivers and cost efficiency improvements, and in evaluations of different strategies for product operation, maintenance, and inspection, and so on [22].

There are two popular swarm inspired methods in computational intelligence areas: ant colony optimization (ACO) and particle swarm optimization (PSO). ACO was inspired by the behaviors of ants and has many successful applications in discrete optimization problems. The particle swarm concept originated as a simulation of simplified social system. The original intent was to graphically simulate the choreography of a bird block or fish school. However, it was found that particle swarm model can be used as an optimizer. A substantial review of the properties of the global optimization problems has been given by Parsopoulos and Vrahatis [23]. As one of the global optimization problems, PSO has been widely used in various kinds of planning problems, especially in the area of substation locating and sizing [24–27]. But in area of heating supply, PSO is mainly applied in heating load forecasting [28, 29], but rarely used in HSP.

The main objective of this paper is to discuss the usefulness of the PSO algorithm for solving the HSP problem. Therefore, based on the LCC approach, an integral mathematical model is presented and PSO algorithm is introduced and improved for solving the problem. In the end, the results of the case study suggest the effectiveness of improved particle swarm optimization (IPSO) application to the optimal planning method for heating system.

2. Mathematical Formulation

2.1. Problem Definition and Assumptions. LCC is related to the systems engineering process, because economic considerations are very important in the process of creating systems. Life cycle economic analyses should be done early in the system or product life cycle, because the outcome of the systems engineering process cannot be influenced very much when the design is completed. Thus, LCC involves evaluation of all future costs related to all of the phases in the system life cycle including design, construction and/or production, distribution, operation, maintenance and support, retirement, and material disposal, and so on [30].

Cost models may range from simple to complex and are essentially predictive in nature. Parameters, such as the system's physical environment, usage demand, reliability, maintainability, labor, energy, taxes, inflation, and the time value of money, may have a great influence on the life cycle costs [17].

The main objective of this paper is to discuss the usefulness of the PSO algorithm for owners in making sustainable heating system investment decisions and to improve their decision-bases for municipal administration. Therefore, we apply LCC approach to describe the HSP problem.

Moreover, HSP considered in this study works under the following definition and assumptions.

(i) A heat consuming installation can connect with any heat source but cannot connect with two or more heat sources at the same time.

(ii) The indirect connection between heat consuming installation and heat source is not allowed.

(iii) A heat source must be connected with more than one heat consuming installation; otherwise, it will be closed.

(iv) Any connection between any two heat sources is not allowed.

(v) The location of heat consuming installation is fixed.

(vi) A heat source can be sited in a given region.

(vii) The elevation difference between heat consuming installation and heat source is ignored.

(viii) Heating system planning and optimization can be achieved by changing the number and the heating capacity of heat source and the distance between the heat source and heat consuming installation.

(ix) The measure between heat source and heat consuming installation is simplified to the Manhattan (or city block) distance.

(x) There is no functional difference between any two heat sources and their products.

2.2. Notation. The notations used in the mathematical formulations are given as follows.

Indices

i: Optional heating source

k: Heating equipment

j: Heat consuming installation

r: Heat load distributing segment.

Parameters

m: Number of heat source

k_i: Number of heating equipment which could be installed at the heating source i; $k_i = \{1, 2, \ldots, P_i\}$

n: Number of heat consuming installation

n_r: Number of heat load distributing segments

F_i: Life cycle fixed cost of the heat source i

F_{ik}: Life cycle fixed cost of the heating equipment k which is in the heat source i

C_{ikjr}: Variable production and transport discounted costs within life cycle of heating equipment k to satisfy the heat load distributing segment r of heat consuming installation j, which is in the heat source i; $C_{ikjr} = P_{ikjr} + t_{ikjr}$, where P_{ikjr} is the variable production discounted cost within life cycle of specific heat load; t_{ikjr} is the transport discounted cost within life cycle per specific heat load

X_{ikjr}: Continuous variable, the load of the heat load distributing segment r of heat consuming installation j, which is supplied by heating equipment k of the heat source i

Q_{jr}: Load of the heat load distributing segment r of heat consuming installation j

S_{ik}: Maximum supply capacity of heating equipment k of the heat source i

$Q_i^{\max}$: Maximum supply capacity of heat source i

C_{zd}: Major repair depreciation discounted costs within life cycle of heat source i

C_{rg}: Labor discounted cost within life cycle of heat source i

u: Coefficient of sum; $u = [(1 + r)^y - 1]/r(1 + r)^y$, where r is the standard discount rate, and y is the life cycle

P_{rl}: Price of fuel

Q_w: Calorific value of fuel

η: Thermal efficiency of heat source

E: Water and electricity consumption costs of specific heat load

h_r: Duration of heat load distributing segment r

β: Sulfur content in fuel

λ: Standard emission charge for SO_2

$t_{rw}(j)$: Pipe network discounted cost per specific heat load, which is supplied by heat source i to heat consuming installation j

$C(L_j)$: The discounted cost of pipe segment L_j

$C_{zd}(L_j)$: The major repair depreciation discounted costs within life cycle of pipe segment L_j

$C_{sr}(L_j)$: The heat loss discounted costs within life cycle of pipe segment L_j

$Q(L_j)$: The heat load-bearing of pipe segment L_j

$C_{dl}(L_j)$: The power consumption discounted cost within life cycle of pipe segment L_j per specific heat load

$t_{rz}(j)$: The transport discounted cost within life cycle per specific heat load, which is supplied to heat consuming installation j

$C_{zd}(j)$: The major repair depreciation discounted costs within life cycle of heat consuming installation j

Q_{ij}: The heat load of pipe network for heat consuming installation j

$C_{dl}(j)$: The power consumption discounted cost within life cycle of heat consuming installation j per specific heat load

$C_{rg}(j)$: The labor discounted cost within life cycle of heat consuming installation j

$a[d(L_j)]^b$: Investment of $d(L_j)$ meters diameter double-pipe per meter length, where a and b are coefficients of pipe laying

γ: Rate of major repair depreciation

ρ: Rate of gross fixed capital formation

ω: Conversion coefficient of the units

R: Specific frictional resistance

$l_{dl}(L_j)$: Equivalent length of local resistance for pipe segment L_j

H_{gl}: Heating period

P_d: Electricity price for industrial uses

η_{xb}: Efficiency of circulating water pump

t_g, t_h: Supply/return water temperature of pipe segment

ξ: Conversion coefficient of the units

k: Heat transfer coefficient

ε: Local heat loss coefficient of pipe fittings

P_{sr}: Annual costs of heat loss

$t_{g,pj}$: Annual mean supply water temperature of pipe segment

$t_{h,pj}$: Annual mean return water temperature of pipe segment

$t_{hj,pj}$: Annual mean temperature

c_1, c_2: Comprehensive coefficient of investment

Q_{ij}: Heat load of pipe network

α: Correction factor

μ: Conversion coefficient of the units

ΔP_j: Pressure difference between supply and return water of pipe network for heat consuming installation j

S_{gz}: Average annual wages of operating personnel and manager

n_{yg}: Number of operating personnel and manager per 1 MW heat load

Ω: Conversion coefficient of the units.

Decision Variables

Y_{ik}: 1, if the equipment k is installed or set up in the heat source i; 0, if the equipment k is not installed or set up in the heat source i

Z_i: 1, if the heat source i is set up; 0, if the heat source i is not set up.

2.3. Mathematical Model of HSP.

In this study, the problem is summarized into a multisource, multifacility, single-commodity, multiraw material plant location problem, and a mixed 0-1 integer planning model has been formulated. The cost model of the heat source and the heat-transmission network concerned in the optimization model are considered in this study. The objective function of heating system planning problem is to minimize the total heat production cost. The proposed mathematical model formulation for HSP problem can be found as follows.

Minimize

$$\text{LCC} = \sum_{i=1}^{m} F_i Z_i + \sum_{i=1}^{m}\sum_{k=1}^{k_i} F_{ik} Y_{ik} + \sum_{i=1}^{m}\sum_{k=1}^{k_i}\sum_{j=1}^{n}\sum_{r=1}^{n_r} C_{ikjr} X_{ikjr} \quad (1)$$

subject to

$$\sum_{i=1}^{m}\sum_{k=1}^{k_i} X_{ikjr} = Q_{jr}, \quad j=1,2,\dots,n;\ r=1,2,\dots,n_r, \quad (2)$$

$$\sum_{j=1}^{n}\sum_{r=1}^{n_r} X_{ikjr} \leq S_{ik} Y_{ik}, \quad i=1,2,\dots,m;\ k=1,2,\dots,k_i, \quad (3)$$

$$\sum_{k=1}^{k_i} S_{ik} Y_{ik} \leq Q_i^{\max}, \quad i=1,2,\dots,m, \quad (4)$$

$$\sum_{k=1}^{k_i} Y_{ik} \leq P_i Z_i, \quad i=1,2,\dots,m, \quad (5)$$

$$Z_i, Y_{ik} = 0 \text{ or } 1, \quad X_{ikjr} \geq 0. \quad (6)$$

Objective function (1) minimizes the discounted costs within life cycle of heating system as the general objective; it is an index of dynamic economy evaluation, where F_i, F_{ik}, and C_{ikjr} are composed of respective discounted costs together. Constraint (2) is each heat consuming installation's heat load, which is heat consumption for each user and the requirements of the heating quantity and quality. Constraint (3) means that each of the heating equipment in the heating system bear heat load should not exceed the maximum heating capacity. Constraint (4) means the maximum heating capacity of heating source, which is allowed under the restrictions of objective conditions. Constraint (5) means that only open heating source first can install equipment in it. In the model, there are two decision variables, in which Z_i is related to heating source, and Y_{ik} is related to heating equipment.

Because the piecewise function of heat load duration curve is introduced in the process of solving the model, this model can be applied to any form of heating system.

2.4. Formulation of Heating System Cost Model

2.4.1. The Heating Source Cost Model.
The heating source cost model is aimed to resolve the calculation problem of F_{ik},

in the objective function (1), and P_{ikjr}, which is a part of C_{ikjr} in the objective function (1). It consists of fixed costs and variable costs, the former refers to all necessary costs of heating source, so long as open a heating source or install a piece of heating equipment, the latter only associated with the size of the heat load and running status of equipment. Consider

$$F_{ik} = C_{zd} + C_{rg},\tag{7}$$

$$P_{ikjr} = u\left(\frac{0.36P_{rl} + 0.72\beta\lambda}{Q_w\eta} + 0.36E\right)h_r.\tag{8}$$

Equation (7) is the formulation of heating source fixed costs, and (8) is the formulation of heating source variable costs.

2.4.2. The Heating Network Cost Model. The heating network cost model is aimed to resolve the calculation problem of t_{ikjr}, which is a part of C_{ikjr} in the objective function (1), and also to optimize the direction of heating network and the pipe diameter. Heating network (heat consuming installation included) cost consists of the heating network operation cost and heat consuming installation costs. Heating network operation cost consists of major repair depreciation discounted cost, power consumption discounted cost, pipe network heat loss discounted cost, and labor discounted cost. By dividing the discounted cost within life cycle of pipe segment allocation to the total heat load bearded by itself directly and evenly, the transport discounted cost within life cycle per specific heat load can be obtained, which is supplied by heat source i to heat consuming installation j. Consider

$$t_{ikjr} = t_{rw}(j) + t_{rz}(j),\tag{9}$$

$$t_{rw}(j) = t_{rw}(j-1) + C(L_j),$$

$$C(L_j) = \frac{C_{zd}(L_j) + C_{sr}(L_j)}{Q(L_j)} + C_{dl}(L_j),\tag{10}$$

$$t_{rw}(0) = 0,$$

$$C_{tz}(L_j) = a\left[d(L_j)\right]^b l(L_j),\tag{11}$$

$$C_{zd}(L_j) = \gamma\rho C_{tz}(L_j)u,\tag{12}$$

$$C_{dl}(L_j) = \frac{2\omega R\left[l(L_j) + l_{dl}(L_j)\right]uH_{gl}P_d}{\eta_{xb}(t_g - t_h)},\tag{13}$$

$$C_{sr}(L_j) = \xi k\pi d(L_j)l(L_j)(1+\varepsilon)$$
$$\times H_{gl}P_{sr}u\left(t_{g,pj} + t_{h,pj} - 2t_{hj,pj}\right).\tag{14}$$

Equation (9) is the heating network transportation cost model. The pipe segment cost model is composed of (10)–(14), where (10) is the pipe network discounted cost per specific heat load supplied by heat source i to heat consuming installation j; (11) is the investment cost of pipe segment L_j; (12) is the major repair depreciation discounted cost of pipe

segment L_j; (13) is the power consumption discounted cost of pipe segment L_j per specific heat load; and (14) is the heat loss discounted cost of pipe segment L_j. Consider

$$t_{rz}(j) = \frac{C_{zd}(j)}{Q_{ij}} + C_{dl}(j) + C_{rg}(j),\tag{15}$$

$$C_{tz}(j) = c_1 + \alpha c_2 Q_{ij},\tag{16}$$

$$C_{zd}(j) = \gamma\rho C_{tz}(j)u,\tag{17}$$

$$C_{dl}(j) = \frac{\mu\Delta P_j}{\eta_{xb}(t_g - t_h)}H_{gl}P_d u,\tag{18}$$

$$C_{rg}(j) = S_{gz}n_{yg}u\Omega.\tag{19}$$

The heat consuming installation cost model is composed between (15) and (19), where (15) is the transport discounted cost within life cycle per specific heat load supplied by heat consuming installation j; (16) is the investment cost of heat consuming installation j; (17) is the major repair depreciation discounted cost of heat consuming installation j; (18) is the power consumption discounted cost of heat consuming installation j per specific heat load; and (19) is the labor discounted cost of heat consuming installation j.

3. PSO and Its Improvement

3.1. PSO Algorithm. The PSO is proposed by Kennedy and Eberhart [31, 32] in 1995, and the motivation for the development of this algorithm was studied based on the simulation of simplified animal social behaviors, such as fish schooling and bird flocking. Similar to other population-based optimization methods such as genetic algorithms, the particle swarm algorithm starts with the random initialization of a population of particles in the search space [33]. However, unlike in other evolutionary optimization methods, in PSO there is no direct recombination of genetic material between individuals during the search. The PSO algorithm works on the social behavior of particles in the swarm. Therefore, it provides the global best solution by simply adjusting the trajectory of each individual toward its own best location and toward the best particle of the entire swarm at each time step (generation) [31, 34, 35]. The PSO method is becoming very popular due to its simplicity of implementation and ability to quickly converge to a reasonably good solution.

3.2. Formulation of General PSO. Specifically, PSO algorithm maintains a population of particles, each of which represents a potential solution to an optimization problem. The position of the particle denotes a feasible, if not the best, solution to the problem. The optimum progress is required to move the particle position in order to improve the value of objective function. The convergence condition always requires setting up the move iteration number of particle.

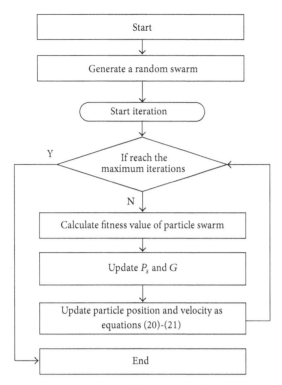

FIGURE 1: Flow chart of general PSO.

The position of particle move rule is shown as follows:

$$V_s(t+1) = wV_s(t) + C_1r_1\left(P_s - X_s(t)\right) + C_2r_2\left(G - X_s(t)\right), \tag{20}$$

$$X_s(t+1) = X_s(t) + V_s(t+1), \tag{21}$$

where $V_s(t)$ represents the velocity vector of particle s in t time; $X_s(t)$ represents the position vector of particle s in t time; P_s is the personal best position of particle s; G is the best position of the particle found at present; w represents inertia weight; C_1, C_2 are two acceleration constants, called cognitive and social parameters, respectively; and r_1 and r_2 are two random functions in the range $[0, 1]$.

The flow chart of general PSO is shown in Figure 1.

3.3. Improvement of Particle Swarm Optimization (IPSO) for HSP Problem. For HSP problem and its model in this paper, the value of LCC depends mostly on the distance between heating source and heat consuming installation, and the number of heating source i. It is necessary to make corresponding improvements on PSO, in order to solve this problem more accurately and effectively.

The evolution of the solution set begins with an initial solution set in the PSO; initial solution set is composed of initial particles. Each solution location is represented by an i-dimensional vector; i represents the number of variables of each solution, and it represents the number of heating sources in particularly in this paper.

The position coordinate of heating source (p) has two components, which is represented by two i-dimensional vectors, where x direction coordinates are represented by

vector px, and y direction coordinates are represented by vector py. Therefore, x direction component for the position vector of particle s in t time can be represented by $px_s(t)$, and the rest can be done in the same manner.

In the same way, the velocity for location change of heating source (Vp) has two components, which is represented by two i-dimensional vectors, where x direction component for the velocity vector is represented by vector Vpx, and y direction component for the velocity vector is represented by vector Vpy. Therefore, x direction component for the velocity vector of particle s in t time can be represented by $Vpx_s(t)$, and the rest can be done in the same manner.

Thus, the update rule of velocity for each particle is indicated by (22)-(23), and the update rule of position for each particle is indicated by (24)-(25). Consider

$$Vpx_s(t+1) = wVpx_s(t) + C_1r_1\left(P_s - px_s(t)\right) \\ + C_2r_2\left(G - px_s(t)\right), \tag{22}$$

$$Vpy_s(t+1) = wVpy_s(t) + C_1r_1\left(P_s - py_s(t)\right) \\ + C_2r_2\left(G - py_s(t)\right), \tag{23}$$

$$px_s(t+1) = px_s(t) + Vpx_s(t+1), \tag{24}$$

$$py_s(t+1) = py_s(t) + Vpy_s(t+1). \tag{25}$$

The meanings of parameters are consistent with previous description.

3.4. Calculated Flow of IPSO. The calculated flow of proposed IPSO is described as follows.

3.4.1. Initial Solution. The initial solution for HSP problem is obtained by random initial position of each heat source; a matrix is employed in recording the coordinates and the heat load-bearing information of heat source, and the calculated flow of initial solution is as follows.

(1) Set up the number of heat source i, and generate an empty matrix for the initial position of heat source.

(2) Based on randomly and evenly distributed manner, generate the position coordinates of heat sources, into the matrix.

(3) Call the decoding function; calculate the heat load-bearing and the cost for each heat source, into the matrix.

(4) Calculate the LCC, the fitness value of the initial particle.

3.4.2. Decoding Function. In this paper, decoding function will call the matrix for current position and heat load of heat consuming installation, and then according to the matrix for the position of heat source, which is represented by current particle, divide the heating range of each heat source, and calculate the LCC.

Information matrix of heat consuming installation (*heat_point*) is a j-line four-column matrix; the first column represents the serial number of heat consuming installation, the second column represents the x coordinate of heat consuming installation, the third column represents the y coordinate of heat consuming installation, and the heat load of heat consuming installation is represented by the fourth column. The calculated flow of initial solution is as follows.

(1) Read matrix $heat\_point$, and let $j = j + 1$.

(2) Calculate the distance to all heat source from the heat consuming installation j, into the vector l_j.

(3) By substituting l_j into (10)–(14), calculate the cost of the heat consuming installation j connected with each heat source.

(4) Find out the minimum cost, and the heat consuming installation j connected with the corresponding heat source.

(5) If j is the last heat consuming installation then stop; otherwise, go to Step 1.

3.4.3. The Evolution of Particle Swarm. After one generation of particles, a new generation is evolved as follows.

(1) Call the decoding function; calculate the fitness value of the particle swarm.

(2) Update the individual optimal solution P_s and the global optimal solution G.

(3) Update the speed vector, by using (22)-(23).

(4) Update the speed vector, by using (24)-(25).

3.4.4. Improvement Approach. The PSO's convergence is fast, so it is liable to fall into local optimal solution. In order to improve the optimizing capability, we add modular arithmetic of velocity vector into each iterative operation. If the norm of velocity vector V is less than the predetermined minimum value V_{min}, then generate a random velocity, let the current particle swarm out of local convergence region, and search other solution spaces. However, after it falls into local optimal solution, the norm of velocity tends to 0 in the general PSO algorithm, the solution stabilized near the local optimal solution, and it cannot explore search space furthermore.

The flow chart of IPSO is shown as Figure 2.

4. Case Study

4.1. Basic Information of Case. This is a heating plan for a new area in China covering the area of 3.346 million square meters, and heat load is 167.3 MW in total. Based on the road network, the new area is divided into 29 heating districts (Figure 3), and the heating load of each district (Figure 4) is supplied by their small gas-fired boiler.

4.2. The Parameters of Algorithms. The role of the inertia weight w, in (20), (22), and (23), is considered critical for the PSO's convergence behaviour. The inertia weight is employed to control the impact of the previous history of

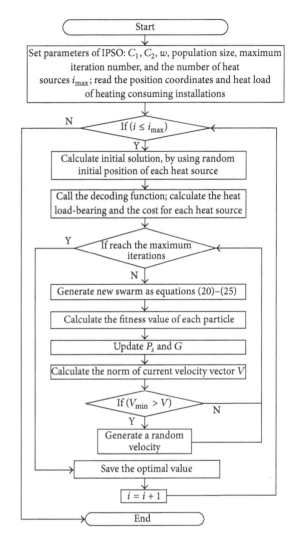

FIGURE 2: Flow chart of IPSO.

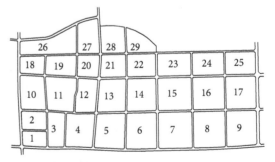

FIGURE 3: Site location plan of 29 heating districts.

velocities on the current one. Accordingly, the parameter w regulates the trade-off between the global and local exploration abilities of the swarm. A large inertia weight facilitates global exploration, while a small one tends to facilitate local exploration. A suitable value for the inertia weight w usually provides balance between global and local exploration abilities resulting in a reduction of the number of iterations required to locate the optimum solution. Initially, the inertia

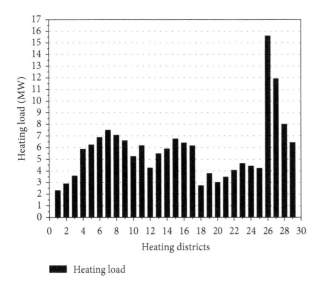

FIGURE 4: Heating load of 29 heating districts.

weight was constant. However, experimental results indicated that it is better to initially set the inertia to a large value, in order to promote global exploration of the search space, and gradually decrease it to get more refined solutions [32, 36]. Thus, an initial value around 1.2 and a gradual decline towards 0 can be considered as a good choice for w. The parameters C_1 and C_2, in (20), (22), and (23), are not critical for PSO's convergence. However, proper fine-tuning may result in faster convergence and alleviation of local minima. A further study of the acceleration parameter in the first version of PSO is given in [37]. As default values, $C_1 = C_2 = 2$ were proposed, but experimental results indicate that $C_1 = C_2 = 0.5$ might provide even better results. Some work reports that it might be even better to choose a larger cognitive parameter, C_1, than a social parameter, C_2, and $C_1 + C_2 \leq 4$ [38, 39], but $(C_1 + C_2)/2 = 1.494$ was suggested by [35]; the strategy of acceleration parameter linear changing with iterations was proposed by Ratnaweera et al. [40], but acceleration parameter is the nonlinear function of the ratio G-to-P_s, which was proposed by Arumugam et al. [41]; Jie et al. [42] suggested to adjust the acceleration coefficient by measuring diversity.

But so far, the research on the most appropriate values for w, C_1, and C_2 has no unified conclusion. And how the variable values impact the solution to HSP problem is unknown. For HSP problem on kinds of values is unknown. So we set the w, C_1, and C_2 to common values in this study.

4.3. Analysis of Results.
By applying PSO and IPSO algorithm, respectively, we solved the HSP problem in this paper. The parameters of PSO and IPSO are summarized in Table 1.

In this study, 29 kinds of schemes of heating (from one heat source to twenty-nine heat sources) were calculated for 10 times through reading initial conditions from the excel file successively, which contains the coordinates and heat load of heat consuming installation, preset maximum number of heat source. The results of LCC and the D-value

TABLE 1: PSO and IPSO parameters.

Variable	Symbol	Value	
		PSO	IPSO
Population size	—	100	100
Maximum iteration number	—	1000	1000
Inertia weight	w	0.7	0.7
Acceleration constant	C_1	2	2
	C_2	2	2

TABLE 2: Algorithm calculation results comparison.

Heat source	LCC (billion Yuan)					
	Optimum value			Average value		
	PSO	IPSO	D-value	PSO	IPSO	D-value
1	1.5320	1.5320	0.0000	1.5320	1.5320	0.0000
2	1.5035	1.5035	0.0000	1.5035	1.5035	0.0000
3	1.4940	1.4940	0.0000	1.4947	1.4945	0.0002
4	1.4881	1.4880	0.0001	1.4893	1.4890	0.0003
5	1.4866	1.4864	0.0002	1.4873	1.4872	0.0001
6	1.4857	1.4848	0.0009	1.4867	1.4863	0.0004
7	1.4857	1.4842	0.0015	1.4865	1.4852	0.0013
8	1.4850	1.4828	0.0022	1.4865	1.4854	0.0011
9	1.4849	1.4832	0.0017	1.4872	1.4857	0.0015
10	1.4847	1.4843	0.0004	1.4875	1.4866	0.0009
11	1.4855	1.4852	0.0003	1.4889	1.4874	0.0015
12	1.4864	1.4856	0.0008	1.4894	1.4880	0.0014
13	1.4883	1.4865	0.0018	1.4915	1.4887	0.0028
14	1.4893	1.4873	0.0020	1.4920	1.4910	0.0010
15	1.4910	1.4903	0.0007	1.4933	1.4917	0.0016
16	1.4931	1.4908	0.0023	1.4952	1.4944	0.0008
17	1.4939	1.4933	0.0006	1.4966	1.4954	0.0012
18	1.4966	1.4944	0.0022	1.5002	1.4971	0.0031
19	1.4987	1.4974	0.0013	1.5025	1.4993	0.0032
20	1.4990	1.4985	0.0005	1.5010	1.5007	0.0003
21	1.5018	1.5001	0.0017	1.5031	1.5027	0.0004
22	1.5032	1.5018	0.0014	1.5044	1.5040	0.0004
23	1.5033	1.5031	0.0002	1.5065	1.5056	0.0009
24	1.5062	1.5050	0.0012	1.5080	1.5075	0.0005
25	1.5075	1.5065	0.0010	1.5100	1.5095	0.0005
26	1.5106	1.5102	0.0004	1.5131	1.5120	0.0011
27	1.5121	1.5110	0.0011	1.5132	1.5130	0.0002
28	1.5135	1.5133	0.0002	1.5152	1.5150	0.0002
29	1.5169	1.5145	0.0024	1.5195	1.5170	0.0025

for the optimum and the average between PSO and IPSO at the same number of heat source are shown as Figures 5 and 6 and Table 2.

From analyzing the results, we can draw the following conclusion about the HSP problem.

(1) The original plan (the heating load of each district is supplied by its small gas-fired boiler) is not an economic and reasonable plan for the case, and the LCC is the second highest in 29 schemes, which is

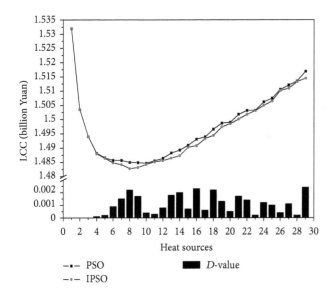

FIGURE 5: Algorithm calculation results comparison (optimum value).

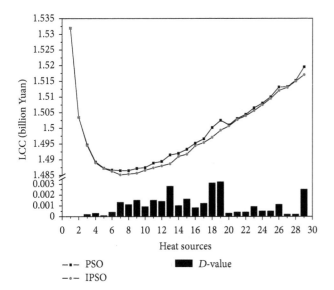

FIGURE 6: Algorithm calculation results comparison (average value).

TABLE 3: The detailed results of 8 heat sources scheme.

Heating source	Coordinate	Supply heat load (MW)	Heat consuming installation
1	(395, 555)	24.38	1, 2, 3, 10, 11, 12
2	(320, 1050)	22.07	18, 19, 26
3	(1030, 315)	24.43	4, 5, 6, 13
4	(760, 1070)	14.92	20, 27
5	(1745, 555)	24.73	7, 14, 15, 23
6	(1040, 1090)	21.94	21, 22, 28, 29
7	(2380, 850)	14.78	17, 24, 25
8	(2145, 340)	20.05	8, 9, 16

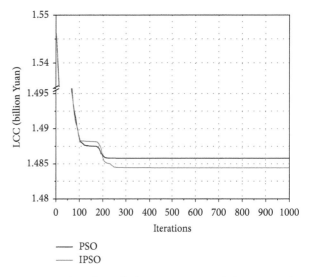

FIGURE 7: Algorithm calculation comparison (7 heat sources).

(1) The optimal solution of IPSO is better than PSO. The optimum LCC which calculated by IPSO is not larger than PSO for all 29 schemes. The maximum D-value is 2.4 million Yuan in the scheme which plans to set up 29 heat sources.

(2) The real minimum LCC was not calculated by PSO. The minimum LCC calculated by PSO is 1.9 million Yuan larger than the minimum LCC calculated by IPSO.

Figure 7 compares the LCC convergence curves of two algorithms in three kinds of schemes, respectively. When the population size and the iteration number of PSO are same as those of IPSO during the HSP optimization process, although the PSO algorithm is faster for giving the optimization results, but the optimal results by IPSO are better than the searcher values by PSO. The main reason for current performance is that IPSO can avoid local optimal solution and then further expand the search space so as to find a better solution.

Hence, it can be concluded that the improvement approach is effective, and the proposed method IPSO has better significance in solving the HSP problem and competitive to PSO algorithm.

only better than the scheme which plans to set up one heat source only.

(2) From one heat source to twenty-nine heat sources, LCC is monotone decreasing until a minimum value first, then monotone increasing.

(3) Only one minimum value of LCC that appeared throughout the change process, which is 1.4828 billion Yuan, the scheme of which plans to set up 8 heat sources, is the best choice for the case. (The detailed calculation results of this scheme are shown in Table 3.)

By observing the algorithms, the following is also concluded.

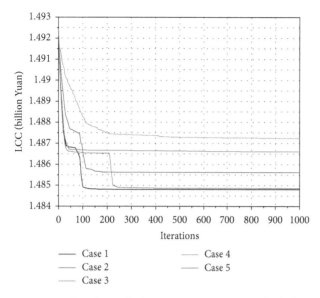

FIGURE 8: Algorithm calculation in comparison with different parameters (6 heat sources).

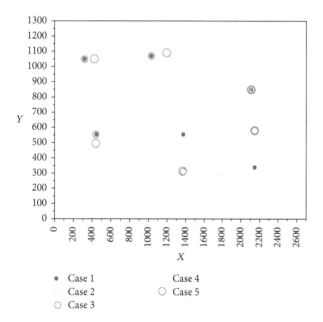

FIGURE 9: Coordinates of heating sources in comparison with different parameters (6 heat sources).

TABLE 4: The parameters of each case in Figures 8 and 9.

Variable	Symbol	Value				
		Case 1	Case 2	Case 3	Case 4	Case 5
Population size	—	100	100	100	100	100
Maximum iteration number	—	1000	1000	1000	1000	1000
Inertia weight	w	0.7	0.4	0.9	0.7	0.7
Acceleration constant	C_1	2	2	2	0.2	3.8
	C_2	2	2	2	0.2	3.8

the more details were not presented here and will be discussed in a separate paper.

6. Conclusions and Prospects

(1) In this paper, we presented an integral mathematical model for solving the heating system planning (HSP) problem taking into account minimizing the cost of heating system for a given life cycle time.

(2) According to the particularity of HSP problem, the particle swarm optimization (PSO) algorithm was introduced and improved, the new definition and update rule of velocity and position vector were proposed, and the improvement approach about generating a random velocity was adopted to avoid particle swarm into local optimal solution. Then an actual case study was calculated to check its feasibility in practical use. The results show that the IPSO algorithm can more preferably solve the HSP problem than PSO algorithm.

(3) Although there is no more discussion about the influence of computational results by changing the values of algorithm parameters (w, C_1, and C_2), but the results of the case study still show the potential to provide useful information when making decisions in the practical planning process. Thus, it is believed that if this approach is applied correctly and in combination with other elements, such as the accurate prediction of heating load, the running efficiency of equipment, and the real operation situation, it can become a powerful and effective optimization tool for HSP problem.

5. Discussion

Section 4.2 referred to the values of w, C_1, and C_2 which may influence the computational results. In Figures 8 and 9, the results obtained by IPSO were also proved. Algorithm calculation comparison with different parameters is shown in Figures 8 and 9, which is a visual display of the coordinates of heating sources with different parameters.

The parameters of each case in the figure are summarized in Table 4.

The influence aspect of the algorithm is worth further study, but because of the major goal of the present study,

References

[1] V. Arroyo, *Agenda for Climate Action*, Pew Centre on Global Climate Change, Arlington, Va, USA, 2006.

[2] Tsinghua University Building Energy Research Center, *2012 Annual Report on China Building Energy Efficiency*, China Architecture & Building Press, 2012.

[3] M. Kleinpeter, *Energy Planning and Policy*, John Wiley & Sons, New York, NY, USA, 1995.

[4] C. Cormio, M. Dicorato, A. Minoia, and M. Trovato, "A regional energy planning methodology including renewable energy sources and environmental constraints," *Renewable and Sustainable Energy Reviews*, vol. 7, no. 2, pp. 99–130, 2003.

[5] O. Helmer, "Kommentar zur Delphi methode," *Science Journal*, no. 10, pp. 49–53, 1967.

[6] Y.-T. Shen and J.-Y. He, *The Optimization of Thermo-Dynamic System and Equipment*, China Machine Press, 1985.

[7] Z.-G. Wang, X.-Y. Xiang, L. Zhou et al., "Optimization design of central heating system in Liaohe oilfield Zhenxing district," *Oil-Gasfield Surface Engineering*, vol. 16, no. 1, pp. 32–36, 1997.

[8] Z.-G. Wang, Y.-T. Ma, W. Lu et al., "Optimization programming for heating system," *Heating Ventilating & Air Conditioning*, vol. 33, no. 1, pp. 2–4, 2003.

[9] Z.-G. Wang, J. Chen, Y.-C. Song, W.-Z. Yang, and X.-Y. Xiang, "The study on the desing method of "duct-station" layout and pipe networt optimization for central heating system," *Journal of Engineering Thermophysics*, vol. 33, no. 2, pp. 302–304, 2012.

[10] K.-X. Xie, L.-X. Han, and Y.-L. Lin, *Optimization Method*, Tianjin University Press, 1998.

[11] Y. Sawaragi, H. Nakayama, and T. Tanino, "Theory of multiobjective optimization," *Mathematics in Science and Engineering*, vol. 176, pp. 1–296, 1985.

[12] S. M. Lee, *Goal Programming for Decision Analysis*, Auer Bach, Philadelphia, Pa, USA, 1972.

[13] Z.-Y. Shi and H.-J. Li, "Application of genetic algorithms in location selection of heating system with multi-heat sources," *District Heating*, no. 2, pp. 11–14, 1998.

[14] Y.-J. Shi and W. Yuan, "Optimal planning of district heating system of water boiler," *Journal of Hebei Institute of Architectural Engineering*, no. 3, pp. 5–10, 1997.

[15] Y.-J. Shi and L.-L. Liu, "Application of LCC to optimization of heating systems," *Heating Ventilating & Air Conditioning*, vol. 29, no. 5, pp. 65–66, 1999.

[16] Q.-Y. Mu, L.-Q. Yue, and F.-S. Zhou, "Applied LCC's concept in optimum planning of heating system," *Journal of Hebei Institute of Architectural Engineering*, vol. 19, no. 2, pp. 46–47, 2001.

[17] Y. S. Sherif and W. J. Kolarik, "Life cycle costing: concept and practice," *Omega*, vol. 9, no. 3, pp. 287–296, 1981.

[18] International Electro technical Commission (IEC), "Dependability management. Part 3-3. Application guide—Life cycle costing," International standard, IEC 60300-3-3, Pronorm AS, 2004.

[19] M. Rausand and A. Høyland, *System Reliability Theory. Models, Statistical Methods, and Applications*, Wiley Series in Probability and Statistics, Wiley-Interscience, 2004.

[20] J. Lutz, A. Lekov, P. Chan, C. D. Whitehead, S. Meyers, and J. McMahon, "Life-cycle cost analysis of energy efficiency design options for residential furnaces and boilers," *Energy*, vol. 31, no. 2-3, pp. 311–329, 2006.

[21] Norsok Standard, "Life cycle cost for systems and equipment," Common requirements, O-CR-001, 1996.

[22] D. Ravemark, "LCC/LCA Experience. Developing and working with LCC tools," DANTES—EU Life Environment Program, 2004.

[23] K. E. Parsopoulos and M. N. Vrahatis, "Recent approaches to global optimization problems through particle swarm optimization," *Natural Computing*, vol. 1, no. 2-3, pp. 235–306, 2002.

[24] B.-Z. Wang, Z.-R. Liang, H.-F. Su, and Y.-Z. Liu, "Application of improved PSO algorithm in location selection of substations," *Electric Power Science and Engineering*, vol. 25, no. 10, pp. 4–7, 2009.

[25] M.-H. Yang, H. Liu, C.-S. Wang, S.-Y. Ge, and T. Zeng, "Optimal substation locating and sizing based on cultural algorithm of particle swarm," *Journal of Tianjin University*, vol. 45, no. 9, pp. 785–790, 2012.

[26] C.-S. Wu, "Multi-objective distributed generation planning based on improved particle swarm optimization algorithm," *Guangdong Electric Power*, vol. 25, no. 1, pp. 54–58, 2012.

[27] H.-F. Su, J.-H. Zhang, Z.-R. Liang, S. Zhang, and S.-S. Niu, "Substation LCC planning based on refined mean clustering random particle swarm algorithm," *Transactions of China Electrotechnical Society*, vol. 27, no. 4, pp. 209–215, 2012.

[28] B.-K. Gao, Y. Li, and M.-Z. Xu, "Application of particle swarm optimization algorithm in the heating load combination forecasting," *Information and Electronic Engineering*, vol. 9, no. 5, pp. 655–659, 2011.

[29] J. Liu, Y. Yang, and Q.-G. Qiu, "Research on heat burden prediction and control of substation based on PSO algorithm," *Energy Conservation*, no. 6, pp. 27–30, 2008.

[30] W. J. Fabrycky and B. S. Blanchard, *Life-Cycle Cost and Economic Analysis*, Prentice Hall, Upper Saddle River, NJ, USA, 1991.

[31] J. Kennedy and R. Eberhart, "Particle swarm optimization," in *Proceedings of IEEE International Conference on Neural Network*, pp. 1942–1948, December 1995.

[32] Y. Shi and R. Eberhart, "A modified particle swarm optimizer," in *Proceedings of IEEE International Conference on Evolutionary Computation (ICEC '98)*, pp. 69–73, May 1998.

[33] D. E. Goldberg, *Genetic Algorithms in Search, Optimization, and Machine Learning*, Addison-Wesley, Reading, Mass, USA, 1989.

[34] M. Clerc, "The swarm and the queen: toward a deterministic and adaptive particle swarm optimization," in *Proceedings of the IEEE International Joint Conference on Evolutionary Computation*, vol. 3, pp. 1951–1957, 1999.

[35] M. Clerc and J. Kennedy, "The particle swarm-explosion, stability, and convergence in a multidimensional complex space," *IEEE Transactions on Evolutionary Computation*, vol. 6, no. 1, pp. 58–73, 2002.

[36] Y. Shi and R. Eberhart, "Parameter selection in particle swarm optimization," in *Evolutionary Programming VII*, vol. 1447 of *Lecture Notes in Computer Science*, pp. 591–600, 1998.

[37] J. Kennedy, "The behavior of particles," in *Evolutionary Programming VII*, vol. 1447 of *Lecture Notes in Computer Science*, pp. 579–589, 1998.

[38] A. Carlisle and G. Dozier, "An off-the-shelf PSO," in *Proceedings of the Particle Swarm Optimization Workshop*, pp. 1–6, 2001.

[39] Y.-X. Shen, G.-Y. Wang, and C.-H. Zeng, "Correlative particle swarm optimization model," *Journal of Software*, vol. 22, no. 4, pp. 695–708, 2011.

[40] A. Ratnaweera, S. K. Halgamuge, and H. C. Watson, "Self-organizing hierarchical particle swarm optimizer with time-varying acceleration coefficients," *IEEE Transactions on Evolutionary Computation*, vol. 8, no. 3, pp. 240–255, 2004.

[41] M. S. Arumugam, M. V. C. Rao, and A. W. C. Tan, "A novel and effective particle swarm optimization like algorithm with extrapolation technique," *Applied Soft Computing Journal*, vol. 9, no. 1, pp. 308–320, 2009.

[42] J. Jie, J.-C. Zeng, and C.-Z. Han, "Self-organized particle swarm optimization based on feedback control of diversity," *Computer Research and Development*, vol. 45, no. 3, pp. 464–471, 2008.

9

Clustering-Based Multiple Imputation via Gray Relational Analysis for Missing Data and Its Application to Aerospace Field

Jing Tian, Bing Yu, Dan Yu, and Shilong Ma

State Key Laboratory of Software Development Environment, Beihang University, No. 37 Xueyuan Road, Haidian District, Beijing 100191, China

Correspondence should be addressed to Jing Tian; tianjing@nlsde.buaa.edu.cn

Academic Editors: Y.-P. Huang, P. Melin, M. F. G. Penedo, and D. Rodriguez

A large number of scientific researches and industrial applications commonly suffer from missing data. Some inappropriate techniques of missing value treatment compromise data quality, which detrimentally influences the knowledge discovery. In this paper, we propose a missing data completion method named CBGMI. Firstly, it separates the nonmissing data instances into several clusters by excluding the missing-valued entries. Then, it utilizes the entropy of the proximal category for each incomplete instance in terms of the similarity metric based on gray relational analysis. Experiments on UCI datasets and aerospace datasets demonstrate that the superiority of our algorithm to other approaches on validity.

1. Introduction

In a variety of application domains, machine learning and data mining algorithms proved to be of great value [1–3]. However, people using real-world databases or datasets repeatedly encounter the data imperfection issue in the form of incompleteness [4, 5]. Therefore, a plenty of resolutions have been devised to cope with the unfavorable phenomenon. Despite the fact that missing data might not cause any major issue particularly when the missing rate is not significantly high, it could not be considered as an ideal case to ensure the data quality. Additionally, some people argue that the fragmentary data should be excluded from further consideration. Nevertheless, the opinion remains as an obvious shortcoming which is articulated that the other observed factual values of the same instance may simultaneously be absent [6]. In some high-missing-rate environment, this strategy is presumed unreasonable and infeasible. Consequently, the handling for substitution or replacement draws increasing attentions, termed as imputation. In broad outline, the methods available can be separated into two categories: single imputation and multiple imputation methods. On one hand, single imputation, that is, filling in precisely one value for each missing one, intuitively has many appealing features. For example, standard complete-data methods can be applied directly, and the substantial effort required to create imputations needs to be carried out only once [7, 8]. On the other hand, multiple imputation generates a quantity of simulated values for each missing item, in order to reflect properly the uncertainty attached to missing data [9, 10]. This has been advocated as a statistically sound approach, but so far its use has been limited mainly to the social and medical sciences.

Recently, multiple imputation has emerged as an interesting and quite visible alternative in missing data analyses. The versions of the sophisticated approach are advantageous to these conventional techniques because they require less stringent assumptions and mitigate the pitfalls of traditional ones [11, 12]. Nevertheless, for the most part of existing solutions, the following facets retain defective. (a) The clustering strategy combining complete instances with incomplete instances violates the formation of good clusters. In other words, the entire instances involved clustering generates unbiased values due to the imperfection [13]. (b) The traditional *Minkowski*'s L_p ($p = 1, 2, \infty$) metric is imprecise to scale the similarity among different instances. (c) The current methodologies are hardly applicable to handling the missing aerospace data due to the their underperformance on validity.

In this paper, data imputation is formulated as a problem of estimation of missing values by multiple operations based on clustering. Furthermore, the prime contribution of this paper could be described as follows. (a) Dividing nonmissing items into a finite number of well-partitioned clusters contributes to make the completion in the optimal tailored area. (b) The gray relational analysis, which signifies the situational variation of the curve, could characterize the relative discrepancy more precisely. (c) CBGMI is adopted to the practical aerospace with accurate performance.

The rest of this paper is structured as follows. Section 2 first briefly introduces both the missingness mechanisms and the emblematic patterns of missing data treatment and then reviews the diverse-related literatures about imputation. In Section 3, the detailed process of the CBGMI algorithm is illustrated in three primary procedural subitems. Section 4 demonstrates a series of experimental results on both UCI datasets and empirical aerospace datasets to compare the performance with other methods. Finally, conclusions are given in Section 5.

2. Related Work

2.1. Missingness Mechanisms. Three different mechanisms, which lead to the introduction of missing values, can be categorized as follows [13, 14].

2.1.1. Missing Completely at Random (MCAR). When the distribution of an example having a missing value for an attribute does not depend on either the observed data or the missing data. When MCAR happens, evidently the set of subjects with no missing data is also a random sample from the source population. Hence, most simple techniques for handling missing data, including complete and available case analyses, yield unbiased results.

2.1.2. Missing at Random (MAR). This mechanism establishes once the distribution of an example having a missing value for an attribute depends on the observed data but does not depend on the missing data. Under this scenario, a complete or available case analysis is no longer based on a random sample from the source population, and selection bias likely occurs. Generally, when missing data are MAR, all simple techniques for handling missing data give biased results.

2.1.3. Not Missing at Random (NMAR). It implies that the pattern of data missingness is nonrandom, and it is not predictable from other variables in the database. If missing data are NMAR, valuable information is lost from the data and there are no universal methods of handling the missing data properly. For instance, participants who are unsatisfied with their company are more likely to not answer the questions about company satisfaction.

2.2. Methods for Missing Data Analysis. Current managements of processing missing data can be approximately divided into three categories: tolerable procedures, procedures based on deletion of cases, and imputation-based procedures.

2.2.1. Tolerance. The straightforward method aims to maintain the source entries in the incomplete fashion. Consequently, the ulterior analysis is directly designed based on the raw data [15]. It is poor when the percentage of missing values per attribute varies considerably.

2.2.2. Ignoring. Missing data ignorance often refers to "*Case Deletion.*" It is the most frequently applied procedure, but it is prone to diminish the data quality. Its strength lies in the ease of application; it simply proposes to delete elements with missing data. The procedure can be applied in two manners [12, 16].

(a) Listwise/Casewise Deletion: it performs indiscriminately deleting from the database any elements with missing data for any of the attributes being examined.

(b) Pairwise Deletion: incomplete cases are removed on an analysis-by-analysis basis, such that any given case may contribute to some analyses but not to others.

2.2.3. Imputation

Mean/Mode Substitution (MMS). This is a simple way to impute the missing data. It replaces the missing values by the mean or mode of all the observations or a subgroup at the same variable. It consists of replacing the unknown value for a given attribute by the mean (quantitative attribute) or mode (qualitative attribute) of all known values of that attribute. Replacing all missing records with a single value distorts the input data distribution [15].

Hot-Deck/Cold-Deck Imputation [13]. Given an incomplete pattern, *hot-deck imputation* (HDI) replaces the missing data with the values from the input vector that is the closest in terms of the attributes that are known in both patterns. This method attempts to preserve the distribution by substituting different observed values for each missing item. Another possibility is the *cold-deck imputation* (CDI) method, which is similar to hot deck, but the data source must be other than the current dataset. For example, in a survey context, the external source can be a previous realization of the same survey.

Regression Imputation. This method uses multiple linear regression to obtain estimates of the missing values. It is applied by estimating a regression equation for each variable, using the others as predictors. This solves the problems concerning variance and covariance raised by the previous method but leads to polarization of all the variables if they are not linked in a linear fashion. Possible errors are due to the insertion of highly correlated predictors to estimate the variables. The advantage of this method is that existing relationships between the variables can be used to calculate missing data, but it is rarely used as it amplifies the correlation between variables [13, 16].

Expectation Maximization Estimation (EME). The technique is on the basis of *expectation maximization* (EM) algorithm proposed by *Dempster*, *Laird*, and *Rubin*. The algorithm can handle parameter estimation in the presence of missing data. These methods are generally superior to case deletion methods, because they utilize all the observed data. However, they suffer from a strict assumption of a model distribution for the variables, such as a multivariate normal model, which has a high sensitivity to outliers [2, 14].

Machine Learning-Based Imputation. It acquires the features of interested unknown data by behavior evolution after sample data processed. The essence is to automatically learn sample for complicated pattern cognition and intelligently predict the missing values. The methods mainly includes decision tree-based imputation, association rules-based imputation, clustering-based imputation, and so forth [6, 8, 17].

Multiple Imputation. It replaces each missing value with two or more plausible values that represent the uncertainty about the right value to impute. Each of the two or more resulting complete datasets is then analyzed using standard complete-data methods. All the analyses become combined to reflect both the interimputation variability and intraimputation variability [16, 18, 19].

2.2.4. State-of-the-Art for Missing Data Imputation. Statistical analysis with missing data has been noted in the literature for more than 70 years. Allison [13] pointed that Walks initiated a study on the maximum likelihood estimation for multivariate normal models with fragmentary data. Thereafter, extensive discussions on this topic continue. A useful reference for general parametric statistical inferences with missing data can be found in Little and Rubin [14].

Zhu et al. [19] made use of Magnani's reviewing on the main missing data techniques, including conventional methods, global imputation, local imputation, parameter estimation, and direct management of missing data. They tried to highlight the advantages and disadvantages for all kinds of missing data mechanisms. However, the main problem of these techniques is the need for strong model assumptions. In recent years, many researchers focused on the topic of imputing missing values. S. M. Chen and H. H. Chen [20] developed an estimating null value method, where a fuzzy similarity matrix is used to represent fuzzy relations, and the method is used to deal with one missing value in an attribute. Embedded methods consist of casewise deletion, lazy decision tree, dynamic path generation, and some popular methods such as C4.5 and CART. Nonetheless, these methods are not a completely satisfactory way to handle missing value problems [21]. Firstly, they are merely designed to deal with the discrete values, and the continuous ones are discretized before imputing the missing value, which may lose the true characteristic during the converting process from the continuous value to discretized one. Secondly, they usually studied the problem of missing covariance.

Huang and Lee [22] employed a grey-based nearest neighbor method to handle the missing data problem. In their opinion, the gray association analysis is employed to determine the nearest neighbors of an instance with missing values. And those unknown values are inferred by the known attribute values derived from these nearest neighbors. Hruschka Jr. et al. [23] used Bayesian networks to

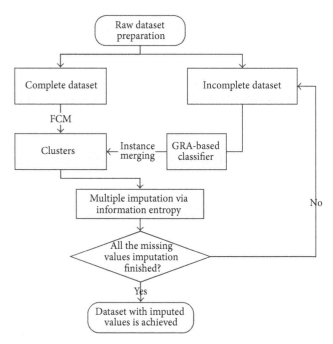

FIGURE 1: The flowchart of the CBGMI algorithm.

fulfill missing values in a hybrid model, which applies the clustering genetic algorithm in objects without missing values and generates Bayesian networks to substitute the missing values. Chen and Huang [24] used the weighted fuzzy rules to estimate null values in relational database. Li et al. [25] borrowed the idea from fuzzy K-means clustering and applied it to the problem of missing data imputation with superior performance to the basic K-means especially when the percentage of missing values are high. Meesad and Hengpraprohm [26] combined K-nearest neighbor-based feature selection and K-nearest neighbor-based imputation, including feature selection and estimation of new values. The results showed that the proposed method had powerful estimation ability on microarray datasets. Di Nuovo [2] made the comparisons among four solutions of the *fuzzy c-means* (FCM) in the psychological research environment. The result revealed that the FCM based on optimal completion strategy leads to effective data imputation instead of deleting elements with missing values. Zhang et al. [18] utilized the information within the incomplete instances since the second imputation iteration. The *non-parametric iterative imputation* (NIIA) is an improvement of the classic multiple imputation, which is based on kernel function. The experimental results on UCI datasets unfolded that the NIIA could easily capture the distribution of a dataset even when there is no prior knowledge of the datasets.

3. The CBGMI Algorithm

In this section, the global procedure of the CBGMI algorithm is schematized in Figure 1. And each of the key components is detailed correspondingly. Firstly, the clustering technique is explained, and then the computation of gray relational analysis with missing values is presented with formulations. After the instructions of the entropy-based multiple imputation comprising of initial and successive estimations, the entire algorithmic information descriptively listed.

3.1. The Clustering Strategy.
The specific clustering schema utilizes the standard FCM [1, 27], which attempts to minimize the following objective function with respect to fuzzy memberships $U^{(r)} = [u_{ij}^{(r)}]$ and cluster centroids $C^{(r)} = c_j^{(r)}: J = \sum_{j=1}^{G} \sum_{i=1}^{M} (u_{ij}^{(r)})^s d(x_i, c_j^{(r)})$. In the function, r is the ordinal number of the iterations with x_k and $c_j^{(r)}$, respectively, denoting the kth complete data instance and the jth cluster, while $d(\cdot, \cdot)$ is the distance metric between two instances, and $u_{ij}^{(r)}$ is the degree of membership in which the ith instance is subordinate to the jth cluster under the "fuzzier" s, as G defines the total number of clusters, and M represents the number of data instances. The algorithm would immediately end with formed clusters under the circumstance that $\|U^{(r)} - U^{(r-1)}\| < \varepsilon$ or r accumulatively reaches the predefined number.

3.2. The Classification of Incomplete Instances.
Each of the incomplete instances is individually incorporated into the closest cluster according to the maximal value of *gray relational grade* (GRG) [22] in (1) and (2)

$$\text{GRC}\left(x_k^{\text{mis}}, c_i\right)$$

$$= \frac{\min_M \min_N \left|x_{kp}^{\text{mis}} - c_{ip}\right| + \zeta \max_M \max_N \left|x_{kp}^{\text{mis}} - c_{ip}\right|}{\left|x_{kp}^{\text{mis}} - c_{ip}\right| + \zeta \max_M \max_N \left|x_{kp}^{\text{mis}} - c_{ip}\right|}$$

$$i = 1, 2, \ldots, M; \quad p = 1, 2, \ldots, N; \quad 0 \leq \zeta \leq 1, \tag{1}$$

where x_k^{mis} is the kth incomplete instance and p is the pth attribute with nonmissing values, while N is the number of attributes, and coefficient ζ is used to decrease the effect of $\max_M \max_N$, which is the maximal value in the matrix.

Consider the following:

$$\text{GRG}\left(x_k^{\text{mis}}, c_i\right) = \frac{1}{N} \sum_{p=1}^{N} \text{GRC}\left(x_k^{\text{mis}}, c_i\right), \quad i = 1, 2, \ldots, M. \tag{2}$$

3.3. The Entropy-Based Multiple Imputation.
When each time one instance has been assigned to the most proximate group, an internal multiple imputation strategic approach starts as follows.

3.3.1. First Imputation.
Algorithms like C4.5 and kNN could be used in the initial round of imputation. Although the MMS was doubted for its potential bias in terms of distributions in the situation, Zhang et al. [18] emphasized that the value of such imputation would be reasonable unless it runs the extraiterative imputation. For this reason, MMS is employed to initialize missing values in the first imputation.

3.3.2. Successive Imputation.
$R = (r_{ij})_{m \times n}$ associates with the data matrix of the cluster, into which $x_i^{\text{mis}} \in X_{ic}$ is attached. That is, it includes $m-1$ complete elements and one initialized element.

Step 1. Calculate the entropy value of the fth data instance [3]

$$I_f = -k * h_f * \ln p_f,$$

$$k = \frac{1}{\ln m}, \quad h_f = \frac{\|r_{fl} - r_{il}\|}{\sum_{i=1}^{m} \|r_{fl} - r_{il}\|}, \quad (l \neq j). \tag{3}$$

Step 2. Compute the coefficient of difference for the fth instance

$$t_f = 1 - I_f, \quad f = 1, 2, \ldots, n. \tag{4}$$

Step 3. Elicit the coefficient of weight for the fth copy

$$w_f = \frac{t_f}{\sum_{f=1}^{n} t_f}. \tag{5}$$

Step 4. Estimate the jth attributive missing value of x_i^{mis}

$$x_{ij}^{\text{mis}} = \sum_{q=1, q \neq j}^{n} w_q x_{iq}^{\text{mis}}. \tag{6}$$

If the estimated values of the individual instance vary beyond a tolerable interval compared with the calculated value of the last iteration or the number of iteration times does not reach the maximal value, the operations from (3) to (6) continue iteratively. On the contrast, the iterative process mentioned above terminates as the assessed value is considered as the imputed one. Consequently, the imputed instance is aggregated into the corresponding cluster afterwards with updated centroids.

3.4. The Framework of the CBGMI Algorithm

Procedure. CBGMI

Input. X_{raw}, the $n \times m$ dimensional dataset with missing values G, the number of clusters

Output. X_{full}, the $n \times m$ dimensional complete dataset with imputed values

$X_{\text{raw}} \rightarrow X_{\text{obs}}, X_{\text{mis}}$, where $X_{\text{raw}} = X_{\text{obs}} \cup X_{\text{mis}}$ and $\emptyset = X_{\text{obs}} \cap X_{\text{mis}}$

FCM $(X_{\text{obs}}, G) \rightarrow C = \{C_1, C_2, \ldots, C_G\}$ according to Section 3.1.

For each element x_k in X_{mis}

Allocate x_k to the closest cluster c_q according to Section 3.2.

Complete the missing values of x_k according to Section 3.3.

Integrate the x_k into corresponding cluster, and update c_q according to Section 3.3.

$$X_{\text{full}} \leftarrow \bigcup_{i=1}^{G} c_i. \tag{7}$$

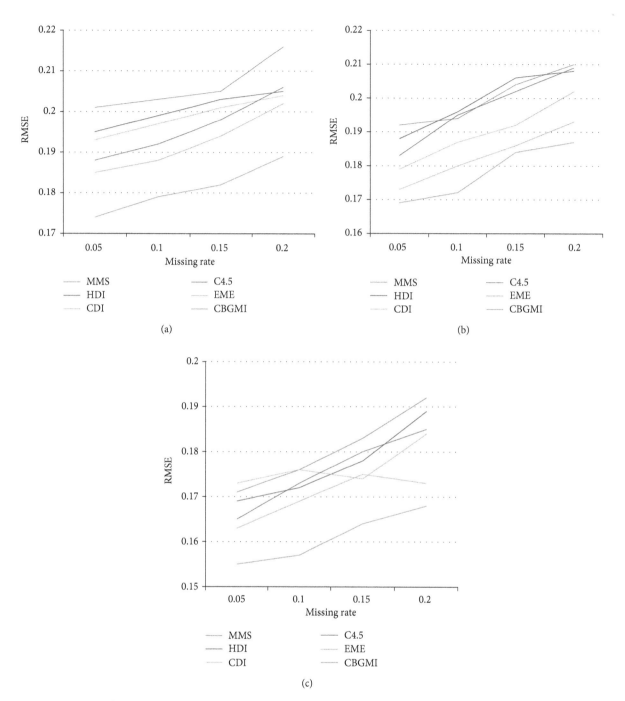

FIGURE 2: The RMSE in dataset Wine under (a) MCAR, (b) MAR, and (c) NMAR with different missing rates.

4. Experimental Evaluation

In this section, the assessment criteria are primarily explained in terms of the types of the attributes in Section 4.1. Then, the general effectiveness of our algorithmic approach is presented by a comparative experiment on two UCI datasets [28], remaining superior to MMS, HDI, CDI, C4.5, and EME in Section 4.2.1. Section 4.2.2 shows the technique which also outperforms these aforementioned approaches by applying CBGMI to a real case analysis in two aerospace datasets.

4.1. The Evaluation Criterion

4.1.1. Missing Data on Numeric Attributes. The *root mean square error* (RMSE) is used to evaluate the predictive ability of the various data imputation algorithms within which the attributes are quantitative

$$\text{RMSE} = \sqrt{\frac{1}{m}\sum_{i=1}^{m}(e_i - \widetilde{e}_i)^2}, \tag{8}$$

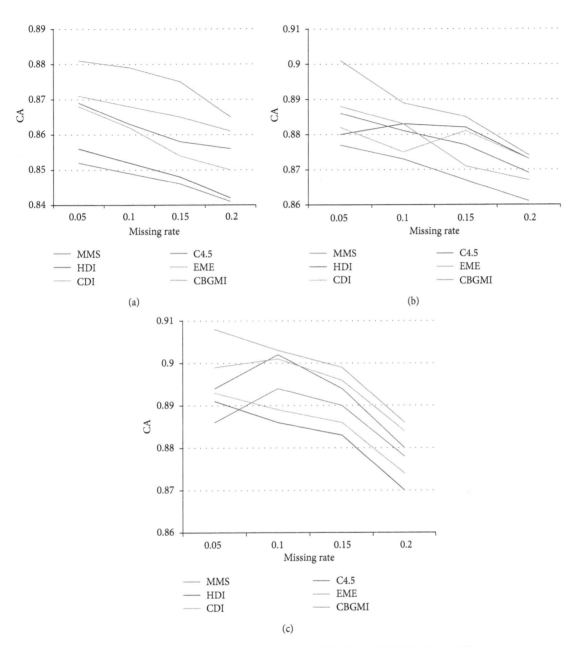

FIGURE 3: The CA in dataset Thyroid Disease under (a) MCAR, (b) MAR, and (c) NMAR with different missing rates.

where e_i is the original value, $\tilde{e}_i$ is the predicted plausible value, and m is the total number of estimations. The larger value of RMSE suggests the less accuracy that the algorithm holds [18, 29].

4.1.2. Missing Data on Nominal Attributes.

The performances of the algorithms for categorical attributes are appraised by the *classification accuracy* (CA)

$$\text{CA} = \frac{1}{n}\sum_{i=1}^{n} l\left(\text{EC}_i, \text{TC}_i\right), \qquad (9)$$

where EC_i and TC_i are the estimated and true class label for the ith missing value, respectively, with n indicating the total

number of the missing values. The function $l(x, y) = 1$ if $x = y$, otherwise $l(x, y) = 0$. For this reason, the larger value of function l indicates the most correct imputed value [18, 29].

4.2. Empirical Result Analysis

4.2.1. UCI Datasets.
Two datasets from UCI, that is, *Wine* and *Thyroid Disease*, are selected to test the validity of the algorithms. *Wine* contains 178 instances and 13 attributes. The variable values are either real or integer. *Thyroid Disease* includes 7200 instances and 21 attributes. The multivariate factual data are either categorical or real.

To intrinsically examine the effectiveness and validity and ensure the systematic nature of the research, we artificially

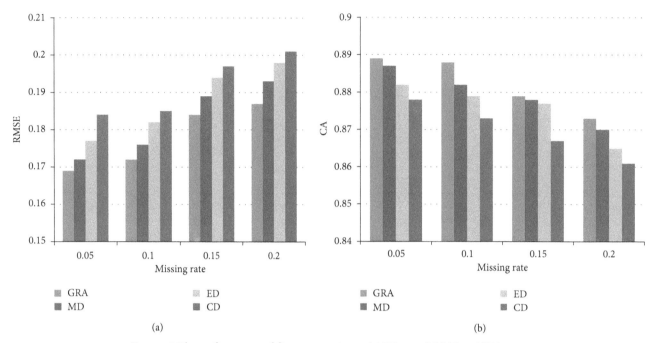

(a)

(b)

FIGURE 4: The performances of distance metrics on (a) Wine and (b) Thyroid Disease.

generated a lack of data at four distinct missing ratios, that is, 5%, 10%, 15%, and 20% under three different modalities, namely, MCAR, MAR, and NMAR in the complete datasets via the means that Twala did [30].

As we specify $G = 3$, fuzzier $s = 1.3$, and $\zeta = 0.5$, which are mentioned in 3.1 and 3.2, the RMSE produced by six methodologies on the two datasets is illustrated in Figures 2 and 3, respectively.

Figure 2 shows that CBGMI performs better than the other five approaches under all the three missingness mechanisms on Wine, since it is prone to identify the corresponding line from the other five tangled ones. Although the RMSE arises when the missing rate increases from a single subfigure, it indicates that the absence of observed values directly undermines the effect of imputation, as more information could promote the final predictions. Moreover, for each method, the minimum value of RMSE at the same missing ratio always appears when data are NMAR distributed, while MCAR yields the maximum value of RMSE. Therefore, CBGMI is effective and superior to the above algorithms in accuracy for numeric attributes.

The result in Figure 3 demonstrates that CBGMI outperforms the other five approaches under all the three missing modalities on *Thyroid Disease*. The phenomenon that increasing proportion of missing instances deteriorates the CA also states that incomplete nominal values negatively impact on the completion. Similarly, each imputation method functions best under NMAR but operates worst under MCAR. Thus, CBGMI is also applicable to categorical attributes.

To clarify the different distance metrics that influence the accuracy of the results, we suppose that the test happens under MAR. Then, the gray relational analysis metric is practically compared with the *Minkowski distance*, which

refers to *Manhattan distance* (MD), *Euclidean distance* (ED), and *Chebyshev distance* (CD).

From Figure 4, we could assume that *gray relational analysis-* (GRA-) based distance metric generates the least bias at different missing rates compared with the other three variants of *Minkowski distance*. Furthermore, the discrimination is even more significant when gray relational analysis is contrasted with CD according to RMSE or CA.

4.2.2. Aerospace Datasets. Since Section 4.2.1 testifies the effectiveness of the proposed CBGMI on distinct mechanisms, missing rates, and distance metrics, in this subsection, the missingness is artificially simulated under MAR at missing rate 15% based on gray relational analysis.

To the authors' best knowledge, there are a few of hybrid models integrating multiple imputation into clustering. Accordingly, we selected the method proposed by Zhang et al. [5] (denoted as CGKMI) and replaced our Section 3.3 by NIIA [18] (denoted as CNIIA) as the competitors in this part of experiment.

The *remote controlling for spacecraft flying* (RCSF) dataset covers the data generated by some particular unmanned spaceship on real-time condition when flying in the outer space with the remote controlling by the experts. Due to the huge amount of the raw data, we just extract the data which was produced within one minute. Subsequently, the experiment is designed on the 953 records of 20 continuous attributes.

When CBGMI is applied to RCSF dataset, the maximum times of the iteration in all the clusters are 18 loops, which is faster than CNIIA's 19 times and CGKMI's 22 times iterations, respectively, in Figure 5(a). What is more, the RMSE achieves slightly lower than the other counterparts.

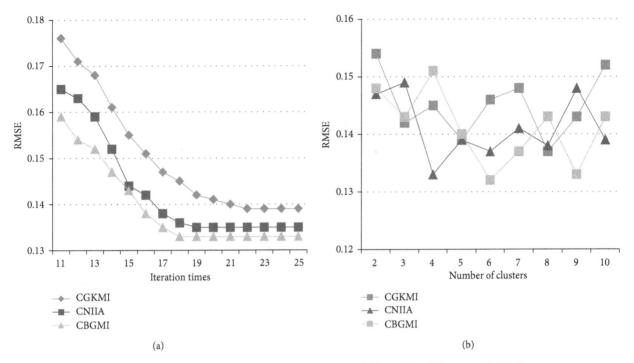

FIGURE 5: The RMSE influenced by (a) imputation times and (b) number of clusters on RCSF dataset.

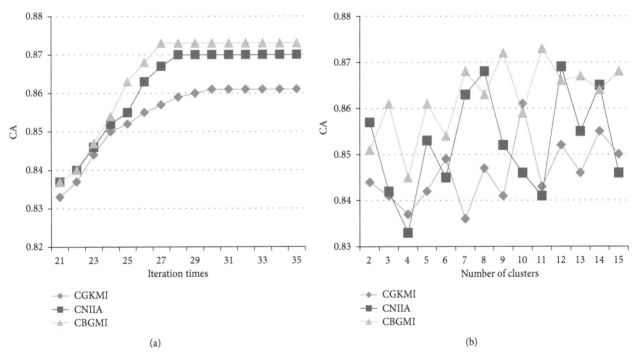

FIGURE 6: The CA influenced by (a) imputation times and (b) number of clusters on SOMD dataset.

As versions of clustering principles, interrelationship between RMSE and the number of clusters in these techniques should be discussed. In Figure 5(b), it appears that when the whole data is agglomerated into 6 groups, the RMSE declines to the minimum. Differently, CGKMI performs best with 8 clusters, while CNIIA requires 4 partitions.

The *spacecraft overall mechanical design* (SOMD) dataset comprises the data related to the assembling and fabrication of one specific model of the manned spaceships. Both the numeric values and categorical values are mixed in the dataset. The total number of instances is beyond 300,000. 1,221 elements with the 30 variables belonging to a certain step of the entire manufacturing process are chosen.

It is easy to perceive that the three algorithms advance CA as the number of iteration aggrandizes until the convergence emerges in Figure 6(a). Simultaneously, CBGMI attains the best CA in the minimum time of the repetitions compared with the other counterparts on SOMD.

When the amount of clusters rises, the CA fluctuates irregularly in the interval (0.83, 0.88). And CBGMI reaches the maximum of CA when 11 clusters exist in Figure 6(b). Generally, CGKMI and CNIIA undulate in an inferior range of CA to CBGMI, which demands the different optimal number of clustered groups, respectively.

5. Conclusion

By investigating missing data analysis techniques, this study advocates the clustering-based imputation via partitioning original data into two nonoverlapped subsets, that is, the missing-valued subsets and the complete-valued subsets. Then, the iterative imputation strategy is combined within the categorized groups after each entry including missing values has been merged into the closest cluster through gray relational analysis-based distance metric. The experimental results demonstrate that CBGMI exceeds the existing methods, for example, MMS, HDI, CDI, C4.5, and EME, in terms of the RMSE (for continuous missing attributes) and the CA (for discrete missing attributes) at different missing ratios in two canonical UCI datasets, namely, *Wine* and *Thyroid Disease*. In particular, CBGMI algorithm has been applied into the aerospace datasets. The RMSE and CA affected by the iteration times indicate that CBGMI converges more rapidly than the other iterative imputation techniques with better accuracy in the real application environment. In future research, we will focus on how to more effectively estimate and impute missing values under massive data circumstance.

Acknowledgments

This work is supported by Project of the State Key Laboratory of Software Development Environment, Beihang University (SKLSDE-2011ZX-09) and National Natural Science Foundation of China (61003016).

References

[1] J. C. Bezdek, J. Keller, R. Krishnapuram, and N. R. Pal, *Fuzzy Models and Algorithms for Pattern Recognition and Image Processing*, The Handbooks of Fuzzy Sets, Springer, 1999.

[2] A. G. Di Nuovo, "Missing data analysis with fuzzy C-Means: a study of its application in a psychological scenario," *Expert Systems with Applications*, vol. 38, pp. 6793–6797, 2011.

[3] E. T. Jaynes, "Information theory and statistical mechanics," *Physical Review*, vol. 106, no. 4, pp. 620–630, 1957.

[4] A. N. Baraldi and C. K. Enders, "An introduction to modern missing data analyses," *Journal of School Psychology*, vol. 48, no. 1, pp. 5–37, 2010.

[5] S. Zhang, Z. Jin, X. Zhu, and J. Zhang, "Missing data analysis: a kernel-based multi-imputation approach," *Transactions on Computational Science*, vol. 5300, pp. 122–142, 2009.

[6] A. Farhangfar, L. Kurgan, and W. Pedrycz, "Experimental analysis of methods for imputation of missing values in databases," in *Proceedings of the Intelligent Computing: Theory and Applications II*, vol. 5421 of *Proceedings of SPIE*, pp. 172–182, April 2004.

[7] P. J. García-Laencina, J. L. Sancho-Gómez, A. R. Figueiras-Vidal, and M. Verleysen, "K nearest neighbours with mutual information for simultaneous classification and missing data imputation," *Neurocomputing*, vol. 72, no. 7–9, pp. 1483–1493, 2009.

[8] J. R. Quinlan, "Induction of decision trees," *Machine Learning*, vol. 1, no. 1, pp. 81–106, 1986.

[9] M. Di Zio, U. Guarnera, and O. Luzi, "Imputation through finite Gaussian mixture models," *Computational Statistics and Data Analysis*, vol. 51, no. 11, pp. 5305–5316, 2007.

[10] Y. Qin, S. Zhang, X. Zhu, J. Zhang, and C. Zhang, "POP algorithm: kernel-based imputation to treat missing values in knowledge discovery from databases," *Expert Systems with Applications*, vol. 36, no. 2, pp. 2794–2804, 2009.

[11] H. Junninen, H. Niska, K. Tuppurainen, J. Ruuskanen, and M. Kolehmainen, "Methods for imputation of missing values in air quality data sets," *Atmospheric Environment*, vol. 38, no. 18, pp. 2895–2907, 2004.

[12] J. L. Schafer, *Analysis of Incomplete Multivariate Data*, Chapman & Hall/CRC Press, London, UK, 1997.

[13] P. D. Allison, *Missing Data*, Sage University Papers, Quantitative Applications in the Social Sciences, Thousand Oaks, Calif, USA, 2001.

[14] R. J. A. Little and D. B. Rubin, *Statistical Analysis with Missing Data*, John Wiley & Sons, Hoboken, NJ, USA, 2nd edition, 2002.

[15] C. Enders, S. Dietz, M. Montague, and J. Dixon, "Modern alternatives for dealing with missing data in special education research," in *Advances in Learning and Behavioral Disorders*, T. E. Scruggs and M. A. Mastropieri, Eds., vol. 19,, pp. 101–130, Elsevier, New York, NY, USA, 2006.

[16] A. R. T. Donders, G. J. M. G. van der Heijden, T. Stijnen, and K. G. M. Moons, "Review: a gentle introduction to imputation of missing values," *Journal of Clinical Epidemiology*, vol. 59, no. 10, pp. 1087–1091, 2006.

[17] J. F. Muñoz and M. Rueda, "New imputation methods for missing data using quantiles," *Journal of Computational and Applied Mathematics*, vol. 232, no. 2, pp. 305–317, 2009.

[18] S. Zhang, Z. Jin, and X. Zhu, "Missing data imputation by utilizing information within incomplete instances," *Journal of Systems and Software*, vol. 84, no. 3, pp. 452–459, 2011.

[19] B. Zhu, C. He, and P. Liatsis, "A robust missing value imputation method for noisy data," *Applied Intelligence*, vol. 36, no. 1, pp. 61–74, 2012.

[20] S. M. Chen and H. H. Chen, "Estimating null values in the distributed relational databases environment," *Cybernetics and Systems*, vol. 31, no. 8, pp. 851–871, 2000.

[21] G. J. McLachlan, K. A. Do, and C. Ambroise, *Analyzing Microarray Gene Expression Data*, John Wiley & Sons, 2004.

[22] C. C. Huang and H. M. Lee, "A grey-based nearest neighbor approach for missing attribute value prediction," *Applied Intelligence*, vol. 20, no. 3, pp. 239–252, 2004.

[23] E. R. Hruschka Jr., E. R. Hruschka, and N. F. F. Ebecken, "A Bayesian imputation method for a clustering genetic algorithm," *Journal of Computational Methods in Sciences and Engineering*, vol. 11, pp. 173–183, 2011.

[24] S. M. Chen and C. M. Huang, "Generating weighted fuzzy rules from relational database systems for estimating null values

using genetic algorithms," *IEEE Transactions on Fuzzy Systems*, vol. 11, no. 4, pp. 495–506, 2003.

[25] D. Li, J. Deogun, W. Spaulding, and B. Shuart, "Towards missing data imputation: a study of fuzzy K-means clustering method," in *Proceedings of the 4th International Conference (RSCTC '04)*, pp. 573–579, June 2004.

[26] P. Meesad and K. Hengpraprohm, "Combination of KNN-based feature selection and KNN-based missing-value imputation of microarray data," in *Proceedings of the 3rd International Conference on Innovative Computing Information and Control (ICICIC '08)*, pp. 341–344, June 2008.

[27] R. J. Hathaway and J. C. Bezdek, "Fuzzy c-means clustering of incomplete data," *IEEE Transactions on Systems, Man, and Cybernetics B*, vol. 31, no. 5, pp. 735–744, 2001.

[28] http://archive.ics.uci.edu/ml/.

[29] C. Zhang, Y. Qin, X. Zhu, J. Zhang, and S. Zhang, "Clustering-based missing value imputation for data preprocessing," in *Proceedings of the IEEE International Conference on Industrial Informatics (INDIN '06)*, pp. 1081–1086, August 2006.

[30] B. Twala, "An empirical comparison of techniques for handling incomplete data using decision trees," *Applied Artificial Intelligence*, vol. 23, no. 5, pp. 373–405, 2009.

10

Reliable Execution Based on CPN and Skyline Optimization for Web Service Composition

Liping Chen,[1] Weitao Ha,[1] and Guojun Zhang[2]

[1] College of Mathematics and Information Science, Network Engineering Technology Center, Weinan Normal University, Weinan 714000, China

[2] College of Communication Engineering, Network Engineering Technology Center, Weinan Normal University, Weinan 714000, China

Correspondence should be addressed to Liping Chen; wnchlp@126.com

Academic Editors: Y.-m. Cheung and Y. Wang

With development of SOA, the complex problem can be solved by combining available individual services and ordering them to best suit user's requirements. Web services composition is widely used in business environment. With the features of inherent autonomy and heterogeneity for component web services, it is difficult to predict the behavior of the overall composite service. Therefore, transactional properties and nonfunctional quality of service (QoS) properties are crucial for selecting the web services to take part in the composition. Transactional properties ensure reliability of composite Web service, and QoS properties can identify the best candidate web services from a set of functionally equivalent services. In this paper we define a Colored Petri Net (CPN) model which involves transactional properties of web services in the composition process. To ensure reliable and correct execution, unfolding processes of the CPN are followed. The execution of transactional composition Web service (TCWS) is formalized by CPN properties. To identify the best services of QoS properties from candidate service sets formed in the TCSW-CPN, we use skyline computation to retrieve dominant Web service. It can overcome that the reduction of individual scores to an overall similarity leads to significant information loss. We evaluate our approach experimentally using both real and synthetically generated datasets.

1. Introduction

Web services are distributed applications that interoperate across heterogeneous networks and that are hosted and executed on remote systems. Service oriented architecture (SOA) is gaining prominence as a key architecture because it allows well-formed and autonomous components to be reused rather than creating new one from scratch. On SOA, web services composition focuses on how to integrate existing web services in diverse and heterogeneous distributed environments, providing different functional, nonfunctional, and behavioral features, to quickly construct workable applications or software for satisfying the requirements which are requested by users and unable to be fulfilled by any single web service.

In order to implement web services composition, component Web services are selected according to user requirements, some constraints and preferences. The selected services usually have the best QoS. However, the interoperation of distributed software systems is always affected by failures,

dynamic changes, and availability of resources [1]. The composite web service will not guarantee reliable execution and consistency if the component services are chosen only according to QoS and functional attributes. Transactional properties of selected service should be considered to ensure reliable execution of composite web services. Besides, numerous web services are spread all over Internet, and it is intractable to select appropriate web services satisfying the goal efficiently. Existing various approaches use aggregating parameters and utility function to get score of service. One direction is to assign weights, determined through user feedback, to individual scores [2, 3]. Appropriate weights are chosen either by assuming a priori knowledge about the user's preferences or by applying expensive machine-learning techniques. Both alternatives face serious drawbacks and raise a series of other issues to be solved. More often, these approaches lead to information loss that significantly affects the retrieved results accuracy. For example, use utility function, and finally return the web services with moderate attributes; thus, service with only one bad attribute will be excluded from the result, even though they are potentially good alternatives.

We will use Colored Petri Net as formalism to represent composite web service and perform a Best-First search, where transactional and QoS properties are both integrated in the selection process. But the selection is done in two separate steps, transactional service selection starts firstly, and the QoS-aware service selection is embedded with the transactional-aware service selection [4]. As a tremendous amount of different QoS web services after transactional-aware service selection are spread all over Internet, it is intractable to find the appropriate web services satisfying the given goal quickly. What is more, using traditional methods, services with only one bad QoS attribute may be excluded from the result set, even though they are potentially good alternatives, and thus leads to information loss that significantly affects the retrieved results accuracy. But skyline computation is a nondiscriminating comparison of several numerical attributes at the same time and treats each service equally. We use skyline computation to reduce the number of candidate services and speed up the selection process.

We find that CPN model allows describing not only a static vision of a system, but also its dynamic behavior, and it is expressive enough to capture the semantics of complex web services combinations and their respective interactions. We incorporate transactional web services properties in the CPN model. To ensure reliable and correct execution, unfolding processes of the CPN are followed. The execution of transactional composition web service (TCWS) is formalized by CPN properties. To identify the best services of QoS properties from candidate service sets formed in the TCSW-CPN, we use skyline computation to retrieve dominant web service. It can overcome that the reduction of individual scores to an overall similarity leads to significant information loss. We also define QoS-based dominance relationships between services. To identify the best services from CPN model in QoS properties, we use skyline computation to retrieve dominant web service.

2. Related Work

In the last years, although the problem of web service selection and composition has received much attention of many researchers, designing a composite web service which ensures not only correct and reliable execution but also optimal QoS remains an important challenge. Indeed, these two aspects of selection are always implemented separately.

Web services transactions have received much attention recently. Industrial web services transaction specifications emerge. WS-atomic transaction, WS-business activity, and WS-TXM rely on ATM to define transactional coordination protocols. Like ATM these protocols are unable in most cases to model Business process due to their limited control structure. It also ensures reliability on behalf of process adequacy or the opposite. Indeed, a transactional pattern taken alone as a composition of transactional patterns can be considered as a transactional protocol.

In one hand, WSBPEL and WS-CDL follow a workflow approach to define services compositions and services choreographies. Like workflow systems these two languages meet the business process need in terms of control structure. However, they are unable to ensure reliability especially according to the designers' specific needs.

Transaction has achieved a great success in the database community [4, 5]. One of the most important reasons is that the operations in database have clear transactional semantics. However, this is not the case in web services. To solve this problem, the extension mechanism of WSDL can be exploited to explicitly describe the transactional semantics of web services operations [6, 7].

There are many works that adopt three kinds of transactional properties proposed in [8] to express the different transactional semantics of web services. Based on this classification, Bhiri et al. [9] analyze the termination property of a composite service. Rusinkiewicz and Sheth [10] define a set of transactional rules to verify the required failure atomicity specified by ATS [11], given the skeleton of a composite service and the transactional properties of its component services. Zeng et al. [12] propose an approach to deduce the required transactional properties of every task based on ATS and then use the result to guide service selection.

For these researches web services composition based on transactional properties ensures a reliable execution; however, an optimal QoS composite web service is not guaranteed.

QoS guarantee for web services is one of the main concerns of the SLA framework. There are projects studying QoS-empowered service selection. In [13], authors present a QoS-aware web service composition which is middleware-supporting quality driven. But the method is based on integer linear programming and best suited for small-size problems as its complexity increases exponentially with the increasing problem size. For [14], the authors propose an extensible QoS computation model that supports an open and fair management of QoS data by incorporating user feedback. However, the problem of QoS-based composition is not addressed by this work. The work of Zeng at al. [15, 16] focuses on dynamic and quality-driven selection of services. The authors use global planning to find the best service components for the composition. They use linear programming techniques [17] to find the optimal selection of component services. Linear programming methods are very effective when the size of the problem is small but suffer from poor scalability due to the exponential time complexity of the applied search algorithms [18]. Despite the significant improvement of these algorithms compared to exact solutions, both algorithms do not scale with respect to the number of candidate web services and hence are not suitable for real-time service composition. The proposed skyline-based algorithm in this paper is complementary to these solutions as it can be used as a preprocessing step to prune noninteresting candidate services and hence reduce the computation time of the applied selection algorithm.

With the above quotation, the approaches implement conventional optimal QoS composition, but composing optimal QoS web services does not guarantee a reliable execution of the resulting composite web service. Therefore, transactional based and QoS based should be integrated.

3. A Colored Petri-Net Model of Web Service Composition

Due to the inherent autonomy and heterogeneity of web service it is difficult to predict the overall behavior of a composite service. Unexpected behavior or failure implement of a component service might not only lead to its failure but also may bring negative impact on all the participants of the composition. Web service composition process must satisfy transactional property to provide reliable and consistent execution.

3.1. Transactional Property Description. A transactional web service is a web service of which the behavior manifests transactional properties. The main transactional properties of a web service we are considering are pivot, compensatable, and retriable [19]. When transactional property of a service is pivot (p for short), the service's effects remain forever and cannot be semantically undone if it completes successfully, and it has no effect at all if it fails. When a service is compensatable (c for short), it offers compensation policies to semantically undo its effects. When a service is said to be retriable (r for short), it ensures successful completing after several finite activations. Moreover, the transactional property can be combined, and the set of all possible combinations is $\{p, c, pr, cr\}$ [4].

El Haddad et al. [4, 20] extended the previous described transactional properties and adapted them to CWS. A CWS is atomic (a for short), if all its component web services complete successfully, they cannot be semantically undone, if one component service cannot complete successfully, previously successful component services have to be compensated. cs is compensatable (c for short) if all its component services are compensatable. A CWS is retriable (r for short), if all its component services are retriable. Transactional composite web service (TCWS) is CWS whose transactional property is in $\{a, ar, c, cr\}$.

3.2. Tolerance Level. In order to provide expression of user transactional criteria, we define tolerance that gives importance of the uncertainty of application completion and recovery for user. A CWS with transactional property a or ar has greater risk of success completion and recovery than the CWS with transactional property c or cr [21]. The reason is that properties a and ar mean once a service has been executed, and it cannot be rolled back. Therefore, we define two levels of tolerance in a transactional system.

Tolerance 0 (T_0). The system guarantees that if the execution is successful, the obtained results can be compensated by the user. In this level the selecting process generates a compensatable workflow [4].

Tolerance 1 (T_1). The system does not guarantee the successful execution, but if it achieves, the results cannot be compensated by the user. In this level the selecting process generates an atomic workflow [4].

In both tolerance cases, if the execution is not successful, then no result is reflected to the system; nothing is changed on the system.

3.3. TCWS-CPN Definition. A colored petri net (CPN) is one of the very useful graphical and mathematical representations, and it has a well-defined semantics for describing states and actions of web service composition. We build a colored petri net model of transactional web service composition (CPN-TWSC). It provides a formalism to depict transactional selections of component services. Besides, functional conditions are expressed as input and output attributes, and transactional properties expressed as a tolerance level. The composite web service will satisfy user's functional requirement and will ensure executing reliably and consistently.

Definition 1 (TCWS-CPN). We define a CPN to transactional composite web services (TCWS-CPN) as a tuple $(P, T, \text{Pre}, \text{Post}, C, cd)$, where

(i) P is a finite nonempty set of places, with colors in the set C. In our case, P is composed input and output attributes of web services in the TCWS, functional and transactional requirement, and colors,

(ii) T is a finite set of transitions, corresponding to candidate component services execution, $P \cap T = \phi$,

(iii) C is a set of color, which is composed of transactional properties of web services and composition pattern, $C = C_1 \cup C_2 = \{p, pr, a, ar, c, cr\} \cup \{\text{sequence}, \text{parallel}\}$,

(iv) $cd : P \cup T \rightarrow C$. cd is a mapping from places or transition set to colors set,

(v) Pre, Post $\in \beta^{|P| \times |T|}$ are backward incidence matrix and forward incidence matrix of CPN. β can be taken as the set of mappings of the form $f : cd(t) \rightarrow \text{Bag}(cd(p))$. $\text{Pre}[p, t] : cd(t) \rightarrow \text{Bag}(cd(p))$ and $\text{Post}[p, t] : cd(t) \rightarrow \text{Bag}(cd(p))$ are mappings for each pair $(p, t) \in P \times T$. $\text{Bag}(cd(p))$ denotes the set of all multisets over $cd(p)$. They indicate the input and output execution dependencies during composite web service formation.

(a) To denote the places connected to a transition, we use the following notation. F is a flow relation $F \subseteq (P \times T) \cup (T \times P)$ for the set of arcs. Given an element $x \in P \cup T$, then $\cdot x := \{y \in P \cup T \mid (y, x) \in F\}$ denotes the set of all input elements of x, and $x \cdot := \{y \in P \cup T \mid (x, y) \in F\}$ denotes the set of all output elements of x. If x is a place, then $\cdot x$ and $x \cdot$ denote the set of input and output transitions, respectively.

(b) Place is labeled as $\{I, O, I_R, O_R, T_R\}$. In our specific model, a TCWS-CPN will have only initially place p_0, such that $p_0 = \phi$, which will be initially marked with one token of color. Because it is clear for transactional requirement of user, it will correspond to the only color of transactional property. As color token of every place is transactional property of composite web service, the color set of places is $\{a, ar, c, cr\}$.

(c) Transition includes two basic activities, selecting new component services by means of transactional property and compositing the present component services. Color of transition denotes transactional property of new selecting component services.

(d) $cd(p)$ expresses color of place p, and $cd(t)$ expresses color of transition t.

(e) Pre$[p, t] \in$ Bag$(cd(p))$: there is an arc with arc color from a place $p \in P$ to some transition $t \in T$, and Post$[p, t] \in$ Bag$(cd(p))$: there is an arc from a transition $t \in T$ to some place $p \in P$. Hence, $F := \{(p, t) \in P \times T \mid \text{Pre}[p, t]\} \cup \{(t, p) \in T \times P \mid \text{Post}[p, t]\}$ is the set of arcs of CPN.

Definition 2. A marking of TCWS-CPN $= (P, T, \text{Pre}, \text{Post}, C, cd)$ is a vector m such that $m[p] \in$ Bag$(cd(p))$ for each $p \in P$, and $m[p]$ is component of vector m which gives the multiset of color token in place p. TCWS-CPN together with a marking m is called a TCWS-CPN system and is denoted by $S = \langle \text{TCWS-CPN}, m \rangle$. $\langle \text{TCWS-CPN}, m \rangle$ assigns a multiset of colors to each place, which represents the current transactional state of web service composition system.

3.4. Services Selection of Transactional Property in the TCWS-CPN. In the section, we focus on web services composition satisfying the user's functional, transactional requirements. We define guard to express transactional restriction of services selection. Binding determines transactional property of selected services. Firing rules are selection rules for component services of transactional property.

Definition 3 (guard). The appropriate restriction is defined by a predicate at the transition which is called a guard. In our TCWS-CPN model, variable "tpattern" is guard of transition, which expressed fired pattern of transition. (That is composition pattern of selected services.)

Definition 4 (binding). A binding is an assignment of values to variables, and variables appear both in the guard of t and in the arc expressions of the arcs connected to t.

Definition 5 (firing rules). A marking of TCWS-CPN and a binding B enable a transition t if and only if all its input places contain tokens such that (for all $p \in (\cdot t), m[p] \neq \phi)$, and at least one of the following conditions is fulfilled:

(1) $m = m_0$ (initial marking),

(2) $(m[p] \in$ Bag$(a, ar)) \wedge (B(tpattern) = $ sequence$) \wedge [cd(t) \in \{pr, ar, cr\}]$,

(3) $(m[p] \in$ Bag$(c, cr) \wedge (B(tpattern) = $ sequence$) \wedge [cd(t) \in \{p, a, c, pr, ar, cr\}]$,

(4) $(m[p] \in$ Bag$(a)) \wedge (B(tpattern) = $ parallel$) \wedge (cd(t) = cr)$,

(5) $(m[p] \in$ Bag$(ar)) \wedge (B(tpattern) = $ parallel$) \wedge [cd(t) \in \{pr, ar, cr\}]$,

(6) $(m[p] \in$ Bag$(c)) \wedge (B(tpattern) = $ parallel$) \wedge [cd(t) \in \{c, cr\}]$,

(7) $(m[p] \in$ Bag$(cr)) \wedge (B(tpattern) = $ parallel$) \wedge [cd(t) \in \{p, a, c, pr, ar, cr\}]$.

Definition 6 (successor marking relation). A successor marking relation is defined by $m \xrightarrow{t,B} m' \Leftrightarrow m \geq \text{pre}[\cdot, t]B \wedge m'$. The m' is obtained after a transition $t \in T$ is fired for binding B in a marking m.

In our web service composition, a concrete service should be selected only one time and the corresponding transition in TCWS-CPN should be fired only one time. For this reason, when a transition is fired, in the successor marking relation tokens of input places are removed and new tokens are added to the output places. Tokens are added to the output places of transition t according to the following rules [20]:

(1) if $(\exists p_i \in (\cdot t) \mid a \in m_{[p]})$, then (for all $p_{i+1} \in (t\cdot) \mid m'_{[p_{i+1}]}) \in$ Bag(a),

(2) if $(\exists p_i \in (\cdot t) \mid ar \in m_{[p]})$, then (for all $p_{i+1} \in (t\cdot) \mid m'_{[p_{i+1}]}) \in$ Bag(ar),

(3) if $(\exists p_i \in (\cdot t) \mid c \in m_{[p]}) \wedge (cd(t) \in \{p, pr, a, ar\}) \wedge (B(tpattern) = $ sequence$)$, then (for all $p_{i+1} \in (t\cdot) \mid m'_{[p_{i+1}]}) \in$ Bag(a),

(4) if $(\exists p_i \in (\cdot t) \mid c \in m_{[p]}) \wedge (cd(t) \in \{c, cr\})$, then (for all $p_{i+1} \in (t\cdot) \mid m'_{[p_{i+1}]}) \in$ Bag(c),

(5) if $(\exists p_i \in (\cdot t) \mid cr \in m_{[p]}) \wedge (cd(t) \in \{pr, ar\})$, then (for all $p_{i+1} \in (t\cdot) \mid m'_{[p_{i+1}]}) \in$ Bag(ar),

(6) if $(\exists p_i \in (\cdot t) \mid cr \in m_{[p]}) \wedge (cd(t) \in \{cr\})$, then (for all $p_{i+1} \in (t\cdot) \mid m'_{[p_{i+1}]}) \in$ Bag(cr),

(7) if $(\exists p_i \in (\cdot t) \mid cr \in m_{[p]}) \wedge (cd(t) \in \{p, a\})$, then (for all $p_{i+1} \in (t\cdot) \mid m'_{[p_{i+1}]}) \in$ Bag(a),

(8) if $(\exists p_i \in (\cdot t) \mid cr \in m_{[p]}) \wedge (cd(t) \in \{c\})$, then (for all $p_{i+1} \in (t\cdot) \mid m'_{[p_{i+1}]}) \in$ Bag(c).

3.5. Composite Sequence in the CPN

Definition 7 (occurrence sequence). We define the set OCC(S) of occurrence sequences to be the set of all sequences of the form $m_0, t_0, m_1, t_1, m_2, t_2, \ldots, t_{n-1}, m_n$ $(n \geq 1)$ such that $m_i \xrightarrow{t_i} m_{i+1}$ for $i \in \{0, \ldots, n-1\}$.

Occurrence sequence in fact represents the selection of several web services, $s_0 \cdots s_{n-1}$, which are components of the resulting TCWS, whose aggregated TP is m_n.

Definition 8 (reachability set). For a TCWS-CPN system $S = \langle \text{TCWS-CPN}, m \rangle$ the set RS(S) $= $ RS(TCWS-CPN, m) $:= \{m \mid \exists w \in T^* \cdot m_0 \xrightarrow{w} m\}$ is the reachability set.

One of the goals in my paper is discovering and selecting the web services whose composition satisfies the functional and the transactional requirements of the user such as follows.

Our problem consists in discovering and selecting the web services of the registry whose composition satisfies the functional, QoS, and the transactional requirements of the user, which ensures reliable execution of composite web servic such as follows.

Definition 9 (transactional composite web services problem). Given a user query Q (it is used to discover component services) and a TCWS-CPN, transactional composite web services problem consists in creating a TCWS-CPN by firing rule of a marking and binding, from the occurrence sequence and reachability set, such that $m_0 \xrightarrow{w} m_F$, where m_0 is the initial marking, m_F is a reachable marking such that: if $T_Q = T_0$, then for all $p \in (P \cap O_Q)$ and $m_F[p] \in \{c, cr\}$ and if $T_Q = T_1$, then for all $p \in (P \cap O_Q)$ and $m_F[p] \in \{a, ar, c, cr\}$, and such that the composition of all the web services corresponding to the transitions of w represents a TCWS.

4. Execution Framework Architecture of TCWS-CPN

4.1. Execution Framework Architecture. During the TCWS component web services exist two composition patterns. In sequential patterns, the results of previous services are inputs of successor services which cannot be invoked until previous services have finished. In parallel scenario, several branch services are executed simultaneously because they do not have data flow dependencies. Hence, to ensure that sequential and parallel execution of TCWS satisfies transactional requirement of user, it is mandatory to follow TCWS-CPN model taken by the composer.

In this paper, we propose execution framework architecture of TCWS-CPN, in which a Composition Engine manages selection and execution of a TCWS. It is in turn a collection of Composition Threads that is assigned to each Wed service in the TCWS. Figure 1 depicts the overall architecture of our Executor. The Composition Engine and its Engine Threads are in charge of initiating, controlling, and monitoring the execution, as well as collaborating with its peers to deploy the TCWS execution. The Composition Engine and its Engine Threads are in charge of initiating, controlling, and monitoring the execution, as well as collaborating with its peers to deploy the TCWS execution. The Composition Engine is responsible for initiating the Engine Threads and the TCWS-CPN system, and then Engine Threads are responsible for the invocation of web services, monitoring its execution, and forwarding results to its peers to continue the execution flow. In the framework, all of components are recovery.

The model of proposed framework can distribute the responsibility of executing a TCWS across several Engine Threads, which is implemented in a distributed memory environment supported by message passing or in a shared memory platform. The logic of Executor can distribute execution and is independent of implementation, which is

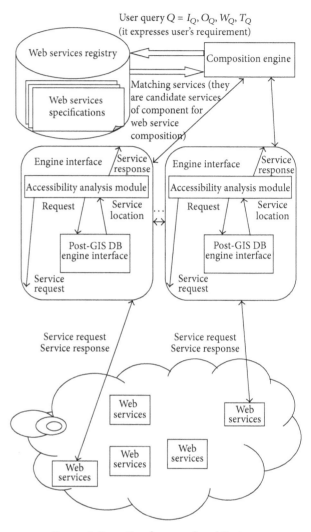

FIGURE 1: Execution framework architecture.

place in different physical nodes from those where actual web services are placed. The Composition Engine needs to have access to the web services Registry, which contains the WSDL and OWLS documents. Engine Threads invoke the component web services remotely from web services Registry. The information needed at runtime by each Engine Thread is extracted from the TCSW-CPN in a shared memory implementation or sent by the composition Engine in a distributed implementation.

Generally, the component web services are categorized into two types, atomic and composite web services. An atomic web service invokes local operations. A composite web service accesses additionally other web services or invokes operations of other web services. Transitions in the TCWS-CPN, representing the TCWS, could be atomic web services or TCWS. Atomic web services have its corresponding WSDL and OWLS documents. TCWS can be encapsulated into an executor. The Composition Engine also has its corresponding WSDL and OWLS documents.

4.2. Example. The example in this paper is based upon a travel-scheduling service composition which is depicted by

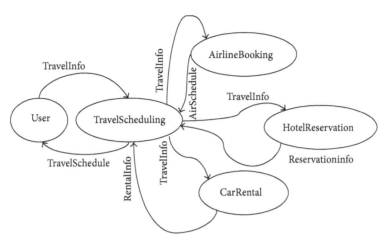

FIGURE 2: Illustrative state diagrams for travel scheduling.

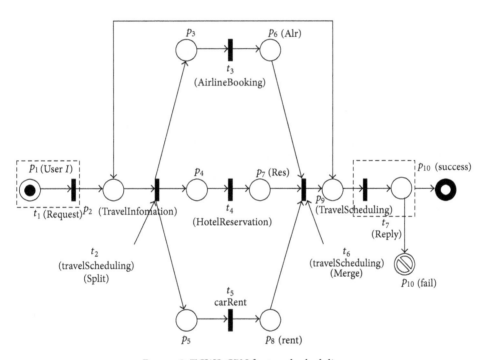

FIGURE 3: TCWS-CPN for travel scheduling.

state diagram in Figure 2. Basic inputs and outputs of candidate service sets which correspond to component services assigned to transitions are shown in Table 1.

Let I_Q = {UserRequest}, O_Q = {User TravelPlan}, T_Q = T_1, m_0 = $(pr, \phi, \phi, \phi, \phi, \phi, \phi, \phi, \phi, \phi)$. According to I and I_Q, place p_1 is created. The set of Candidate services for p_1 is also formed by query from registry. In order to satisfy transactional request transition t_1 is added to TCWS-CPN based on m_0 and firing rule (1), and token of t_1 is $cd(t_1) \in \{a, ar, c, cr\}$. As web service of user request is retriable shown in Figure 3, let $cd(t_1)$ = ar. Meanwhile candidate services of t_1 are pruned, which are

kept with transactional property cr and deleted with other transactional properties. Then an arc is created from p_1 to t_1. One of candidate services is assigned to transition t_1 and takes part in web service composition. Place of p_2 is created after t_1 is fired, and $pre[\cdot, t_1]$ of the arc is also created. Rule of successor marking relation enables m_1 = $(\phi, ar, \phi, \phi, \phi, \phi, \phi, \phi, \phi, \phi)$. Generating the rest parts of TCWS-CPN, including marking of places, token and binding of transitions, and backward and forward matrix of arcs is shown as (1). Marking of places and token and binding of transitions are expressed in occurrence sequence (Definition 8):

$$m_o = \begin{pmatrix} pr \\ \phi \\ \phi \\ \phi \\ \phi \\ \phi \\ \phi \\ \phi \\ \phi \\ \phi \end{pmatrix} \xrightarrow{t_1(cd(t_1)=pr \wedge B(tparttern)=sequence)} m_1 = \begin{pmatrix} \phi \\ ar \\ \phi \\ \phi \\ \phi \\ \phi \\ \phi \\ \phi \\ \phi \\ \phi \end{pmatrix} \xrightarrow{t_2(cd(t_2)=cr \wedge B(tparttern)=sequence)}$$

$$m_2 = \begin{pmatrix} \phi \\ \phi \\ ar \\ ar \\ ar \\ \phi \\ \phi \\ \phi \\ \phi \\ \phi \end{pmatrix} \xrightarrow{t_3(cd(t_3)=ar \wedge B(tparttern)=parallel)} m_5 = \begin{pmatrix} \phi \\ \phi \\ \phi \\ \phi \\ \phi \\ ar \\ ar \\ ar \\ \phi \\ \phi \end{pmatrix}$$

$$m_3 = \begin{pmatrix} \phi \\ \phi \\ ar \\ ar \\ ar \\ \phi \\ \phi \\ \phi \\ \phi \\ \phi \end{pmatrix} \xrightarrow{t_4(cd(t_4)=cr \wedge B(tparttern)=parallel)} m_6 = \begin{pmatrix} \phi \\ \phi \\ \phi \\ \phi \\ \phi \\ ar \\ ar \\ ar \\ \phi \\ \phi \end{pmatrix} \xrightarrow{t_5(cd(t_5)=pr \wedge B(tparttern)=sequence)}$$

$$m_4 = \begin{pmatrix} \phi \\ \phi \\ ar \\ ar \\ ar \\ \phi \\ \phi \\ \phi \\ \phi \\ \phi \end{pmatrix} \xrightarrow{t_5(cd(t_5)=cr \wedge B(tparttern)=parallel)} m_7 = \begin{pmatrix} \phi \\ \phi \\ \phi \\ \phi \\ \phi \\ ar \\ ar \\ ar \\ \phi \\ \phi \end{pmatrix}$$

$$m_8 = \begin{pmatrix} \phi \\ \phi \\ \phi \\ \phi \\ \phi \\ \phi \\ \phi \\ \phi \\ ar \\ \phi \end{pmatrix} \xrightarrow{t_6(cd(t_6)=cr \wedge B(tparttern)=sequence)} m_9 = \begin{pmatrix} \phi \\ \phi \\ \phi \\ \phi \\ \phi \\ \phi \\ \phi \\ \phi \\ \phi \\ ar \end{pmatrix}.$$

(1)

TABLE 1: Example.

Service class name	Input	Output
s1	UserRequest	TravelScheduling
s2	TravelScheduling	AirlineRequest, HotelRequest, CarRentRequest
s3	AirlineRequest	AirlineScheduling
s4	HotelRequest	HotelScheduling
s5	CarRentRequest	CarRentScheduling
s6	AirlineScheduling, HotelScheduling, CarRentScheduling	TravelPlan
s7	TravelPlan	User TravelPlan

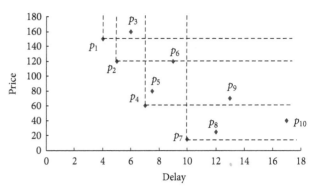

FIGURE 4: Skyline Services.

5. Qos-Based Skyline Web Services

5.1. The Skyline Computation Problem. The basic skyline consists of all nondominated database objects. That means all database objects for which there is no object in the database that is better or equal in all dimensions, but in at least one aspect strictly better. Assuming every database object to be represented by a point in n-dimensional space with the coordinates for each dimension given by its scores for the respective aspect, we can formulate the problem as follows.

The Skyline Problem. Given set $O := \{o_1, \ldots, o_N\}$ of N database objects, n score functions $s_1, \ldots, s_n$ with $s_i : O \rightarrow [0, 1]$ and n sorted lists $S_1, \ldots, S_n$ containing all database objects and their respective score values using one of the score function is for each list; all lists are sorted descending by score values starting with the highest scores. Wanted is the subset P of all non-dominated objects in O, that is, $\{o_i \in P \mid \neg \exists o_j \in O : (s_1(o_i) \leqslant s_1(o_j) \wedge \cdots \wedge s_n(o_i) \leqslant s_n(o_j) \wedge \exists q \in [1, \ldots, n] : s_q(o_i) < s_q(o_j))\}$.

5.2. Skyline Web Services for Qos-Based Composition. QoS-based service composition is a constraint optimization problem which aims at selecting individual services that meet QoS constraints and also provide the best value for the utility. For a composite web service with n activities and l candidate services per activity, there are l^n possible combinations to be examined. Hence, performing an exhaustive search can be very expensive in terms of computation time and, therefore, inappropriate for run-time service selection in applications with many services and dynamic needs. Skyline computation offers a new solution of finding optimal data from huge data sets, whose computation can be expensive and whose applications require fast response times.

The main idea in our approach is to perform a skyline query on the services in each activity to distinguish between those services that are potential candidates for the composition and those that cannot possibly be part of the final solution. The latter can effectively be pruned to reduce the search space.

Definition 10 (dominance). Given a service set S_{A_i} assigned to activity A_i having n candidate services: $S_{A_{i1}}, S_{A_{i1}}, \ldots, S_{A_{in}}$, QoS vector is d dimensions: $q_1(S_{A_{il}}), q_2(S_{A_{il}}), \ldots, q_d(S_{A_{il}})$. $S_{A_{iu}}$ is said to dominate $S_{A_{iv}}$, denoted as $S_{A_{iu}} \prec S_{A_{iv}}$ if and only if $S_{A_{iu}}$ is better than or equal to $S_{A_{iv}}$ in all attributes and strictly better in at least one attribute, that is, for all $k \in [1, d]$: $q_k(S_{A_{iu}}) \leq q_k(S_{A_{iv}})$ and $\exists l \in [1, d] : q_k(S_{A_{iu}}) < q_k(S_{A_{iv}})$.

If $S_{A_{iv}}$ is neither dominated by nor dominates $S_{A_{iu}}$, then $S_{A_{iv}}$ and $S_{A_{iu}}$ are incomparable. The notion of dominance handles requirement since comparing between matched services takes into consideration the degrees of match in all parameters, instead of calculating and using a single, overall score.

Definition 11 (skyline web services [22]). The skyline web services of a service set S_{Ai}, denoted by SWS, comprise the set of those services that are not dominated by any other services, that is, $SWS = \{S_{A_{iu}} \in S_{A_i} \mid \neg \exists S_{A_{iv}} \in S_{A_i} : S_{A_{iv}} \prec S_{A_{iu}}\}$. Services in SWS are skyline web services of a service set S_{A_i}.

We observe that only those services that belong to the SWS are not dominated by any other functionally equivalent service and are valid candidates for the composition. This provides a valid pruning of the number of candidate services. Figure 4 shows an example of skyline services of candidate services for a certain activity. Each service is described by two QoS attributes, namely, delay and price. Hence, the services are represented as points in the 2-dimensional space, with the coordinates of each point corresponding to the values of the service in these two parameters. SWS includes four elements, SWS = $\{p_1, p_2, p_4, p_7\}$, because they are not dominated by any other service. On the other hand, service p_6 is not contained in the SWS because it is dominated by the services p_2 and p_4.

The skyline web services provide different tradeoffs between the QoS attributes and are incomparable to each other, as long as there is no prespecified preference scheme regarding the relative importance of these attributes. For example, for a specific user, a service may be the most suitable choice, due to its very low delay and despite its high price, while for the other user, a service may be the most preferred one due to its low price.

5.3. Skyline Algorithm of Qos-Based Web Service Selection

(0) Initialize a data structure SWS := Φ containing records with an identifier and n real values indexed by the identifiers, initialize n lists $K_1, \ldots, K_n := \Phi$ containing records with an identifier and a real value, and initialize n real values $p_1, \ldots, p_n := 1$.

(1) Initialize counter $i := 1$.

(2) Get the next object $S_{A_{i_{new}}}$ by sorted access on list S_{A_i}.

(3) If $S_{A_{i_{new}}} \in$ SWS, update its record's ith real value with $S_{A_i}(S_{A_{i_{new}}})$, else create such a record in SWS.

(4) Append $S_{A_{i_{new}}}$ with $S_{A_i}(S_{A_{i_{new}}})$ to list K_i.

(5) Set $p_i := S_{A_{i_{new}}}$ and $i := (i \mod n) + 1$.

(6) If all scores $S_{A_i}(S_{A_{i_{new}}})$ $(1 \leq i \leq n)$ are known, proceed with Step (2) else with Step(4)

(7) For $i = 1$ to n do.

(8) While $p_i = S_{A_i}(S_{A_{i_{new}}})$ do sorted access on list S_{A_i} and handle the retrieved objects like in Step (2) to (3).

(9) If more than one object is entirely known, compare pairwise and remove the dominated objects from SWS.

(10) For $i = 1$ to n do.

(11) Do all necessary random accesses for the objects in K_i that are also in SWS, and immediately discard objects that are not in SWS.

(12) Take the objects of K_i and compare them pairwise with the objects, in K_i. If an object is dominated by another object remove it from K_i and SWS.

(13) Output SWS as the set of skyline web services.

6. Experimentation

In the section, we use two scenarios to evaluate the behavior of TCWS-CPN and the efficiency of our approach. We have conducted experiments in two scenarios. The first scenario: different services are generated to verify the validity of our TCWS-CPN model. In the second one, we use the OWL-S service retrieval test collection OWLS-TC v2[2]. The execution time of QoS services selection with skyline computation is compared with that without skyline computation.

The first scenario is implemented as follows. In order to evaluate the behavior of transactional selection approach based on TCWS-CPN, 10 user queries are generating with various kinds of inputs and outputs. The services are generating randomly from an ontology containing 20 generated elements each of which has between 1 and 5 inputs and between 1 and 3 outputs [20]. Every generated service is independently from the others. Experiments are conducted by implementing the proposed service selection approach with the program on a PC Core i3 with 2 GB RAM, Windows 7, and Java 2 Enterprise Edition V1.5.0. JDK 1.6 virtual machine is used to develop and run the program. The experiments involved composite services varying the number of activities and varying the number of web services.

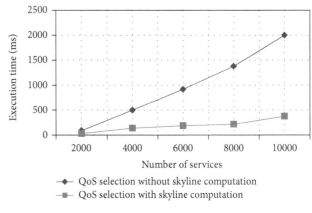

FIGURE 5: Execution time.

In the first scenario, every web service has between 1 and 5 inputs and outputs, randomly generated from an ontology containing 10 generated elements. QoS attribute and transactional property of every service are also generated randomly but there are the relations between them. To model the fact, we assume that the execution price of service whose transactional property is c is more expensive than whose transactional property is p or a, because the former provides additional functionality in order to guarantee that the result can be compensatable. Similarly, we believe that a pr, ar, or cr web service has execution duration higher than a nonretriable one, because the former provides additional operation in order to guarantee that it successfully finishes after a finite number of invocations. In addition, user's requirement and QoS weight have been randomly generated by varying number of inputs and outputs between 1 and 3.

Relationship of utility value and duration weight with different tolerance are depicted the more important the duration criteria to the user, the better a composition with tolerance T_0 compared to a composition with tolerance T_1.

For the second scenario, we use the OWL-S service retrieval test collection OWLS-TC v2[2]. This collection contains services retrieved mainly from public IBM UDDI registries and semiautomatically transformed from WSDL to OWL-S. We apply skyline to select the best candidates for QoS selection. We compare execution time of QoS selection using skyline computation with the time without using Figure 5 illustrates the running time of QoS selection with (and without) skyline computation. Observe that the time without using skyline computation is higher than that using it.

7. Conclusion

CPN model allows describing not only a static vision of a system, but also its dynamic behavior, and it is expressive enough to capture the semantics of complex web services combinations and their respective interactions. In the paper we propose a hybrid solution that takes advantage of search metaheuristics techniques to consider functional conditions expressed as input and output attributes, and transactional properties expressed as a tolerance level. We incorporate transactional web services properties in the CPN model. To ensure reliable and correct execution, unfolding processes of the CPN are followed. The execution of transactional composition web service (TCWS) is formalized by CPN properties. To identify the best services of QoS properties from candidate service sets formed in the TCSW-CPN, we use skyline computation to retrieve dominant web service. It can overcome that the reduction of individual scores to an overall similarity lead to significant information loss. We also define QoS-based dominance relationships between services. To identify the best services from CPN model in QoS properties, we use skyline computation to retrieve dominant web service. We have shown how the best matches can be identified efficiently by a skyline computation algorithm, and we have addressed common tasks involved in the service selection process, referring both to the requesters' and the providers' perspectives.

In the experimentation, our intention is to compare both implementations under different characterizations of CPNs. Experimental evaluation on real and synthetic data shows that the best matches can be identified very efficiently, with a significant increase in recall and precision.

At the same time, the next step is to add automatic data mapping functionality into our system, using the semantic-based approach. In this paper, we utilize product-specific property to facilitate mediator service generation. To improve our prototype of the service selection process, by facilitating the user in expressing and refining his/her queries and providing faceted browsing capabilities.

Acknowledgments

This work is partially supported by Shaanxi Education department, Foundation of China, no. 12JK0745 and no. 12JK0746, by the projects of Weinan Teachers University, no. 10YKS005, by the Education Reform Project of Weinan Teachers University, no. JG201147.

References

[1] A. Liu, Q. Li, L. Huang, and M. Xiao, "FACTS: a framework for fault tolerant composition of transactional web services," *IEEE Transactions on Services Computing*, vol. 3, no. 1, pp. 46–59, 2009.

[2] X. Dong, A. Y. Halevy, J. Madhavan, E. Nemes, and J. Zhang, "Similarity search for web services," in *Proceedings of the VLDB*, pp. 372–383, 2004.

[3] A. Elmagarmid, *Transaction Models for Advanced Database Applications*, Morgan-Kaufmann, 1992.

[4] J. EI Haddad, M. Manouvrier, and M. Rukoz, "TQoS: transactional and QoS-aware selection algorithm for automatic Web service composition," *IEEE Transactions on Services Computing*, vol. 3, no. 1, pp. 73–85, 2010.

[5] T. Mikalsen, T. Tai, and I. Rouvellou, "Transactional attitudes: reliable composition of autonomous web services," in *Proceedings of the Workshop on Dependable Middleware-Based Systems at the Dependable Systems and Network Conference*, 2002.

[6] P. F. Pires, M. R. F. Benevides, and M. Mattoso, "Building reliable web services compositions," in *Proceedings of the Web, Web-Services, and Database Systems, NODe Web and Database-Related Workshops*, pp. 59–72.

[7] S. Mehrotra, R. Rastogi, A. Silberschatz, and H. Korth, "A transactional model for multidatabase systems," in *Proceedings of the International Conference on Distributed Computing Systems (ICDCS '92)*, pp. 56–63, 1992.

[8] K. Vidyasankar and G. Vossen, "A multi-level model for web services composition," in *Proceedings of the IEEE International Conference on Web Services (ICWS '04)*, pp. 462–469, 2004.

[9] S. Bhiri, O. Perrin, and C. Godart, "Ensuring required failure atomicity of composite web services," in *Proceedings of the International Conference World Wide Web (WWW '05)*, pp. 138–147, 2005.

[10] M. Rusinkiewicz and A. Sheth, *Specification and Execution of Transactional Workflows*, Modern Database Systems: The Object Model, Interoperability, and Beyond, ACM Press/ Addison-Wesley, 1995.

[11] F. Montagut and R. Molva, "Augmenting Web services composition with transactional requirements," in *Proceedings of the IEEE International Conference on Web Services (ICWS '06)*, pp. 91–98, September 2006.

[12] L. Zeng, B. Benatallah, A. H. H. Ngu, M. Dumas, J. Kalagnanam, and H. Chang, "QoS-aware middleware for web services composition," *IEEE Transactions on Software Engineering*, vol. 30, no. 5, pp. 311–327, 2004.

[13] Y. Liu, A. H. H. Ngu, and L. Zeng, "QoS computation and policing in dynamic web service selection," in *Proceedings of the 13th International World Wide Web Conference (WWW '04)*, pp. 66–73, May 2004.

[14] L. Zeng, B. Benatallah, M. Dumas, J. Kalagnanam, and Q. Z. Sheng, "Quality driven web services composition," in *Proceedings of the International World Wide Web Conference*, pp. 411–421, 2003.

[15] L. Zeng, B. Benatallah, A. H. H. Ngu, M. Dumas, and J. Kalagnanam, "Qos-aware middleware for web services composition," *IEEE Transactions on Software Engineering*, vol. 30, no. 5, pp. 311–327, 2004.

[16] G. L. Nemhauser and L. A. Wolsey, *Integer and Combinatorial Optimization*, Wiley-Interscience, New York, NY, USA, 1988.

[17] I. Maros, *Computational Techniques of the Simplex Method*, Springer, 2003.

[18] S. Mehrotra, R. Rastogi, H. F. Korth, and A. Silberschatz, "A transaction model for multidatabase systems," in *Proceedings of the ICDCS*, pp. 56–63, 1992.

[19] P. Albert, L. Henocque, and M. Kleiner, "Configuration based workflow composition," in *Proceedings of the IEEE International Conference on Web Services (ICWS '05)*, pp. 285–292, July 2005.

[20] Y. Cardinale, J. El Haddad, and M. Manouvrier, "CPN-TWS: a colored petri-net approach for transactional-QoS driven Web Service composition," *Web and Grid Services*, vol. 7, no. 1, pp. 91–115, 2011.

[21] G. Zhang, L. Chen, and W. Ha, "Service selection of ensuring transactional reliability and QoS for web service composition," *Mathematical Problems in Engineering*, vol. 2012, Article ID 641361, 15 pages, 2012.

[22] M. Alrifai, D. Skoutas, and T. Risse, "Selecting skyline services for QoS-based Web service composition," in *Proceedings of the 19th international conference on World Wide Web*, pp. 88–101, ACM, 2010.

11

Music Identification System Using MPEG-7 Audio Signature Descriptors

Shingchern D. You,[1] Wei-Hwa Chen,[2] and Woei-Kae Chen[1]

[1] *Department of Computer Science and Information Engineering, National Taipei University of Technology, Taipei 104, Taiwan*
[2] *Hon-Hai Precision Industry Co. Ltd, Tucheng District, New Taipei City 236, Taiwan*

Correspondence should be addressed to Shingchern You; you@csie.ntut.edu.tw

Academic Editors: P. Melin, J. Pavón, and K. Polat

This paper describes a multiresolution system based on MPEG-7 audio signature descriptors for music identification. Such an identification system may be used to detect illegally copied music circulated over the Internet. In the proposed system, low-resolution descriptors are used to search likely candidates, and then full-resolution descriptors are used to identify the unknown (query) audio. With this arrangement, the proposed system achieves both high speed and high accuracy. To deal with the problem that a piece of query audio may not be inside the system's database, we suggest two different methods to find the decision threshold. Simulation results show that the proposed method II can achieve an accuracy of 99.4% for query inputs both inside and outside the database. Overall, it is highly possible to use the proposed system for copyright control.

1. Introduction

With the SOPA (stop online piracy act) bill [1] proposed in 2011, the protection of copyrighted intellectual property, such as digital content, once again brought to public attention. Despite the controversial issues of the SOPA bill, it is commonly agreed that copyrighted digital content should be protected. However, the first step toward the protection of copyrighted content is to identify whether a piece of digital content is copyrighted, and if so, who owns it. In this regard, it is important to identify (detect) whether a digital work is copyrighted or not.

Among digital content, soundtracks (usually in the form of audio files) are one type of content that is easily to be illegally reproduced. Owing to the advanced techniques in audio compression, music soundtracks are usually distributed over the Internet in compressed form rather than in uncompressed form. Therefore, any approach for copyright detection must be able to deal with both compressed and uncompressed audio files.

A typical method to attach the copyright information to a piece of music is by embedding watermarks [2]. Though effective, this method has some limitations, such as the watermarks must be embedded into the source soundtracks before release. Therefore, it is not possible to identify the rights owner of a piece of music without watermarks. Another concern is that the embedding process usually introduces distortion. Thus, the quality of the embedded audio may be degraded.

In addition to the watermarking technique, it is also possible to identify rights owner by comparison. For example, if an unknown soundtrack is very similar to a soundtrack owned by a company, then the unknown soundtrack is highly likely copyrighted in that company's name. This type of approach is especially suitable for audio files because, in practice, tremendous amount of records currently available do not embed watermarks or any kind of copyright information.

When comparing a piece of music with a music database, the comparison may be accomplished based on the melody (i.e., musical notes) of the music [3]. For this type of comparison, however, if two persons sing the same song, these two works will be recognized as the same one. Since different artists may perform the same song, known as the cover version, a comparison based on melody cannot solve this problem.

Another type of comparison is based on the waveform of the music. This technique is also known as music identification. In this case, the same song performed by different artists generally does not have the same waveforms, and therefore they can be correctly identified. Though conceptually simple, it is not plausible to directly compare PCM samples of two pieces of music because it would take too much time for the comparison. For example, a typical compact disc (CD) has about 600 M bytes of PCM samples to store about ten songs. If a database contains 10,000 different songs, then the PCM samples occupy about 600 G bytes of space. A piece of unknown music with duration of ten seconds has about 880 k bytes of data. It is obvious that it requires a huge amount of computation to sequentially compare the 880 k bytes of data with the 600 G bytes of data in the database. Therefore, dimension-reduced representations of the PCM waveforms, known as fingerprints, are used in comparison. Among the fingerprints, most of them are defined by individual companies or groups. Some of them are briefly explained in the following.

Researchers in Google develop a fingerprinting scheme for audio called Waveprint [4] based on wavelets. With the aid of wavelets, the fingerprint is invariant to timescale change. In other words, whether the audio piece is played faster or slower than the normal speed, the fingerprint is unchanged. The fingerprint of a piece of 4-minute music is around 64 k bytes, equivalently 2133 bits per second.

Shazam [5] is a company (and service) dedicated for music identification. Its database contains around eleven million soundtracks. As described in [6], the fingerprints used are sets of triplets based on spectrogram peaks. For example, if (t_1, f_1) and (t_2, f_2) are two peaks at time t_1 and t_2 and frequency f_1 and f_2, then the triplet $((t_2 - t_1), f_1, (f_2 - f_1))$ is a feature. Based on the realization of [7], the fingerprint in this scheme uses 400 bits per second.

Researchers in Philips also propose a fingerprinting scheme [8]. The computation of the fingerprints includes: framing, windowing (von Hann window), FFT (fast fourier transform), band decision, energy computation, and then quantization (into binary). In the typical setting, one second of audio has around 2,730 bits of fingerprint.

Microsoft's Robust Audio Recognition Engine (RARE) [9] divides the incoming audio into overlapping frames. Each frame is converted to spectral domain by MCLT (modulated complex lapped transform). The spectral values are applied to two layers of OPCA (oriented principle component analysis) to reduce the dimensionality of the spectral data. For this method, 344 features (11,008 bits if one feature is stored in 4 bytes in a floating point) are obtained per second.

In addition to the above methods, there are actually many more different types of audio fingerprinting schemes available, such as Music Brainz [10], Audible Magic [11], and Gracenote's MusicID [12]. According to [13], there are more than ten different audio fingerprinting schemes available.

Since there are vast amount of different fingerprinting schemes available, some researchers then conducted experiments to compare the relative performance among some of them. The results show that, if the schemes use the same number of bits to represent fingerprints, they have comparable performance [14]. Therefore, the selection of the fingerprinting schemes should also consider other factors

(such as interoperability to be addressed below) rather than merely the minor performance difference.

With the ever-increasing amount of multimedia content over the Internet and in the multimedia databases, it is an important task to exchange multimedia content. To respond the public demands, ISO's (International Standardization Organization) working group developed MPEG-7 standard [15, 16]. In the audio part of the standard [17], a high-level tool is developed for audio identification called audio signature description scheme. The fingerprints used in the scheme are called audio signature descriptors, and they have good identification accuracy [18, 19]. In the following, we interchangeably use descriptors and fingerprints without distinction.

Although proprietary audio fingerprints have excellent identification performance, the MPEG-7 audio descriptors offer some advantages. First, being an international standard ensures the open and fair use (subject to license fee) of the technology. Second, such an international standard makes the interoperability possible. For example, if a mobile phone installs an application program to convert a piece of recorded audio to MPEG-7 descriptors, the descriptors can be sent to any website accepting the descriptors. On the other hand, it is not possible to send proprietary fingerprints used in one company to database systems owned by competitors. Third, different companies may share or exchange their audio descriptors (fingerprints) in their databases without any difficulties. In the current situation, each company has to compute fingerprints for newly released albums. With the use of MPEG-7 descriptors, the redundant efforts of computing fingerprints can be minimized.

Although a music identification system based on audio fingerprints has several applications [8], we concentrate on the issue of detecting if a piece of circulated music is highly similar to a copyrighted work or not. In a typical case, the similarity is measured by a distance metric. If the distance is shorter than a threshold, the two pieces of music are considered as similar. Although it is not trivial to determine a suitable threshold [20], this problem is not fully studied. For example, [20] does not indicate any approach to determine the threshold. In addition, the audio files to be compared may be very large; therefore it is very important to reduce the comparison time while maintaining high identification accuracy. Since not many papers address these two issues based on MPEG-7 descriptors, we report in this paper our approaches and experimental results.

This paper is organized as follows. Section 2 is an overview of the MPEG-7 audio signature descriptors. Section 3 is the system model for music identification. Section 4 describes the dimensionality reduction method used in the paper. Section 5 is the proposed strategy to determine the threshold. Section 6 covers the experiments and results. Section 7 is the conclusion.

2. Overview of MPEG-7 Audio Signature Descriptors

Part 4 [17] of the MPEG-7 standard includes low-level and high-level descriptors for various applications. Low-level descriptors are derived from the temporal and spectral characteristics of the waveform, whereas the high-level descriptors are constructed based on low-level descriptors. In this section, we will briefly describe the descriptors related to music identification.

2.1. Low-Level and High-Level Descriptors of the MPEG-7 Audio. There are 17 low-level audio descriptors defined in the standard. All of these low-level descriptors are derived from the waveform of the music. They can be divided into six different categories: basic, basic spectral, signal parameter, temporal timbral, spectral timbral, and spectral basis representation. These low-level features may be directly used or may serve as the basics for constructing high-level descriptors.

Based on low-level descriptors, MPEG-7 audio standard also defines high-level description schemes for various applications. These include audio signature description, instrument timbre description, general sound recognition and indexing description, and spoken content description. The audio signature descriptors, one type of fingerprints, are used for music identification.

2.2. MPEG-7 Audio Signature Descriptors. Although low-level descriptors in MPEG-7 audio may also be used to identify music, it is shown that the audio signature descriptors provide better identification performance [18, 19]. Therefore, the audio signature descriptors are adopted in the proposed system.

The MPEG-7 audio signature descriptors are computed as follows.

(1) Time-to-frequency conversion: this step is based on audio spectrum envelope descriptors, including the following substeps.

    (i) Determine the hop length between two consecutive windows in the unit of samples. The default value is equivalent to 30 ms.

    (ii) Define the window length l_w. This value is set to three times the hop length. The chosen window is Hamming window.

    (iii) Determine the length of FFT, denoted as N_{FFT}. To reduce the computational complexity, N_{FFT} is the smallest power-of-2 number equal to or greater than l_w. For example, if the sample rate of the audio is 44,100 s/s, then $l_w = 44100 \cdot 0.03 \cdot 3 = 3969$. Therefore, $N_{\text{FFT}} = 4096$. The extra samples after l_w are padded with zeros.

    (iv) Perform the FFT on the windowed samples.

(2) Divide the FFT coefficients into subbands, with each subband having a bandwidth of one-fourth of an octave. In addition, the bandwidths of two consecutive subbands should overlap each other by 10%. That is, the computed bandwidth for each subband must be multiplied by 1.1. The beginning frequency of the first subband, denoted as loEdge, is fixed at 250 Hz. Table 1 lists the frequency range of the first three subbands before and after (spectral) overlapping.

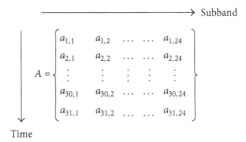

FIGURE 1: MPEG-7 audio signature descriptors in a matrix.

(3) Find the flatness measure $F(b)$ for subband b by

$$F(b) = \frac{\sqrt[h(b)-l(b)+1]{\prod_{i=l(b)}^{h(b)} c(i)}}{(1/(h(b) - l(b) + 1)) \sum_{i=l(b)}^{h(b)} c(i)}, \tag{1}$$

where $c(i)$ is the power spectrum computed by FFT (in step 1), and $h(b)$ and $l(b)$ are the lower and upper indices of $c(i)$ within subband b.

(4) Find the mean and variance of $F(b)$ for subband b over a certain number of successive FFT windows, called scaling ratio. The default value of the scaling ratio is 16.

(5) The series of mean and variance values are the audio signature descriptors.

With the computational steps of the audio signature descriptor, we may compute the number of descriptors in a piece of 15-second music. In the time domain, about $(15-0.09)/0.03 = 497$ windows are used to cover the 15-second signal because the hop size is 30 ms. Since the scaling ratio is set to 16, there are $497/16 \approx 31$ values per subband. In the spectral domain, since there are four subbands per octave and we use six octaves (250 Hz ~ 16 kHz), there are totally 24 subbands in the spectral domain. Thus, the 15-second signal produces $24 \times 31 = 744$ mean values and other 744 variance values. The descriptors are arranged in a matrix form, as shown in Figure 1.

Since the mean values are sufficient for the identification purpose [21], we will not consider the variance descriptors in the following. The obtained descriptors are referred to as high-resolution (or full-dimensional) descriptors. According to [21], if a piece of query music is to be compared with a reference piece, it should be done with a sliding comparison, as shown in Figure 2. In the figure, one segment of line represents descriptors in a piece of music arranged in one dimensional structure. Using the representation in Figure 1, the query segment is arranged as

$$Q = [q_{1,1} \cdots q_{1,24} \cdots q_{31,1} \cdots q_{31,24}]. \tag{2}$$

Since only descriptors from the same subband are to be compared, the hop size between two query segments in Figure 2 is 24 descriptors, or $0.03 \cdot 16 = 0.48$ second. In other words, one descriptor (in a subband) represents 0.48 second of audio samples. The smallest Euclidean distance

$$\begin{array}{|llllllll|}
\hline
a_{1,1}\dots a_{1,24} & a_{2,1}\dots a_{2,24} & a_{3,1}\dots a_{3,24} & \dots & a_{31,24} & a_{32,24} & \dots & a_{62,24} \\
\hline
\end{array}$$

$$\begin{array}{|llll|}
\hline
q_{1,1}\dots q_{1,24} & q_{2,1}\dots q_{2,24} & \cdots & q_{31,24} \\
\hline
\end{array}$$

$$\begin{array}{|llll|}
\hline
q_{1,1}\dots q_{1,24} & q_{2,1}\dots q_{2,24} & \cdots & q_{31,24} \\
\hline
\end{array}$$

$$\begin{array}{|lll|}
\hline
q_{1,1}\cdots & q_{1,24} & \cdots & q_{31,24} \\
\hline
\end{array}$$

FIGURE 2: The sliding operation to compare the query input Q (15 seconds) and the reference music A (30 seconds).

obtained during the sliding operation is recorded as the distance between the query input and the reference music. For example, if the query Q is to be compared with reference A, then we may obtain the Euclidean distance $E_{A,B}(k)$ for the k-th sliding comparison as

$$E_{Q,A}(k) = \sum_{i=1}^{31}\sum_{j=1}^{24} \left| q_{i,j} - a_{(i+k),j} \right|. \tag{3}$$

The recorded distance between these two pieces of music is

$$d_{Q,A} = \min_{k} E_{Q,A}(k). \tag{4}$$

Although using audio signature descriptors greatly reduces the computational burden for comparison, the required computation using (3) is still very large. According to [21], suppose that a database contains 1,000 audio files, with each one having duration of 30 seconds, and the music to be identified has a duration of 15 seconds, then 47, 616, 000 arithmetic operations are required. Therefore, it is beneficial to further reduce the number of comparison, which can be accomplished by employing a multiresolution strategy.

3. Music Identification Based on Multiresolution Strategy

As discussed previously, the computational cost is still very high even if we use the MPEG-7 descriptors. Therefore, we will use the multiresolution strategy to reduce the computational complexity. To do so, in addition to the above-mentioned high-resolution descriptors, we also need to generate low-resolution descriptors (see also Section 4). Therefore, the music database contains high-resolution and low-resolution descriptors for each soundtrack to be identified. This step can be accomplished during the setup of the database. In addition, a training process is conducted to find a distance threshold to determine whether the query input is in the database or not. Section 5 has a detailed description about the training process.

Once the database is constructed, as shown in Figure 3, the music identification procedure consists of the following steps:

(1) When a query input is sent to the system, it computes the MPEG-7 audio signature descriptors and low-resolution descriptors for the query music. If a mobile device is used to record the music, usually the

TABLE 1: Bandwidth of the first three subbands.

Bandwidth of subband (nonoverlapped)	Bandwidth of subband (overlapped)
250–297.3 Hz	237.5–312.2 Hz
297.3–353.6 Hz	282.4–371.2 Hz
353.5–420.4 Hz	335.9–441.5 Hz

descriptors (fingerprints) are sent instead of the PCM samples to reduce the size of the transmitted data.

(2) The computed low-resolution descriptors are compared with those in the database. Based on the distance metric, a list of candidates is obtained. Since the query music may start at any position of the soundtrack, a sliding comparison, as shown in Figure 2, is necessary.

(3) After obtaining the candidate list, high-resolution descriptors are used to find the distances between the query input and the candidates. The shortest distance and its associated soundtrack are recorded.

(4) If the shortest distance is less than the threshold, the query input is considered as highly similar to the recorded soundtrack in the database. Otherwise, the query input is not in the database.

During the low-resolution comparison, it is also possible to use an existing algorithm to reduce the comparison time. For example, we may arrange the descriptors in k-d tree (k-dimensional binary search tree) [22, 23] structure to reduce the search time. However, using the k-d tree structure implies that every segment of music in the database has the same number of descriptors, or same duration. Note that the unit to be compared is one segment, and one soundtrack can be divided into many overlapped segments, as shown in Figure 2. Therefore, if the duration of the segment is set to 15 seconds, then the query music must also have a duration of 15 seconds to use the system. In a practical situation, if the query input is longer than 15 seconds, then only 15 seconds of the music is used for computing the descriptors and comparison.

4. Dimensionality Reduction Method for MPEG-7 Audio Signature Descriptors

This section briefly explains the dimensionality reduction technique used in the experiments. Although a block-average method is proposed in [21] for this purpose, we use a different technique in this paper.

4.1. Problems of Reducing Dimensionality Using Scaling Ratio. Conceptually we may increase the scaling ratio (given in Section 2) to reduce the number of descriptors during computing them. For example, by increasing the scaling ratio from 16 to 256, the number of descriptors is reduced by 16 times. Unfortunately, this approach does not yield satisfactory results because of insufficient time resolution. Recall that the descriptors are derived based on the windowed waveform. Therefore, if two segments of the soundtrack are

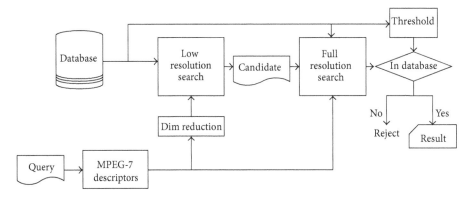

FIGURE 3: Procedure for multiresolution music identification.

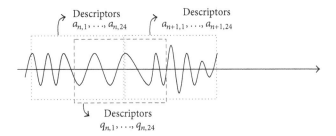

FIGURE 4: The audio samples and the descriptors. In a real application, $a_{n,k}$ is stored in the database, whereas $q_{n,k}$ is computed from the query input. Usually $a_{n,k}$ is not equal to $q_{n,k}$ due to different scopes of the windows even though they are all derived from the same soundtrack.

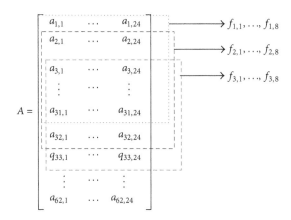

FIGURE 5: Low-resolution descriptors. In the figure, each temporal-spectral block corresponds to descriptors from 15-second music.

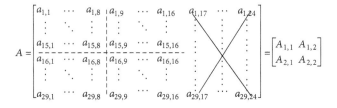

FIGURE 6: Partition of a temporal-spectral block into four subblocks in the experiments.

not highly similar, their corresponding descriptors usually have large differences. With a scaling ratio of 256, each descriptor represents around 7.7 seconds of audio samples. Therefore, unless the query input also starts at a point very close to the segment boundary of a soundtrack, a comparison based on these descriptors may fail. As illustrated in Figure 4, descriptors of $a_{n,k}$ (or $a_{n+1,k}$) and $q_{n,k}$ are quite different, and therefore the descriptor-based identification scheme cannot identify the query input. Therefore, a suitable time resolution, for example, 0.48 second, should be maintained.

4.2. Proposed Dimensionality Reduction Method. In contrast to reduce the number of descriptors by increasing the scaling ratio, we may reduce them in each temporal-spectral block (i.e., the matrix in Figure 1) representing a segment of (15-second) music. However, to maintain a high time resolution, successive temporal-spectral block should have a small time difference, as shown in Figure 5. With this arrangement, we achieve both high identification rate and low comparison complexity.

For each temporal-spectral block, we use PCA (principal component analysis) [21, 24] to reduce the number of descriptors. Since it is difficult to directly use PCA to obtain good low-resolution descriptors [21], we use an alternative approach. Its basic idea is to partition the entire block into

four subblocks, as shown in Figure 6, and then use PCA to reduce the number of descriptors of each subblock into two values (descriptors), called low-resolution descriptors. Also, high-frequency descriptors in the original temporal-spectral block are all discarded because they are susceptible to noise [21]. With this arrangement, totally eight descriptors are used to represent a segment of 15-second music. Note that the actual duration of a segment used in the experiments is 14.04 seconds (though we still say 15 seconds) because some audio samples are lost after MP-3 compression and decompression in the experiments.

TABLE 2: Identification accuracy using high-resolution features.

	Uncompressed		192 k MP-3		96 k MP-3	
High-frequency descriptors	Used	Not used	Used	Not used	Used	Not used
Match in first one	100%	100%	100%	100%	94%	100%
Match in first 15	100%	100%	100%	100%	98%	100%

TABLE 3: Comparison of identification accuracies using low-resolution descriptors obtained by the proposed approach and by the averaging (avg) method [21].

	Uncompressed		192 k MP-3		96 k MP-3	
Method	Proposed	Avg.	Proposed	Avg.	Proposed	Avg.
Match in first one	99.3%	99.5%	99.1%	99.3%	90.1%	89.8%
Match in first 15	100%	100%	100%	100%	99.6%	99.5%

We now describe how to calculate low-resolution descriptors. Since using PCA for dimensionality reduction is a well-known approach, we only describe how to construct the covariance matrix for PCA computation and omit the computation of finding principal components. Suppose that there are N segments of music pieces in the database, with their descriptor matrices denoted as $A^{(1)}$ to $A^{(N)}$. To simplify the argument, we consider the subblock matrix $A_{1,1}^{(k)}$ (referring to Figure 6) in the following. Other subblocks can be computed by the same procedure. First, collect all subblocks from $A_{1,1}^{(k)}$ to form a big matrix as follows:

$$B = \begin{bmatrix} a_{1,1}^{(1)} & \cdots & a_{1,8}^{(1)} & a_{1,1}^{(2)} & \cdots & a_{1,8}^{(2)} & \cdots & a_{1,1}^{(N)} & \cdots & a_{1,8}^{(N)} \\ \vdots & \ddots & \vdots & \vdots & \ddots & \vdots & \cdots & \vdots & \ddots & \vdots \\ a_{15,1}^{(1)} & \cdots & a_{15,8}^{(1)} & a_{15,1}^{(2)} & \cdots & a_{15,8}^{(2)} & \cdots & a_{15,1}^{(N)} & \cdots & a_{15,8}^{(N)} \end{bmatrix}$$

$$= \begin{bmatrix} \uparrow & \cdots & \uparrow \\ \mathbf{b}_1 & \cdots & \mathbf{b}_{8N} \\ \downarrow & \cdots & \downarrow \end{bmatrix}.$$

(5)

Then, we may consider column vectors of matrix B as $\mathbf{b}_i$ vectors. Having the data vectors $\mathbf{b}_i$, the covariance matrix and, subsequently, the principal components can be found. By keeping only two principal components, we can obtain $\mathbf{c}_i = [c_{i,1} \ c_{i,2}]$ from $\mathbf{b}_i$. Since there are eight column vectors in a subblock, descriptors in $A_{1,1}^{(k)}$ are reduced to eight $\mathbf{c}_i$ ($8k-7 \le i \le 8k$) vectors. Next, we can rearrange the obtained $\mathbf{c}_i$ vectors as

$$C = \begin{bmatrix} c_{1,1} & c_{1,2} & c_{9,1} & c_{9,2} & \cdots & c_{8N-7,1} & c_{8N-7,2} \\ \vdots & \vdots & \vdots & \vdots & \cdots & \vdots & \vdots \\ c_{8,1} & c_{8,2} & c_{16,1} & c_{16,2} & \cdots & c_{8N,1} & c_{8N,2} \end{bmatrix}.$$

(6)

Again, by treating each row of matrix C as the data to be processed by PCA, we can compute the covariance matrix, and finally reduce each column vector to one value. Since there are two columns originally from one subblock, there are totally two (low-resolution) descriptors per subblock. Equivalently, a segment of 15-second music is represented by eight descriptors. During the computation, the principal components obtained in the first and the second steps should be stored in the database. When a query input (in the form of high-resolution descriptors) is supplied, these components are used to obtain the low-resolution descriptors for the input.

5. Threshold to Determine the Membership of the Query Input

Since, in practice, the database cannot collect all music soundtracks in the world, we have to have a strategy to determine if the query input is actually in the database or not. In our case, the decision is accomplished with the aid of a threshold. If the shortest distances between the input and the candidates are greater than a threshold, then the query input is not in the database; otherwise, it is in the database. Though the concept is simple, it is not trivial to determine the threshold [20].

Recall that when a query input is applied to the proposed system, the system computes the Euclidean distances between the low-resolution descriptors of the query input and those in the database. Accordingly, m (say, $m = 20$) segments of soundtracks from distinct titles are selected based on the computed distances. Next, the Euclidean distances between the query and the selected segments are computed again using full-resolution descriptors. By sorting the distances from small to large, the system creates a candidate list for the query input.

To compute the previously mentioned threshold, we examine two different methods. In the first method (method I), we define the "first" distance d_1 as the (full-resolution) distance associated with the first candidate in the list. Similarly, the "second" distance d_2 is the distance associated with the second candidate, as shown in Figure 7. The method to compute the first and second distances is used both in training and in identification. For the training phase, assume that there are N_T soundtracks used. For a segment from a soundtrack indexed n, let the first distance be $d_1(n)$ and the second distance be $d_2(n)$. The threshold T_A is then computed as

$$T_A = 0.5 \cdot \left(\sum_{n=1}^{N_T} d_1(n) + \sum_{n=1}^{N_T} d_2(n) \right).$$

(7)

During the identification phase, the first distance for the query input is computed. If the first distance is smaller than the threshold T_A, the query input is determined to be highly similar to the top soundtrack title in the candidate list. Otherwise, the query input is not inside the database.

In addition to method I, we also propose an alternative method (method II) to compute the first and second distances

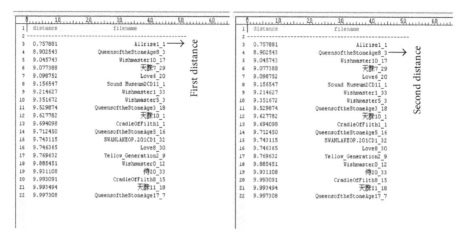

FIGURE 7: The first and second distances in method I.

and the threshold. Referring to Figure 8, the first distance $d'_1(n)$ of method II for a training segment in soundtrack n is

$$d'_1(n) = d_1(n) \div \frac{\sum_{m=2}^{M} d_m(n)}{M-1}, \tag{8}$$

where $d_m(n)$ is the distance associated with the mth candidate in the list, and M is a constant. Based on our experiment, $M = 10$ is sufficient. By the same arrangement, the second distance $d'_2(n)$ is calculated as

$$d'_2(n) = d_2(n) \div \frac{\sum_{m=3}^{M+1} d_m(n)}{M-1}. \tag{9}$$

Similar to (7), the threshold T'_A is determined as

$$T'_A = 0.5 \cdot \left(\sum_{n=1}^{N_T} d'_1(n) + \sum_{n=1}^{N_T} d'_2(n) \right). \tag{10}$$

During identification phase, if the computed distance d'_1 is greater than T'_A, the query input is determined as not in the database. Otherwise, the query input is highly similar to the top soundtrack title in the candidate list.

6. Experiments and Results

Before conducting the experiments, we collect 750 soundtracks from many CD titles for constructing the database and for identification. In the experiments, 30 seconds of music is excerpted from the soundtracks as the reference items to be identified. Then, low- and full-resolution descriptors of the reference items are calculated and stored in the database. We also randomly excerpt 15-second query items from the reference items. Note that a query item may start from any sample on the first half of the reference. To test the identification accuracy for compressed audio, the 15-second query inputs are also encoded and then decoded with an MP-3 coder with bitrates of 192 k and 96 k, respectively. However, the database only contains descriptors from the uncompressed items. In addition, the principal components are also obtained using uncompressed items.

TABLE 4: Comparison of search time between k-d tree search and linear search.

	K-d tree	Linear search
Average time	0.255 sec	3.23 sec

Several experiments are conducted to examine the performance of the proposed system. The first experiment checks the identification accuracy using high-resolution descriptors. The second one compares the relative identification accuracy between the proposed method (in Section 4.2) and the method given in [21]. The third experiment compares the search speed by using the linear search and k-d tree search. The next experiment intends to determine a suitable value of M used in (8) and (9). Having the value of M, we report the identification accuracy using a multiresolution strategy in experiment five. In this experiment, both method I and method II are examined. To have a complete comparison between method I and II, we also report the results in terms of the ROC (receiver operating characteristics) [25] curve and the DET-like (detection error tradeoff) [26] curve but without logarithm.

6.1. Experiment One: Identification Accuracy Using High-Resolution Descriptors. The first experiment is to examine the identification accuracy using the high-resolution MPEG-7 audio signature descriptors (without reduction). To evaluate the influences of high-frequency descriptors, we also examine the accuracies with and without using high-frequency (greater than 2.5 kHz) descriptors. The results are given in Table 2. In the table, "match in first one" is the rate that the query input is correctly identified with the shortest distance among all reference items. Similarly, "match in first 15" is the rate that the query is correctly identified within a list of 15 reference items sorted by distance. The results indicate that high-resolution descriptors have very good identification accuracy. Also, for uncompressed or 192 k MP-3 items, whether using high-frequency descriptors does not affect the identification accuracy. However, for 96 k MP-3 items, discarding high-frequency descriptors greatly improves the accuracy.

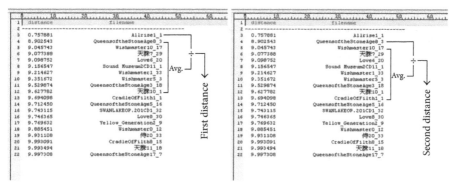

FIGURE 8: The first and second distances in method II.

6.2. Experiment Two: Identification Accuracy Using Low-Resolution Descriptors.

The second experiment compares the relative identification accuracies of the proposed dimensionality reduction technique and the averaging method proposed in [21]. In this experiment, eight descriptors are used to represent one segment of music (15 seconds). The results are shown in Table 3. For this experiment, the accuracy rate in "match in first 15" is more important than the figure in "match in first one" because the low-resolution descriptors are used to produce a candidate list. Therefore, it is acceptable as long as the correct item is within the list, as the high-resolution descriptors are to be used in the second stage. In this regard, the proposed approach is slightly better than the averaging method proposed in [21] for 96 k MP-3 query inputs.

6.3. Experiment Three: Time for k-d Tree Search and Linear Search.

The third experiment compares the time to generate a list of 20 candidates by using k-d tree search and linear (exhausted) search for low-resolution descriptors. The computing time is obtained by averaging the required time in ten trials. For each trial, 500 query items are randomly selected among the 750 available items. The experimental platform is a personal computer with a 1.6 GHz Pentium CPU and 1.5 GB memory. The program is written in C with a Borland C++ compiler. The results are shown in Table 4. The results show that we can increase the search time by 10-fold if the low-resolution descriptors are embedded in the k-d tree structure.

6.4. Experiment Four: Determination of M in Method II.

The fourth experiment is to determine the number M in method II. Recall that the thresholds in both methods are computed based on high-resolution descriptors. To determine the optimal value of M, we vary this value from one to eighteen in (8) and (9) to compute the threshold T'_A and then to perform identification. Note that method II is degenerated to method I if $M = 1$. In this experiment, 96 k MP-3-coded items are used as the query. In addition, we deliberately keep the high-frequency descriptors in computing the distances because keeping them makes it easier to examine the influence of M versus identification rate (defined in experiment five). The experimental results are given in Figure 9. The results show that when M is equal or greater than 10, the identification rate

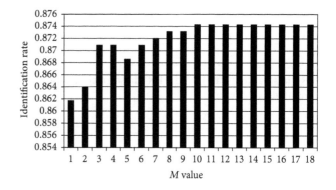

FIGURE 9: The identification rate versus the number M for 96 k MP-3 query inputs.

remains almost constant. Therefore, $M = 10$ is sufficient for method II. This value is then used in experiment five.

6.5. Experiment Five: Comparison between Method I and Method II.

The fifth experiment compares the identification rates between method I and method II. The thresholds are calculated using (7) and (10), respectively. In this experiment, 375 of the 750 15-second items are randomly chosen for training (i.e., to obtain the thresholds). The rest of 375 items are for query. Note that all of the items are excerpted from the reference items in the database. In addition, we test other 500 query items (also with duration of 15 sec) not excerpted from database references.

Since some query inputs are not in the database, we also need to consider the situations of falsely identifying an outside database item as one inside the database, and vice versa. Suppose that T_d query items are actually inside the database and T_o query items are not inside the database. Assume that the identification system correctly identifies N_d inside-database query item, erroneously rejects N_r inside-database query items, and erroneously accepts N_a outside database query items. Then, the IDR (identification rate),

Table 5: Comparison of identification performance using method I and method II with the use of high-frequency descriptors.

	Uncompressed		192 k MP-3		96 k MP-3	
	Method I	Method II	Method I	Method II	Method I	Method II
IDR	98.8%	99.9%	99%	99.7%	84.1%	87.4%
FAR	2.1%	0.2%	1.8%	0.2%	0.4%	0.2%
FRR	0.0%	0.0%	0.0%	0.5%	36.6%	29.6%
ACC	98.4%	99.9%	98.9%	99.5%	71.8%	76.8%

Table 6: Comparison of method I and method II for IDR, FAR, and FRR with high-frequency descriptors removed.

	Uncompressed		192 k MP-3		96 k MP-3	
	Method I	Method II	Method I	Method II	Method I	Method II
IDR	99.1%	99.7%	98.9%	99.7%	99.0%	99.7%
FAR	1.5%	0.2%	1.9%	0.2%	1.6%	0.2%
FRR	0.3%	0.4%	0.2%	0.4%	0.3%	0.6%
ACC	98.7%	99.5%	98.5%	99.5%	98.6%	99.4%

FAR (false-accept rate), and FRR (false-rejection rate) are computed as follows:

$$IDR = \frac{N_d}{T_d - N_r} \qquad (11)$$

$$FAR = \frac{N_a}{T_o} \qquad (12)$$

$$FRR = \frac{N_r}{T_d}. \qquad (13)$$

In addition, the accuracy of the system is computed as

$$ACC = \frac{N_d + N_o}{T_d + T_o}, \qquad (14)$$

where N_o is the number of query items correctly identified as outside-database items and can be computed as $N_o = T_o - N_a$.

In this experiment, the low-resolution descriptors are used to find 20 candidates. Next, high-resolution descriptors are used to find the best-matched one in the list. If the distance associated with the best-match is greater than the threshold, the query input is determined as not in the database. Otherwise, the query input is identified as the best-matched one. In this experiment, high-frequency descriptors are kept in the comparison. With the use of (11) to (14), the average values after four trials are given in Table 5. From the results we know that the system does not perform well for identifying 96 k MP-3 query items. This is mainly due to high distortion in high-frequency descriptors. A similar phenomenon can also be observed in Table 2. Later on, we will repeat this experiment but discard high-frequency descriptors.

To further examine the performance differences between method I and method II, we again use 96 k MP-3 items as the query inputs. But this time we vary the threshold values (for both methods) and then record the IDR, FAR, and FRR values. The results are presented as ROC curves [25] and DET-like curves [26] (but without logarithm), as shown in

Figures 10 and 11, respectively. The ROC curve plots FAR versus TPR (true positive rate), which is defined as

$$TPR = \frac{N_d}{T_d}. \qquad (15)$$

Conceptually, a better classifier should have a higher TPR for a fixed FAR. Therefore, a better classifier should have an ROC curve closer to the left-upper corner. With this interpretation, from Figure 10 we know that method II is a better classifier.

In this experiment, we also show DET-like curves. A "true" DET curve plots FAR versus FRR using logarithm scales. In our case, however, we do not use logarithm scales to exhibit the similarity between ROC and DET curves. Again, conceptually we know that a better classifier should have a lower FRR over a fixed FAR. Thus, a better classifier should have a curve closer to the left-bottom corner. By examining Figure 11, we again confirm that method II is a better method.

Since the high-frequency descriptors actually affect the identification rate at low bitrates, we again repeat this experiment without using high-frequency descriptors. The results are given in Table 6. By comparing the results in Tables 5 and 6, we know that removing high-frequency descriptors slightly reduces the accuracy of uncompressed items. However, it greatly improves the accuracy for 96 k MP-3 items. Since method II has an accuracy of at least 99.4% in all cases, it is highly plausible to identify copyrighted audio materials using this method.

7. Conclusion

In this paper, we propose a system using a multiresolution strategy to identify whether a piece of unknown music is identical to one of the pieces in the database. In the system, high-resolution descriptors are MPEG-7 audio signature descriptors, and the low-resolution descriptors are obtained from high-resolution descriptors with the aid of PCA to reduce their dimensionality. Experimental results show that

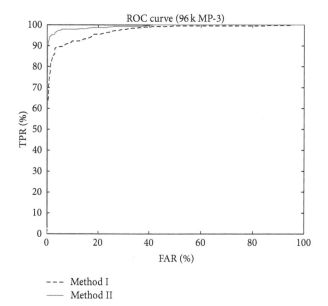

FIGURE 10: The ROC curves for both methods.

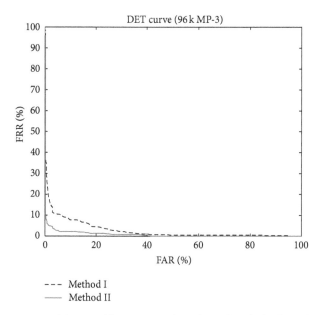

FIGURE 11: The DET-like curves without logarithm for both methods.

low-resolution descriptors still have high identification accuracies. To reduce the time to generate the candidate list, we use the k-d tree structure to store low-resolution descriptors. Experimental results show that using k-d tree structure increases the search time by ten-folds. Since not every piece of query input is within the database, we also proposed two methods to determine the distance thresholds. Experimental results show that the proposed method II provides an accuracy of 99.4%. Therefore, the proposed system can be used in real applications, such as identifying copyrighted audio files circulated over the Internet. As it can be easily extended to operate with multiple computers, the proposed system is a plausible starting point to construct a large, operable database.

Acknowledgment

This work was supported in part by National Science Council of Taiwan through Grants NSC 94-2213-E-027-042 and 99-2221-E-027-097.

References

[1] For a brief description of the bill, please refer to, http://en.wikipedia.org/wiki/SOPA.

[2] R. Eklund, "Audio watermarking techniques," http://www.musemagic.com/papers/watermark.html.

[3] J. S. R. Jang and H. R. Lee, "A general framework of progressive filtering and its application to query by singing/humming," *IEEE Transactions on Audio, Speech and Language Processing*, vol. 16, no. 2, pp. 350–358, 2008.

[4] S. Baluja and M. Covell, "Audio fingerprinting: combining computer vision & data stream processing," in *Proceedings of the IEEE International Conference on Acoustics, Speech and Signal Processing (ICASSP '07)*, pp. II213–II216, Honolulu, Hawaii, USA, April 2007.

[5] Shazam, http://www.shazam.com/music/web/home.html.

[6] A. Wang, "The Shazam music recognition service," *Communications of the ACM*, vol. 49, no. 8, pp. 44–48, 2006.

[7] V. Chandrasekha, M. Sharifi, and D. A. Ross, "Survey and evaluation of audio fingerprinting schemes for mobile query-by-example applications," in *Proceedinjgs of the 12th International Conference on Music Information Retrieval*, pp. 801–806, Miami, Fla, USA, October 2011.

[8] J. A. Haitsma and T. Kalker, "A highly robust audio fingerprinting system," in *Proceedinjgs of the 12th International Conference on Music Information Retrieval*, pp. 107–115, Paris, France, October 2002.

[9] C. J. C. Burges, J. C. Platt, and S. Jana, "Distortion discriminant analysis for audio fingerprinting," *IEEE Transactions on Speech and Audio Processing*, vol. 11, no. 3, pp. 165–174, 2003.

[10] Official website: http://musicbrainz.org/.

[11] Official website: http://www.audiblemagic.com/.

[12] Official website: http://www.gracenote.com/.

[13] http://en.wikipedia.org/wiki/Acoustic_fingerprint.

[14] P. J. O. Doets, M. M. Gisbert, and R. L. Lagendijk, "On the comparison of audio fingerprints for extracting quality parameters of compressed audio," in *Security, Steganography, and Watermarking of Multimedia Contents VIII*, vol. 6072 of *Proceedings of SPIE*, pp. 60720L-1–60720L-12, San Jose, Calif, USA, January 2006.

[15] F. Nack and A. T. Lindsay, "Everything you wanted to know about MPEG-7: part 1," *IEEE Multimedia*, vol. 6, no. 3, pp. 65–77, 1999.

[16] F. Nack and A. Lindsay, "Everything you wanted to know about MPEG-7: part 2," *IEEE Multimedia*, vol. 6, no. 4, pp. 64–73, 1999.

[17] ISO/IEC, Information Technology—Multimedia Content Description Interface -Part 4: Audio, IS 15938-4, 2002.

[18] H. Crysandt, "Music identification with MPEG-7," in *Proceedings of the 115th AES Convention*, October 2003, Paper 5967.

[19] O. Hellmuth, E. Allamance, M. Cremer, H. Grossmann, J. Herre, and T. Kastner, "Using MPEG-7 audio fingerprinting in real-world application," in *Proceedings of the 115th AES Convention*, October 2003, Paper 5961.

[20] H.-G. Kim, N. Moreau, and T. Sikora, *MPEG-7 Audio and Beyond*, John Wiley & Sons, 2005.

[21] J.-Y. Lee and S. D. You, "Dimension-reduction technique for MPEG-7 Audio Descriptors," in *Proceedings of the 6th Pacific Rim Conference on Multimedia (PCM '05)*, vol. 3768 of *Lecture Notes in Computer Science*, pp. 526–537, 2005.

[22] J. L. Bentley, "Multidimensional binary search trees used for associative searching," *Communications of the ACM*, vol. 18, no. 9, pp. 509–517, 1975.

[23] Open source program for k-d tree, http://www.cs.umd.edu/~mount/ANN.

[24] J. Shlens, "A tutorial on principal component analysis," http://www.snl.salk.edu/~shlens/pca.pdf.

[25] T. Fawcell, "ROC graphs: notes and practical considerations for researchers," Tech. Rep., HP Lab, 2004.

[26] A. Martin, G. Doddington, T. Kamm, M. Ordowski, and M. Przybocki, "The DET curve in assessment of detection task performance," in *Proceedings of the Eurospeech*, vol. 4, pp. 1899–1903, Rhodes, Greece, September 1997.

12

Memory-Based Multiagent Coevolution Modeling for Robust Moving Object Tracking

Yanjiang Wang, Yujuan Qi, and Yongping Li

College of Information and Control Engineering, China University of Petroleum, No. 66, Changjiang West Road, Economic and Technological Development Zone, Qingdao 266580, China

Correspondence should be addressed to Yujuan Qi; qiyj@upc.edu.cn

Academic Editors: P. Agarwal, S. Balochian, V. Bhatnagar, J. Yan, and Y. Zhang

The three-stage human brain memory model is incorporated into a multiagent coevolutionary process for finding the best match of the appearance of an object, and a memory-based multiagent coevolution algorithm for robust tracking the moving objects is presented in this paper. Each agent can remember, retrieve, or forget the appearance of the object through its own memory system by its own experience. A number of such memory-based agents are randomly distributed nearby the located object region and then mapped onto a 2D lattice-like environment for predicting the new location of the object by their coevolutionary behaviors, such as competition, recombination, and migration. Experimental results show that the proposed method can deal with large appearance changes and heavy occlusions when tracking a moving object. It can locate the correct object after the appearance changed or the occlusion recovered and outperforms the traditional particle filter-based tracking methods.

1. Introduction

The problem of object tracking is often posed as that of estimating the trajectory of objects in an image plane as objects move in a scene [1]. Although considerable efforts have been made in establishing a robust tracking framework in the research literature, the problem still remains challenging when appearance abrupt changes or occlusions occur. To address these challenges, in the literature tremendous attempts have been made in characterizing appearance models which are able to handle appearance changes. In this context, most of the extant methods tend to apply a total model updating mechanism for template updating in which the initial template model is updated gradually based on the estimated information, for example particle filters (PF). However, if an object is heavily occluded or its appearance changes abruptly, the total model updating based PF (TMU-PF) will gradually deviate from the target.

Recently, a lot of modifications have been made for improving the performance of particle filters. For example, Zhou et al. [2] presented an approach that incorporated appearance-adaptive models to stabilize the tracker. They made three extensions: (a) an observation model arising from an adaptive appearance model, (b) an adaptive velocity motion model with adaptive noise variance, and (c) an adaptive number of particles. Li et al. [3] proposed a robust observation model to address appearance changes. Wang et al. [4, 5] developed an SMOG appearance model and an SMOG-based similarity measure to deal with appearance variations. Zhang et al. [6] embedded an adaptive appearance model into a particle filter to address the appearance changes and proposed an occlusion handling scheme to deal with occlusion situations. On the other hand, some researchers have incorporated other optimization algorithms into particle filer to enhance the performance. For example, in [7], CamShift was used into the probabilistic framework of particle filter as an optimization scheme for proposal distribution such that both the tracking robustness and computational efficiency are improved. Shan et al. [8] incorporated the mean-shift (MS) optimization algorithm into a particle filter framework to improve the sampling efficiency. Zhou et al. [9] presented a scale invariant feature transform (SIFT) based mean shift algorithm for object tracking, which improved the tracking performance of the classical mean shift and SIFT tracking algorithms in complicated real scenarios. Zhao and Li [10] applied particle swarm optimization (PSO) to find high likelihood areas where the particles could be distributed even though the dynamic model of the object could not be obtained. Zhou et al. [11] combined multiband Generalized Cross Correlation, KF, and Weighted Probabilistic Data Association within the particle filtering framework, which improves the performance of the algorithm in noisy scenarios. Most of the above methods applied a total model updating mechanism for template updating in which the initial template model is updated gradually based on the estimated information by particle filters. However, if an object is heavily occluded or its appearance changes abruptly, the total model updating based PF (TMU-PF) will gradually deviate from the target.

To tackle the drawback of the TMU-PF, Montemayor et al. [12] introduced memory strategies into PF to store the states of particles, which can deal with some occlusion situations. Mikami et al. [13] proposed a memory-based particle filter (MPF) to handle facial pose variation by predicting the prior distribution of the target state in future time steps. However, both of the methods are neither biologically motivated nor cognitively inspired. They just apply memory to store the states of particles and could not cope with situations with sudden changes.

It is well known that humans can track and recognize an object with little difficulty in the case of appearance changes and partial occlusions. This capability of human beings benefits from the human's memory system. When humans perceive something, the related information which is stored in their memory can be recalled. As a function of information retention organs in the brain, the mechanism of memory system has been extensively studied in neural science, biopsychology, cognitive science, and cognitive informatics [14, 15].

Inspired by the way humans perceive the environment, in this paper, we present a memory-based multiagent coevolution model for tracking the moving objects. The three-stage human brain memory mechanism is incorporated into a multiagent coevolutionary process for finding a best match of the appearance of the object. Each agent can remember, retrieve, or forget the appearance of the object through its memory system by its own experience. A number of such memory-based agents are randomly distributed nearby the located object region and then mapped onto a 2D lattice-like environment for predicting the new location of the object by their coevolutionary behaviors, such as competition, recombination, and migration. Experimental results show that the proposed method can deal with large appearance changes and heavy occlusions when tracking a moving object. It can locate the correct object after the appearance changed or the occlusion recovered.

The remainder of this paper is organized as follows. In Section 2, we will first propose the memory-based multiagent coevolution model including the definitions of each behavior involved. Section 3 gives the detailed description of the memory modeling of an agent and the object appearance template updating process for each agent. Then the color object modeling and the proposed tracking algorithm are described in Section 4. Finally, the performance of our tracking algorithm is verified on different standard video

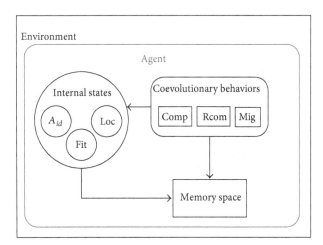

FIGURE 1: Memory-based agent model.

sequences and some conclusions are summarized in Sections 5 and 6.

2. Memory-Based Multiagent Coevolution Modeling

2.1. Memory-Based Multiagent Model. According to [16], an agent can be defined as an intelligent entity that resides in an environment and can act autonomously and collaboratively. It is driven by certain purposes and has some reactive behaviors. Based on this idea, many agent-based applications are reported during past years, such as image feature extraction [17], image segmentation [18], and optimization problems [19–24]. In our previous work [25, 26], we also proposed an evolutionary agent model for color-based face detection and location.

In this paper, we will present a memory-based multiagent model (MMAM) for moving object tracking. Each agent represents a candidate target region in a video frame; it lives in a lattice-like environment, and its main task is to compete or cooperate with its neighbor agents to continuously improve its own fitness by exhibiting its behaviors.

The schematic diagram of the proposed MMMA is shown in Figure 1.

More specifically, the memory-based multiagent model (MMAM) for object tracking can be defined as a 7-tuples: $\langle A_{id}, \text{Loc}, \text{Fit}, \text{MS}, \text{Comp}, \text{Rcom}, \text{Mig} \rangle$. Where A_{id} denotes the identity of an agent; Loc represents the position of an agent in the image, that is, the center of a candidate target; Fit symbolizes its fitness, which is defined by the similarity between the candidate target and the object template; and MS = {USTMS, STMS, LTMS} is a set of hominine memory spaces of an agent for information storage, where USTMS, STMS, and LTMS stand for the ultrashort-term memory space, short-term memory space, and long-term memory space, respectively.

The above 4 parameters describe the internal states of an agent. While Comp, Rcom, and Mig describe the external coevolutionary behaviors of an agent, where Comp represents the competition behavior, Rcom denotes the recombination behavior, while Mig refers to the migration behavior.

Suppose all the agents inhabit in a lattice-like environment, A, which is called an agent lattice, as shown in Figure 2. Each agent is fixed on a lattice point and it can only interact with its 4 neighbors. The size of A is $N \times N$ and the agent located at (i, j) is denoted by $A_{i,j}, i, j = 1, 2, \ldots, N$. Each agent can compete or cooperate with its 4 neighbors in order to improve its fitness.

The mapping process is described as follows.

First, it randomly generates $N \times N$ agents near the located object region at begining. The first generated agent is placed at $A_{1,1}$, the second agent is placed at $A_{1,2}, \ldots$, the Nth agent is placed at $A_{1,N}$, the $(N + 1)$th agent is placed at $A_{2,1}, \ldots$, and the final agent $(N \times N)$th is placed at $A_{N,N}$. The neighbors of agent $A_{i,j}$ are defined as $Nb_{i,j} = \{A_{i-1,j}, A_{i+1,j}, A_{i,j-1}, A_{i,j+1}\}$. For the agents at the four edges of the lattice, we define

$$
\begin{aligned}
A_{0,j} &= A_{N,j}, & A_{i,0} &= A_{i,N}, \\
A_{N+1,j} &= A_{1,j}, & A_{i,N+1} &= A_{i,1}.
\end{aligned}
\tag{1}
$$

According to the above definition, the neighbors of an agent on the lattice are not its real neighbors in the video image. Because each agent is generated randomly and can only evolve with its neighbors on the lattice-like environment, the mapping process can also be thought as a natural selection before their coevolution.

2.2. Multiagent Coevolutionary Behaviors. There are three coevolutionary behaviors for each agent, that is, competition, recombination, and migration. The three behaviors are defined as follows.

Definition 1 (Comp (competition behavior)). Comp means that an agent will contend with other agents for its survival.

For each agent $A_{i,j}$, if $\text{Fit}(A_{i,j}) < \text{Fit}(Nb\max_{i,j})$, where $Nb\max_{i,j}$ is the agent with maximum fitness among its 4 neighbors, then $A_{i,j}$ will be replaced by the following:

$$
A_{i,j}^l = \begin{cases}
\underline{l}, & \left(Nb\max_{i,j}^l + U(-1, 1) \right. \\
& \left. \times \left(Nb\max_{i,j}^l - A_{i,j}^l\right)\right) < \underline{l}, \\
\bar{l}, & \left(Nb\max_{i,j}^l + U(-1, 1) \right. \\
& \left. \times \left(Nb\max_{i,j}^l - A_{i,j}^l\right)\right) > \bar{l}, \\
Nb\max_{i,j}^l + U(-1, 1) & \\
\times \left(Nb\max_{i,j}^l - A_{i,j}^l\right), & \text{otherwise,}
\end{cases}
\tag{2}
$$

where $U(-1, 1)$ is a uniform random number in $[-1, 1]$, l denotes the location of agent $A_{i,j}$ in the video frame, $l = (x, y)$, $L = [\underline{l}, \bar{l}]$ represents the whole searching space, that is, the video size, $\underline{l} = [\underline{x}, \underline{y}], \bar{l} = [\bar{x}, \bar{y}]$.

Definition 2 (Rcom (recombination behavior)). Rcom means that an agent may exchange the x or y coordinate with other agents. It is similar to the crossover operator in genetic algorithms.

For each agent $A_{i,j}$, given a recombination probability P_r, if $U(0, 1) < P_r$, exchange the x or y coordinate of $A_{i,j}$ and $Nb\max_{i,j}$, a new agent will be created, $Ar_{i,j}$. If $\text{Fit}(A_{i,j}) > \text{Fit}(Ar_{i,j})$, $A_{i,j}$ will continue to exist in the lattice; otherwise it will be replaced by the following:

$$
Ar_{i,j} = \begin{cases}
\left(A_{i,j}^x, Nb\max_{i,j}^y\right), & U(0, 1) < 0.5, \\
\left(Nb\max_{i,j}^x, A_{i,j}^y\right), & \text{else.}
\end{cases}
\tag{3}
$$

Definition 3 (Mig (migration behavior)). Mig means that an agent can move to another location by some random steps in the image other than the lattice it locates at. It is similar to the mutation operator in genetic algorithms.

For each agent $A_{i,j}$, the migration behavior will occur according to a migration probability P_m. if $U(0, 1) < P_m$, $A_{i,j}$ will be replaced by the following:

$$
Am_{i,j}^l = \begin{cases}
\underline{l}, & A_{i,j}^l + U^l(-10, 10) < \underline{l}, \\
\bar{l}, & A_{i,j}^l + U^l(-10, 10) > \bar{l}, \\
A_{i,j}^l + U^l(-10, 10), & \text{otherwise,}
\end{cases}
\tag{4}
$$

where $U(-10, 10)$ is a uniform random number in $[-10, 10]$; that is, the migration steps are randomly generated within $(-10, 10)$ pixels for i and j, respectively.

3. Memory Modeling for an Agent

3.1. Three-Stage Human Brain Memory Modeling for Appearance Updating. As a faculty of information retention organs in the brain, memory has been intensively studied in psychology, neural science, and cognitive science, and several memory models have been proposed since the late 19th century. In 1890, James first divided the human memory into three components: after-image memory, the primary memory, and the secondary memory [27]. Atkinson and Shiffrin modeled the human memory as a sequence of three stages: the sensory memory, short-term memory, and long-term memory [28] (also known as the multistore model). Baddeley and Hitch proposed a multicomponent model of working memory where a central executive responsible for control processes and two slave systems providing modality-specific buffer storage [29]. Recently, Wang proposed a logical architecture of memories in the brain which includes four parts: (a) the sensory buffer memory; (b) the short-term memory; (c) the long-term memory; and (d) the action buffer memory [15, 30]. According to contemporary cognitive psychology, the popular model of a basic human brain memory includes three stages: ultrashort-term memory (USTM), short-term memory (STM), and long-term memory (LTM), as shown in Figure 3 [31].

Each stage includes three processes: (a) encoding, (b) storage, and (c) retrieval. "Encoding" (also referred to as registration) is the process of forwarding physical sensory input into one's memory. It is considered as the first step in memory information processing. "Storage" is the process of retaining information whether in the sensory memory,

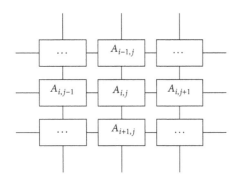

FIGURE 2: Model of the agent lattice.

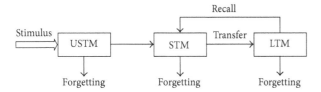

FIGURE 3: Three-stage human brain memory model.

the short-term memory, or the more permanent long-term memory. "Retrieval" (also referred to as "recall") is to call back the stored information in response to some cues for use in a process or activity.

The memorization process can be described as follows.

(1) USTM is used to store the basic cognitive information.

(2) STM, which in the recent literature has been referred to as working memory, is used to make decision. The information stored in STM includes the new information from USTM, the information processed in STM, or the information recalled from LTM. Therefore, STM can be considered as a complicated system for information storing and processing.

(3) LTM is a library used to store experienced knowledge which can inspire the individual to recall every thing that had happened, cognize all kinds of models, and solve problems (e.g., tracking problems in our work).

(4) Forgetting is a special function of memory which helps the information either not always recalled or not commonly used to be lost from memory.

According to the above three-stage human memory model, the appearance template updating model of an agent can be described as shown in Figure 4,

where the input of the model is the candidate template estimated by the Loc of an agent in the current video frame while the output is the updated template for prediction in the next frame. USTMS, STMS, and LTMS represent the three-stage memories, respectively. They are defined as follows.

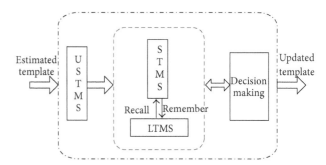

FIGURE 4: Three-stage memory model for appearance template updating.

Definition 4 (memory space (MS)). A 3-tuple which is used to store the current estimated appearance template and the past templates. Each element in MS is a memory space:

$$MS = \{USTMS, STMS, LTMS\}. \tag{5}$$

Definition 5 (USTMS). A one-element set for storing the estimated model p in the current video frame, which simulates the stage of ultrashort-term memory of human brain:

$$USTMS = \{p\}. \tag{6}$$

Definition 6 (STMS). A set of K_s temporary templates, which imitates the stage of short-term memory of human brain. Let q_i denote the ith template in STMS; then

$$STMS = \{q_i, i = 1, 2, \ldots, K_s\}. \tag{7}$$

Definition 7 (LTMS). A set of K_l remembered templates, which simulates the dynamic stage of the long-term memory of human brain. Let q_{Mj} stand for the jth remembered template in LTMS:

$$LTMS = \{q_{Mj}, j = 1, 2, \ldots, K_l\}. \tag{8}$$

The templates stored in STMS include the estimated template transferred from USTMS, the updated templates in STMS, or the templates recalled from LTMS.

According to the theory of cognitive psychology, only the information which is stimulated repeatedly can be stored into LTMS. Therefore, we define a parameter β for each template in STMS to determine whether the templates in STMS can be stored into LTMS or not, where β is a counter indicating the number of successful matches. The bigger β is, the more probably the template can be stored into LTMS.

More specifically, for all $q_i \in$ STMS, $i = 1, 2, \ldots, K_s$, If $q_i.\beta > T_M$ (a predefined threshold), the template will be remembered and stored into LTMS.

The process of template updating can be briefly described as follows.

First, the estimated template of the current frame is stored into USTMS and checked against the current template in STMS (the first one). If they are matched, update the template; otherwise check against the remaining templates in STMS and then LTMS in turn for a match. If a match exists, it will

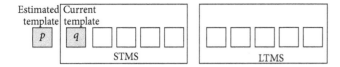

FIGURE 5: Initialization step.

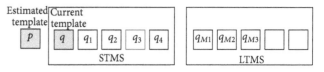

(a) A match is found in STMS

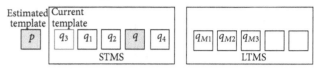

(b) Updating STMS

FIGURE 6: Illustration of updating process in STMS.

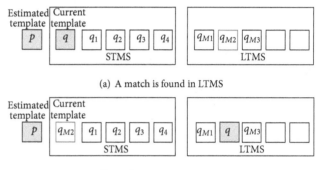

(a) A match is found in LTMS

(b) Updating STMS and LTMS

FIGURE 7: Illustration of recalling and remembering.

be selected for the new template. Meanwhile the STMS and LTMS are updated by some behaviors, such as remembering, recall, and forgetting. These behaviors are defined as follows.

Definition 8 (remembering). An action that a template is stored into LTMS.

If there is no match in STMS and LTMS, and the STMS is full and the last template in STMS (denoted by q_{K_s}) is satisfied with $q_{K_s}.\beta > T_M$, then q_{K_s} will be remembered into LTMS and replaced by q_{K_s-1}. In such a circumstance, the estimated template will be reserved for the next estimation.

Definition 9 (recall). An action that a matched template is loaded from LTMS.

If a match is found in LTMS, the matched template will be extracted and used as the current object template.

Definition 10 (forgetting). An action that a template is removed from either of STMS or LTMS.

If the LTMS is full and $q_{K_s}.\beta > T_M$, the oldest template in LTMS will be forgotten in order to remember q_{K_s}.

3.2. Detailed Description of Memory-Based Appearance Updating. According to the above model, the memory-based appearance template updating algorithm can be described as follows.

Step 1 (Initialization). For each agent, store the estimated template (candidate object) p into the USTMS and the current template q into the STMS; set $q.\beta = 1$ and the LTMS to be empty, where p and q are determined by the initial target region, as shown in Figure 5. It is worth mentioning that the STMS and LTMS will be filled up gradually after several time steps during tracking.

Step 2. Calculate the similarity coefficient $\rho = \rho[p, q]$, if $\rho > T_{dc}$, update the current object template by the following:

$$q = (1 - \alpha)q + \alpha \cdot p,$$
$$q.\beta = q.\beta + 1, \tag{9}$$

where T_{dc} is a predefined threshold for current template matching and α is the updating rate.

Step 3. If $\rho \leq T_{dc}$, check against the remaining templates in STMS for a match, if

$$\rho[p, q_i] > T_{ds}, \quad i = 1, \ldots, K_s - 1, \tag{10}$$

update the matched template by the following:

$$q_i = (1 - \alpha) \cdot q_i + \alpha \cdot p,$$
$$q_i.\beta = q_i.\beta + 1, \tag{11}$$

where T_{ds} is the threshold for template-matching in STMS.

Then, exchange the current template and the matched one, as shown in Figure 6.

For example, if q_3 is a matched template found in STMS (as shown in Figure 6(a)), then it will be moved to the top location in STMS and used as the current template, while the previous current template q will be moved to the original location of q_3 as shown in Figure 6(b).

Step 4. If $\rho[p, q_i] \leq T_{ds}$, check in LTMS for a match, if

$$\rho[p, q_{Mj}] > T_{dl}, \quad j = 1, \ldots, K_l, \tag{12}$$

where T_{dl} is the threshold for template-matching in LTMS. Then update the matched template by the following:

$$q_{Mj} = (1 - \alpha)q_{Mj} + \alpha \cdot p,$$
$$q_{Mj}.\beta = q_{Mj}.\beta + 1, \tag{13}$$

and then recall the matched one to use as the new object template and remember the current template q, as shown in Figure 7.

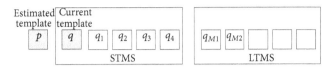

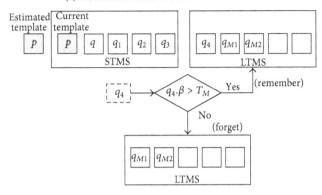

(a) No match is found in both STMS and LTMS

(b) Updating STMS and LTMS

FIGURE 8: Illustration of updating STMS and LTMS when no match is found in both memory spaces.

Step 5. If $\rho[p, q_{Mj}] \leq T_{dl}$, it means that there is no any match in STMS and LTMS. The estimated template p is stored into STMS and used as the new object template (set $p.\beta = 1$), as seen in Figure 8. Meanwhile, if the STMS reaches its maximum capacity, remember or forget the oldest template in STMS (i.e., q_{K_s-1}) by the following substeps.

(1) If $q_{K_s-1}.\beta > T_M$ and the LTMS is full, forget the oldest template in LTMS (i.e., q_{MK_l}) and remember q_{K_s-1}.

(2) If $q_{K_s-1}.\beta \leq T_M$, forget q_{K_s-1}.

As shown in Figure 8, when no match is found in both memory spaces, the current estimated template p is stored into STMS, while q_4 (i.e., $K_s - 1 = 4$) is either remembered ($q_4.\beta > T_M$) or forgotten ($q_4.\beta \leq T_M$).

Note that the templates in STMS and LTMS are stored in chronological order; that is, if a template is stored into STMS or LTMS earlier, it will move to the subsequent locations in order to make rooms for the newly reached templates.

4. Moving Object Tracking by MMAM

4.1. Object Detection and Modeling. To detect a color object, it is very important to obtain an effective color model to accurately represent and identify the object under various illumination conditions. In this paper, we use a histogram-based nonparametric modeling technique in YCbCr color space to model an object [32], which is much robust to lighting variations.

Giving the distribution of colors in an object region, let $px_{i,j}$ be a pixel location inside the object region with the origin at the center of the object region, the non-parametric

distribution of the object, Q, can be represented by the following [32]:

$$Q = \{q_u; u = 1, 2, \ldots, m\}, \tag{14}$$

where

$$q_u = C \sum_{i=1,j=1}^{x,y} k\left(\left\|px_{i,j}\right\|^2\right) \delta\left[b\left(px_{i,j}\right) - u\right], \tag{15}$$

where k is the Epanechnikov kernel function, δ is the Kronecker delta function, and the function $b : R^2 \to \{1, \ldots, m\}$ associates the pixel at location $px_{i,j}$ with its color's index $b(px_{i,j})$ in the histogram. The normalization constant C is derived by imposing the condition $\sum_{u=1}^{m} q_u = 1$.

Suppose P_y is the non-parametric distribution of the candidate object at position y in the image, then the similarity or Bhattacharyya coefficient can be decided by the following [32]:

$$\rho(y) = \rho\left[P_y, Q\right] = \sum_{u=1}^{m} \sqrt{p_u(y) q_u}. \tag{16}$$

For tracking by agents, $\rho(y)$ can be used to compute the fitness of an agent and the similarity coefficient between two appearance templates.

4.2. Implementation of the Tracking Algorithm. The memory-based multiagent model for object tracking can be described as follows.

Step 1. First locate the object in a video scene and then build the object appearance model by (14).

Step 2. Randomly generate $N \times N$ agents near the located object region by adding a 2D Gaussian distribution $G_{x,y}(0, 10)$, as shown in Figure 9(a), and then map the agents onto the 2D lattice-like environment.

Step 3. For each agent on the lattice, first retrieve the appearance template from its memory spaces, then compute the fitness of the agent, and then perform the competition, recombination, and migration behaviors when the object moves. A snapshot of multiagent coevolution is shown in Figure 9(b).

Step 4. Compute the final target by weighted averaging of all the agents on the lattice, and the tacking result after the end of coevolution is shown in Figure 9(c).

5. Experimental Results and Discussions

In this section, we aim to experimentally verify the efficacy of the proposed object tracking method. We compare the performance of the proposed method with the total model updating PF (TMU-PF) in practical tracking problems. We use some standard video sequences [33, 34] as testing dataset and the experiments are conducted on a computer with a P4 3.0 G Processor.

(a) Randomly distributed agents (yellow points)   (b) A snapshot of multiagent coevolution   (c) Tacking result after the end of coevolution

FIGURE 9: Object tracking by multiagent coevolution.

It is worth noting that the parameters for the algorithms are set initially as follows in our experiments:

(a) m is the number of the bins for modeling the object using histogram and is set as $m = 16 \times 16$;

(b) T_{dc} is used to measure the similarity between the estimated template and the current object template and is set as $T_{dc} = 0.9$;

(c) T_{ds} and T_{dl} are the thresholds used to find a match in STMS and LTMS, respectively, and are set as $T_{ds} = T_{dl} = 0.8$;

(d) K_s and K_l are the capacity of the STMS and LTMS, respectively, and are set as $K_l = K_s = 5$;

(e) T_M is a predefined threshold used to decide whether the template in STMS can be stored into LTMS or not and is initially set as $T_M = 1$;

(f) the total number of agents is 49; that is, the size of the lattice A is 7×7, the recombination probability P_r is 0.6, and the migration probability P_m is 0.05.

(g) the number of the particles used in particle filter-based tracking is set as 50 (almost equal to the number of agents used).

5.1. Tracking a Person with Large Appearance Change. The first sets of experiments are to track a person with abrupt appearance changes. The video used in this experiment is clipped from the standard sequence "seq_dk" (The video sequences can be downloaded from http://www.ces.clemson.edu/~stb/research/headtracker/seq/) [33]. The tracking results of the man by traditional PF, TMU-PF, and the proposed method at frames 21, 58, 82, 83, 87, and 96 are shown in Figures 10(a), 10(b), and 10(c), respectively (the template is initialized manually). The human appearance changes very abruptly from frame 82 to frame 83. The results show that when the appearance is far from the initialized template, PF and TMU-PF deviate from the target gradually, while the original templates are remembered by the proposed method and when the appearance changes abruptly the relevant template can be recalled from the memory space of an agent.

Figure 11 displays experiments to track a person whose pose changes continuously in Head Pose Image Database

(The video sequences can be downloaded from http://www-prima.inrialpes.fr/perso/Gourier/Faces/HPDatabase.html) [34]. Experimental results show that our proposed method can track more precisely than the other two methods.

5.2. Tracking a Person with Heavy Occlusions by Others. The second set of experiments aims at tracking persons who are occasionally occluded by another object.

The sequence used in the first experiment is also a standard sequence "seq_jd" [33]. In this sequence, the man is occluded twice by another person. The tracking results by PF, TMU-PF and the proposed MMAM are shown in Figures 12(a), 12(b), and 12(c), respectively (the template is initialized manually). It is worth noting that the man is totally occluded at frame 52 and frame 253. The results show that the proposed MMAM can still track the person correctly after recovered from the occlusion at frame 55 and frame 256.

Figure 13 shows the results of tracking a face which is fully occluded by another person (The templates are initialized manually).

Finally, unlike the particle filter-based tracking method, the proposed approach has no restrictions to the face moving direction and speed. The face will be located and tracked at any time.

6. Conclusions

In this paper, we propose a different approach for visual tracking inspired by the way human perceive the environment. A number of memory-based agents are distributed nearby the located object region and then mapped onto a 2D lattice-like environment for predicting the new location of the object by their coevolutionary behaviors, such as competition, recombination, and migration, which imitate the process when many people search for a target in real world. The three-stage of human brain memory model is incorporated into a multiagent coevolutionary process for finding a best match of the appearance of the object. Each agent can remember, retrieve, or forget the appearance of the object through its memory system by its own experience. Experimental results show that the proposed method can deal with large appearance changes and heavy occlusions when tracking a moving object. It can locate the correct object

(a) Tracking results by PF

(b) Tracking results by TMU-PF

(c) Tracking results by MMAM

FIGURE 10: Tracking results of "seq_dk" sequence.

(a) Tracking results by PF

(b) Tracking results by TMU-PF

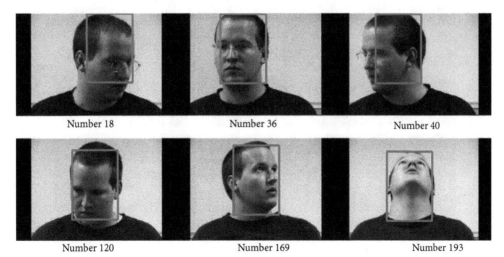

(c) Tracking results by MMAM

FIGURE 11: Tracking a person with pose changes.

(a) Tracking results by PF

(b) Tracking results by TMU-PF

(c) Tracking results by MMAM

FIGURE 12: Tracking a fully occluded person.

Number 16 Number 87 Number 131

Number 173 Number 198 Number 229

(a) Tracking results by PF

(b) Tracking results by MTU-PF

(c) Tracking results by MMAM

FIGURE 13: Tracking a fully occluded face.

after the appearance changed or the occlusion recovered and outperforms the traditional particle filter based tracking.

Acknowledgments

The paper is funded by the National Natural Science Foundation of China (no. 60873163, no. 61271407) and the Fundamental Research Funds for the Central Universities (no. 27R1105019A, no. R1405008A).

References

[1] A. Yilmaz, O. Javed, and M. Shah, "Object tracking: a survey," *ACM Computing Surveys*, vol. 38, no. 4, pp. 1–45, 2006.

[2] S. K. Zhou, R. Chellappa, and B. Moghaddam, "Visual tracking and recognition using appearance-adaptive models in particle filters," *IEEE Transactions on Image Processing*, vol. 13, no. 11, pp. 1491–1506, 2004.

[3] A. Li, Z. Jing, and S. Hu, "Robust observation model for visual tracking in particle filter," *International Journal of Electronics and Communications*, vol. 61, no. 3, pp. 186–194, 2007.

[4] H. Wang, D. Suter, and K. Schindler, "Effective appearance model and similarity measure for particle filtering and visual tracking," in *Proceedings of the 9th European Conference on Computer Vision, Part III (ECCV '06)*, vol. 3953 of *Lecture Notes in Computer Science*, pp. 606–618, Graz, Austria, May, 2006.

[5] H. Wang, D. Suter, K. Schindler, and C. Shen, "Adaptive object tracking based on an effective appearance filter," *IEEE Transactions on Pattern Analysis and Machine Intelligence*, vol. 29, no. 9, pp. 1661–1667, 2007.

[6] B. Zhang, W. Tian, and Z. Jin, "Robust appearance-guided particle filter for object tracking with occlusion analysis," *International Journal of Electronics and Communications*, vol. 62, no. 1, pp. 24–32, 2008.

[7] Z. Wang, X. Yang, Y. Xu, and S. Yu, "CamShift guided particle filter for visual tracking," *Pattern Recognition Letters*, vol. 30, no. 4, pp. 407–413, 2009.

[8] C. Shan, T. Tan, and Y. Wei, "Real-time hand tracking using a mean shift embedded particle filter," *Pattern Recognition*, vol. 40, no. 7, pp. 1958–1970, 2007.

[9] H. Zhou, Y. Yuan, and C. Shi, "Object tracking using SIFT features and mean shift," *Computer Vision and Image Understanding*, vol. 113, no. 3, pp. 345–352, 2009.

[10] J. Zhao and Z. Li, "Particle filter based on particle swarm optimization resampling for vision tracking," *Expert Systems with Applications*, vol. 37, no. 12, pp. 8910–8914, 2010.

[11] H. Zhou, M. Taj, and A. Cavallaro, "Target detection and tracking with heterogeneous sensors," *IEEE Journal on Selected Topics in Signal Processing*, vol. 2, no. 4, pp. 503–513, 2008.

[12] A. S. Montemayor, J. J. Pantrigo, and J. Hernamdez, "A memory-based particle filter for visual tracking through occlusion," in *Proceedings of the International Work-Conference on the Interplay Between Natural and Artificial Computation, Part II (IWINAC '09)*, vol. 5602 of *Lecture Notes in Computer Science*, pp. 274–283, 2009.

[13] D. Mikami, K. Otsuka, and J. Yamato, "Memory-based particle filter for face pose tracking robust under complex dynamics," in *Proceedings of IEEE Conference on Computer Vision and Pattern Recognition*, pp. 999–1006, Miami, FL, USA, 2009.

[14] Y. Wang and V. Chiew, "On the cognitive process of human problem solving," *Cognitive Systems Research*, vol. 11, no. 1, pp. 81–92, 2010.

[15] Y. X. Wang, "Formal description of the cognitive process of memorization," *Transactions on Computational Intelligence*, vol. 1, no. 3, pp. 1–15, 2009.

[16] M. Wooldridge and N. R. Jennings, "Intelligent agents: theory and practice," *The Knowledge Engineering Review*, vol. 10, no. 2, pp. 115–152, 1995.

[17] J. Liu, Y. Y. Tang, and Y. C. Cao, "An evolutionary autonomous agents approach to image feature extraction," *IEEE Transactions on Evolutionary Computation*, vol. 1, no. 2, pp. 141–158, 1997.

[18] E. G. P. Bovenkamp, J. Dijkstra, J. G. Bosch, and J. H. C. Reiber, "Multi-agent segmentation of IVUS images," *Pattern Recognition*, vol. 37, no. 4, pp. 647–663, 2004.

[19] J. Liu, H. Jing, and Y. Y. Tang, "Multi-agent oriented constraint satisfaction," *Artificial Intelligence*, vol. 136, no. 1, pp. 101–144, 2002.

[20] J. Liu, X. Jin, and K. C. Tsui, "Autonomy-oriented computing (AOC): formulating computational systems with autonomous components," *IEEE Transactions on Systems, Man, and Cybernetics A*, vol. 35, no. 6, pp. 879–902, 2005.

[21] K. C. Tsui and J. Liu, "An evolutionary multiagent diffusion approach to optimization," *International Journal of Pattern Recognition and Artificial Intelligence*, vol. 16, no. 6, pp. 715–733, 2002.

[22] W. Zhong, J. Liu, M. Xue, and L. Jiao, "A multiagent genetic algorithm for global numerical optimization," *IEEE Transactions on Systems, Man, and Cybernetics B*, vol. 34, no. 2, pp. 1128–1141, 2004.

[23] J. Liu, W. Zhong, and L. Jiao, "A multiagent evolutionary algorithm for constraint satisfaction problems," *IEEE Transactions on Systems, Man, and Cybernetics B*, vol. 36, no. 1, pp. 54–73, 2006.

[24] J. Liu, W. Zhong, and L. Jiao, "An organizational evolutionary algorithm for numerical optimization," *IEEE Transactions on Systems, Man, and Cybernetics B*, vol. 37, no. 4, pp. 1052–1064, 2007.

[25] Y. Wang and B. Yuan, "A novel approach for human face detection from color images under complex background," *Pattern Recognition*, vol. 34, no. 10, pp. 1983–1992, 2001.

[26] Y. Wang and B. Yuan, "Fast method for face location and tracking by distributed behaviour-based agents," *IEE Proceedings*, vol. 149, no. 3, pp. 173–178, 2002.

[27] W. James, *Principles of Psychology*, Holt, New York, NY, USA, 1890.

[28] R. C. Atkinson and R. M. Shiffrin, "Human memory: a proposed system and its control processes," in *The Psychology of Learning and Motivation*, K. W. Spence, Ed., vol. 2, pp. 89–195, Academic Press, New York, NY, USA, 1968.

[29] A. D. Baddeley and G. J. Hitch, "Working memory," in *The Psychology of Learning and Motivation*, G. H. Bower, Ed., vol. 8, pp. 47–89, 1974.

[30] Y. X. Wang and Y. Wang, "Cognitive informatics models of the brain," *IEEE Transactions on Systems, Man and Cybernetics C*, vol. 36, no. 2, pp. 203–207, 2006.

[31] M. W. Eysenck and M. T. Keane, *Cognitive Psychology: A Student's Handbook*, Psychology Press, New York, NY, USA, 6th edition, 2010.

[32] C. Lerdsudwichai, M. Abdel-Mottaleb, and A. Ansari, "Tracking multiple people with recovery from partial and total occlusion," *Pattern Recognition*, vol. 38, no. 7, pp. 1059–1070, 2005.

[33] S. Birchfield, "Elliptical head tracking using intensity gradients and color histograms," in *Proceedings of the IEEE Computer Society Conference on Computer Vision and Pattern Recognition*, pp. 232–237, Santa Barbara, Calif, USA, June 1998.

[34] N. Gourier, D. Hall, and J. L. Crowley, "Estimating face orientation from robust detection of salient facial features," in *Proceedings of the Pointing International Workshop on Visual Observation of Deictic Gestures*, Cambridge, UK, 2004.

13

A Fragile Zero Watermarking Scheme to Detect and Characterize Malicious Modifications in Database Relations

Aihab Khan[1] and Syed Afaq Husain[2]

[1] Department of Computing & Technology, Iqra University, Islamabad 44000, Pakistan
[2] Faculty of Computer Science & IT, King Faisal University, Ahsaa 31982, Saudi Arabia

Correspondence should be addressed to Aihab Khan; aihabkhan@yahoo.com

Academic Editors: P. Melin and Y. Zhu

We put forward a fragile zero watermarking scheme to detect and characterize malicious modifications made to a database relation. Most of the existing watermarking schemes for relational databases introduce intentional errors or permanent distortions as marks into the database original content. These distortions inevitably degrade the data quality and data usability as the integrity of a relational database is violated. Moreover, these fragile schemes can detect malicious data modifications but do not characterize the tempering attack, that is, the nature of tempering. The proposed fragile scheme is based on zero watermarking approach to detect malicious modifications made to a database relation. In zero watermarking, the watermark is generated (constructed) from the contents of the original data rather than introduction of permanent distortions as marks into the data. As a result, the proposed scheme is distortion-free; thus, it also resolves the inherent conflict between security and imperceptibility. The proposed scheme also characterizes the malicious data modifications to quantify the nature of tempering attacks. Experimental results show that even minor malicious modifications made to a database relation can be detected and characterized successfully.

1. Introduction

Digital watermarking is a class of information hiding technique that provides measures for copyright protection, broadcast monitoring, covert communication, copy control, tamper, and integrity proof of digital assets. The watermarking techniques were primarily proposed for multimedia content [1–4]; however, in the last decade, the research community has extended these techniques to relational databases for its copyright protection, temper detection, and integrity proof. Most of the existing watermarking schemes for relational databases [5–20] introduce intentional errors or distortions as marks in the underlying data with some error tolerance so that it does not have a significant impact on the usefulness of data. However, this results in degrading data quality as the integrity of a relational database is violated. A large collection of real-world datasets has a strong usability constraint that disallows any permanent distortions or intentional errors. For example, the safety critical datasets are designed to minimize errors rather than to introduce intentional errors. Similarly, a business application may require that local properties like item-cost, ordered-quantity, and so forth, are preserved as well as global properties like natural join between item and sales, employees and department, and so forth. Moreover, in business datasets, the semantic constraints are not violated, like dissimilarity in attribute value for two similar transactions [21]. Query processing is sensitive due to selection criteria and has well-defined semantics; therefore, the watermarking schemes that introduce distortion into the database original content are not appropriate for certain applications.

Based on the intent of marking, the watermarking schemes presented in the literature can be categorized into robust and fragile schemes. The robust schemes [5–16] are aimed at copyright protection, whereas the fragile schemes [17–25] are used for tamper detection and integrity proof of database relations. Most of the robust schemes for copyright protection [5–16] introduce distortions into the database original content which affects data integrity and usability. These robust schemes may work for numeric [5–10] and categorical attributes [11, 12] of relational databases to embed watermarks. Some techniques embed meaningless bit pattern [5, 6]; whereas in other techniques meaningful bit patterns like image [13–15] and owner's speech [16] are used as watermarks for embedding in relational databases. In data sales environment, some of these robust schemes are extended to fingerprinting domain for unique identification of each buyer and also for traitor detection [21, 26–28]. Compared with the robust schemes, the fragile watermarking schemes are not adequately addressed and relatively little work is available for integrity proof of relational databases [20]. In this paper, we focus on fragile watermarking schemes for temper detection and integrity proof of database relations.

The initial work on fragile watermarking schemes can be found on images [29–31], which is extended to audio [32, 33] and video [3, 34] schemes. Recently, the importance of other data domains is recognized and fragile schemes for text [35, 36] and relational databases [17–20, 22–25] are proposed. Like robust schemes, most of the fragile schemes for relational databases [17–20] introduce distortion into the database original contents that degrades data quality and also affects data usability. These schemes are based on the content characteristics of database relation itself to create a secure hash (used as a watermark) which is stored in Least Significant Bits (LSBs) of database original contents, thus introducing distortion.

A fragile watermarking scheme presented by Guo et al. [17] detects malicious modifications made to a database relation. In their scheme, the watermark generation is based on the content characteristics of the database relation itself. The generated watermarks are embedded in at most two LSBs of all attributes in the database relation that introduces considerable distortion in the database original contents. The fragile scheme presented by Khataeimaragheh and Rashidi [18] is also a distortion-based scheme for integrity proof of database relations. Like [17], the watermarks are embedded in at most two LSBs of all attributes in the relation that forms a two-bit watermark grid. The fragile scheme presented by Iqbal et al. [19] logically partitions the database relation into three groups and generates self-constructing fragile watermark information from each group. The generated watermarks are embedded at LSBs of numerical attributes in each group of a database relation which introduces distortion in database original contents. Prasannakumari [20] presented a fragile scheme for temper detection in database relations. This technique also introduces distortion as it inserts a fake attribute in database relation to act as a watermark. The data values for the newly inserted attribute are determined by applying aggregate function on original database content.

Beside distortion-based techniques, some researches also presented distortion free fragile watermarking schemes [22–25] for integrity proof of database relations. The main feature of these schemes is that the watermark embedding in actual fact is the tuples or attributes reordering based on the content characteristics of database relation. A fragile scheme proposed by Li et al. [22] detects and localizes malicious modifications made to the database relations. Their scheme partitions the database relation into disjoint groups and the watermark is embedded and verified in each group

independently. In their scheme, the watermark is embedded as tuple reordering and the order of each tuple pair in group is changed or unchanged depending on the tuple hash values and the corresponding group hash value. Though their technique does not introduce any distortion in the database relation, but it works only for categorical data type. Kamel [23] presented a fragile scheme to protect the integrity of database relations. Their scheme divides the database relations in groups and each group is marked independently. As in [22], the watermark embedding is reordering of tuples in each group that corresponds to the value of some secret watermark. The fragile scheme proposed by Bhattacharya and Cortesi [24] detects malicious modifications in database relations having categorical attributes. Their scheme divides the database relation into groups on the basis of categorical attribute values. Like [22, 23], tuple hash value is used to obtain a watermark as permutation of tuples. A fragile zero watermarking scheme is presented by Hamadou et al. [25] for authentication of database relations. Their technique is distortion-free and is based on attribute reordering method. Initially, the attributes of database relation are virtually sorted on hash values of attribute names to define a secret initial order of attributes. For each attribute in database relation, the Most Significant Bits (MSBs) are extracted and used for watermark generation. The generated watermark is then registered with the Certification Authority (CA) for certification purpose. As their technique is based on virtual sorting of attributes by their names, so any change in attribute name by attacker would fail the temper detection process.

In the previous discussion, we have identified two important issues in existing fragile watermarking schemes. First, the fragile schemes are distortion based [17–20] that inevitably degrade data integrity and thus affect data usability; therefore, these schemes are not applicable to non-error-tolerant data like safety critical datasets, and so forth. Second, though there exist some fragile schemes like [22–25] that are distortion-free, but the watermarking approach is based on reordering of tuples or attributes; so, they are vulnerable to sorting attacks. Also, if the modification is small, such that, it does not affect the order of tuples, the temper detection would fail. To address these issues, we propose a fragile scheme based on zero watermarking approach that does not modify any part or properties of the database relations itself; therefore, the proposed scheme assures imperceptibility and overcomes weaknesses like data integrity and data usability in existing fragile watermarking schemes. Also, the proposed scheme is independent of tuple ordering as well as attributes ordering and naming, so it is not vulnerable to sorting attacks. The watermark generation in the proposed scheme is based on algorithmically evaluating the local characteristics of database relation like frequency distribution of digit count, length and range of data values. This enables us to characterize the malicious data modifications on parameters like the fraction of digit, length and range of data values attacked, the type of attack (insertion, deletion, or update), and the effect of attack (low to high, high to low, or no change) on data values. Also, to the best of our knowledge, there is no such distortion-free fragile watermarking scheme that can characterize the tempering attacks, that is, the nature of tempering. Experimental results show that the proposed scheme can detect and characterize malicious data modifications successfully.

2. Materials and Methods

In this section, we present our proposed fragile zero watermarking scheme to detect and characterize malicious modifications made to a database relation. The proposed scheme exhibits the following important properties of a fragile watermarking system as discussed in [17].

(1) *Fragility.* The proposed scheme is designed to be fragile; that is, if there are any malicious data modifications, the embedded watermark is not detectable (destroyed).

(2) *Imperceptibility.* As the proposed scheme is based on zero watermarking approach, it does not introduce any distortion in the underlying data; therefore, the embedded watermark is invisible or imperceptible.

(3) *Key-Based System.* The watermark generation and verification in the proposed scheme is a key-based system. Also, to detect and characterize malicious data modifications, a secret key is required.

(4) *Blindness.* In the proposed scheme, the original database relation is not required to detect and characterize malicious data modifications.

(5) *Tuple and Attribute Ordering.* The existing fragile schemes are based on tuple ordering [22–24] and attribute ordering and naming [25]. The proposed scheme is independent of tuple and attributes ordering so it is not vulnerable to sorting attacks.

(6) *Characterization.* The proposed scheme not only detects but also characterizes the malicious data modifications in database relation to quantify the nature of tempering attacks.

2.1. Watermark Generation. Let R be a database relation with primary key PK and v attributes denoted by $R(\text{PK}, A1, A2, \ldots, A_v)$. The watermark generation in the proposed scheme is based on the content characteristics of numeric data values, so we assume that some attributes of the database relation are numeric. Figure 1 shows the watermark generation process that comprises of subwatermark generation for digit count, length, and range of data values. The generated watermark is registered with the Certification Authority (CA) for certification purpose. Table 1 presents the list of notations used in our algorithms and discussion.

The algorithm for watermark generation is presented in Algorithm 1. At lines 1–3, the digit, length, and range of data values in a database relation are algorithmically evaluated to generate the subwatermarks as presented in Algorithms 2–4. These subwatermarks are then used to generate a database relation watermark ω_R as shown at line 4. At line 5, the relation watermark ω_R is encrypted with a secret key SK known only to the database owner. We assume that the secret key is selected from large key space such that it is

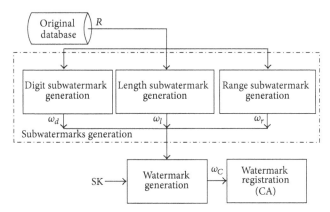

FIGURE 1: Proposed model for watermark generation and registration.

(1) ω_d = *digit sub-watermark generation*()
               //See Algorithm 2
(2) ω_l = *length sub-watermark generation*()
               //See Algorithm 3
(3) ω_r = *range sub-watermark generation*()
               //See Algorithm 4
(4) $\omega_R = \omega_d \parallel \omega_l \parallel \omega_r$
(5) $E\omega_R = Encrypt(\omega_R, SK)$
(6) $\omega_C = E\omega_R \parallel owner\_id \parallel date \parallel time$
(7) *Register* ω_C *to CA*

ALGORITHM 1: Watermark generation.

computationally infeasible for attacker to guess a key. At lines 6-7, the encrypted relation watermark $E\omega_R$ is concatenated with owner Id along with date and time stamp to generate a watermark certificate ω_C, which is then registered with the CA before publishing the database for certification purpose.

Algorithm 2 generates a digit subwatermark which is based on digit frequency for all data values present in adatabase relation. At lines 1–3, the length of each data value is determined which is then used to extract the individual digits as shown at lines 4-5. Lines 6-7 compute the frequency of each digit and the total number of digits present in the database relation. At line 11, the relative frequency of each digit rfd_i is determined which is then used to generate a digit subwatermark ω_d as shown at line 13. At lines 15-16, the digit subwatermark ω_d is concatenated with total digit count and is returned to the watermark generation algorithm. It is to be noted that the digit subwatermark is composed of each digit relative frequency rfd_i and the total count of all digits. In fact, this information is used for characterization of attacks as discussed in Section 3.

The subwatermark generation for length of data values in a database relation is presented in Algorithm 3. At lines 1–3, the length of each data value is determined. Lines 4-5 determine the frequency for each length of data values and the total count of data values length present in the database relation. At line 9, the relative frequency for each length of data value rfl_j is computed which is then used to generate

```
(1)  For Each tuple r_i ∈ relation R Do
(2)    For Each attribute A_j ∈ relation R Do
(3)      length = Len(r_i · A_j)
(4)      For i = 0 to length − 1 Do
(5)        d_i = Mid$(r_i · A_j, i, 1)
(6)        digit_frequency[d_i]++
(7)        total_digit_count++
(8)      End For
(9)    End For
(10)  End For
(11)  For Each i ∈ digit Do
(12)    rfd_i = (digit_frequency[i]/total_digit_count) * 100
(13)    ω_d = ω_d ‖ rfd_i
(14)  End For
(15)  ω_d = ω_d ‖ total_digit_count
(16)  Return ω_d
```

ALGORITHM 2: Digit sub-watermark generation.

TABLE 1: Notations.

Symbol	Description
R	Database relation
PK	Primary key attribute
r_i	The ith tuple
A_j	The jth attribute
η	Number of tuples in a database relation
ν	Number of attributes in a database relation
ω_d	Digit sub-watermark
ω_l	Length sub-watermark
ω_r	Range sub-watermark
ω_R	Watermark for database relation R
ω_C	Watermark certificate
SK	Secret key
d_i	The ith digit
l_j	The jth length
r_k	The kth range
fd_i	Frequency for digit i of data values
fl_j	Frequency for length j of data values
fr_k	Frequency for range k of data values
rfd_i	Relative frequency for digit i of data values
rfl_j	Relative frequency for length j of data values
rfr_k	Relative frequency for range k of data values
Δfd_i	Change in frequency of digit i
Δfl_j	Change in frequency for length j
Δfr_k	Change in frequency for range k
$\Delta \mathscr{F}d_i$	Fractional change in digit frequency for digit i
$\Delta \mathscr{F}l_j$	Fractional change in length frequency for length j
$\Delta \mathscr{F}r_k$	Fractional change in range frequency for range k
CA	Certification authority
WAR	Watermark accuracy rate
WDR	Watermark distortion rate

```
(1)  For Each tuple r_i ∈ relation R do
(2)    For Each attribute A_j ∈ relation R do
(3)      length = Len(r_i · A_j)
(4)      length_frequency[length]++
(5)      total_length_count++
(6)    EndFor
(7)  End For
(8)  For Each i ∈ length do
(9)    rfl_j = (length_frequency[i]/total_length_count) * 100
(10)   ω_l = ω_l ‖ rfl_j
(11)  End For
(12)  ω_l = ω_l ‖ total_length_count
(13)  Return ω_l
```

ALGORITHM 3: Length sub-watermark generation.

length subwatermark ω_l as shown at line 10. At lines 12-13, the length subwatermark ω_l is concatenated with total length count and is returned.

Algorithm 4 presents the algorithm for subwatermark generation for range of data values in a database relation. At line 1, different data ranges are defined in which the data value of a database relation may fall. It is to be noted that the defined data ranges may be adjusted as per the nature of data values in the database relation and also for more precise characterization of malicious data modifications, as discussed in Section 3. Lines 1–3 determine the attribute value, within each tuple. Lines 5–13 determine the frequency for different data ranges in which the data value may fall and the total number of data ranges present in the database relation. At lines 16-17, the relative frequency for each range of data value rfr_k is computed, which is then used to generate range subwatermark ω_r. Lines 19-20 show that the range subwatermark ω_r is concatenated with total range count and is returned.

```
(1)    range = {0–99, 100–999, 1000–9999, 10000–99999, 100000–999999}
(2)    For Each tuple r_i € relation R do
(3)    For Each attribute A_j € relation R do
(4)        x = r_i · A_j
(5)        Select Case x
(6)            x in range 0: range_frequency[0]++
(7)            x in range 1: range_frequency[1]++
(8)            x in range 2: range_frequency[2]++
(9)            x in range 3: range_frequency[3]++
(10)           x in range 4: range_frequency[4]++
(11)       End Select
(12)       total_range_count++
(13)   End For
(14)   End For
(15)   For Each i € range do
(16)       rfr_k = (range_frequency[i]/total_range_count) * 100
(17)       ω_r = ω_r ‖ rfr_k
(18)   End For
(19)   ω_r = ω_r ‖ total_range_count
(20)   Return ω_r
```

ALGORITHM 4: Range sub-watermark generation.

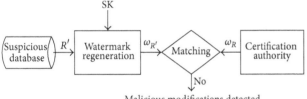

FIGURE 2: Proposed model for detection of malicious tempering.

2.2. Watermark Verification. Figure 2 shows the model for detection of malicious modifications in suspicious database relation R'. For detection of malicious data modifications, the relation watermark $\omega_R{}'$ is regenerated for suspicious database relation R' and compared with the relation watermark ω_R registered at CA; if both watermarks are different then the suspicious database relation R' is considered as a tempered relation.

The algorithm for watermark detection is presented in Algorithm 5. At line 1, the watermark $\omega_R{}'$ is generated by using Algorithm 1 for suspicious database relation R'. The watermark certificate ω_C which is already registered at CA is used to extract database relation watermark ω_R as shown at lines 2–4. At lines 5–10, each digit of ω_R is compared with the corresponding digit of $\omega_R{}'$ and match_count is incremented on each successful match. At line 9, the total_count is computed to know the number of digits tested. At lines 11-12, the WAR (Watermark Accuracy Rate) and WDR (Watermark Distortion Rate) are computed. If the distortion exists in the suspicious database relation R', then R' is rejected as a tempered relation with distortion rate WDR as shown at lines 13–15.

The algorithm for characterization of malicious data modifications is presented in Algorithm 6. At line 2, the relative frequency of each digit rfd_i is extracted from digit subwatermark ω_d as $\omega_d \subseteq \omega_R$ and ω_R is already registered at CA. The frequency distribution of each digit fd_i in relation R is determined at line 3. At line 4, the frequency distribution of each digit $fd_i{}'$ for suspicious database relation R' is determined. The change in frequency distribution of each digit Δfd_i is computed at line 5 and the fractional change in each digit $\Delta \mathscr{F}d_i$ is determined at line 6. The computed value of $\Delta \mathscr{F}d_i$ is then used to characterize the malicious modifications made to the database relation R. For example, if $\Delta \mathscr{F}d_i$ is zero, then the suspicious relation R' is not tempered. A positive $\Delta \mathscr{F}d_i$ indicates that $\mathscr{F}$ fraction of digit d_i is maliciously inserted by attacker as an attempt to transform low data values to high in database relation R. Similarly, a negative $\Delta \mathscr{F}d_i$ indicates that $\mathscr{F}$ fraction of digit d_i is maliciously deleted by attacker as an attempt to transform high data values to low in database relation R. At lines 8–14 and 15–21, a similar method as discussed earlier is used to determine $\Delta \mathscr{F}l_j$ and $\Delta \mathscr{F}r_k$ to characterize the attacks on length and range of data values in database relation R. The characterization of malicious data modifications is further elaborated in Section 3.2 with experimental results.

3. Results and Discussion

Suppose that Alice is the database owner and she has used the proposed algorithms along with the secret key to generate a watermark for the database relation R. The attacker Mallory for his own nefarious objectives may attempt to make malicious modifications in Alice watermarked database relation. We conducted our experiments in Microsoft Visual Basic and Microsoft Access, on 3.2 GHz Intel core i3 CPU with 2 GB of RAM. The proposed watermarking scheme is evaluated on a real-life dataset namely Forest Cover Type data set, available at UCI Machine Learning Repository [37]. This dataset has

```
(1)   Compute $\omega_R'$ for $R'$ (by using Algorithm 1)
(2)   Obtain $\omega_C$ from CA
(3)   Extract $E\omega_R$ from $\omega_C$
(4)   $\omega_R = Decrypt(E\omega_R, SK)$
(5)   For $i$ = 1 to length($\omega_R$) Do
(6)       If $\omega_R[i] = \omega_R'[i]$ Then
(7)           match_count = match_count + 1
(8)       End if
(9)       total_count = total_count + 1
(10)  End For
(11)  WAR = match_count/total_count $*$ 100
(12)  WDR = 1 – WAR
(13)  If WDR $\neq$ 0 Then
(14)      Database Relation $R'$ is tempered with distortion rate WDR
(15)  End if
```

ALGORITHM 5: Watermark verification.

```
(1)   For Each $d_i \in digit$ do
(2)       Extract $rfd_i$ from $\omega_d$
(3)       $fd_i = rfd_i$/total_digit_count
(4)       Generate $fd_i'$ from $R'$ (by using Algorithm 2)
(5)       $\Delta fd_i = fd_i - fd_i'$
(6)       $\Delta \mathcal{F}d_i = \Delta fd_i / fd_i * 100$
(7)   End For
(8)   For Each $l_j \in length$ do
(9)       Extract $rfl_j$ from $\omega_l$
(10)      $fl_j = rfl_j$/total_length_count
(11)      Generate $fl_j'$ from $R'$ (by using Algorithm 3)
(12)      $\Delta fl_j = fl_j - fl_j'$
(13)      $\Delta \mathcal{F}l_j = \Delta fl_j / fl_j * 100$
(14)  End For
(15)  For Each $r_k \in range$ do
(16)      Extract $rfr_k$ from $\omega_r$
(17)      $fr_k = rfr_k$/total_range_count
(18)      Generate $fr_k'$ from $R'$ (by using Algorithm 4)
(19)      $\Delta fr_k = fr_k - fr_k'$
(20)      $\Delta \mathcal{F}r_k = \Delta fr_k / fr_k * 100$
(21)  End For
```

ALGORITHM 6: Characterization of malicious data modifications.

TABLE 2: Detection of malicious insertion of tuples with different attack rates ($\eta = 10^6$).

Insertion attack rate	WAR	WDR	Temper detection
10%	18.14	81.86	Yes (High)
30%	18.56	81.44	Yes (High)
50%	20.41	79.59	Yes (High)
70%	16.67	83.33	Yes (High)
90%	16.32	83.68	Yes (High)

TABLE 3: Detection of malicious deletion of tuples with different attack rates ($\eta = 10^6$).

Deletion attack rate	WAR	WDR	Temper detection
10%	24.32	75.68	Yes (High)
30%	17.88	82.12	Yes (High)
50%	20.95	79.05	Yes (High)
70%	13.08	86.92	Yes (High)
90%	14.14	85.86	Yes (High)

581,102 tuples, each with 10 integer attributes, 44 Boolean attributes, and 1 categorical attribute. In our experiments, we have used all 10 integer attributes. It is to be noted that in robust watermarking schemes, the aim of Mallory is to destroy the Alice watermark without affecting the database relation, whereas in fragile schemes, Mallory attempts to make malicious modifications in Alice watermarked database relation without affecting the watermark. The experimental results presented in this section show that the watermark is adversely affected by even minor malicious data modifications; therefore, the generated watermark is fragile.

3.1. Detection of Malicious Modifications. In this set of experiments, we randomly introduce malicious modifications in

Forest Cover Type data set [37]. As discussed in Algorithm 5, these malicious modifications are detected by generating the watermark for the suspicious database relation R' to obtain ω_R', which is then compared with the registered watermark ω_R to determine the WAR (Watermark Accuracy Rate) and WDR (Watermark Distortion Rate).

Table 2 shows the WAR and WDR for the malicious insertions made to the database relation with different attack rates. For example, when 10% of the fake but similar tuples are randomly inserted into the database relation R, the WDR is found to be high and malicious insertions are detected with low WAR.

Tables 3-4 show similar results as of insertion attack for malicious deletions and updates made to the database relation R.

Figure 3 summarizes the insertion, deletion, and update attacks and shows that the WDR is always high for different volume of malicious data modifications.

TABLE 4: Detection of malicious update of tuples with different attack rates ($\eta = 10^6$).

Update attack rate	WAR	WDR	Temper detection
10%	20.42	79.58	Yes (High)
30%	19.89	80.11	Yes (High)
50%	19.89	80.11	Yes (High)
70%	18.94	81.06	Yes (High)
90%	14.13	85.87	Yes (High)

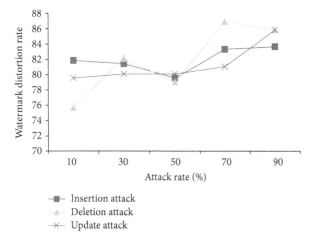

FIGURE 3: Watermark distortion rate for malicious insertion, deletion, and update of tuples with different attack rates ($n = 10^6$).

In another set of attacks, we simultaneously perform malicious insertion, deletion, and update of tuples with different attack rates in database relation R. Table 5 shows the WDR for this set of attack.

The experimental results presented in Tables 2–5 show that the malicious modifications are always detected and fragility of the registered watermark ω_R is observed for even low volumes of attack. The WAR is low and WDR is high for different volume of malicious insertions, deletions, and updates made to the database relation. The low WAR indicates the extent to which the database relation has been attacked, whereas the high WDR indicates that the database relation has been tampered and is not authentic. The accuracy of watermark is adversely affected even with minor malicious data modifications and the watermark fragility proves that the database relation has been attacked.

3.2. Characterization of Malicious Modifications. One of the important features of the proposed watermarking scheme is to characterize the malicious modifications made to the database relations. As discussed in Algorithm 1, the watermark generation is based on the content characteristics of database relation itself which enable us to characterize the malicious data modifications. Algorithm 6 elaborates the algorithm for characterization of malicious data modifications by evaluating the fractional change in each digit $\Delta\mathscr{F}d_i$, length $\Delta\mathscr{F}l_j$ and range $\Delta\mathscr{F}r_k$ of data values in the tempered database relation R'.

We have conducted experiments for both random and deterministic attacks for characterization of malicious data modifications. In random tempering attacks, we randomly attack the digit frequency, length, and range of data values in the database relation, whereas in deterministic attacks, the attack is performed with the specific attack rates. The random tempering attacks are presented in this section and the results of detailed deterministic attacks are shown in the Appendix for reference.

3.2.1. Attacks on Digit Frequency. In this set of attacks, Mallory randomly performs malicious insertion, deletion, and update attacks on digit frequency in Alice's watermarked relation R. For example, in insertion attack, Mallory may attempt to maliciously insert some digits in R. Table 6 shows the experimental results obtained for characterization of malicious insertion attack on digits 9 and 0 as discussed in Algorithm 6. A positive value of $\Delta\mathscr{F}d_i$ indicates that $\mathscr{F}$ fraction of digits 9 and 0 is maliciously inserted by Mallory in the database relation R. The characteristic of this attack is an attempt to relatively increase the low data values to high in database relation R as an increase of 35.84% and 24.42% is observed in $\Delta\mathscr{F}d_i$ of digits 9 and 0, respectively. As the other digits are not attacked, so $\Delta\mathscr{F}d_i$ is zero for digits 1–8 and there is no change in the digit frequency Δfd_i of these digits. This characteristic of attack, when combined with the nature of data, may provide useful information about the attacker intention. For example, in the product sales environment, these malicious insertions indicate that the attacker may have attempted to increase the low volume and amount of product sales.

Table 7 shows the result for random malicious deletions of digits 9 and 0 made to the database relation R. A negative value of $\Delta\mathscr{F}d_i$ indicates that $\mathscr{F}$ fraction of digits 9 and 0 is maliciously deleted by the attacker. The characteristic of this attack is an attempt to relatively decrease the high data values to low in the database relation R. In this attack, 14.70% of digit 9 and 12.44% of digit 0 are randomly deleted from the database relation. As the other digits are not deleted, so $\Delta\mathscr{F}d_i$ is zero for digits 1–8. Table 8 shows similar result for random malicious update for digits 9 and 0 made to the database relation. In this attack, digits 9 and 0 are randomly replaced with some other digits, so the digit frequency Δfd_i of digits 9 and 0 is decreased (high to low), where as the digit frequency Δfd_i of digits 1–8 is increased (low to high).

Figure 4 summarizes the malicious insertion, deletion, and update attacks on digits 9 and 0. The insertion attack shows a positive increase (low to high) on attacked digits, where as a negative trend (high to low) is observed in attacked digits for deletion attack. In update attack, both negative (high to low) and positive trends (low to high) are observed for attacked and unattacked digits, respectively.

In another set of attacks, we randomly insert, delete and update 10% (lower bound) and 90% (upper bound) of the tuples from the database relation R. Table 9 shows the effect on fractional change in digit frequency $\Delta\mathscr{F}d_i$ for each digit. It is to be noted that, in insertion attack, a k fraction of positive trend (low to high) is being observed in each digit frequency of database relation R. For example, when 10% of

TABLE 5: Detection of malicious data modifications with different attack rates ($\eta = 10^6$).

Insertion attack rate	Deletion attack rate	Update attack rate	WAR	WDR	Temper detection
10%	10%	10%	15.85	84.15	Yes (High)
30%	30%	30%	10.98	89.02	Yes (High)
50%	50%	50%	10.28	89.72	Yes (High)
70%	70%	70%	13.33	86.67	Yes (High)
90%	90%	90%	10.98	89.02	Yes (High)

TABLE 6: Characterization of malicious insertion attacks on digit frequency.

d_i	rfd_i	fd_i	$rfd_i{'}$	$fd_i{'}$	Δfd_i	$\Delta \mathscr{F} d_i$	Characteristic
0	**8.63**	**1435163**	**10.28**	**1785659**	**+350496**	**+24.42%**	**↑Low to High**
1	18.02	2995771	17.24	2995771	0	0	No change
2	19.48	3238818	18.64	3238818	0	0	No change
3	11.70	1945572	11.20	1945572	0	0	No change
4	8.22	1366062	7.86	1366062	0	0	No change
5	7.48	1244089	7.16	1244089	0	0	No change
6	6.65	1105210	6.36	1105210	0	0	No change
7	6.45	1072363	6.17	1072363	0	0	No change
8	6.60	1097669	6.32	1097669	0	0	No change
9	**6.76**	**1123819**	**8.78**	**1526545**	**+402726**	**+35.84%**	**↑Low to High**

TABLE 7: Characterization of malicious deletion attacks on digit frequency.

d_i	rfd_i	fd_i	$rfd_i{'}$	$fd_i{'}$	Δfd_i	$\Delta \mathscr{F} d_i$	Characteristic
0	**8.63**	**1435163**	**7.72**	**1256568**	**−178595**	**−12.44%**	**↓High to Low**
1	18.02	2995771	18.40	2995771	0	0	No change
2	19.48	3238818	19.89	3238818	0	0	No change
3	11.70	1945572	11.95	1945572	0	0	No change
4	8.22	1366062	8.39	1366062	0	0	No change
5	7.48	1244089	7.64	1244089	0	0	No change
6	6.65	1105210	6.79	1105210	0	0	No change
7	6.45	1072363	6.59	1072363	0	0	No change
8	6.60	1097669	6.74	1097669	0	0	No change
9	**6.76**	**1123819**	**5.89**	**958569**	**−165250**	**−14.70%**	**↓High to Low**

TABLE 8: Characterization of malicious update attacks on digit frequency.

d_i	rfd_i	fd_i	$rfd_i{'}$	$fd_i{'}$	Δfd_i	$\Delta \mathscr{F} d_i$	Characteristic
0	**8.63**	**1435163**	**5.71**	**948993**	**−486170**	**−33.88%**	**↓High to Low**
1	18.02	2995771	19.01	3159784	+164013	+5.47%	↑Low to High
2	19.48	3238818	20.97	3485451	+246633	+7.61%	↑Low to High
3	11.70	1945572	11.91	1980325	+34753	+1.79%	↑Low to High
4	8.22	1366062	8.52	1416889	+50827	+3.72%	↑Low to High
5	7.48	1244089	8.22	1365803	+121714	+9.78%	↑Low to High
6	6.65	1105210	6.90	1146565	+41355	+3.74%	↑Low to High
7	6.45	1072363	7.14	1187586	+115223	+10.74%	↑Low to High
8	6.60	1097669	6.78	1127651	+29982	+2.73%	↑Low to High
9	**6.76**	**1123819**	**4.85**	**805489**	**−318330**	**−28.33%**	**↓High to Low**

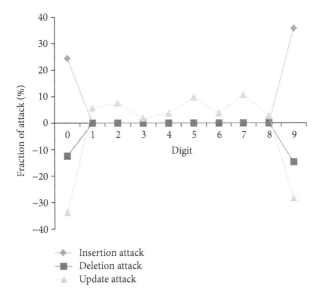

FIGURE 4: Characterization of malicious insertion, deletion, and update attacks on digits 9 and 0 of data values.

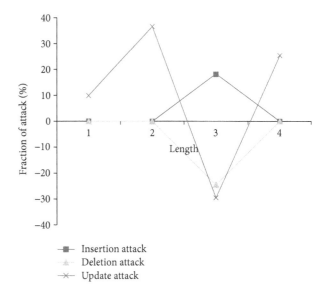

FIGURE 5: Characterization of malicious insertion, deletion, and update attacks on length 3 of data values.

similar tuples are inserted in database relation, an increase of approximately 10% is being observed in $\Delta\mathcal{F}d_i$ for each digit of database relation. Similarly, in deletion attack, a k fraction of negative trend (high to low) is observed in $\Delta\mathcal{F}d_i$ for each digit of database relation. In update attack, no specific trend is observed in $\Delta\mathcal{F}d_i$ as k fractions of digits are randomly replaced by some other digits.

It is to be noted that the attack on digit frequency (as discussed above) can be characterized on parameters like the digits being attacked, the fraction of each digit attacked, the type of attack (insertion, deletion, or update) on each digit, and the effect of attack (low to high, high to low, or no change) on data values.

3.2.2. Attack on Length of Data Values.
In this set of attacks, Mallory randomly performs malicious insertion, deletion, and update attacks on length of data values. Table 10 shows the experimental result for characterization of malicious insertion on data values of length 3 in the database relation R. A positive value of $\Delta\mathcal{F}l_j$ indicates that $\mathcal{F}$ fraction of length l_j is maliciously inserted in the database relation R. The characteristic of this attack is to relatively increase the low data values to high as an increase of 18.27% is observed in $\Delta\mathcal{F}l_j$ for data values of length 3. Also, $\Delta\mathcal{F}l_j$ is zero for lengths 1, 2, and 4, which shows that the data values of these lengths are not attacked.

Table 11 shows result of random malicious deletion for data values of length 3. As in deletion of digit frequency attack, a negative value of $\Delta\mathcal{F}l_j$ indicates that $\mathcal{F}$ fraction of length l_j is maliciously deleted with characteristic of decreasing high data values to low in database relation. Also, as in malicious insertion, the $\Delta\mathcal{F}l_j$ is zero for lengths 1, 2, and 4, which indicates that the data values of these lengths are not deleted. Table 12 shows results for malicious updates on data values of length 3. In this attack, the data values of length 3 are randomly replaced by lengths 1, 2, and 4. This attack shows

a decrease in $\Delta\mathcal{F}l_j$ for length 3, where as the $\Delta\mathcal{F}l_j$ for lengths 1, 2, and 4 is increased.

Figure 5 summarizes the malicious insertion, deletion, and update attacks on length 3 of data values. The insertion attack shows a positive increase (low to high) in attacked length, where as a negative trend (high to low) on attacked length is observed in deletion attack. In modification attack, a negative trend (high to low) is observed on attacked length, where as a positive trend (low to high) is observed on un-attacked length of data values.

Table 13 shows the effect on fractional change in length frequency $\Delta\mathcal{F}l_j$, when 10% (lower bound) and 90% (upper bound) of tuples are maliciously inserted, deleted, and updated in the database relation. In insertion attack, the fractional change in length frequency $\Delta\mathcal{F}l_j$ has a k fraction of positive trend (low to high) for each length of data values. Similarly, in deletion attack, a k fraction of negative trend (high to low) is observed for each length of data values. For example, when 10% of tuples are randomly deleted from a database relation, a decrease of approximately 10% is observed in $\Delta\mathcal{F}l_j$ for each length of data values. The update attack does not show any specific trend as k fraction of different length of data values are randomly replaced by some other length of data values.

It is to be noted that the attack on length of data values can be characterized on parameters like the length of data values being attacked, the fraction of each length of data values attacked, the type of attack (insertion, deletion, or update), and the effect of attack (low to high, high to low, or no change) on each length of data values.

3.2.3. Attack on Range of Data Values.
In this set of attacks, Mallory randomly performs insertion, deletion, and update attack on range 1, that is, (100–999) of data values present in the database relation R. Table 14 shows the experimental results for characterization of malicious insertion for range 1

TABLE 9: Characterization of malicious modifications on digit frequency.

	Insertion attack		Deletion attack		Update attack	
Attack rate	10%	90%	10%	90%	10%	90%
d_i	$\Delta\mathscr{F}d_i\%$	$\Delta\mathscr{F}d_i\%$	$\Delta\mathscr{F}d_i\%$	$\Delta\mathscr{F}d_i\%$	$\Delta\mathscr{F}d_i\%$	$\Delta\mathscr{F}d_i\%$
0	+9.51	+90.77%	−9.63%	−89.65%	+0.41	+0.45
1	+10.51	+94.47%	−10.11%	−89.05%	+0.80	+15.91
2	+10.49	+90.14%	−10.67%	−90.20%	−0.57	−3.72
3	+9.63	+94.72%	−9.87%	−90.30%	−2.12	+3.39
4	+9.47	+83.78%	−10.07%	−90.82%	−0.28	−7.34
5	+9.01	+82.00%	−9.43%	−91.26%	+0.40	−11.43
6	+9.08	+81.84%	−9.48%	−91.01%	+0.13	−7.78
7	+10.17	+88.20%	−9.95%	−89.83%	+0.05	+1.46
8	+10.23	+88.86%	−10.06%	−89.89%	−0.22	+2.16
9	+10.25	+88.36%	−10.37%	−90.66%	−0.96	−2.62

The detailed experiments for this set of attacks are presented in the Appendix (Tables 18(a)–18(f)).

TABLE 10: Characterization of malicious insertion attacks on length of data values.

l_j	rfl_j	fl_j	$rfl_j{}'$	$fl_j{}'$	Δfl_j	$\Delta\mathscr{F}l_j$	Characteristic
1	5.74	325894	5.27	325894	0	0	No change
2	20.19	1146469	18.54	1146469	0	0	No change
3	**48.66**	**2762791**	**52.85**	**3267609**	**+504818**	**+18.27%**	**↑Low to High**
4	25.41	1442906	23.34	1442906	0	0	No change

of data values. The characteristic of this attack is to relatively increase the low data values to high as an increase of 17.33% is observed in $\Delta\mathscr{F}r_k$ for range 1 of data values. The $\Delta\mathscr{F}r_k$ for range 0 and 2 is zero as the data values of these ranges are not attacked.

Table 15 shows the results of random malicious deletion for data values of range 1. As in deletion of digit frequency attack, a negative value of $\Delta\mathscr{F}r_k$ indicates that $\mathscr{F}$ fraction of range 1 is maliciously deleted with characteristic of transforming high data values to low in database relation R. As the data values of ranges 0 and 2 are not attacked, so the $\Delta\mathscr{F}r_k$ is zero for these ranges. Table 16 shows the results for malicious updates on data values of range 1. In this attack, the data values of range 1 are randomly replaced by ranges 0 and 2. This attack shows a decrease in $\Delta\mathscr{F}r_k$ for range 1, where as the $\Delta\mathscr{F}r_k$ for range 0 and 2 is increased.

The malicious insertion, deletion, and update attacks on range 1 of data values are summarized in Figure 6. A positive increase is observed in the attacked range for insertion attack (low to high) and a negative trend (high to low) is observed in attacked range for deletion attack. The modification attack shows a negative trend (high to low) for attacked range, that is, range 1 of data values and a positive increase for nonattacked ranges, that is, range 0 and 2 of data values.

In another set of attacks, we randomly inserted, deleted, and updated 10% (lower bound) and 90% (upper bound) of tuples from the database relation R. Table 17 shows the effect on fractional change in range frequency $\Delta\mathscr{F}r_k$, for each range of data values. The fractional change in range frequency $\Delta\mathscr{F}r_k$ has a k fraction of positive trend (low to high) for malicious insertion in each range of data values. Similarly, in deletion

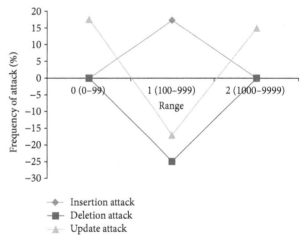

FIGURE 6: Characterization of malicious insertion, deletion, and update attacks on range 1 (100–999) of data values.

attack, a k fraction of negative trend (high to low) is observed for each range of data values. For example, when 10% of tuples are randomly deleted from a database relation, a decrease of approximately 10% is observed in $\Delta\mathscr{F}r_k$ for each range of data values. The update attack does not show any specific trend as k fraction of different range of data values are randomly replaced by some other range of data values.

It is to be noted that the data characteristics used for our experiments like digit, length, and range of data values are cohesive to each another. Due to this relationship, we evaluated the effect of malicious data modifications on these three data characteristics. For example, if Mallory maliciously

TABLE 11: Characterization of malicious deletion attacks on length of data values.

l_j	rfl_j	fl_j	$rfl_j{}'$	$fl_j{}'$	Δfl_j	$\Delta \mathscr{F}l_j$	Characteristic
1	5.74	325894	6.52	325894	0	0.00	No change
2	20.19	1146469	22.92	1146469	0	0.00	No change
3	**48.66**	**2762791**	**41.71**	**2085761**	**−677030**	**−24.51%**	**↓High to Low**
4	25.41	1442906	28.85	1442906	0	0.00	No change

TABLE 12: Characterization of malicious update attacks on length of data values.

l_j	rfl_j	fl_j	$rfl_j{}'$	$fl_j{}'$	Δfl_j	$\Delta \mathscr{F}l_j$	Characteristic
1	5.74	325894	6.31	358142	+32248	+9.90%	↑Low to High
2	20.19	1146469	27.57	1565462	+418993	+36.55%	↑Low to High
3	**48.66**	**2762791**	**34.27**	**1945657**	**−817134**	**−29.58%**	**↓High to Low**
4	25.41	1442906	31.86	1808799	+365893	+25.36%	↑Low to High

TABLE 13: Characterization of malicious modifications on length of data values.

Attack rate	Insertion attack		Deletion attack		Update attack	
	10%	90%	10%	90%	10%	90%
l_j	$\Delta \mathscr{F}l_j\%$	$\Delta \mathscr{F}l_j\%$	$\Delta \mathscr{F}l_j\%$	$\Delta \mathscr{F}l_j\%$	$\Delta \mathscr{F}l_j\%$	$\Delta \mathscr{F}l_j\%$
1	+9.55	100.58	−8.94	−91.25	−3.65	−38.67
2	+10.20	89.64	−10.21	−89.28	1.89	6.13
3	+10.35	89.91	−9.98	−88.92	1.57	11.03
4	+9.41	87.71	−10.16	−91.93	−2.94	−12.33

The detailed experiments for this set of attacks are presented in the Appendix (Tables 19(a)–19(f)).

TABLE 14: Characterization of malicious insertion attacks on range of data values.

Range	r_k	rfr_k	fr_k	$rfr_k{}'$	$fr_k{}'$	Δfr_k	$\Delta \mathscr{F}r_k$	Characteristic
0	0–99	25.59	1436986	23.60	1436986	0	0	No change
1	**100–999**	**48.73**	**2736731**	**52.72**	**3210988**	**+474257**	**+17.33%**	**↑Low to High**
2	1000–9999	25.68	1442223	23.68	1442223	0	0	No change

TABLE 15: Characterization of malicious deletion attacks on range of data values.

Range	r_k	rfr_k	fr_k	$rfr_k{}'$	$fr_k{}'$	Δfr_k	$\Delta \mathscr{F}r_k$	Characteristic
0	0–99	25.59	1436986	29.12	1436986	0	0	No change
1	**100–999**	**48.73**	**2736731**	**41.65**	**2054875**	**−681856**	**−24.92%**	**↓High to Low**
2	1000–9999	25.68	1442223	29.23	1442223	0	0	No change

TABLE 16: Characterization of malicious update attacks on range of data values.

Range	r_k	rfr_k	fr_k	$rfr_k{}'$	$fr_k{}'$	Δfr_k	$\Delta \mathscr{F}r_k$	Characteristic
0	0–99	25.59	1436986	30.07	1688965	251979	+17.54%	↑Low to High
1	**100–999**	**48.73**	**2736731**	**40.42**	**2269854**	**−466877**	**−17.06%**	**↓High to Low**
2	1000–9999	25.68	1442223	29.51	1657121	214898	+14.91%	↑Low to High

TABLE 17: Characterization of malicious data modifications on range of data values.

Attack rate		Insertion attack		Deletion attack		Update attack	
		10%	90%	10%	90%	10%	90%
Range	r_k	$\Delta \mathscr{F}r_k\%$	$\Delta \mathscr{F}r_k\%$	$\Delta \mathscr{F}r_k\%$	$\Delta \mathscr{F}r_k\%$	$\Delta \mathscr{F}r_k\%$	$\Delta \mathscr{F}r_k\%$
0	0–99	+9.97	+92.33	−9.84	−89.76	0.39	−5.91
1	100–999	+10.34	+89.86	−9.99	−88.90	1.48	10.46
2	1000–9999	+9.41	+87.71	−10.16	−91.93	−2.94	−12.41

The detailed experiments for this set of attacks are presented in the Appendix (Tables 20(a)–20(f)).

TABLE 18: Characterization of malicious attacks on digit frequency (deterministic).

(a) Characterization of malicious insertion attacks on digit frequency ($\eta = 10^6$, attack rate = 10%)

d_i	rfd_i	fd_i	$rfd_i{}'$	$fd_i{}'$	Δfd_i	$\Delta \mathcal{F} d_i$	Characteristic
0	8.44	247345	8.40	270858	23513	+9.51%	↑Low to High
1	16.28	477362	16.37	527535	50173	+10.51%	↑Low to High
2	19.88	582616	19.97	643745	61129	+10.49%	↑Low to High
3	11.37	333378	11.34	365471	32093	+9.63%	↑Low to High
4	8.83	258748	8.79	283251	24503	+9.47%	↑Low to High
5	8.31	243554	8.24	265510	21956	+9.01%	↑Low to High
6	7.14	209399	7.09	228418	19019	+9.08%	↑Low to High
7	6.40	187586	6.41	206659	19073	+10.17%	↑Low to High
8	6.49	190268	6.51	209737	19469	+10.23%	↑Low to High
9	6.86	201050	6.88	221653	20603	+10.25%	↑Low to High

(b) Characterization of malicious insertion attacks on digit frequency ($\eta = 10^6$, attack rate = 90%)

d_i	rfd_i	fd_i	$rfd_i{}'$	$fd_i{}'$	Δfd_i	$\Delta \mathcal{F} d_i$	Characteristic
0	8.44	247345	8.51	471852	224507	+90.77%	↑Low to High
1	16.28	477362	16.73	928331	450969	+94.47%	↑Low to High
2	19.88	582616	19.97	1107797	525181	+90.14%	↑Low to High
3	11.37	333378	11.70	649150	315772	+94.72%	↑Low to High
4	8.83	258748	8.57	475532	216784	+83.78%	↑Low to High
5	8.31	243554	7.99	443279	199725	+82.00%	↑Low to High
6	7.14	209399	6.86	380768	171369	+81.84%	↑Low to High
7	6.40	187586	6.36	353031	165445	+88.20%	↑Low to High
8	6.49	190268	6.48	359339	169071	+88.86%	↑Low to High
9	6.86	201050	6.83	378696	177646	+88.36%	↑Low to High

(c) Characterization of malicious deletion attacks on digit frequency ($\eta = 10^6$, attack rate = 10%)

d_i	rfd_i	fd_i	$rfd_i{}'$	$fd_i{}'$	Δfd_i	$\Delta \mathcal{F} d_i$	Characteristic
0	8.44	247345	8.48	223528	−23817	−9.63%	↓High to Low
1	16.28	477362	16.27	429114	−48248	−10.11%	↓High to Low
2	19.88	582616	19.74	520475	−62141	−10.67%	↓High to Low
3	11.37	333378	11.40	300483	−32895	−9.87%	↓High to Low
4	8.83	258748	8.83	232703	−26045	−10.07%	↓High to Low
5	8.31	243554	8.37	220577	−22977	−9.43%	↓High to Low
6	7.14	209399	7.19	189555	−19844	−9.48%	↓High to Low
7	6.40	187586	6.41	168921	−18665	−9.95%	↓High to Low
8	6.49	190268	6.49	171131	−19137	−10.06%	↓High to Low
9	6.86	201050	6.83	180196	−20854	−10.37%	↓High to Low

(d) Characterization of malicious deletion attacks on digit frequency ($\eta = 10^6$, attack rate = 90%)

d_i	rfd_i	fd_i	$rfd_i{}'$	$fd_i{}'$	Δfd_i	$\Delta \mathcal{F} d_i$	Characteristic
0	8.44	247345	8.89	25612	−221733	−89.65%	↓High to Low
1	16.28	477362	18.14	52276	−425086	−89.05%	↓High to Low
2	19.88	582616	19.80	57072	−525544	−90.20%	↓High to Low
3	11.37	333378	11.22	32342	−301036	−90.30%	↓High to Low
4	8.83	258748	8.24	23758	−234990	−90.82%	↓High to Low
5	8.31	243554	7.38	21281	−222273	−91.26%	↓High to Low

(d) Continued.

d_i	rfd_i	fd_i	$rfd_i{}'$	$fd_i{}'$	Δfd_i	$\Delta \mathcal{F} d_i$	Characteristic
6	7.14	209399	6.53	18815	−190584	−91.01%	↓High to Low
7	6.40	187586	6.62	19071	−168515	−89.83%	↓High to Low
8	6.49	190268	6.67	19239	−171029	−89.89%	↓High to Low
9	6.86	201050	6.52	18780	−182270	−90.66%	↓High to Low

(e) Characterization of malicious update attacks on digit frequency ($\eta = 10^6$, attack rate = 10%)

d_i	rfd_i	fd_i	$rfd_i{}'$	$fd_i{}'$	Δfd_i	$\Delta \mathcal{F} d_i$	Characteristic
0	8.438048	247345	8.49	248357	1012	+0.41%	↑Low to High
1	16.28496	477362	16.46	481186	3824	+0.80%	↑Low to High
2	19.87565	582616	19.81	579315	−3301	−0.57%	↓High to Low
3	11.37302	333378	11.16	326311	−7067	−2.12%	↓High to Low
4	8.827055	258748	8.82	258020	−728	−0.28%	↓High to Low
5	8.30872	243554	8.36	244519	965	+0.40%	↑Low to High
6	7.143539	209399	7.17	209680	281	+0.13%	↑Low to High
7	6.3994	187586	6.42	187678	92	+0.05%	↑Low to High
8	6.490895	190268	6.49	189845	−423	−0.22%	↓High to Low
9	6.858718	201050	6.81	199111	−1939	−0.96%	↓High to Low

(f) Characterization of malicious update attacks on digit frequency ($\eta = 10^6$, attack rate = 90%)

d_i	rfd_i	fd_i	$rfd_i{}'$	$fd_i{}'$	Δfd_i	$\Delta \mathcal{F} d_i$	Characteristic
0	8.438048	247345	8.46	248462	1117	+0.45%	↑Low to High
1	16.28496	477362	18.84	553334	75972	+15.91%	↑Low to High
2	19.87565	582616	19.10	560965	−21651	−3.72%	↓High to Low
3	11.37302	333378	11.74	344665	11287	+3.39%	↑Low to High
4	8.827055	258748	8.16	239767	−18981	−7.34%	↓High to Low
5	8.30872	243554	7.35	215727	−27827	−11.43%	↓High to Low
6	7.143539	209399	6.58	193116	−16283	−7.78%	↓High to Low
7	6.3994	187586	6.48	190330	2744	+1.46%	↑Low to High
8	6.490895	190268	6.62	194384	4116	+2.16%	↑Low to High
9	6.858718	201050	6.67	195785	−5265	−2.62%	↓High to Low

inserts a digit in a data value, the length and range of the data value are also increased. Similarly, if Mallory maliciously decreases the length of a data value, the digit count and range of the data value are also decreased (Tables 9, 13, and 17).

At the end, we summarize our findings and observations for characterization of malicious data modifications as follows.

(i) If there is a positive trend in fractional change $\Delta \mathcal{F}$ of data values in tempered database relation R', it means that $\mathcal{F}$ fraction of digit, range, and length of data values is maliciously inserted by Mallory in Alice's watermarked relation R. The characteristic of this attack is to relatively increase the low data values to high in database relation R (Tables 6, 10, and 14).

(ii) If there is a negative trend in fractional change $\Delta \mathcal{F}$ of data values in tempered database relation R', it means that $\mathcal{F}$ fraction of digit, range, and length of data values is maliciously deleted by Mallory from Alice's watermarked relation R. The characteristic of

this attack is to relatively decrease the high data values to low in database relation R (Tables 7, 11, and 15).

(iii) If there is both positive and negative trends in fractional change $\Delta \mathcal{F}$ for digit, range, and length of data values in tempered database relation R', it means that the negative trend fractional change $\Delta \mathcal{F}$ of data values is maliciously replaced (updated) by positive trend fractional change $\Delta \mathcal{F}$ of data values (Tables 8, 12, and 16).

(iv) If there is a uniform increase of k in fractional change $\Delta \mathcal{F}$ of all data values in tempered database relation R', it means that k fraction of similar tuples is maliciously inserted by Mallory in Alice's watermarked relation R. The characteristic of this attack is to relatively increase the low data values to high in database relation R (Tables 9, 13, and 17).

(v) If there is a uniform decrease of k in fractional change $\Delta \mathcal{F}$ of all data values in tempered database relation R', it means that k fraction of tuples is maliciously deleted by Mallory from Alice's watermarked relation

TABLE 19: Characterization of malicious attacks on length of data values (deterministic).

(a) Characterization of malicious insertion attacks on length of data values ($\eta = 10^6$, attack rate = 10%)

l_j	rfl_j	fl_j	rfl_j'	fl_j'	Δfl_j	$\Delta \mathscr{F}l_j$	Characteristic
1	7.11	71085	7.08	77875	6790	+9.55%	↑Low to High
2	19.76	197605	19.80	217767	20162	+10.20%	↑Low to High
3	45.18	451787	45.32	498531	46744	+10.35%	↑Low to High
4	27.95	279523	27.80	305827	26304	+9.41%	↑Low to High

(b) Characterization of malicious insertion attacks on length of data values ($\eta = 10^6$, attack rate = 90%)

l_j	rfl_j	fl_j	rfl_j'	fl_j'	Δfl_j	$\Delta \mathscr{F}l_j$	Characteristic
1	7.11	71085	7.50	142584	71499	+100.58%	↑Low to High
2	19.76	197605	19.72	374737	177132	+89.64%	↑Low to High
3	45.18	451787	45.16	857986	406199	+89.91%	↑Low to High
4	27.95	279523	27.62	524693	245170	+87.71%	↑Low to High

(c) Characterization of malicious deletion attacks on length of data values ($\eta = 10^6$, attack rate = 10%)

l_j	rfl_j	fl_j	rfl_j'	fl_j'	Δfl_j	$\Delta \mathscr{F}l_j$	Characteristic
1	7.11	71085	7.19	64733	−6352	−8.94%	↓High to Low
2	19.76	197605	19.71	177421	−20184	−10.21%	↓High to Low
3	45.18	451787	45.19	406721	−45066	−9.98%	↓High to Low
4	27.95	279523	27.90	251125	−28398	−10.16%	↓High to Low

(d) Characterization of malicious deletion attacks on length of data values ($\eta = 10^6$, attack rate = 90%)

l_j	rfl_j	fl_j	rfl_j'	fl_j'	Δfl_j	$\Delta \mathscr{F}l_j$	Characteristic
1	7.11	71085	6.22	6221	−64864	−91.25%	↓High to Low
2	19.76	197605	21.19	21186	−176419	−89.28%	↓High to Low
3	45.18	451787	50.04	50039	−401748	−88.92%	↓High to Low
4	27.95	279523	22.55	22554	−256969	−91.93%	↓High to Low

(e) Characterization of malicious update attacks on length of data values ($\eta = 10^6$, attack rate = 10%)

l_j	rfl_j	fl_j	rfl_j'	fl_j'	Δfl_j	$\Delta \mathscr{F}l_j$	Characteristic
1	7.11	71085	6.85	68488	−2597	−3.65%	↓High to Low
2	19.76	197605	20.13	201333	3728	+1.89%	↑Low to High
3	45.18	451787	45.89	458869	7082	+1.57%	↑Low to High
4	27.95	279523	27.13	271310	−8213	−2.94%	↓High to Low

(f) Characterization of malicious update attacks on length of data values ($\eta = 10^6$, attack rate = 90%)

l_j	rfl_j	fl_j	rfl_j'	fl_j'	Δfl_j	$\Delta \mathscr{F}l_j$	Characteristic
1	7.11	71085	4.36	43599	−27486	−38.67%	↓High to Low
2	19.76	197605	20.97	209711	12106	+6.13%	↑Low to High
3	45.18	451787	50.16	501622	49835	+11.03%	↑Low to High
4	27.95	279523	24.51	245068	−34455	−12.33%	↓High to Low

R. The characteristic of this attack is to relatively decrease the high data values to low in database relation *R* (Tables 9, 13, and 17).

4. Conclusions

In this paper, a fragile watermarking scheme to detect and characterize malicious tempering made in database relations is presented. The proposed scheme is based on zero watermarking approach that does not alter the database original content, and thus it overcomes the limitation of data integrity and data usability in existing watermarking schemes. In the proposed scheme, the watermarks are generated by using the local characteristics of database relation itself, like frequency distribution of various digits, lengths, and ranges of data values. This enables us to characterize the malicious modifications made to the database relations. Experimental results showed that the proposed scheme can detect and characterize malicious data modifications successfully. In the future, we intend to work on some other local characteristics

TABLE 20: Characterization of malicious attacks on range of data values (Deterministic).

(a) Characterization of malicious insertion attacks on range of data values ($\eta = 10^6$, attack rate = 10%)

Range No	r_k	rfr_k	fr_k	$rfr_k{'}$	$fr_k{'}$	Δfr_k	$\Delta \mathscr{F}r_k$	Characteristic
0	0–99	25.59	1436986	26.49	288506	26164	+9.97%	↑Low to High
1	100–999	48.73	2736731	45.43	494709	46373	+10.34%	↑Low to High
2	1000–9999	25.68	1442223	28.08	305806	26304	+9.41%	↑Low to High

(b) Characterization of malicious insertion attacks on range of data values ($\eta = 10^6$, attack rate = 90%)

Range No	r_k	rfr_k	fr_k	$rfr_k{'}$	$fr_k{'}$	Δfr_k	$\Delta \mathscr{F}r_k$	Characteristic
0	0–99	25.59	1436986	26.83	504566	242224	+92.33%	↑Low to High
1	100–999	48.73	2736731	45.27	851193	402857	+89.86%	↑Low to High
2	1000–9999	25.68	1442223	27.90	524663	245161	+87.71%	↑Low to High

(c) Characterization of malicious deletion attacks on range of data values ($\eta = 10^6$, attack rate = 10%)

Range No	r_k	rfr_k	fr_k	$rfr_k{'}$	$fr_k{'}$	Δfr_k	$\Delta \mathscr{F}r_k$	Characteristic
0	0–99	25.59	1436986	26.54	236532	−25810	−9.84%	↓High to Low
1	100–999	48.73	2736731	45.28	403562	−44774	−9.99%	↑Low to High
2	1000–9999	25.68	1442223	28.18	251104	−28398	−10.16%	↓High to Low

(d) Characterization of malicious deletion attacks on range of data values ($\eta = 10^6$, attack rate = 90%)

Range No	r_k	rfr_k	fr_k	$rfr_k{'}$	$fr_k{'}$	Δfr_k	$\Delta \mathscr{F}r_k$	Characteristic
0	0–99	25.59	1436986	27.08	26857	−235485	−89.76%	↓High to Low
1	100–999	48.73	2736731	50.18	49757	−398579	−88.90%	↑Low to High
2	1000–9999	25.68	1442223	22.74	22547	−256955	−91.93%	↓High to Low

(e) Characterization of malicious update attacks on range of data values ($\eta = 10^6$, attack rate = 10%)

Range No	r_k	rfr_k	fr_k	$rfr_k{'}$	$fr_k{'}$	Δfr_k	$\Delta \mathscr{F}r_k$	Characteristic
0	0–99	25.59	1436986	26.61	263370	1028	+0.39%	↑Low to High
1	100–999	48.73	2736731	45.97	454956	6620	+1.48%	↑Low to High
2	1000–9999	25.68	1442223	27.41	271271	−8231	−2.94%	↓High to Low

(f) Characterization of malicious update attacks on range of data values ($\eta = 10^6$, attack rate = 90%)

Range No	r_k	rfr_k	fr_k	$rfr_k{'}$	$fr_k{'}$	Δfr_k	$\Delta \mathscr{F}r_k$	Characteristic
0	0–99	25.59	1436986	25.01	246838	−15504	−5.91%	↓High to Low
1	100–999	48.73	2736731	50.18	495248	46912	+10.46%	↑Low to High
2	1000–9999	25.68	1442223	24.81	244819	−34683	−12.41%	↓High to Low

of relational databases for watermark generation and to extend the proposed scheme to semifragile watermarking schemes.

Appendix

(i) Characterization of malicious attacks on digit frequency (deterministic) (see Table 18).

(ii) Characterization of malicious attacks on length of data values (deterministic) (see Table 19).

(iii) Characterization of malicious attacks on range of data values (deterministic) (see Table 20).

References

[1] J. Dittmann, P. Schmitt, E. Saar, J. Schwenk, and J. Ueberberg, "Combining digital watermarks and collusion secure fingerprints for digital images," *SPIE Journal of Electronic Imaging*, vol. 9, no. 4, pp. 456–467, 2000.

[2] E. T. Lin and E. J. Delp, "Temporal synchronization in video watermarking," *IEEE Transactions on Signal Processing*, vol. 52, no. 10, pp. 3007–3022, 2004.

[3] M. Chen, Y. He, and R. L. Lagendijk, "A fragile watermark error detection scheme for wireless video communications," *IEEE Transactions on Multimedia*, vol. 7, no. 2, pp. 201–211, 2005.

[4] F. Hartung, P. Eisert, and B. Girod, "Digital watermarking of mpeg-4 facial animation parameters," *Computers and Graphics*, vol. 22, no. 4, pp. 425–435, 1998.

[5] R. Agrawal, P. J. Haas, and J. Kiernan, "Watermarking relational data: framework, algorithms and analysis," *VLDB Journal*, vol. 12, no. 2, pp. 157–169, 2003.

[6] G. Gupta and J. Pieprzyk, "Database relation watermarking resilient against secondary watermarking attacks," in *Proceedings of the 5th International Conference on Information Systems

Security (ICISS '09), vol. 5905 of Lecture Notes in Computer Science, pp. 222–236, Springer, Kolkata, India, 2009.

[7] Y. Zhang, X. Niu, and D. Zhao, "A method of protecting relational databases copyright with cloud watermark," International Journal of Information and Communication Engineering, vol. 1, pp. 337–341, 2005.

[8] F. Guo, J. Wang, Z. Zhang, X. Ye, and D. Li, "An improved algorithm to watermark numeric relational data," in Proceedings of the 6th International Workshop on Information Security applications (WISA '05), vol. 3786 of Lecture Notes in Computer Science, pp. 138–149, Springer, Jeju Island, Republic of Korea, 2005.

[9] M. Huang, J. Cao, Z. Peng, and Y. Fang, "A new watermark mechanism for relational data," in Proceedings of the 4th International Conference on Computer and Information Technology (CIT '04), pp. 946–950, IEEE Computer Society, Wuhan, China, 2004.

[10] T. Hu, G. Chen, K. Chen, and J. Dong, "Garwm: towards a generalized and adaptive watermark scheme for relational data," in Proceedings of the 6th International Conference in Advances in Web-Age Information Management (WAIM '05), vol. 3739 of Lecture Notes in Computer Science, pp. 380–391, Springer, Hangzhou, China, 2005.

[11] R. Sion, "Proving ownership over categorical data," in Proceedings of the 20th International Conference on Data Engineering (ICDE '04), pp. 584–595, IEEE Computer Society, Boston, Mass, USA, April 2004.

[12] R. Sion, M. Atallah, and S. Prabhakar, "Rights protection for categorical data," IEEE Transactions on Knowledge and Data Engineering, vol. 17, no. 7, pp. 912–926, 2005.

[13] C. Wang, J. Wang, M. Zhou, G. Chen, and D. Li, "Atbam: an arnold transform based method on watermarking relational data," in Proceedings of the International Conference on Multimedia and Ubiquitous Engineering (MUE '08), pp. 263–270, IEEE Computer Society, Beijing, China, 2008.

[14] X. Zhou, M. Huang, and Z. Peng, "An additive-attack-proof watermarking mechanism for databases copyrights protection using image," in Proceedings of the ACM symposium on Applied Computing (SAC '07), pp. 254–258, ACM Press, Seoul, Republic of Korea, March 2007.

[15] A. Al-Haj and A. Odeh, "Robust and blind watermarking of relational database systems," Journal of Computer Science, vol. 4, no. 12, pp. 1024–1029, 2008.

[16] H. Wang, X. Cui, and Z. Cao, "A speech based algorithm for watermarking relational databases," in Proceedings of the International Symposiums on Information Processing (ISIP '08), pp. 603–606, IEEE Computer Society, Moscow, Russia, 2008.

[17] H. Guo, Y. Li, A. Liu, and S. Jajodia, "A fragile watermarking scheme for detecting malicious modifications of database relations," Information Sciences, vol. 176, no. 10, pp. 1350–1378, 2006.

[18] H. Khataeimaragheh and H. Rashidi, "A novel watermarking scheme for detecting and recovering distortions in database tables," International Journal of Database Management Systems, vol. 2, no. 3, pp. 1–11, 2010.

[19] S. Iqbal, A. Rauf, S. Mahfooz, S. Khusro, and S. H. Shah, "Self-constructing fragile watermark algorithm for. relational database integrity proof," World Applied Sciences Journal, vol. 19, no. 9, pp. 1273–1277, 2012.

[20] V. Prasannakumari, "A robust tamperproof watermarking for data integrity in relational databases," Research Journal of Information Technology, vol. 1, no. 3, pp. 115–121, 2009.

[21] J. Lafaye, D. Gross-Amblard, C. Constantin, and M. Guerrouani, "WATERMILL: an optimized fingerprinting system for databases under constraints," IEEE Transactions on Knowledge and Data Engineering, vol. 20, no. 4, pp. 532–546, 2008.

[22] Y. Li, H. Guo, and S. Jajodia, "Tamper detection and localization for categorical data using fragile watermarks," in Proceedings of the 4th ACM Workshop on Digital Rights Management (DRM '04), pp. 73–82, ACM Press, Washington, DC, USA, October 2004.

[23] I. Kamel, "A schema for protecting the integrity of databases," Computers and Security, vol. 28, no. 7, pp. 698–709, 2009.

[24] S. Bhattacharya and A. Cortesi, "A distortion free watermark framework for relational databases," in Proceedings of the 4th International Conference on Software and Data Technologies (ICSOFT '09), pp. 229–234, INSTICC Press, Sofia, Bulgaria, July 2009.

[25] A. Hamadou, X. Sun, L. Gao, and S. A. Shah, "A fragile zero-watermarking technique for authentication of relational databases," International Journal of Digital Content Technology and its Applications, vol. 5, no. 5, pp. 189–200, 2011.

[26] Y. Li, V. Swarup, and S. Jajodia, "Fingerprinting relational databases: schemes and specialties," IEEE Transactions on Dependable and Secure Computing, vol. 2, no. 1, pp. 34–45, 2005.

[27] S. Liu, S. Wang, R. H. Deng, and W. Shao, "A block oriented fingerprinting scheme in relational database," in Proceedings of the 7th International Conference in Information Security and Cryptology (ICISC '04), vol. 3506 of Lecture Notes in Computer Science, pp. 455–466, Springer, Seoul, Republic of Korea, 2004.

[28] F. Guo, J. Wang, and D. Li, "Fingerprinting relational databases," in Proceedings of the ACM symposium on Applied Computing (SAC '06), pp. 487–492, ACM Press, Dijon, France, 2006.

[29] C. T. Li, F. M. Yang, and C. S. Lee, "Oblivious fragile watermarking scheme for image authentication," in Proceedings of the IEEE International Conference on Acoustics, Speech, and Signal Processing, pp. 3445–3448, IEEE Press, Orlando, Fla, USA, 2002.

[30] H. Yang, X. Sun, B. Wang, and Z. Qin, "An image-adaptive semi-fragile watermarking for image authentication and tamper detection," in Proceedings of the International Conference on Computational Science and its Applications, Kuala Lumpur, Malaysia, 2007.

[31] J. Hu, J. Huang, D. Huang, and Y. Q. Shi, "Image fragile watermarking based on fusion of multi-resolution tamper detection," Electronics Letters, vol. 38, no. 24, pp. 1512–1513, 2002.

[32] J. Zhang and H. Bin, "Fragile audio watermarking scheme based on sample mean sequence," in Proceedings of the IEEE International Conference on Multimedia Technology (ICMT '11), pp. 333–336, 2011.

[33] H. Wang and M. Fan, "Centroid-based semi-fragile audio watermarking in hybrid domain," Science in China F, vol. 53, no. 3, pp. 619–633, 2010.

[34] S. Lian, Z. Liu, Z. Ren, and H. Wang, "Commutative encryption and watermarking in video compression," IEEE Transactions on Circuits and Systems for Video Technology, vol. 17, no. 6, pp. 774–778, 2007.

[35] X. Huazheng, S. Xingming, and T. Chengliang, "New fragile watermarking scheme for text documents authentication," Wuhan University Journal of Natural Sciences, vol. 11, no. 6, pp. 1661–1666, 2006.

[36] H. Yang, A. C. Kot, and J. Liu, "Semi-fragile watermarking for text document images authentication," in Proceedings of the IEEE International Symposium on Circuits and Systems (ISCAS '05), pp. 4002–4005, May 2005.

[37] http://archive.ics.uci.edu/ml/datasets/Covertype.

14

Immunity-Based Optimal Estimation Approach for a New Real Time Group Elevator Dynamic Control Application for Energy and Time Saving

Mehmet Baygin[1] and Mehmet Karakose[2]

[1] *Computer Engineering Department, Ardahan University, Ardahan, Turkey*
[2] *Computer Engineering Department, Firat University, Elazig, Turkey*

Correspondence should be addressed to Mehmet Baygin; mehmetbaygin@ardahan.edu.tr

Academic Editors: P. Agarwal, S. Balochian, V. Bhatnagar, and Y. Zhang

Nowadays, the increasing use of group elevator control systems owing to increasing building heights makes the development of high-performance algorithms necessary in terms of time and energy saving. Although there are many studies in the literature about this topic, they are still not effective enough because they are not able to evaluate all features of system. In this paper, a new approach of immune system-based optimal estimate is studied for dynamic control of group elevator systems. The method is mainly based on estimation of optimal way by optimizing all calls with genetic, immune system and DNA computing algorithms, and it is evaluated with a fuzzy system. The system has a dynamic feature in terms of the situation of calls and the option of the most appropriate algorithm, and it also adaptively works in terms of parameters such as the number of floors and cabins. This new approach which provides both time and energy saving was carried out in real time. The experimental results comparatively demonstrate the effects of method. With dynamic and adaptive control approach in this study carried out, a significant progress on group elevator control systems has been achieved in terms of time and energy efficiency according to traditional methods.

1. Introduction

The scheduling of the group elevator systems, which has been used for vertical transportation at high-rise buildings, has an important place in our daily lives. Aiming to give rapid service to the crowd population in the building, such systems have very complex structure. One of the issues that people usually complain inside building is vertical transportation service of the building [1]. The studies on this topic continue for a long time, and important developments are provided.

The group elevator systems are structures, which elevate the population in the building from one floor to another by using more than one cabin in the widest sense. Generally managed from one control center in a coordinated manner, such systems are finding optimal ways according to the condition of calls, and they apply such ways on cabins. However, the width of the optimal way space makes this problem hard to solve in the best way. Because there are the option of n^p different ways in a building having n storey and p cabin [2, 3]. Actually, what is expected from the group elevator systems is the average performance of such cabins instead of individual performance of elevator. In addition, the basic criteria at such performances are to minimize the average waiting time of passengers and energy consumption values of cabins [3, 4]. Generally, by considering such parameters, the most optimum way is selected from the way space, and these are applied to the system. Actually, there are many factors, which affect average waiting time; these can be counted as lack of some information like number of passengers, elevator speed, and so on. For instance, the passengers have to wait new coming elevator for a long time because they missed the elevator a few minutes ago. In addition to this case, although no one uses elevator because of call of any empty floor, the passengers often wait for closing

Immunity-Based Optimal Estimation Approach for a New Real Time Group Elevator Dynamic Control Application for Energy and Time Saving

139

the doors [5]. All of this and similar circumstances are caused by lack of traffic information, and those waiting directly affect the average waiting time. However, despite all such circumstances, average waiting time can be approximately calculated as shown in the following equation [6, 7]:

$$AWT = 0.4 \, INT, \quad \text{for car loads} < 50\%,$$

$$AWT = \left[0.4 + \frac{1.8 \, P}{CC} - 0.77^2 \right] INT, \quad \text{for car loads} > 50\%,$$

$$(1)$$

where AWT, average waiting time, P, numbers of passenger, INT, interval (the main floor average time), and CC, car capacity.

For the most suitable car allocation at the past, although some mathematical approaches are thought, today soft computing techniques and artificial intelligence algorithms are often applied to this kind of system. In addition, such calculations can be made in shortest time with advanced computer systems, and the most optimum car can be allocated to the users [3].

One other criterion of the group elevator systems is energy consumption values in cabins. Although the energy consumption of the elevator occurs at the moment of stop start, it consists of two sections as travel and standby position. The consumption during travel (stop-travel-start) compromises more than 70% of total energy consumption [8]. The most important problem here is irregular energy consumption of cabins. For example, working of elevators without any pattern causes some cabins to operate more and to wear off. This parameter is considered in applications to be made for the removal of this condition, and load distribution of cabins is attempted to be equalized in parallel with average waiting time. Generally, it is very hard to determine daily energy consumption of elevator. However, Schroeder makes many measurements in many elevators and creates a formula to calculate this value. In (2), according to the Schroeder method, daily energy consumption amount of an elevator has been given. In this equation, TP shows general course time, and this term varies depending on drive mechanism type and speed of elevator [7]. The strongest point in the Schroeder method is to determine the ST value. Because the incoming calls are not known earlier, accordingly, how much the lifts operate during day is not predetermined. For this reason, this value is determined by either making certain measurements or by using certain approaches [7, 9]. Because the energy consumption of elevators is mostly caused by stop-start movements, this value directly affects the equation [9]

$$EC = N * \frac{R * ST * TP}{3600},$$

$$(2)$$

where EC is energy consumption (kWh/day), N is cabin number, R is motor ratings (kW), ST is daily start number, and TP = time factor.

The most important factor affecting both the average waiting time of passengers and energy consumption in group elevator systems is traffic time of buildings [2, 9]. This is very important issue because passengers use elevators much in certain hours, and they rarely use cabins in rest of their times. In the observations, 4 different traffic times are determined in any building, and such traffic hours and passenger density created depending on those hours are considered in either real world or computer simulations. Depending on those hours, the first of created density is uppeak, and it includes the hours when people come to work at mornings at the office building [1, 4, 6, 8]. The calls made in traffic are generally upward position, and these upward calls reach peak points at mornings. The second traffic movement is downpeak. This situation includes arrival time from work, and calls from floors are generally downward [5, 9]. Other traffic time is seen at lunch times. It contains the time frame at which building population is going out at lunch break and is coming back to work [10]. Traffic condition is random situation between floors. This traffic condition is caused by passing of people inside building between floors, and it is traffic condition, which is seen during working hours [3, 8].

There are various studies made in literature on group elevator systems. Either reduction of average waiting time of passengers or reduction of energy consumption is wide in literature. In such studies on which certain traffic conditions are considered, the soft computing techniques like genetic algorithms, fuzzy logic, particle swarm optimization, and artificial intelligence [4, 6, 8]. However, sheer number of parameters in elevator systems, width of solution space, and failure to determine incoming calls earlier make scheduling problem hard to solve [2, 3]. Despite these lacks, an important development has been performed from the first day of appearance of group elevator systems, and still continues to develop. Some studies, which have been made on literature within scope of working has been examined, such studies have been classified as aim, used method, traffic condition, number of elevator, and simulation forms. However, some lacks have been found in studies performed in literature in this classification. This study aims at elimination of lacks in literature with this study, and brings a new point of view to the solution of scheduling problems for group elevator systems. Two examples have been given to the studies which have been made in the literature Figure 1.

As seen in Figure 1, the procedures in the studies made in literature are performed over one algorithm with certain number of cabins. These limitations bring many problems. For example, subjecting to only one algorithm does not guarantee that the application always gives best results. Because each algorithm has different ways to reach better, and for this reason, the best results, which have been found by each algorithm, are different from each other. In this kind of system, it is evident that better results can be obtained by using different algorithms together. One other lack in the studies made on group elevator systems is limited number of cabins. This situation is directly associated with use of only one algorithm in the system. The largest lack here is that the algorithm selected gives better results in the designated number of algorithm. However, the results are reverse from one expected when you exclude the number of cabins. This study makes clear all this and similar conditions, and the studies made on literature gains new dimension. The artificial immune systems, genetic algorithms, and DNA

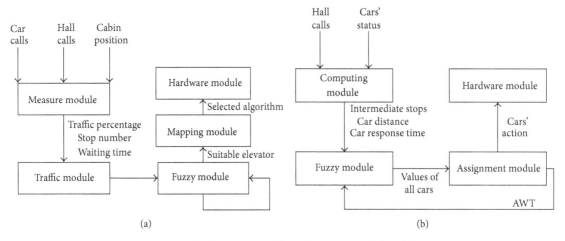

FIGURE 1: The closest two studies in literature (a) [2] (b) [4].

computing algorithm have been used in the study performed for reduction of average waiting time of passengers and providing energy efficiency in group elevator systems. In addition to these methods, an estimation algorithm has been developed, the relation of such methods has been provided with fuzzy logic, and the most suitable algorithm has been aimed according to the calls and cabin conditions of the system in adaptive way. The results which have been obtained from fuzzy logic are sent to the microprocessor-based experiment set, and the performance and accuracy of the system have been observed. The system procedure and methods used for control algorithm, which is recommended in 2nd section within scope of this study, have been examined; the simulation results and test results which have been obtained from these algorithms in 3rd section have been given. The obtained results are assessed in 4th and final section of the study.

2. Proposed Approach

The group elevator systems have a very complex structure. The sheer number of input parameters and many options as output makes these systems hard to solve. Especially the conditions as unknown building population or unknown floor by a passenger are basic factors in creation of wide solution space. However the developed electronic and computer world is useful for similar problems and used to solve this. Especially, making computational procedures about milliseconds makes detection of most suitable option from wide solution space.

There are some basic principles required to perform by system while group elevator systems are in service. These principles, which have been given in list below, are considered in this study.

(i) The elevator cannot pass up cabin call. It must complete these until all calls in present direction, and the cabin calls in reverse direction must be ignored

in this process. After present direction of elevator returns reverse, the rest of calls must be completed.

(ii) If there is enough space inside cabin before change of direction of system, it can collect floor calls in same direction.

(iii) If there is no one at the point where floor call is made, this floor call can be ignored.

(iv) It is required to do less stop-start movement as much as possible to provide energy efficiency of system. To perform this, no more than one cabin goes to the same floor call.

(v) It is required to do feasibility study before for population inside building and frequency to use elevator by this population in order to increase efficiency of methods to be used in the system.

This study aims at reduction of average waiting time of passengers and providing energy efficiency. The proposed control approach primarily consists of 3 main modules. The first module is optimization module, and calls are evaluated here according to the 4 different optimization methods. The results which have been obtained from the assessment made according to the average waiting time and energy efficiency are sent to the 2nd module, the fuzzy module. In this module, the method to be applied on call pool is determined, and optimum way must be given as exit. The optimal way obtained from the fuzzy module is sent to the hardware module and is tested on experiment set. A flow diagram is given in Figure 2, which summarizes the system.

2.1. Optimization Module. A group elevator system is modeled with modules designated within scope of this study. The optimization methods, which are often used in wide problems where solution space is wide, are used within scope of study. Three different optimization methods and 1 estimation algorithm are used in this performed optimization module. As optimization methods, clonal selection algorithm, genetic

Immunity-Based Optimal Estimation Approach for a New Real Time Group Elevator Dynamic Control Application
for Energy and Time Saving

141

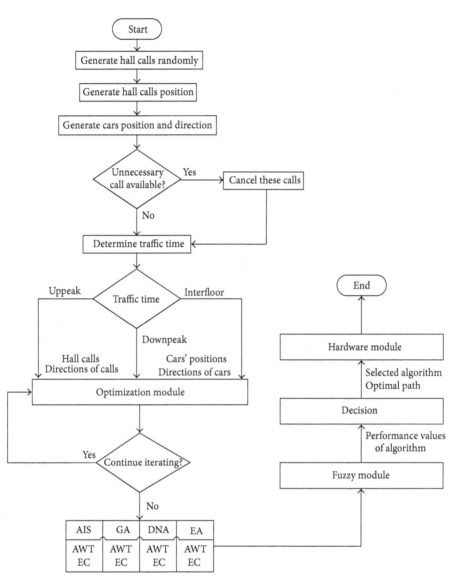

FIGURE 2: Flow chart of the proposed approach.

algorithms, and DNA computing algorithm are used from artificial immune system.

2.1.1. Clonal Selection Algorithm.
The artificial immune algorithms which are proposed by taking human immune system as example incorporate negative and clonal selection algorithms. While negative selection algorithm is used in determination of undesired situations, the clonal selection algorithms are often used in optimization and pattern recognition problems [11, 12]. The pseudocode of the clonal selection algorithm, which has been used for optimization purpose in this study, has been given below.

Step 1. The antibodies compromising body antibody repertoire constitute the initial solution set.

Step 2. Degree of similarity of antibodies is calculated.

Step 3. n pieces of highest similar antibody are selected.

Step 4. Proportional to the degree of similarity of the n pieces of the selected antibody, the high degree of similarity cloning of antibody is carried out.

Step 5. Antibodies with a high degree of similarity are exposed to the mutation as a manner to become less.

Step 6. The degrees of similarity of mutated clones are determined.

Step 7. n pieces of highest similar antibody are selected again.

Step 8. Change of d pieces of antibodies in lowest degree of similarity with newly produced antibodies is realized.

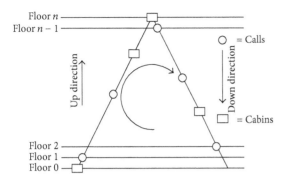

FIGURE 3: Proposed estimation algorithm.

2.1.2. Genetic Algorithm.
Genetic algorithms are search and optimization methods are aiming to find the best result from the problem space in the widest sense [13, 14]. Offering extremely fast and efficient solutions, this method has been used in this study as one of the optimization methods, which have been used during simulation. A pseudocode, which summarizes the operating principle of genetic algorithms, is given below.

Step 1. Initial population of randomly generated sequences of binary numbers.

Step 2. A certain amount of element is selected for the solution.

Step 3. Crossing is applied to new population.

Step 4. Mutation process is applied for the same population.

Step 5. Affinity values of elements of these populations are found.

Step 6. Step 2 is repeated until it reaches the maximum number of transactions.

2.1.3. DNA Computing Algorithm.
DNA computing algorithm is a method, which is mainly used in literature, and it is soft computing technique used in solution of the NP hard problems [15, 16]. The operating principle of this method used in this study as assessment criteria is similar to the genetic algorithms, and the pseudocode which summarizes this algorithm is given below.

Step 1. First population is created.

Step 2. DNA sequences are converted to numeric values.

Step 3. Affinity value is calculated for each element.

Step 4. Crossing process is applied to individuals in the population and the new population is obtained.

Step 5. Mutation of the enzyme is applied to new population.

Step 6. Mutation of the virus instead of the deleted elements is applied.

Step 7. Affinity value of population is determined. If newly found population value is better than original value, it is changed and it is continued from 3rd step until maximum procedure number is reached.

2.1.4. Proposed Estimation Algorithm.
Within the scope of the study, an estimation algorithm has been proposed in order to bring a different point of view to group elevator systems. Together with this algorithm, it has been aimed to enable the energy efficiency of the cabins. Since the results obtained by optimization methods used bring overload to some cabins, it causes some cars work more and some cars work less. This is an undesired situation and it both directly reflects to average waiting time and energy consumption values of the cabins. In principle, it is expected from an elevator system that energy consumption values should resemble each other so that all the cabins can work efficiently to decrease waiting time of the passengers. For this reason, a diagram, which summarizes the estimation algorithm performed, has been given in Figure 3.

Proposed estimation algorithm considers the longest route that the elevators can follow. As it is shown in Figure 3, left side of the triangle shows upper direction, and right side of the triangle shows the down direction. The rectangles present in these sides show the instant position of the cabins and rounds show the calls made. The longest route that the elevators can follow is to go to the top floor and turn back to the ground floor, and this situation has been shown with an arrow in the triangle. In other words, the cabins in the triangle move clockwise and calls settle into the edges of the triangle according to the directions. Proposed estimation algorithm is based on answering calls available to the current direction of movement of the cabins. Pseudocode, which summarizes working principle of this algorithm, has been given below.

Step 1. Determine number of user floor, number of cabins, position of cabins, and their directions.

Step 2. Randomly directed calls are created.

Step 3. Calls at ground floor are always arranged upwards and calls at top floor of building are arranged downwards.

Step 4. Cabins and randomly produced calls are placed on triangle according to directions.

Step 5. The arrival time to calls is calculated according to affinity function of cabins.

Step 6. Calls having low arrival time are shared to proper cabins and these calls are deleted from call pools.

Step 7. If there are remaining calls, proceed from the 5th step.

Step 8. Proceed from Step 2 until maximum iteration number is reached.

Immunity-Based Optimal Estimation Approach for a New Real Time Group Elevator Dynamic Control Application for Energy and Time Saving

143

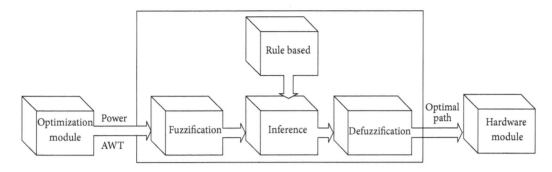

FIGURE 4: Fuzzy logic module.

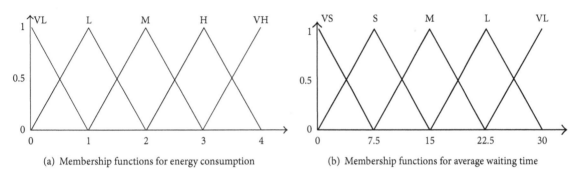

(a) Membership functions for energy consumption

(b) Membership functions for average waiting time

FIGURE 5: Input membership functions.

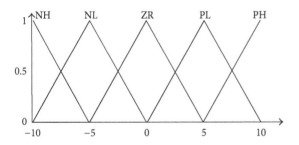

FIGURE 6: Output membership functions.

TABLE 1: Rule base of fuzzy logic module.

Input	Energy consumption				
	VL	L	M	H	VH
Average waiting time					
VS	NH	NH	NL	NL	ZR
S	NH	NL	NL	ZR	PL
M	NL	NL	ZR	PL	PL
L	NL	ZR	PL	PL	PH
VL	ZR	PL	PL	PH	PH

2.2. Fuzzy Module. Another part in proposed control algorithm for group elevator systems is fuzzy module. The diagram which summarizes fuzzy systems consisting of generally four fundamental parts has been given in Figure 4 [17, 18].

Fuzzy module in the system takes energy consumption values and average waiting time coming from optimization module and sends to fuzzy part. In step of fuzzification, there is energy membership input function and average waiting time membership input function. The input functions have been given in Figure 5.

The values obtained from membership input function are sent to inference part to be evaluated. Here, Mamdani method is used and the system has defined 25 different rules for this procedure. The values obtained from inference part are sent to clarification part to be converted into reel values. In this part, optimal route is defined according to exit membership functions defined. In Table 1 given below, rule base used in fuzzy module has been given and membership exit function has been shown in Figure 6.

2.3. Hardware Module. The final part of the practice performed within the scope of the study is hardware part. In this part, optimal path coming from fuzzy logic module has been evaluated in the microprocessor-based experiment set and the accuracy of the system is tested. Also, led mechanism connected to experiment set represents a building and the cabins in the building. The practice made with this module has been brought into practicable condition by taking from being simulation. A diagram, which summarizes a hardware module used in the system, is as given in Figure 7.

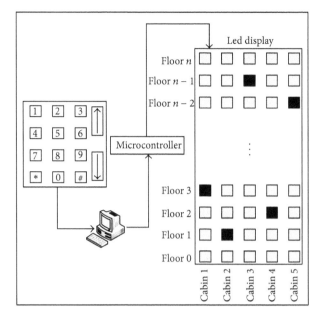

FIGURE 7: Hardware module.

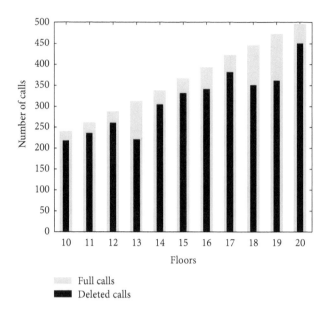

FIGURE 8: Calls according to number of floors.

3. Experimental Results

Within the scope of the study done, it has been aimed to decrease the average waiting time of the passengers and enable energy efficiency with proposed control approach. In direction of these purposes, the application performed has been performed by using 3 modules and the results are perceptibly observed. Simulation stage of the application has been prepared in a computer environment with Windows 7 operating system including 2,53 GHZ speed, 4 GB RAM, Intel Core i5. The study done has been performed in Matlab R2009b platform. An experiment set has been used for hardware stage of the application. This experiment set has been worked in 20 MHZ speed, and RS-232 serial communication line in 9600 bandwidth has been used for communication. The results coming from simulation stage are transmitted to microprocessor-based experiment set through serial communication line. In addition to this, in order to be able to define the starting status of the cabins and let them make call after the system starts, a numeric keypad is used. Building and cabin specifications used as base at simulation stage are as given in Tables 2 and 3.

With the application performed within the scope of the study, total average waiting times and energy efficiencies of the cabins have been calculated. Random 500 numbers of calls have been created within the frame of the application, and approximately 80% of these calls have been arranged as to be downside and upside to be able to obtain up and down traffic condition. For traffic condition in inter floors, half of 500 numbers of calls have been arranged so as to be downward and the other half has been arranged so as to be upward. The distribution of the calls according to the floor has been shown in Figure 8.

Depending on the number of floors, the number of the calls increases. In the study done, if there is nobody in the floor to be made, the cabins are enabled to pass over this call.

TABLE 2: Building parameters.

Number of elevators	From 10 to 20
Number of cabins	From 2 to 5
Floor height	3,5 m
Building type	Office
Building population	500
Building occupancy	80%

TABLE 3: Cabin parameters.

Cabin rate	13 person
Velocity	1,6 m/sn
Door open	3 sn
Door close	4 sn
Passenger transfer time	1,2 sn
One floor passing time	2,2 sn

In order to perform this purpose, 20% of the current calls have been cancelled, computational procedures are started after this point. The cancellation of invalid calls provides an important advantage regarding energy efficiency and average waiting time. In Table 4, average waiting time changing to the floor situations and algorithms have been shown.

The performance of algorithms according to the number of traffic peak hours and floors is shown in Figure 9. In the application performed, 3 different traffic times, genetic algorithm, DNA computing algorithm, artificial immune system algorithm, and estimation algorithm have, respectively, been applied. At practice stage, total 11 different floor conditions have been considered, and algorithms through 2, 3, 4, and 5 cabins for each floor have been applied. Average waiting times obtained for each cabin and floor have been added separately and divided into total cabin number. When Table 4 is examined, it has been seen that waiting time increases

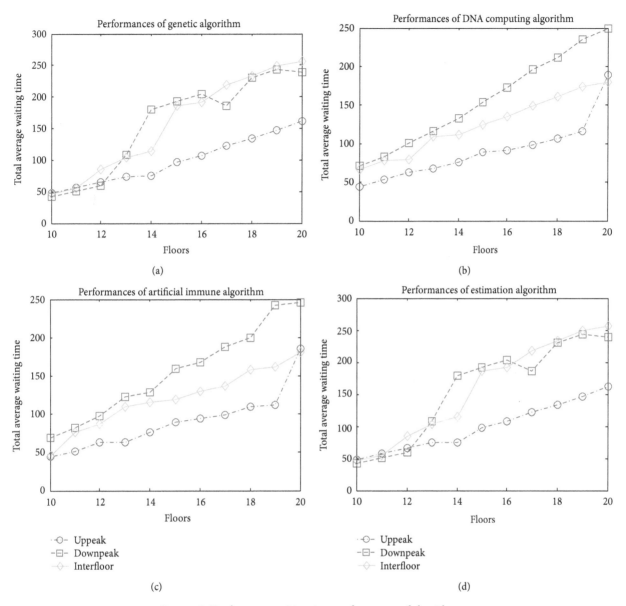

FIGURE 9: Total average waiting time performances of algorithms.

in parallel with the floor number. Furthermore, the performances that algorithms have shown under different traffic conditions are different from each other. For example, while artificial immune system algorithm gives the best result in uppeak traffic condition, estimation algorithm in downpeak traffic algorithm shows the best performance. There are so many factors which affect average waiting times in group elevator systems. As the complete of factors such as number of passengers or hall calls are not known, it cannot completely be calculated regarding which algorithm that provides the best solution. With this study done, a system with adaptive structure has been created and significant results have been obtained from the point of waiting time and energy efficiency.

Another parameter within the scope of the study done is the energy efficiency of the cabins. One of the most important disadvantages of the group elevator systems is the lowness in

energy performances arising from working principles. 70% of the energy that elevator systems consumed occurs while the cabins stop and start. Furthermore, this stop and start movements are seen more frequent in some cabins compared to the others. This situation causes some cabins to consume more energy and wear down. In principle, it is expected from group elevator systems that total energy to be consumed is provided to be stably distributed to the cabins according to the stop-and-start number. Because of working principles of optimization methods, some cabins are overloaded. With the study performed, this situation is aimed to be removed and the energy is provided to be distributed as efficiently. An example of the energy distributions that the cabins consumed has been shown in Figure 10 according to the traffic and algorithm conditions.

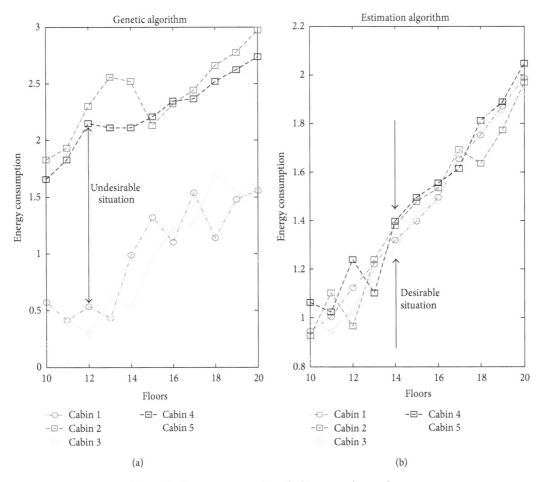

FIGURE 10: Energy consumption of cabins according to floors.

TABLE 4: Average waiting time of passengers (s).

Floor	GA			DNA			AIS			EA		
	Uppeak	Downpeak	Inter floor	Uppeak	Downpeak	Inter floor	Uppeak	Downpeak	Inter floor	Uppeak	Downpeak	Inter floor
10	52,1	75,1	68,7	**44,8**	71,5	66,2	44,4	69,9	**45,7**	48,5	**42,7**	46,8
11	59,2	87,7	79,7	53,3	82,7	78,3	**51,2**	82,2	76,3	57,2	**50,4**	**55,4**
12	**62,3**	101,5	91	63,5	100,6	**79,6**	62,8	97,5	86,5	65,9	**59,2**	85,5
13	72,9	117,2	**103,7**	67,6	**115,7**	108,5	**63,6**	122,8	109,2	74,5	108,3	104,1
14	78,3	135,9	**110,9**	75,9	133,1	111,4	76,4	**128,8**	115,4	**75,4**	179,7	114,3
15	**88,3**	159,9	127,6	89,4	**154,1**	124,7	89,2	159	**119**	97,6	192,6	186,6
16	93,8	174,6	137,9	**91,1**	172,8	134,7	93,9	**167,9**	129,2	107,3	203,9	192,2
17	**97,5**	198,4	147,2	99	196,2	149,5	98,4	188,3	**137,2**	122,5	**185,8**	218,4
18	109,6	211,1	**154,3**	**107,1**	211,3	161,1	109,1	**200**	157,6	133,8	231,1	233,6
19	115,7	**234,4**	171,6	115,7	235,3	174,5	**112,2**	242,4	**161,3**	147,1	243	248,6
20	188,5	250	186,8	189,3	249	**179,6**	185	245,9	181,2	**162,1**	**239,3**	256,1

As it can be understood from the figure, there is an unbalanced load distribution between the cabins according to the optimization methods. With the proposed estimation algorithm, this situation is prevented and it has been enabled to make the cabins share the calls equally. The equal distribution of the calls to all the cabins provides a significant efficiency from the point of energy. By this means, a development occurs in the usage times of the cabins and the wearing times of the cabins extremely decrease.

It is expected from group elevator systems that average waiting time of the system and energy efficiency should be provided at the same time. Because of the fact that in

Immunity-Based Optimal Estimation Approach for a New Real Time Group Elevator Dynamic Control Application for Energy and Time Saving

147

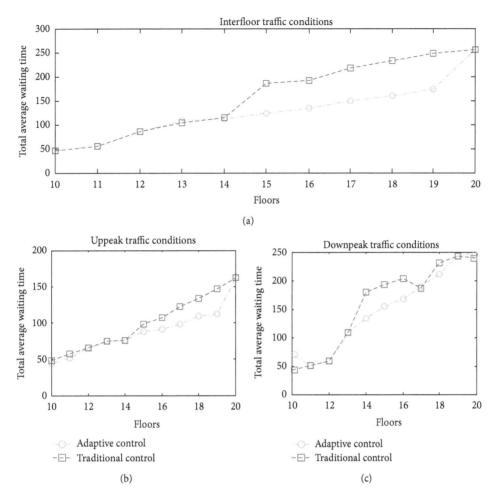

FIGURE 11: Comparative results for classical methods and the proposed approach.

TABLE 5: The results obtained from the fuzzy controller.

Floor	GA			DNA			AIS			EA		
	Uppeak	Downpeak	Inter floor	Uppeak	Downpeak	Inter floor	Uppeak	Downpeak	Inter floor	Uppeak	Downpeak	Inter floor
10	−27,5	−26,7	−27,2	−26,1	−22,7	−26,1	**−28,0**	**−27,5**	**−28,0**	−25,8	−26,0	−25,9
11	−24,8	−21,1	−22,7	−24,7	−20,1	−24,7	**−26,6**	−23,4	−24,4	−25,2	**−25,2**	**−25,2**
12	−24,8	−10,5	−21,1	−22,0	−14,2	−22,0	−23,9	−16,5	−20,2	**−25,0**	**−25,0**	**−25,0**
13	−21,4	−3,1	−10,3	−19,5	−6,11	**−19,5**	−20,9	−2,84	−7,30	**−25,1**	**−7,96**	−10,8
14	−18,5	0,25	−6,17	−18,6	**0,03**	**−18,6**	−16,7	2,92	0,35	**−22,1**	15,1	−3,17
15	**−17,5**	9,56	2,31	−16,3	6,76	**−16,3**	−12,2	8,09	1,22	−16,5	19,6	17,3
16	−11,7	15,2	6,91	**−16,4**	12,3	**−16,4**	−16,1	**11,3**	2,26	−4,37	24,3	19,8
17	**−6,97**	25,7	8,54	−6,5	22,2	**−6,58**	−6,4	**17,8**	6,64	8,4	20,1	24,5
18	0,33	26,9	12,6	0,6	**24,0**	0,64	**−1,1**	26,3	11,6	11,6	25,1	25,0
19	4,9	26,3	16,2	3,3	25,3	**3,30**	**0,7**	25,4	15,5	15,7	**23,1**	22,7
20	22,19	**24,1**	21,4	22,5	25,2	22,5	21,6	25,3	20,3	**18,7**	27,8	**20,1**

some circumstances, while average waiting time is good, energy efficiency shows inverse proportion to this time. To prevent this situation, a fuzzy system has been designed. The fuzzy system designed takes energy values and average waiting times coming from 4 different algorithms to the traffic conditions as input parameter. Then, it evaluates these parameters and provides the most optimal path to be determined. The basic purpose in fuzzy system designed is to find the lowest average waiting time and the best result of energy efficiency. In Table 5, the values rising from fuzzy logic

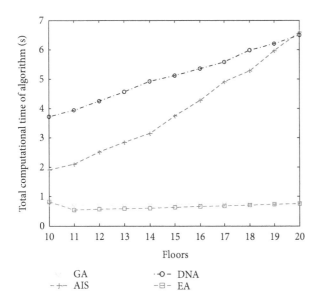

FIGURE 12: Total computational time of algorithms.

and the methods to be applied according to these values have been shown.

Thanks to this performed study, an adaptive approach is developed related to group elevator control systems. It is aimed at making this approach reduces the average waiting time of passengers and provides energy efficiency. The proposed adaptive approach and four different algorithms are combined and fuzzy logic module of the system and the results from these different algorithms are provided to evaluate. In Figure 11, traditional methods on group elevator control systems and changing total average waiting times depending on number of floors of proposed adaptive approach.

These findings obtained in simulation platform are sent to the experiment set and the accuracy of the system has been tested. Figure 12 shows the computing time passing from simulation platform to the experiment set according to the floor number and traffic condition for each algorithm separately.

4. Conclusions

The elevator systems have a structure that constantly renews itself since day one of the emergence. Today, the increase of high-rise buildings is the biggest factor for this situation. Group elevator control systems which were developed in order to provide faster service to resident are computerized to provide both time saving and energy efficiency. Group elevator control systems which have very large place in the literature are not incomplete in terms of efficiency because all of parameters are not taken into consideration.

In this study, an immune system-based approach for the control of group elevator control systems is conducted, and reducing of the average waiting times of passengers and providing of energy efficiency of system are aimed to provide. In the scope of this study, the adaptability of this

application to all building structure is aimed to provide by creating building models from 10 floors to 20 floors and from 2 cabins to 5 cabins. In the next step, calls randomly generated according to traffic hours are sent to optimization module which includes immune system algorithm, genetic algorithm, and DNA computing algorithm to determine average waiting times and energy consumption values of cabins. The average waiting time and cabin energy consumption values that they are acquired from optimization module due to each algorithm are sent to fuzzy system module which is designed in the scope of the study to determine system performance. The optimum way for formed building models and traffic hours are aimed to determine by providing obtained values of fuzzy system. Finally, this optimum way obtained from fuzzy module is tested with hardware module.

This adaptive and dynamic control approach for elevator systems provides efficiency approximately between 5% and 20% on average waiting times of passengers in comparison with traditional methods. In addition to this, a significant gain was achieved related to energy efficiency which is another expected parameter in elevator systems, provided that calls to cabins are as evenly distributed as possible. Future studies target to further increase the efficiency of the system and perform these applications which are performed on a real elevator system.

References

[1] P. B. Luh, B. Xiong, and S. C. Chang, "Group elevator scheduling with advance information for normal and emergency modes," *IEEE Transactions on Automation Science and Engineering*, vol. 5, no. 2, pp. 245–258, 2008.

[2] D. M. Muñoz, C. H. Lianos, M. A. Rincón et al., "Distributed approach to group control of elevator systems using fuzzy logic and FPGA implementation of dispatching algorithms," *Engineering Applications of Artificial Intelligence*, vol. 21, no. 8, pp. 1309–1320, 2008.

[3] P. Cortes, L. Onieva, J. Munuzuri, and J. Guadix, "A viral system algorithm to optimize the car dispatching in elevator group control systems of tall buildings," *Computers & Industrial Engineering*, vol. 64, no. 1, pp. 403–411, 2013.

[4] J. Jamaludin, N. A. Rahim, and W. P. Hew, "An elevator group control system with a self-tuning fuzzy logic group controller," *IEEE Transactions on Industrial Electronics*, vol. 57, no. 12, pp. 4188–4198, 2010.

[5] J. Sun, Q. C. Zhao, and P. B. Luh, "Optimization of group elevator scheduling with advance information," *IEEE Transactions on Automation Science and Engineering*, vol. 7, no. 2, pp. 352–363, 2010.

[6] G. Barney, Ed., *Elevator Traffic Handbook: Theory and Practice*, Taylor & Francis, New York, NY, USA, 2003.

[7] M. Baygin and M. Karakose, "A new intelligent group elevator control approach," in *Proceedings of the 15th International Symposium (MECHATRONIKA '12)*, pp. 1–6, December 2012.

[8] Y. Liu, Z. Hu, Q. Su, and J. Huo, "Energy saving of elevator group control based on optimal zoning strategy with interfloor traffic," in *Proceedings of the 3rd International Conference on Information Management, Innovation Management and Industrial Engineering (ICIII '10)*, vol. 3, pp. 328–331, November 2010.

Immunity-Based Optimal Estimation Approach for a New Real Time Group Elevator Dynamic Control Application
for Energy and Time Saving

149

[9] J. Wang, X. Mu, J. Xu, and S. Wang, "Design and optimization of dispatching rules for elevator group control aiming at energy saving," in *Proceedings of the International Conference on Information Science and Technology (ICIST '12)*, pp. 124–127, March 2012.

[10] P. E. Utgoff and M. E. Connell, "Real-time combinatorial optimization for elevator group dispatching," *IEEE Transactions on Systems, Man, and Cybernetics A*, vol. 42, no. 1, pp. 130–146, 2012.

[11] I. Aydin, M. Karakose, and E. Akin, "An adaptive artificial immune system for fault classification," *Journal of Intelligent Manufacturing*, vol. 23, no. 5, pp. 1489–1499, 2010.

[12] I. Aydin, M. Karakose, and E. Akin, "Artificial immune classifier with swarm learning," *Engineering Applications of Artificial Intelligence*, vol. 23, no. 8, pp. 1291–1302, 2010.

[13] B. Bolat and P. Cortés, "Genetic and tabu search approaches for optimizing the hall call—car allocation problem in elevator group systems," *Applied Soft Computing*, vol. 11, no. 2, pp. 1792–1800, 2011.

[14] K. Hirasawa, T. Eguchi, Z. Jin et al., "A double-deck elevator group supervisory control system using genetic network programming," *IEEE Transactions on Systems, Man and Cybernetics C*, vol. 38, no. 4, pp. 535–550, 2008.

[15] M. S. Muhammad, Z. Ibrahim, S. Ueda, O. Ono, and M. Khalid, *DNA Computing for Complex Scheduling Problem*, Springer, Berlin, Germany, 2005.

[16] H. Jiao, Y. Zhong, and L. Zhang, "Artificial DNA computing-based spectral encoding and matching algorithm for hyperspectral remote sensing data," *IEEE Transactions on Geoscience and Remote Sensing*, vol. 50, no. 10, pp. 4085–4104, 2012.

[17] M. M. Rashid, N. A. Rashid, A. Farouq et al., "Design and implementation of fuzzy based controller for modern elevator group," in *Proceedings of IEEE Symposium on Industrial Electronics and Applications (ISIEA '11)*, pp. 63–68, September 2011.

[18] T. Chen, Y. Hsu, A. Lee, and P. Hong, "Real-time self-tuning approach for intelligent elevator group control system," in *Proceedings of the 5th International Conference on New Trends in Information Science and Service Science (NISS '11)*, pp. 420–424, October 2011.

15

A Danger-Theory-Based Immune Network Optimization Algorithm

Ruirui Zhang,[1] **Tao Li,**[1] **Xin Xiao,**[1] **and Yuanquan Shi**[2]

[1] *College of Computer Science, Sichuan University, Chengdu 610065, China*
[2] *College of Computer Science, Huaihua University, Huaihua 418000, China*

Correspondence should be addressed to Ruirui Zhang; zhangruiruisw@gmail.com

Academic Editors: C. W. Ahn and P. Melin

Existing artificial immune optimization algorithms reflect a number of shortcomings, such as premature convergence and poor local search ability. This paper proposes a danger-theory-based immune network optimization algorithm, named dt-aiNet. The danger theory emphasizes that danger signals generated from changes of environments will guide different levels of immune responses, and the areas around danger signals are called danger zones. By defining the danger zone to calculate danger signals for each antibody, the algorithm adjusts antibodies' concentrations through its own danger signals and then triggers immune responses of self-regulation. So the population diversity can be maintained. Experimental results show that the algorithm has more advantages in the solution quality and diversity of the population. Compared with influential optimization algorithms, CLONALG, opt-aiNet, and dopt-aiNet, the algorithm has smaller error values and higher success rates and can find solutions to meet the accuracies within the specified function evaluation times.

1. Introduction

In the practice of engineering, there are a wide variety of complex optimization problems to be solved, such as multimodal optimization, high-dimensional optimization, and dynamic optimization of time-varying parameters. These problems are manifested in the form of minimization of energy consumption, time, or risk, or maximization of the quality or efficiency, and usually can be expressed by getting the maximum or minimum of multivariable functions with a series of equations and (or) inequality constraints. In order to solve such problems, optimization theories and technologies have been rapidly developed, and its impact on society is also increasing.

Current research focus of optimization algorithms is evolutionary computation methods represented by genetic algorithms (GAs) [1–3]. The genetic algorithm simulates the biological evolution process, is a random search optimization method, and shows excellent performance in solving typical problems. Although GA has characteristics of global search and probabilistic choice, the performance of GA is sensitive to some key parameters which are crossover rate and mutation rate. Moreover, it is difficult for GA to solve multimodal function optimization due to its random crossover pairing mechanism. So, on one hand, researchers hope to make continuous improvements on existing genetic algorithms, and on the other hand, they try to build new algorithm models based on new biological theories.

Artificial immune system (AIS) is one of bionic intelligent systems inspired by biological immune system (BIS), and is new frontier research in artificial intelligence areas. The study of AIS has four major aspects, including negative selection algorithms (NSAs), artificial immune networks (AINEs), clonal selection algorithms (CLONALGs), the danger theory (DT), and dendritic cell algorithms (DCAs) [4]. It cannot only detect and eliminate nonself-antigens regarded as illegal intrusions, but also has the evolutionary learning mechanism [5–7]. There have been a great progress by applying the artificial immune to optimization problems, and many research papers have been sprung up. In artificial immune optimization algorithms, solutions to optimization problems which are to be solved and are usually expressed as high-dimensional functions are viewed as antigens, candidate solutions are viewed as antibodies, and qualities of candidate solutions correspond with affinities between antibodies and antigens [8, 9]. The process of seeking feasible solutions is the process of immune cells recognizing antigens and making immune responses in the immune system. The following works are typical. de Castro and Fernando proposed the basic structure named CLONALG [10] of function optimization and pattern recognition based on the clonal selection mechanism. Halavati et al. [11] added the idea of symbiosis to CLONALG. This algorithm is initialized with a set of partially specified antibodies, each with one specified property, and then the algorithm randomly picks antibodies to add to an assembly. This work showed better performance than CLON-ALG. de Castro and Von Zuben proposed an optimized version of aiNet [12], named opt-aiNet [9]. This algorithm introduces the idea of network suppression to CLONALG and can dynamically adjust the population size, having strong multivalued search capabilities. The work in [13] presented an algorithm called dopt-aiNet to suit the dynamic optimization. This algorithm introduces a line search procedure and two mutation operators, enhances the diversity of the population, and refines individuals of solutions.

Existing artificial immune optimization algorithms have maintained many merits of BIS, such as fine diversity, strong robustness, and implicit parallelism, but also reflect a number of shortcomings, such as premature convergence and poor local search ability [14, 15]. By introducing the danger theory into the optimization algorithm and integrating the clonal selection theory and the immune network theory, this paper proposes a danger-theory-based immune network optimization algorithm, named dt-aiNet. The main contributions of this paper are (1) introducing the danger theory into the optimization algorithms by simulating the danger zone and danger signals; (2) giving a new antibody concentration mechanism.

The remainder of this paper is organized as follows. The principles of artificial immune theories and influential artificial immune based optimization algorithms are described in Section 2. The flow description and optimization strategies of dt-aiNet are described in Section 3. The computational complexity, convergence, and robustness analyses of dt-aiNet are presented in Section 4. The effectiveness of dt-aiNet is verified using typical problems in Section 5. Finally, the conclusion is given in the last section.

2. Related Works

In this section, three artificial immune theories being adopted in this paper are introduced, including the clonal selection, the immune network, and the danger theory. And three influential artificial immune based optimization algorithms, including CLONALG, opt-aiNet, and dopt-aiNet which are to be compared with the proposed algorithm in the experiments are described.

2.1. Artificial Immune Theories. From the humoral immune response in the biological immune mechanism, the main idea of the clonal selection [5–7, 16] is that, when immune cells are stimulated by antigens, clonal proliferation occurs, which result in a large number of clones, and then these clones differentiate into effect cells and memory cells through the high-frequency variation. In the process of proliferation, effect cells generate a large number of antibodies, and then the antibodies duplicate and mutate to make affinities gradually increase and eventually reach affinity maturation. The clonal selection theory simulates the process of evolution of immune cells, which can learn and memorize the modes of antigens. In optimization algorithms, we simplify the concept of immune cells and use antibodies to represent a variety of immune cells. Antibodies evolve through the clonal selection theory, which means search in the solution space.

The main idea of the immune network [5–7, 17] is that, when antibodies recognize invasive antigens, a variety of antibodies constitute a dynamic network through interactions between themselves. The immune system is viewed as a mutual influential and mutual restricted network. The network can maintain a balance according to the immune regulation mechanism. When similarity between antibodies is higher, the network will produce inhibition. When similarity is low, the network will produce stimulus. So, the network can maintain population diversity and equilibrium, and ultimately becomes stable, composed of a variety of memory cells. The theory is an important complement and development to the clonal selection theory. In the optimization algorithms, the concept that the immune network can delete redundant solutions and maintain the balance of global and local search is used.

The danger theory [18] proposed by Matzinger indicated that the key why the immune system is able to distinguish the nonself-antigens and self-antigens is that these nonself-antigens make the body produce biochemical reactions different from natural rules and the reactions will make the body produce danger signals of different levels. So, the immune system produces danger signals based on the environmental changes and then leads to the immune responses. In essence, the danger signal creates a danger zone around itself and immune cells within this danger zone will be activated to participate in the immune response. Compared with the clonal selection theory and the immune network theory, the danger theory introduces the environmental factors of the body, describes some important characteristics of the biological immune system, and explains some immune phenomena which the traditional immune theory cannot explain, such as autoimmune diseases. Therefore, through combination of the clonal selection theory and the immune network theory, the danger theory can simulate the biological immune mechanism more completely and accurately. The theory is a new addition to artificial immune algorithms. The danger theory is introduced in this paper to express the ambient environmental state of antibodies, which can better simulate the biological immune system, maintain the population diversity, and accelerate the convergence of the algorithm. In danger theory, there are not any specific definitions of danger signals. So, using the danger theory is crucial to defining the suitable danger signals and danger zones according to the actual situation.

(1) Initialize. Randomly generate the initial network population;
(2) While (termination conditions are not meet) do
Begin
  (2.1) While (changes of the average fitness of the population compared with that of the last generation is greater than the specified value) do
  Begin
    (2.1.1) Compute the fitness of every individual in the population;
    (2.1.2) Clone the same number for every individual, and get clone groups;
    (2.1.3) Mutate the clone groups, and get mutated groups;
    (2.1.4) Compute the fitness of every clone in the mutated groups;
    (2.1.5) Select the clone with highest fitness in every mutated group, and form a new population;
    (2.1.6) Compute the average fitness of the population;
  End;
  (2.2) Compute the distance between any two individuals; if the distance is less than the threshold, retain one;
  (2.3) Randomly generate a certain number of antibodies;
End;

ALGORITHM 1: The description of opt-aiNet.

2.2. Influential Optimization Algorithms. CLONALG [10] proposed by de Castro simulates the activation process of immune cells. Only those immune cells that can recognize antigens split and amplify. Clones of immune cells with high affinity are more, and the variation rate is small; clones of cells with low affinity are less, and the variation rate is large. This algorithm searches for the global optimal solutions through the cloning and high-frequency variation of immune cells, which makes full use of the diversity mechanism in the immune system. This algorithm is simple, and the disadvantage is the premature convergence [8, 14].

opt-aiNet [9] introduces the concept of immune network based on the clonal selection theory into optimization problems. This algorithm is described in Algorithm 1.

opt-aiNet includes two loops. At first, the algorithm enters into the first loop. Implant a specific number of antibodies (real-valued vectors) in the definition domain of the objective function, constituting the artificial immune network. Then, the algorithm enters into the second loop. In order to obtain the local optimal solution, perform the clonal selection to every antibody in the network. The process continues until the average fitness of the population is close to that of the previous generation, which means that the network is stabilized. Then, the algorithm jumps out of the second loop. Antibodies in the network interact with each other, and the network suppression occurs. At last, randomly introduce new antibodies. Repeat the process until the termination conditions are met. Due to the nested loops, the algorithm increases unnecessary function evaluation times. The algorithm maintains the diversity of the population, but has disadvantages of slow convergence and low search accuracy [8, 14].

dopt-aiNet extends opt-aiNet to deal with time-varying fitness functions [13]. This algorithm introduces a line search procedure called golden section and two mutation operators, which are one-dimensional mutation and gene duplication. The golden section is to choose the best step size of mutation. The one-dimensional mutation performs similarly to the traditional Gaussian mutation but only for one direction at a time. In the operation of gene duplication, a randomly chosen element (coordinate) is copied to another element, simulating the chromosome behavior in the evolution of species. This algorithm increases the search accuracy, but the two mutation operations waste too much function evaluation times, which makes the algorithm converge slowly.

3. Description of the Proposed Algorithm

This section describes the basic idea of dt-aiNet. The flow of the algorithm is described in Section 3.1. The simulation of optimization algorithm for the immune system is introduced in Section 3.2. And the optimization strategies of dt-aiNet are introduced in Section 3.3. These strategies are complementary to each other and are applied in the process of the algorithm.

3.1. Flow Description. In this paper, the danger theory is introduced into the optimization algorithm and the clonal selection theory and the immune network theory are integrated. All the antibodies which interact with each other form the immune network. First, the algorithm defines the danger zone to calculate danger signals for each antibody and then adjusts antibodies' concentrations through its own danger signals. Second, the algorithm performs the clonal proliferation operation, generating clone groups by duplicating a certain number of random antibodies, and then mutates each clone, but keeps the parent antibody. Third, the algorithm selects the antibody with highest fitness which is in the parent antibody's danger zone and selects antibodies with higher fitness than the parent antibody which are not in the parent antibody's danger zone. Fourth, the algorithm adds randomly generated antibodies to adjust the population size, recalculates danger signals for all antibodies, and then removes antibodies whose concentration equals to zero. All the individuals in the population constitute the immune network which improves the affinities of the population in

---

1. Initialize. Randomly generate the initial network population within the definition domain, and set initial concentrations;
2. While (termination conditions are not meet) do
Begin
    2.1. Compute the affinity and danger signals of each antibody in the population;
    2.2. Select better individuals to clone, and make them active. The number of clones is related to concentrations;
    2.3. Perform the mutation operation to the clones, and then affinity mutation occurs. The mutation rate is related
    to affinities and can be adaptively adjusted;
    2.4. Perform the clonal suppression, and select better individuals to add into the network;
    2.5. Update the fitness, danger signals and concentrations of the population, and perform the network suppression;
    2.6. Randomly generate a certain number of antibodies, and add them into the network;
End;
3. Update the fitness, danger signals and concentrations of the population, and perform the network suppression;
4. Output the population.

ALGORITHM 2: The description of dt-aiNet.

constant evolution. The network makes antibodies with low concentration and low affinity dead, and survival antibodies are viewed as memory individuals. When the number of memory individuals does not change, these individuals are the optimization solutions of the multimodal function. Therefore, the algorithm composes of seven elements, danger signals and concentrations calculation, clonal selection (T_s), clonal proliferation (T_c), hypermutation (T_m), clonal suppression (T_{cs}), network suppression (T_{ns}), and population updating (T_u). The termination conditions are that the function evaluation times (FEs) reach the maximum or the function error of the found optimal solution reaches or is less than a specified value (Algorithm 2).

3.2. Representations of Antibodies, Antigens, and Affinities.

The optimization function is expressed as $P = \min f(x)$. The variable $x = (x_1, x_2, \ldots, x_n) \in R^n$ is the decision variable, and the variable n is the variable dimension. The function min represents obtaining minimum of function $f(x)$, and we can also obtain maximum of function $f(x)$. The algorithm uses real coding. Assumed that Ab represents the antibodies set which is also the population of the network, Ag represents the antigens set. For the rest of the paper, population always means the collection of antibodies. So, antibody Ab_i and antigen Ag_j are n-dimensional real vectors, and i, j are natural integers. The antibody population is of R^n scale. So the optimization problem can be transformed to $\min\{f(Ab_i), Ab_i \in R^n\}$ or $\max\{f(Ab_i), Ab_i \in R^n\}$.

The affinity between antibody and antigen is the binding strength between antibody and antigen, which is the solution fitness to the problem. It is expressed by affinity(Ab_i), and is the normalized representation of function value $f(Ab_i)$. The affinity of Ab_i is calculated according to (1)

$$\text{affinity}\left(Ab_i\right) = \begin{cases} \dfrac{f\left(Ab_i\right) - f_{\min}}{f_{\max} - f_{\min}}, & P = \max f\left(x\right), \\[4mm] 1 - \dfrac{f\left(Ab_i\right) - f_{\min}}{f_{\max} - f_{\min}}, & P = \min f\left(x\right), \end{cases} \tag{1}$$

where $f(Ab_i)$ is the function value of antibody Ab_i, $f_{\min}$ is the minimum of the current population, and $f_{\max}$ is the maximum of the current population.

The affinity between antibody and antibody represents the similarity degree between the two antibodies and is expressed by affinity(Ab_i, Ab_j). For real coding, it is usually related to the distance between the two antibodies and is calculated as follows:

$$\text{affinity}\left(Ab_i, Ab_j\right) = \frac{1}{\text{dis}\left(Ab_i, Ab_j\right)}, \tag{2}$$

where dis is the Euclidean distance between antibody Ab_i and antibody Ab_j and is expressed as follows:

$$\text{dis}\left(Ab_i, Ab_j\right) = \sqrt{\sum_{k=1}^{n}\left(Ab_{ik} - Ab_{jk}\right)^2}. \tag{3}$$

3.3. Optimization Strategies.

This section describes some of the steps in the process of the algorithm, which are different from the influential artificial immune based optimization algorithms.

3.3.1. Danger Zone and Danger Signals. Because danger signals are associated with the environment, we use the proximity measurement to simulate the danger zone. The concentrations of antibody populations in the danger zone reflect the environment condition for the optimization problem. According to the danger theory [18], if an antigen Ag_i necrotizes, the nearby area Ag_i-centered will become a danger zone $D(Ag_i)$. Because antigens are invisible for the optimization problem, we assume that each antibody is the peak point, and the vicinity around the peak is the danger zone. The danger zone is defined as follows:

$$D\left(Ab_i\right) = \left\{Ab_j \mid \text{dis}\left(Ab_i, Ab_j\right) < r_{\text{danger}}\right\}, \tag{4}$$

where r_{danger} is the danger zone radius, and the value is related to the intensity of the peak points.

Interactions between antibodies within Ab_i's danger zone are Ab_i's environmental state. Then, the danger signal function ds is defined by (5). This function takes the concentration con(Ab_j) of antibody Ab_j whose affinity is greater than affinity(Ab_i) in Ab_i's danger zone and the distance

$dis(Ab_i, Ab_j)$ between Ab_i and Ab_j as inputs and then produces the danger signal of antibody Ab_i:

$$ds(Ab_i)$$

$$= \sum_{Ab_j \in D(Ab_i) \cap \text{affinity}(Ab_j) > \text{affinity}(Ab_i)} con(Ab_j) \quad (5)$$

$$\cdot \left(r_{\text{danger}} - \text{dis}(Ab_i, Ab_j) \right),$$

where con is the antibody concentration. In the population, only if antibody Ab_j is within the danger zone of antibody Ab_i, and the affinity between Ab_j and antigens is greater than the affinity between Ab_i and antigens, antibody Ab_j will exert an influence on antibody Ab_i. The higher the concentration of Ab_j is, the greater the impact on the environment of antibody Ab_i is. The closer Ab_i and Ab_j are, the greater the impact on the environment of antibody Ab_i is.

3.3.2. Concentration Calculation. The antibody concentration is dynamic and is related to the danger signal of the antibody and the affinity between the antibody and antigens. These two factors are the main reasons for the dynamically changing of antibody concentration.

When the surroundings change, the antibody concentration will change. If the danger signal of an antibody is not zero; that is to say, there are better solutions around the antibody and the danger signal will inhibit the antibody, the concentration of the antibody will decay with the evolution. The greater the danger signal is, the greater the impact on the environment of the antibody is. When the surroundings do not change, the antibody is in a relatively stable environment; that is to say, there are not better solutions around the antibody. So, the antibody is regarded as a candidate peak point, and the concentration of the antibody will increase with the evolution.

The affinity between the antibody and antigens will affect the antibody's concentration as well. The greater the affinity is, the better the fitness of the antibody as a solution is. When the antibody is regarded as a candidate peak point, the increment of the antibody's concentration will be proportional to the affinity. When the danger signal of the antibody exists, the attenuation of the antibody's concentration will be inversely proportional to the affinity.

The concentration $con(Ab_i)$ of antibody Ab_i is calculated according to (6). In the equation, $con(Ab_i)$ depends on the iteration. The variable t represents evolution generation, and $t + 1$ means the next generation after t. So, $con(Ab_i)_t$ means the concentration of antibody Ab_i at generation t:

$$con(Ab_i)_{t+1}$$

$$= \begin{cases} con(Ab_i)_t \left(1 + \exp\left(\text{affinity}(Ab_i)^{0.25} \right) \right) \\ \qquad\qquad\qquad\qquad\qquad ds(Ab_i) = 0, \\ con(Ab_i)_t \left(1 - \dfrac{\ln(1 + \text{affinity}(Ab_i))}{\text{affinity}(Ab_i)} \right) - ds(Ab_i) \\ \qquad\qquad\qquad\qquad\qquad ds(Ab_i) > 0. \end{cases}$$

$$(6)$$

For the initial population, each antibody is set an initial concentration con_0. When the danger signal of the antibody exists, the antibody's concentration will gradually decrease and ultimately to zero. When it does not exist, the antibody's concentration will gradually increase and up to 1. Therefore, $con(Ab_i) \in [0, 1]$. Danger signals provide the changes of concentrations of antibodies a baseline and maintain the diversity of the population.

3.3.3. Mutation Operation. The mutation operation simulates high-frequency variation mechanism in the immune response. And this operator generates antibodies with higher affinities and enhances the diversity of antibody population. The algorithm of opt-aiNet [9] adopts Gaussian variation, and the related formulas are as follows:

$$c' = c + \alpha N(0, 1),$$

$$\alpha = \left(\frac{1}{\beta} \right) \exp(-f^*), \quad (7)$$

where c' is a mutated cell c, $N(0, 1)$ is the Gaussian random variable with mean 0 and deviation of 1, and f^* is the fitness of an individual normalized in the interval $[0, 1]$. β is the control parameter to adjust the mutation range and is an user-specified value in the algorithm of opt-aiNet.

There are certain shortcomings in this method. For different functions, β is difficult to determine. In the search process, if β is too large, individuals will search with higher probability, which is more conducive to global search and leads to a slow rate of convergence. If β is too small, individuals will search with smaller probability, which is more conducive to local search and makes the algorithm searching around the local minimums, impossible to escape from the local minima and result in precociousness. Therefore, this paper adopts dynamic self-adaptive β, and the mutation mechanism is expressed as follows:

$$Ab_i(t + 1) = Ab_i(t) + \alpha N(0, 1),$$

$$\alpha = \beta(t) \exp(-\text{affinity}(Ab_i)),$$

$$\beta(t) = \frac{\beta_0}{1 + \exp((t - t_0)/k)}, \quad (8)$$

where t is the number of iteration times. $Ab_i(t)$ means the antibody Ab_i at generation t, and $Ab_i(t + 1)$ means the antibody Ab_i at generation $t + 1$. In the initial stage of the algorithm, β is large, and the algorithm approaches toward the peak points with higher probability, which speeds up the convergence rate. When the algorithm iterates a certain number of times, β becomes small, and the algorithm searches in the neighborhood of the peak points, which improves the accuracy of solutions. Because affinity$(Ab_i) \in [0, 1]$, $\exp(-\text{affinity}(Ab_i)) \in [0.3679, 1]$. β_0 is the control parameter and determines the range of β, and $\beta \in [0, \beta_0]$. k is the regulation parameter and adjusts the rate of change of $\exp(t - t_0)$. t_0 is the demarcation point of β changes, that is, global search with large probability and local search with small probability. When $t < t_0$, $\beta \in [\beta_0/2, \beta_0]$, and the algorithm

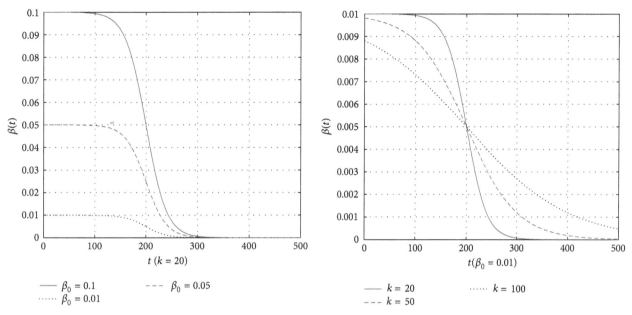

FIGURE 1: Changing curves of β.

should search into the neighborhood of peak points. When $t > t_0$, $\beta \in [0, \beta_0/2]$, and the algorithm starts to do a small-scale search near the peaks. Figure 1 shows the changing curves of β under different initial values of k and β_0. In the first chart, k is stable, and β_0 varies between 0.1, 0.01, and 0.05. As can be seen, the range of β is $[0, \beta_0]$. So, we need to select the appropriate β_0. In the second chart, β_0 is 0.01, and k varies between 20, 50, and 100. The larger the value of k is, the more evidently β changes. The smaller k is, the smaller the change rate of β is.

3.3.4. Suppression Operation. In artificial immune optimization algorithms, the suppression operations are divided into two kinds, which are clonal suppression and network suppression.

Performing the clone operation to every antibody in the population will produce clone groups. Then, variations of clone groups will create antibodies with higher affinity. The clone suppression means retaining antibodies with higher affinity from clone groups, and giving up the rest of the clone individuals. In opt-aiNet, clonal suppression means selecting the antibody with highest affinity from the temporary set which is composed of the parent antibody and its clonal group to join the network. dt-aiNet still chooses this way to add antibodies into the network, and meanwhile selects antibodies into the network which have higher affinity than the parent antibody and are not in the parent antibody's danger zone. So, clonal suppression operation T_{cs} can be expressed as follows:

$$T_{cs}\left(Ab_{\{i\}}\right) = Ab_{\{i\}}{}' + Ab_{\{i\}}{}'', \tag{9}$$

where $Ab_{\{i\}}$ is the collection of antibody Ab_i and its clonal group. $Ab_{\{i\}}{}'$ and $Ab_{\{i\}}{}''$ are expressed by (10) and (11). In (10), it selects antibodies with highest affinity in the parent antibody's danger zone. In (11), it selects antibodies with higher

affinity than that of the parent antibody and not in the parent antibody's danger zone. After the two selection operations, clonal suppression operation retains better antibodies and discards the other ones:

$$Ab_{\{i\}}{}' = \left\{ Ab_{\{i\}k} \mid \text{affinity}\left(Ab_{\{i\}k}\right) = \max\left(\text{affinity}\left(Ab_j\right)\right) \right. $$
$$\left. \cap Ab_j \in Ab_{\{i\}} \cap Ab_{\{i\}k} \in D\left(Ab_i\right) \right\}, \tag{10}$$

$$Ab_{\{i\}}{}'' = \left\{ Ab_{\{i\}k} \mid \text{affinity}\left(Ab_{\{i\}k}\right) > \text{affinity}\left(Ab_i\right) \right. $$
$$\left. \cap Ab_{\{i\}k} \notin D\left(Ab_i\right) \right\}. \tag{11}$$

Network suppression operation simulates the immune network regulation principle, which reduces the redundant antibodies and eliminates similar solutions. In dt-aiNet, this operation deletes antibodies with concentrations equaling to zero. An antibody's concentration is zero indicates that the danger signals of this antibody always exist, and there are better individuals around this antibody. This antibody is redundant. Network suppression operation T_{ns} can be expressed as follows:

$$T_{ns}\left(Ab\right) = Ab - \left\{ Ab_i \mid \text{con}\left(Ab_i\right) = 0 \right\}. \tag{12}$$

4. Algorithm Analyses

This section analyzes the algorithm from three aspects, including the computational complexity, the convergences and the robustness.

4.1. Computational Complexity Analysis

Theorem 1. *The computational complexity of dt-aiNet is $O(t' \cdot N^2 \cdot n)$ or $O(t' \cdot N \cdot Nc \cdot n)$, where t' is the total number of iterations, N is the population size, n is the dimension of the*

TABLE 1: Calculation complexities of the algorithms.

Algorithms	Complexities
CLONALG	$O(t' \cdot N \cdot Nc \cdot n)$ [10]
opt-aiNet	$O(t' \cdot N^2 \cdot n)$ or $O(t' \cdot N \cdot Nc \cdot n)$ [9]
dt-aiNet	$O(t' \cdot N^2 \cdot n)$ or $O(t' \cdot N \cdot Nc \cdot n)$

problem to be solved, and Nc is the max number of clones which an antibody generates.

Proof. As shown in the algorithm flow, dt-aiNet consists of six major components: the clonal selection operation, the cloning operation, the mutation operation, the suppression operations, the population updating operation, and the danger signals and concentrations adjusting operations. In iteration t, the number of calculation times of the clonal selection operation is N. The number of the calculation times of the cloning operation does not exceed $N \cdot Nc$. The number of calculation times of the mutation operation does not exceed $N \cdot Nc \cdot n$ because each dimension of a vector needs to mutate. The number of calculation times of the suppression operations does not exceed $N \cdot Nc$. □

Supposing the population size is N_1, $N_1 \geq N$, and N_1 is related to N, after the suppression operations. The calculation number of the population updating operation is $d\% \cdot N_1 \cdot N_1$, where d is the percentage of population updating and is a user-specified value. The calculation number of the danger signals and concentrations adjusting operations is $N_1 \cdot (N_1 - 1) \cdot n$, where we first calculate the danger zone of each antibody, then compute the danger signal of each antibody, and at last adjust the concentration of each antibody. In iteration t, the total number $g(t)$ of calculation times meets

$$g(t) \leq N + N \cdot Nc + N \cdot Nc \cdot n + N \cdot Nc \\ + d\% \cdot N_1 \cdot N_1 + N_1 \cdot (N_1 - 1) \cdot n. \tag{13}$$

Therefore, if the total number of iterations is t', the computational complexity of algorithm is $O(t' \cdot N^2 \cdot n)$ or $O(t' \cdot N \cdot Nc \cdot n)$. This expression shows that the time complexity of the algorithm is related to the population size N.

Similarly, the calculation complexities of CLONALG and opt-aiNet can be analyzed. Table 1 shows the contrasts of the calculation complexities of the three algorithms. In the case of a certain dimension, reducing the population size can greatly reduce the complexity of the algorithm.

4.2. Convergence Analysis. From the running mechanism of dt-aiNet, each generation of the population consists of two parts. One is the memory antibodies from the previous generation, and another is the new antibodies randomly added. Antibodies with higher affinities from the mutation operation are mainly in the neighborhood of the parent antibody. After the clonal suppression operation, population affinities will be higher than those of the previous generation. The antibodies with higher affinities will change the surrounding environments and then make danger signals of antibodies with lower affinities in the danger zone stronger and their

concentrations lower. As the generation increases, if antibodies with lower affinities cannot escape from the danger zone under strengthened danger signals, their concentrations will decay to zero and then they will die. Antibodies with high affinities will retain in the memory population due to the unchanged environments. In this mechanism, antibodies in the memory population basically have high affinities and are peak points. It will be ensured that new antibodies randomly added to the population in each generation are not in the danger zone of memory antibodies. So, they will develop a new search space, and then the algorithm will eventually find all the peaks with the evolution.

Same as before, we assume that t is the number of generation. So, $Ab(t)$ represents the population Ab at generation t. Due to the state of population, $Ab(t + 1)$ is only related to that of the previous generation $Ab(t)$, and has nothing to do with those of the past generations, the entire population sequences $\{Ab(t)\}$ constitute a random process of the Markov chain [19].

Theorem 2. *For any distribution of the initial population, dt-aiNet is the weak convergence of probability, that is to say,*

$$\lim_{t \to \infty} P\left(Ab(t) \cap Ab^* \neq \emptyset\right) = 1, \tag{14}$$

where Ab^* is a set which contains the optimal solution.

Proof. Known from the total probability formula,

$$P\left(Ab(t + 1) \cap Ab^* = \emptyset\right) \\ = P\left(Ab(t) \cap Ab^* = \emptyset\right) \\ \cdot \left(1 - P\left(Ab(t + 1) \cap Ab^* \neq \emptyset \mid Ab(t) \cap Ab^* = \emptyset\right)\right) \\ + P\left(Ab(t) \cap Ab^* \neq \emptyset\right) \\ \cdot P\left(Ab(t + 1) \cap Ab^* = \emptyset \mid Ab(t) \cap Ab^* \neq \emptyset\right). \tag{15}$$

After operations of selection, clone, mutation, and suppressions, affinities of population $Ab(t)$ will arise, That is to say,

$$\text{affinity}\left(Ab(t + 1)\right) \geq \text{affinity}\left(Ab(t)\right). \tag{16}$$

So,

$$P\left(Ab(t + 1) \cap Ab^* = \emptyset \mid Ab(t) \cap Ab^* \neq \emptyset\right) = 0. \tag{17}$$

From the above equation, we have

$$P\left(Ab(t + 1) \cap Ab^* = \emptyset\right) \\ = P\left(Ab(t) \cap Ab^* = \emptyset\right) \\ \cdot \left(1 - P\left(Ab(t + 1) \cap Ab^* \neq \emptyset \mid Ab(t) \cap Ab^* = \emptyset\right)\right). \tag{18}$$

Suppose $Ab_i \in Ab^*$, $Ab_i \in Ab(t + 1)$, and $Ab_i \notin Ab(t)$, then,

$$P\left(Ab(t + 1) \cap Ab^* \neq \emptyset \mid Ab(t) \cap Ab^* = \emptyset\right) \\ = P\left(T_{c,m,s,cs,ns,u}\left(Ab(t)\right) = Ab(t + 1)\right) \tag{19} \\ \geq P\left(T_m\left(Ab_j\right) = Ab_i\right) = \varepsilon,$$

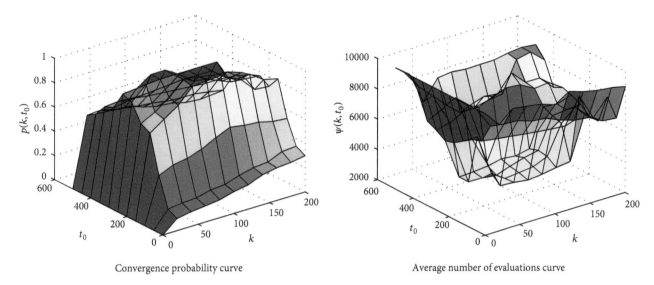

FIGURE 2: Charts of changes of parameter robustness.

where $T_{c,m,s,cs,ns,u}$ means these operations including clone, mutation, selection, suppression, and updating.   □

Known from the induction,

$$P\left(Ab\left(t\right)\cap Ab^{*}=\emptyset\right)\le\left(1-\varepsilon\right)^{t}. \tag{20}$$

So,

$$\lim_{t\to\infty}P\left(Ab\left(t\right)\cap Ab^{*}=\emptyset\right)=0; \tag{21}$$

that is,

$$\lim_{t\to\infty}P\left(Ab\left(t\right)\cap Ab^{*}\ne\emptyset\right)=1-\lim_{t\to\infty}P\left(Ab\left(t\right)\cap Ab^{*}=\emptyset\right)=1. \tag{22}$$

4.3. Robustness Analysis. The algorithm contains a number of parameters. Most of them have little effect on the search performance and can be set conventionally. But the two parameters k and t_0 are more critical and will affect the algorithm performance. k is the adjustable parameter of mutation rate β and decides the change rate of β. t_0 is demarcation point of changes of β, that is, cutoff point of the global search with a high probability and the local search with a small probability. There are two evaluation indicators of robustness measurement, which are the relationship between the convergence probability and the parameter set (k, t_0) and the relationship between the average evaluation number of the function and the parameter set (k, t_0).

Here are three definitions to more clearly explain the evaluation indicators [20].

Definition 3 (successful test). Given the parameters and the max iterative times to be allowed, if the function error between the optimal solution and the best solution gained from running the algorithm is not greater than ε, the test is successful, and then the algorithm stops.

Definition 4 (convergence probability). It means the success ratio in tests of m times.

Definition 5 (the average number of evaluation times). Given the parameters and the max iterative times to be allowed, the average number of evaluation times is the average times of computing the objective function in tests of m times.

We choose the ninth function $F_9(x)$ defined in the work [21] as the testing function. And the work in [21] provides the optimization accuracy $1e-2$ for this function. Here is the definition of this function:

$$F_9\left(x\right)=\sum_{i=1}^{D}\left(z_i{}^2-10\cos\left(2\pi z_i\right)+10\right)+f_{\text{bias}_9}, \tag{23}$$

where $z=x-o$, $x=[x_1, x_2, \ldots, x_D]$, D is the dimension, and $x\in[-5, 5]^D$. o is the extreme point of the function, and $o=[o_1, o_2, \ldots, o_D]$. $F_9(o)=f_{\text{bias}_9}=-330$.

Given $\varepsilon=0.01$ and $m=25$, this function includes a large number of local optimal solutions and a global optimal solution. These solutions are relatively evenly distributed, and there are many local optimal solutions near the global optimal solution. The minimum of the function is -330. We select this function for the robustness test, mainly because this function is relatively more complex, and its features are poor, and general intelligent algorithms are difficult to get satisfactory results. Figure 2 shows the relationships with the convergence probability $p(k, t_0)$ and the relationships with the average evaluation number $\psi(k, t_0)$.

As can be seen from Figure 2, when $k\to0$ and $t_0\to0$, the convergence probability is basically zero, and the average evaluation number is close to the maximum evaluation number of 10000. This range is the nonconvergence zone. Because the variation is very small and almost negligible in this range, only immune selection operation and population updating operation contribute to the search process, and the search process is completely random. Thus, the algorithm is basically impossible to guarantee the convergence. When $k\to200$ and $t_0\to500$, the convergence probability is greater than zero but small, and the average evaluation number is close to

TABLE 2: Accuracies of functions.

Functions	Accuracies
F_2	$-450 + 1e - 6$
F_4	$-450 + 1e - 6$
F_9	$-330 + 1e - 2$
F_{12}	$-460 + 1e - 2$

the maximum evaluation number of 10000 as well. This range is the danger zone. In this range, the mutation rate is large, and the algorithm is easy to jump out of the neighborhood of peak points. So, it will search for a long time to get the optimal solution. When k and t_0 is in the middle range, the convergence probability approaches 1, and the average evaluation number is close to 3400, which is the minimum evaluation number to find the optimal solution. So, for these two parameters, we should choose values of the middle range.

5. Experiments

This section applies the algorithm to the benchmark functions, which run in 2-dimensional spaces and 10-dimensional spaces. The selection of functions and the evaluation criteria of algorithms are described in Section 5.1. The experimental results are shown in Section 5.2 as well as comparisons with the other three artificial immune based optimization algorithms.

5.1. Function Selection and Evaluation Criteria. For that the performance evaluation criteria of optimizing algorithms are not uniform, Suganthan et al. [21] jointly published the report about problem definitions and evaluation criteria on real-parameter optimization in the 2005 IEEE Congress on Evolutionary Computation. In this report, 25 benchmark functions are given, and a common termination criterion, size of problems, initialization scheme, and so forth are specified. We choose F_2, F_4, F_9, and F_{12} and related evaluation criteria, including function error values of the optimal solution, the gained peak numbers, success rates, and convergence graphs to assess the quality and the efficiency of the algorithms.

The termination conditions are that FEs reach $n*10^4$ (n is the dimension), or the function error value of the found optimal solution reaches or is less than the required function errors [21].

We select the influential optimization algorithms based on artificial immune to do the experiments, including CLONALG, opt-aiNet, and dopt-aiNet. The accuracies of the optimization functions are shown in Table 2. The parameters of the four algorithms are as follows:

$$F_2(x) = \sum_{i=1}^{D}\left(\sum_{j=1}^{i} z_j\right)^2 + f_{\text{bias}_2}, \quad (24)$$

where $z = x - o$, $x = [x_1, x_2, \ldots, x_D]$, $x \in [-100, 100]^D$, $F_2(o) = f_{\text{bias}_2} = -450$

$$F_4(x) = \left(\sum_{i=1}^{D}\left(\sum_{j=1}^{i} z_j\right)^2\right) * (1 + 0.4\,|N(0,1)|) + f_{\text{bias}_4}, \quad (25)$$

where $z = x - o$, $x = [x_1, x_2, \ldots, x_D]$, $x \in [-100, 100]^D$, $F_4(o) = f_{\text{bias}_4} = -450$

$$F_9(x) = \sum_{i=1}^{D}\left(z_i^2 - 10\cos(2\pi z_i) + 10\right) + f_{\text{bias}_9}, \quad (26)$$

where $z = x - o$, $x = [x_1, x_2, \ldots, x_D]$, $x \in [-5, 5]^D$, $F_9(o) = f_{\text{bias}_9} = -330$

$$F_{12}(x) = \sum_{i=1}^{D}\left(A_i - B_i(x)\right)^2 + f_{\text{bias}_{12}},$$

$$A_i = \sum_{j=1}^{D}\left(a_{ij}\sin\alpha_j + b_{ij}\cos\alpha_j\right), \quad (27)$$

$$B_i(x) = \sum_{j=1}^{D}\left(a_{ij}\sin x_j + b_{ij}\cos x_j\right), \quad \text{for } i = 1, \ldots, D,$$

where A and B are two $D * D$ matrices, a_{ij} and b_{ij} are integer random numbers in the range $[-100, 100]$, $\alpha = [\alpha_1, \alpha_2, \ldots, \alpha_D]$, α_j are random numbers in the range $[-\pi, \pi]$, $x = [x_1, x_2, \ldots, x_D]$, $x \in [-\pi, \pi]^D$, $F_{12}(\alpha) = f_{\text{bias}_{12}} = -460$.

The parameters of dt-aiNet are N (initial population size) = 50, k (regulation of mutation rate) = 20, t_0 (demarcation point of mutation rate) = 200, β_0 (range of mutation rate) = 0.01, con_0 (initial concentration) = 0.5, Nc (number of clones) = 10, r_{danger} (radius of danger zone) = 0.1, and $d\%$ (percentage of updating population) = 0.3.

The parameters of CLONALG are N (initial population size) = 50, β (mutation rate) = 0.01, and Nc (number of clones) = 10.

The parameters of opt-aiNet are N (initial population size) = 50, Nc (number of clones) = 10, β (mutation rate) = 100, σ_s (network suppression threshold) = 0.2 or 0.05, and $d\%$ (percentage of updating population) = 0.4.

The parameters of dopt-aiNet are N (initial population size) = 50, Nc (number of clones) = 10, β (mutation rate) = 100, σ_s (network suppression threshold) = 0.5, and $d\%$ (percentage of updating population) = 0.4.

5.2. Results of Performance Tests. The algorithms run in 2-dimensional space and 10-dimensional space for the above functions in order to accurately assess the performances.

Table 3 shows the results of performing 25 times for the four algorithms in 2-dimensional space, including function error values $(f - f^*)$ of the optimal solution and peak numbers, where values in brackets are variances. From Table 3, we can see that errors of opt-aiNet are lower than those of CLONALG and dopt-aiNet, and errors of dt-aiNet are lower than those of opt-aiNet. Although dopt-aiNet has local search operation, the two new mutation operations, one-dimensional mutation and gene duplication, take up too much evaluation times; so the algorithm usually cannot find the optimal solution yet when reaches the maximum number of evaluation times. In addition, for the two unimodal functions, F_2 and F_4, dt-aiNet can only find the optimal solution, while CLONALG, opt-aiNet, and dopt-aiNet not

TABLE 3: Results (errors) in 2-dimensional spaces.

		Function errors of the optimal solution	Number of peaks
F_2	dt-aiNet	$1.62 * 10^{-11}$ $(2.1 * 10^{-11})$	1 (0)
	CLONALG	$5.78 * 10^1$ $(3.34 * 10^1)$	1 (1.46)
	opt-aiNet	$6.01 * 10^{-5}$ $(4.61 * 10^{-5})$	5 (1.42)
	Dopt-aiNet	$2.13 * 10^{-1}$ $(4.5 * 10^{-1})$	2.41 (1.2)
F_4	dt-aiNet	$5.86 * 10^{-11}$ $(1.25 * 10^{-11})$	1 (0.2)
	CLONALG	$6.93 * 10^1$ $(3.38 * 10^1)$	3.6 (2.21)
	opt-aiNet	$4.57 * 10^{-5}$ $(4.32 * 10^{-5})$	5.8 (2.2)
	dopt-aiNet	$1.03 * 10^{-1}$ $(5.81 * 10^{-1})$	3.69 (1.3)
F_9	dt-aiNet	$1.2 * 10^{-9}$ $(1.03 * 10^{-9})$	82.54 (8.22)
	CLONALG	$2.12 * 10^0$ $(4.58 * 10^0)$	45.6 (20.28)
	opt-aiNet	$3.99 * 10^{-5}$ $(2.47 * 10^{-5})$	60.11 (23.87)
	dopt-aiNet	$6.87 * 10^{-1}$ $(3.9 * 10^{-1})$	32.09 (12.7)
F_{12}	dt-aiNet	$1.68 * 10^{-11}$ $(1.06 * 10^{-11})$	7.22 (0.43)
	CLONALG	$7.56 * 10^1$ $(4.35 * 10^1)$	4.6 (3.10)
	opt-aiNet	$5.01 * 10^{-2}$ $(2.23 * 10^{-2})$	5 (1.43)
	dopt-aiNet	$7.61 * 10^{-1}$ $(5.84 * 10^{-1})$	8.67 (1.33)

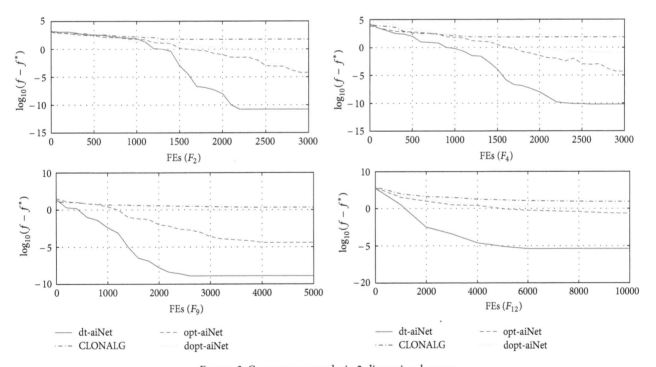

FIGURE 3: Convergence graphs in 2-dimensional spaces.

only find the optimal solution, but also some redundancy solutions.

Table 4 shows the results of performing 25 times for the four algorithms in 2-dimensional space, including success rates and success performances. Known from the work [21], the optimization success rate is defined by *Success Rate = successful runs/total runs*, and the optimization success performance is defined by *Success Performance = mean (FEs for successful runs)*(total runs)/(successful runs)*. It can be seen from Table 4 that only dt-aiNet can find the solution which meets the accuracies when limiting the maximum number of function evaluation times.

Figure 3 shows the convergence graphs in 2-dimensional space of the four algorithms. As can be seen, after initial populations are randomly generated, the convergence curve of each algorithm continues to lower with the evolution. CLONALG is easily trapped in local minima. Opt-aiNet maintains a good diversity of the population, but converges slowly due to the nested loops and increasing unnecessary function evaluation times. dopt-aiNet can find solutions with

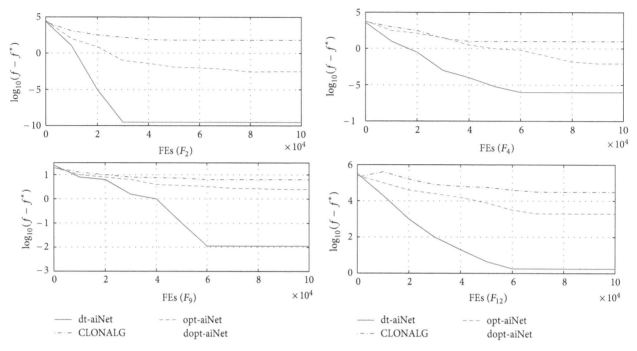

FIGURE 4: Convergence graphs in 10-dimensional spaces.

TABLE 4: Results (success rates) in 2-dimensional spaces.

	dt-aiNet		CLONALG		opt-aiNet		dopt-aiNet	
	Success rates	Success performance	Success rates	Success performance	Success rates	Success performance	Success rates	Success performance
F_2	100%	$2.209 * 10^3$	0%	—	0%	—	0%	—
F_4	100%	$2.576 * 10^3$	0%	—	0%	—	0%	—
F_9	100%	$3.413 * 10^3$	0%	—	0%	—	0%	—
F_{12}	100%	$5.278 * 10^3$	0%	—	0%	—	0%	—

greater accuracies because of the local search operation, but it wastes a large number of function evaluation times for performing the two mutation operations to the memory population and the nonmemory population. So dopt-aiNet converges more slowly. dt-aiNet maintains a better diversity of the population by extracting the environmental information and mutating in a dynamic rate and makes the population quickly converge to the optimal solution.

Tables 5 and 6 show the results of performing 25 times for the four algorithms in 10-dimensional space. Seen from the tables, dt-aiNet still possesses preferable optimization performances in high-dimensional space and is better than CLONALG, opt-aiNet, and dopt-aiNet. In addition, the average function error values and variances are relatively stable and are able to maintain a high level in the 25 times of independently running.

Figure 4 shows the convergence graphs in 10-dimensional space of the four algorithms. As seen from the graphs, dt-aiNet still possesses preferable optimization performances with the increase of dimensions and is better than CLONALG, opt-aiNet, and dopt-aiNet.

6. Conclusions

This paper proposes a danger-theory-based immune network optimization algorithm, named dt-aiNet, for solving multimodal optimization problems. In order to increase the solution quality and the population diversity, the proposed algorithm introduces the danger theory into the optimization algorithms and integrates the clone selection theory and the immune network theory. It simulates the danger zones and the danger signals and adopts concentrations to comprehensively evaluate antibodies. Experimental results show that compared with influential optimization algorithms based on artificial immune, including CLONALG, opt-aiNet, and dopt-aiNet, the proposed algorithm has smaller error values and higher success rates and can find solutions to meet the accuracies within the specified FEs. However, the algorithm cannot apply to any kind of optimization problems, and with the increase of dimension, the success rates of the algorithm are not always 100%. The next steps will be improving the efficiency of the algorithm in the high-dimensional space and extending the application scopes, such

TABLE 5: Results (errors) in 10-dimensional spaces.

		Function errors of the optimal solution	Number of peaks
F_2	dt-aiNet	$7.52 * 10^{-10}$ $(1.84 * 10^{-10})$	1 (0)
	CLONALG	$9.74 * 10^1$ $(2.67 * 10^1)$	57.80 (7.26)
	opt-aiNet	$5.32 * 10^{-3}$ $(4.61 * 10^{-3})$	13.76 (6.81)
	dopt-aiNet	$1.56 * 10^{-2}$ $(5.77 * 10^{-2})$	46.49 (1.33)
F_4	dt-aiNet	$9.65 * 10^{-7}$ $(3.24 * 10^{-7})$	1 (0.1)
	CLONALG	$1.32 * 10^1$ $(5.79 * 10^1)$	123.6 (11.02)
	opt-aiNet	$8.68 * 10^{-3}$ $(3.54 * 10^{-3})$	5 (1.17)
	dopt-aiNet	$7.14 * 10^{-1}$ $(2.94 * 10^{-1})$	12.2 (2.32)
F_9	dt-aiNet	$1.12 * 10^{-2}$ $(2.11 * 10^{-2})$	188.33 (0.31)
	CLONALG	$3.17 * 10^2$ $(4.58 * 10^2)$	45.6 (20.28)
	opt-aiNet	$5.66 * 10^1$ $(2.47 * 10^1)$	433.55 (3.43)
	dopt-aiNet	$7.43 * 10^1$ $(2.80 * 10^1)$	52.5 (4.67)
F_{12}	dt-aiNet	$1.83 * 10^0$ $(5.66 * 10^0)$	193.5 (5.65)
	CLONALG	$3.22 * 10^4$ $(6.43 * 10^4)$	376.67 (5.19)
	opt-aiNet	$2.06 * 10^3$ $(1.33 * 10^3)$	379.43 (0.33)
	dopt-aiNet	$5.69 * 10^3$ $(2.14 * 10^3)$	41.61 (2.26)

TABLE 6: Results (success rates) in 10-dimensional spaces.

	dt-aiNet		CLONALG		opt-aiNet		dopt-aiNet	
	Success rates	Success performance	Success rates	Success performance	Success rates	Success performance	Success rates	Success performance
F_2	100%	$2.677 * 10^4$	0%	—	0%	—	0%	—
F_4	100%	$5.542 * 10^4$	0%	—	0%	—	0%	—
F_9	100%	$4.798 * 10^4$	0%	—	0%	—	0%	—
F_{12}	93%	$5.415 * 10^4$	0%	—	0%	—	0%	—

as dynamic optimization, combinatorial optimization, and constrained optimization.

Acknowledgments

This work has been supported by the National Natural Science Foundation of China under Grants nos. 61173159 and 60873246 and the Cultivation Fund of the Key Scientific and Technical Innovation Project, Ministry of Education of China under Grant no. 708075.

References

[1] D. E. Goldberg, *Genetic Algorithms in Search, Optimization, and Machine Learning*, House of Addison-Wesley, Reading, Mass, USA, 1989.

[2] L. Z. Li and Q. L. Ding, "Routing optimization algorithm for QoS anycast flows based on genetic algorithm," *Computer Engineering*, vol. 6, no. 34, pp. 45–47, 2008.

[3] Y. T. Kao and E. Zahara, "A hybrid genetic algorithm and particle swarm optimization for multimodal functions," *Applied Soft Computing Journal*, vol. 8, no. 2, pp. 849–857, 2008.

[4] D. Dasgupta, S. Yu, and F. Nino, "Recent advances in artificial immune systems: models and applications," *Applied Soft Computing Journal*, vol. 11, no. 2, pp. 1574–1587, 2011.

[5] T. Li, *Computer Immunology*, House of Electronics Industry, Beijing, China, 2004.

[6] L. N. de Castro and J. Timmis, *Artificial Immune Systems: A New Computational Intelligence Approach*, Springer-Verlag, London, UK, 2002.

[7] N. Sun, *Artificial Immune Optimization Algorithm and Applications*, Harbin Institute of Technology, Shandong, China, 2006.

[8] F. Freschi, C. A. C. Coello, and M. Repetto, "Multiobjective optimization and artificial immune systems: a review," in *Multiobjective Optimization*, pp. 1–12, 2009.

[9] L. N. de Castro and J. Timmis, "An artificial immune network for multimodal function optimization," in *Proceedings of the IEEE World Congress on Evolutionary Computation (WCCI '12)*, pp. 699–704, 2002.

[10] L. N. de Castro and J. Fernando, "Learning and optimization using the clonal selection principle," *IEEE Transactions on Evolutionary Computation*, vol. 6, no. 3, pp. 239–251, 2002.

[11] R. Halavati, S. B. Shouraki, M. J. Heravi, and B. J. Jashmi, "An artificial immune system with partially specified antibodies," in *Proceedings of the 9th Annual Genetic and Evolutionary Computation Conference (GECCO '07)*, pp. 57–62, July 2007.

[12] L. N. de Castro and F. J. Von Zuben, "aiNet: artificial immune network for data analysis," in *Data Mining: A Heuristic Approach*, pp. 231–259, 2001.

[13] F. O. de Franca, F. J. Von Zuben, and L. N. de Castro, "An artificial immune network for multimodal function optimization
on dynamic environments," in *Proceedings of the Conference
on Genetic and Evolutionary Computation, ACM*, pp. 289–296,
2005.

[14] J. Timmis, C. Edmonds, and J. Kelsey, "Assessing the performance of two immune inspired algorithms and a hybrid genetic
algorithm for function optimisation," in *Proceedings of the 2004
Congress on Evolutionary Computation (CEC '04)*, vol. 1, pp.
1044–1051, June 2004.

[15] I. Aydin, M. Karakose, and E. Akin, "A multi-objective artificial
immune algorithm for parameter optimization in support vector machine," *Applied Soft Computing Journal*, vol. 11, no. 1, pp.
120–129, 2011.

[16] F. Burnet, *The Clonal Selection Theory of Acquired Immunity*,
Vanderbilt University Press, Nashville, Tenn, USA, 1959.

[17] N. K. Jerne, "Towards a network theory of the immune system,"
Annals of Immunology, vol. 125, no. 1-2, pp. 373–389, 1974.

[18] P. Matzinger, "The danger model: a renewed sense of self,"
Science, vol. 296, no. 5566, pp. 301–305, 2002.

[19] W. X. Zhang and Y. Liang, *Mathematical Foundation of Genetic
Algorithms*, Xi'an Jiaotong University Press, Shaanxi, China,
2001.

[20] Z. H. Zhang, *Study on theory and applications of intelligent
optimization and immune network algorithms in artificial immune systems [Ph.D. thesis]*, Chongqing University, Chongqing,
China, 2004.

[21] P. N. Suganthan, N. Hansen, J. J. Liang et al., "Problem definitions and evaluation criteria for the CEC, 2005 special session
on real-parameter optimization," Tech. Rep., Nanyang Technological University, Singapore, 2005.

16

Query-Biased Preview over Outsourced and Encrypted Data

Ningduo Peng, Guangchun Luo, Ke Qin, and Aiguo Chen

School of Computer Science and Engineering, University of Electronic Science and Technology of China, Chengdu, Sichuan 611731, China

Correspondence should be addressed to Ningduo Peng; nindo_academia@163.com

Academic Editors: T.-Y. Chang and C. L. Hsu

For both convenience and security, more and more users encrypt their sensitive data before outsourcing it to a third party such as cloud storage service. However, searching for the desired documents becomes problematic since it is costly to download and decrypt each possibly needed document to check if it contains the desired content. An informative query-biased preview feature, as applied in modern search engine, could help the users to learn about the content without downloading the entire document. However, when the data are encrypted, securely extracting a keyword-in-context snippet from the data as a preview becomes a challenge. Based on private information retrieval protocol and the core concept of searchable encryption, we propose a single-server and two-round solution to securely obtain a query-biased snippet over the encrypted data from the server. We achieve this novel result by making a document (plaintext) previewable under any cryptosystem and constructing a secure index to support dynamic computation for a best matched snippet when queried by some keywords. For each document, the scheme has $O(d)$ storage complexity and $O(\log(d/s) + s + d/s)$ communication complexity, where d is the document size and s is the snippet length.

1. Introduction

Cloud storage provides an elastic, highly available, easily accessible, and cheap data repository to users who do not want to maintain their own storage or just for convenience, and such a way of storing data becomes more and more popular. In many cases, especially when the users want to store their sensitive data such as business documents, it requires the security guarantees against the cloud provider since an internal staff may access to the data maliciously. Directly encrypting the sensitive documents using traditional encryption techniques such as AES is not an ideal solution since the user will lose the ability to effectively search for the desired documents.

One solution for effectively searching over encrypted data is *searchable encryption* technique. It enables a user to securely outsource his private documents to a third party while maintaining the ability to search the documents by keywords. The scenario is simple: the user submits some encrypted keywords to the server, and then the server performs the search and returns the encrypted documents which contain the queried keywords. However, current searchable encryption techniques either directly return the matched documents or return in the first round some limited information (guided mode) which is prestored in metadata, such as the name and a short static abstract for each matched document. The more documents stored, the more possible matched results will be, and finding the desired documents also becomes a problem. Moreover, the bandwidth cost must be taken into consideration such that returning a large amount of matched documents seemed to be impractical.

Another solution for effectively searching for the desired data is through content preview, which is the main topic of this paper. In modern search engine, if a user searches for a web page by keywords, the search engine will return the name, URI, and a small *query-biased snippet* for each matched page. The snippet explains why such page is matched. Then the user could make a final choice and selectively browse the needed pages without opening all matched links. The same way could be used for searching the desired encrypted documents since the scenario is the same. It could also be combined with searchable encryption to improve the user experience.

However, obtaining a query-biased snippet from an encrypted data is quite challenging. For a general search engine, in order to get a query-biased snippet from a plaintext, it must scan each matched document dynamically, extract the snippets where the keywords occur, then rank the results and finally return the *top-ranking snippet*. While data is encrypted, dynamic scanning becomes quite impossible. Precomputing a snippet file for preview is also impossible because there is no way to know in advance what the queried keywords are, and building all static (keyword, snippet) pairs for each document costs too much storage space even far more than the document itself. Thus, we consider dividing a document to many equal-size encrypted snippets and preconstruct an index to address each snippet. The index stores the information about the keyword frequency in each snippet, which enables the server to dynamically calculate the best snippet for the user when queried by multiple keywords.

There are two major security problems. First, the snippet is the part of a document; therefore the encryption scheme used may affect the snippet retrieval. We use a pad-and-divide scheme to preprocess the document to make it compatible with any cryptosystem such as DES and RSA. Second, the information in the index is private, and no partial information about the document should be leaked to the server. Therefore, we encrypt the index based on the core method of searchable encryption. Since each keyword maps an entry in the index, if queried by some keywords, directly returning the related score information without calculating leaks the information about the number of queried keywords (equals to the number of returned entries) to an eavesdropper, and it also costs multiple communication bandwidth as the number of requested keywords increases. A *homomorphic encryption* scheme could be adopted such that the server could directly operate over the encrypted data and produce a single result, while keeping the ciphertext still secure. However, homomorphic encryption scheme is often costly when dealing with a large amount of data. Observing that all the data are very small, we propose a novel lightweight substitution for homomorphic encryption to construct such secure index.

In this paper, our contributions are the following. (1) To the best of our knowledge, we formalize the problem of securely retrieving query-biased snippet over encrypted data for the first time. We generalize the notion of *secure query-biased preview* (SecQBP) and its security model. (2) We propose a lightweight solution to deal with matrix data with partial homomorphic property, named *matrix additive coding* (Matrix-AC), which could efficiently add two rows of small numbers while keeping the data still encrypted. (3) Based on Matrix-AC and private information retrieval protocol, we construct a *secure additive ranking index* (SecARI) that enables the server to efficiently compute the top-ranking snippet over encrypted data while no partial information about the document is leaked, and then we propose the complete construction to realize SecQBP and prove that it is secure under our security model. (4) We propose a high level solution to combine the preview scheme with searchable encryption technique, which greatly improves the user experience.

The rest of the paper is organized as follows. Section 2 presents the related work. Section 3 presents the notations and preliminaries. Section 4 presents our proposed additive coding scheme. In Section 5 we formally define the preview scheme and its security model and present the construction in detail. We present the application in searchable encryption and analyze the performance in Section 6. Section 7 concludes this paper.

2. Related Work

We categorize the related work into four topics, and each topic is summarized separately.

2.1. Query-Biased Snippet. Query-biased snippet refers to a piece of the content in a document that contains the queried keywords. Query-biased snippet generation schemes are widely used in modern search engine. It is also named *dynamic summary* or *keyword-in-context* (KWIC) snippet generation. The term was used firstly in [1]. The improvements were introduced in [2–6]. However, as far as we know, all query-biased schemes are focused on dynamically retrieving snippets from the plaintext. If the document is encrypted, dynamic scanning becomes impossible. Static preview refers to a snippet summarizing the content in advance, which is always the same regardless of the query. It is generally composed of either a subset of the content or metadata associated with the document. A lightweight static preview scheme over the encrypted data was introduced in [7]. For more details, please refer to [8] for a survey of the recent preview schemes.

2.2. Searchable Encryption. Our proposed scheme and security model are based on searchable encryption technique. The basic goal of searchable encryption is to enable a user to privately search over encrypted data by keywords. The first scheme was introduced in [9]. Later on, many index-based symmetric searchable encryption schemes were proposed. The first secure index was introduced in [10], and the security model of adaptive chosen keyword attack (IND-CKA) was also introduced. Reference [11] introduced two constructions to realize symmetric searchable encryption: the first is SSE-1 which is nonadaptive and the second is SSE-2 which is adaptive. A generalization for symmetric searchable encryption was introduced in [12]. Another type of searchable encryption schemes is public-key based. The first scheme was introduced in [13], the improved definition was introduced in [14], and the strongest security model was introduced in [15].

There are many functional extensions for the basic searchable encryption schemes. Reference [16] introduced a scheme supporting conjunctive keyword search. References [17–19] introduced ranked keyword search over encrypted data. References [20–22] introduced fuzzy keyword search over encrypted data. Similar to fuzzy keyword search but different, [23, 24] introduced similarity search over encrypted data.

2.3. Homomorphic Encryption. Our proposed additive coding method is based on the core concept of homomorphic encryption. The classical homomorphic encryption schemes are based on group operation such as the unpadded RSA in [25], the variant of ElGamal introduced in [26], Goldwasser and Micali's bit homomorphic encryption scheme introduced in [27, 28], and Paillier's encryption scheme introduced in [29]. Many improvements have been proposed based on these classical series of schemes. The referred schemes are public-key based, and few symmetric homomorphic schemes have been proposed. The series of symmetric homomorphic schemes which is based on one-time pad was introduced in [30]. Some ring-based homomorphic schemes have been proposed recently, which are also referred to as full homomorphic encryption, such as the one in [31] that is based on ideal lattices and the one in [32] that does not require ideal lattices.

2.4. Private Information Retrieval. We encapsulate a private information retrieval (PIR) protocol and extend the use of it in our scheme. PIR schemes allow a user to privately retrieve the ith bit of an n-bit database. The notion was fist introduced in [33] by Chor et al., and the notion of private block retrieval (PBR) was also introduced. Kushilevitz and Ostrovsky introduced a single-server and single-round computational PIR scheme in [34], which achieves communication complexity of $O(\sqrt{n})$ for the basic scheme and could achieve $O(n^{\epsilon})$ with arbitrary small ϵ theoretically ($2^{O(\sqrt{\log n \log\log n})}$ is achieved assuming security parameter is polylogarithmic in n). In [35], Cashin et al. introduced a single-database PIR scheme with polylogarithmic communication complexity for the first time, about $O(\log^8 n)$ as suggested. Gentry and Ramzan introduced a PBP scheme with $O(k + d)$ communication cost in [36], where $k \geq \log n$ is a security parameter that depends on n, which is nearly optimal.

3. Notations and Preliminaries

3.1. Basic Notations. We write $x \leftarrow_U X$ to represent sampling element x uniformly random from a set X and write $x \leftarrow \mathcal{A}$ to represent the output of an algorithm $\mathcal{A}$. We write $a \parallel b$ to refer to the concatenation of two strings a and b. We write $|A|$ to represent its cardinality when A is a set and write $|a|$ to represent its bit length if a is a string. We write $\oplus$ to represent bitwise exclusive OR (XOR) and "$\ll n$" to represent bitwise shift left for n bits. We write $\lceil x \rceil$ to represent the least integer less than or equal to x. We write $\underline{s_b}$ to represent a bit string that contains either 0 or 1 (e.g., $\underline{001101_b}$). A function $\mu(k)$: $\mathbb{N} \rightarrow \mathbb{R}$ is negligible if for every positive polynomial $p(\cdot)$ there exists an inter $N > 0$ such that for all $k > N$, $|\mu(k)| < 1/p(k)$. We write $\text{poly}(k)$ and $\text{negl}(k)$ to denote polynomial and negligible functions in k, respectively.

We write $\Delta = (w_1, \ldots, w_n)$ to present a dictionary of n words in lexicographic order. We assume that all words are of length polynomial in k. We write d to refer to a document that contains $\text{poly}(k)$ words. We write $\overline{d}$ to represent the identifier of d that uniquely identifies the document, such as a memory location. We write s to refer to a snippet (50 characters in general) extracted from the document and write $\overline{s}$ to represent the identifier of s, such as the position in the document.

3.2. Cryptographic Primitives. A function $f : \{0, 1\}^k \times \{0, 1\}^n \rightarrow \{0, 1\}^m$ is pseudorandom if it is computable in polynomial time in k and for all polynomial size adversaries $\mathcal{A}$, it cannot be distinguished from random functions. If f is bijective then it is a pseudorandom permutation. We write the abbreviation PRF for pseudorandom functions and PRP for pseudorandom permutations.

Let ES represent an encryption scheme. Let $\text{ES.Gen}(1^k)$ represent the key generation algorithm (k is the secure parameter). Let $\text{ES.Enc}_K(d)$ represent the encryption algorithm that encrypts data d using key K, and let $\text{ES.Dec}_K(c)$ represent the decryption algorithm that decrypts data c to gain the plaintext d. In our scheme, a lot of data will be encrypted using the same key; therefore the encryption scheme must be at least CPA (chosen plaintext attack) and CCA (chosen ciphertext attack) secure. For example, ECB (electronic codebook) mode in DES or RSA without OAEP (optimal asymmetric encryption padding) should not be used.

3.3. Homomorphism. Let $\mathcal{M}$ denote the set of the plaintexts, let $\mathcal{C}$ denote the set of the ciphertexts, let $\odot$ denote the operation between the plaintexts and $\otimes$ the operation between the ciphertexts, and let "$\leftarrow$" denote "directly compute" without any intermediate decryption. An encryption scheme is said to be homomorphic if for any given encryption key k, the encryption function E or the decryption function D satisfies

$$\forall m_1, m_2 \in \mathcal{M}, \quad E(m_1 \odot m_2) \leftarrow E(m_1) \otimes E(m_2), \quad (1)$$

$$\forall c_1, c_2 \in \mathcal{C}, \quad D(c_1 \otimes c_2) \leftarrow D(c_1) \odot D(c_2). \quad (2)$$

Sometimes, property (2) is also referred to as homomorphic decryption. If the operation is upon a group, we say it is a group homomorphism. If the operation is upon a ring, we say it is a ring homomorphism and is also referred to as full homomorphism. If the operator is addition, we say it is additively homomorphic, and if the operator is multiplication, we say it is multiplicatively homomorphic.

3.4. Private Block Retrieval Protocol. Let $B = (B_1, \ldots, B_n)$ represent a database of n blocks; all blocks have equal size d. The user wants to privately retrieve the ith block from the server; therefore he runs a private block retrieval protocol. At a high level, we define the single database and single round computational PBR as follows.

Definition 1 (computational PBR protocol). A computational PBR protocol scheme is a collection of four polynomial-time algorithms $\text{CPBR} = (\text{Setup}, \text{Query}, \text{Response}, \text{Decode})$ such that we have the following.

> $P \leftarrow \text{Setup}(B)$ is a probabilistic algorithm that takes as input the database B and outputs a parameter set P. It is run by the database owner, and P is known to all users.
>
> $t \leftarrow \text{Query}(i)$ is a probabilistic algorithm that takes as input a block index i and outputs a token t. It is run by the user. t is sent to the server.

$r \leftarrow \text{Response}(t)$ is a deterministic algorithm that takes as input the requested token t and outputs a result r. It is run by the server. r is sent to the user.

$B_i \leftarrow \text{Decode}(r)$ is a deterministic algorithm that takes as input the response r from the server and outputs the requested data block B_i. It is run by the user.

In our preview scheme, we adopt the computational PBP scheme as a primitive introduced in [36]. In the setup algorithm, we set the database size as the maximal possible document size (e.g., 10 MB) and reuse prime number set and prime power set in all documents. The communication complexity is $O(\log|d| + |s|)$ where $|d|$ is the document length and $|s|$ is the snippet length.

4. Secure Additive Coding

Before introducing the preview scheme, we first introduce a novel coding method called matrix additive coding (Matrix-AC) that enables addition of two rows in a matrix in a homomorphic fashion, which is very fast and suitable for dealing with small numbers (the integer is coded to a specific bit string) and is especially useful for computing statistical table in encrypted form. Since all operated integers are correlative, it is not a homomorphic encryption scheme which could encrypt data independently.

Matrix-AC is used in the preview scheme to construct the secure additive ranking index (SecARI). Becouse a large number of small numbers will be calculated in the preview scheme, using homomorphic encryption schemes is costly. Therefore, we use Matrix-AC scheme as a substitution for homomorphic encryption scheme to achieve optimal performance.

We note that, for all the schemes (including the preview scheme in the next section), we only consider the confidentiality of the data. Mechanism about protecting data integrity is out of the scope of this paper.

4.1. Basic Idea. The basic idea of coding small integers $\mathbb{S}_N = (0, 1, 2, \ldots, N)$ with homomorphic property is simple: we consider an integer vector $\mathbf{m} = (m_1, \ldots, m_n)$, where $m_i \in \mathbb{S}_N$ and $\sum_{i=1}^{n} m_i \leq N$. We define a "vernier" that has N bits, and each integer m_i is mapped to such vernier for m_i bits in different position. A global cursor g is autoincreased to process the mapping. To code a message, a random string as a one-time-pad key is used and XORed with the mapped data. The decoding is simple: just operate $\oplus$ with the key and count the number of bit-1 to make reverse mapping.

For example (as shown in Figure 1), consider a vernier that has 8 bits, and we map three integers $(2, 1, 3)$ as a vector to three pairs $(2, \underline{00000011}_b)$, $(1, \underline{00000100}_b)$, and $(3, \underline{00111000}_b)$. It is easy to see that the homomorphic property holds as $2 + 3 = 5$, and $\underline{00000011}_b \oplus \underline{00111000}_b = \underline{00111011}_b$, which has exactly 5 bit-1. Thus, let the vector be $(m_1 = 2, m_2 = 1, m_3 = 3)$, and let the keys be (K_1, K_2, K_3) that each key is a random string; then the ciphertext vector will be $(c_1 = \underline{00000011}_b \oplus K_1, c_2 = \underline{00000100}_b \oplus K_1,$

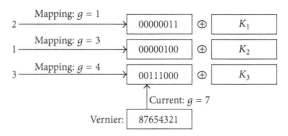

FIGURE 1: Example of vernier mapping and the basic coding procedure.

$c_3 = \underline{00111000}_b \oplus K_1)$. To perform addition for any two plaintexts $m = m_1 + m_2$, the server could directly compute the corresponding ciphertexts $c = c_1 \oplus c_2$ and the decryption key becomes $K = K_1 \oplus K_2$. Using the new key, it is easy to decrypt the ciphertext and count the number of bit-1 to restore the result.

The problem of the basic scheme is that the vernier may be used up. That is why we set the restriction that a vernier is just used in a single vector. Another drawback is that, as the max N increases, the length of the vernier also increases in linear $O(N)$. Thus, the targeted data must be small enough to save storage space. A good application is not for dealing with few such integers but for computing a large number of small data in parallel.

4.2. Coding a Matrix. We extend the basic idea to code the data matrix. Let $A_{m \times n}$ represent a matrix with m rows and n columns, let a_{ij} represent the element in row i and column j, and a_i represent the ith row. Matrix-AC scheme is described in Algorithm 1. Note that there are n cursors that control the mapping for each column.

Let us check the homomorphism for decoding: let D represent the decryption algorithm, for arbitrary two ciphertext rows c_1 and c_2, $D(c_1 \oplus c_2) = D(c_1) + D(c_2)$, where the decryption key for $c_1 \oplus c_2$ is $K_1 \oplus K_2$.

There is a problem if the scheme is directly used in the application. In the real world, there is no way to directly represent, for example, data of 5 bits (there is an extended "bitset" class in C++, but it treats the bits as a set, and all operations are performed over set, and it is very slow). In computer, the data is represented by "byte" that a valid number is stored in such a byte. Thus, 5-bit data is stored in one byte (8 bits) as a "character," 12-bit data is stored in two bytes (16 bits) as a "short integer," and a 20-bit data is stored in four bytes (32 bits) as an "integer." Thus, the XOR operation is performed over byte, and the data should be extended to such standard length. However, since all data in Matrix-AC are in fact a bit string, sometimes the data in the same row could be "chained" together. For example, suppose $N = 5$ and there are 6 data in a row; the row could be chained to a 30-bit string and stored in a 32-bit integer. Another problem is that the "bit-counting" algorithm is realized indirectly by "mod 2" operation or setting N masks to see if the masked bit is 1. Therefore, the performance would be improved if some dedicated hardware directly dealing with bits is used.

Input m random strings $\mathbf{K} = (K_1, \ldots, K_m)$ of length $n \cdot N$

$\mathbf{Code}_{\mathbf{K}}(X_{m \times n})$:

  (1) check the validity of the input, continue if $m_{ij} \in \mathbb{S}_N$ and for all j,
      $\sum_{k=1}^{m} c_{kj} \leq N$, or output $\varnothing$ otherwise

  (2) initialize a ciphertext matrix $C_{m \times n} = (c_{ij})$, each element is set to 0
      (N bits), and initialize n cursors $g_1, \ldots, g_n$ and set each $g_j = 1$ (N bits)

  (3) **for** $(i = 1; i \leq m; i + +)$ **do**

  (4)   **for** $(j = 1; j \leq n; j + +)$ **do**

  (5)   **for** $\left(k = 1; k \leq x_{ij}; k + +\right)$ **do**

  (6) $c_{ij} \leftarrow c_{ij} \oplus g_j$

  (7) $g_j \leftarrow g_j << 1$

  (8)   **end for**

  (9)   **end for**

  (10) encrypt the ith row as $c_i \leftarrow c_i \oplus K_i$

  (11) **end for**

  (12) output $C_{m \times n}$

$\mathbf{Decode}_{K_i}(c_i)$:

  (1) initialize a temporary data row $\mathbf{t} = (t_1, \ldots, t_n)$ with each element
     be N bits, and set $\mathbf{t} = c_i \oplus K_i$

  (2) for each t_j in $\mathbf{t}$, let the binary form of t_j be $b_N b_{N-1} \ldots b_1$, then
     $x_{ij} = \sum_{k=1}^{N} b_k$

  (3) output $\mathbf{x_i} = (x_{i1}, \ldots, x_{in})$

ALGORITHM 1: Secure additive coding for matrix.

4.3. Proof of Security. Intuitively, the scheme is secure if any two matrices (the numbers of elements are the same) prepared by the adversary are indistinguishable, which also implies that any two elements from the same matrix are indistinguishable. We define the security of Matrix-AC as follows.

Lemma 2. *If $K_1, \ldots, K_n$ are random strings, then Matrix-AC is CPA secure.*

Proof (sketch). We briefly prove the scheme since the mechanism is simple. We describe a PPT simulator $\mathcal{S}$ for all PPT adversaries $\mathcal{A}$. $\mathcal{S}$ generates matrix $\mathbf{X}^*_{m \times n}$ with m random strings of length $n \cdot N$. For any row x_i in the original matrix $\mathbf{X}_{m \times n}$, no matter how it maps, the last computation is a string XORed with a one-time-pad random string K_i; thus the result is indistinguishable from random. For any two rows x_i and x_j from the same matrix, each row is XORed with different random strings such that the results are indistinguishable from each other. For any two rows x_i and x_i^* from two matrices, as discussed previously, x_i is indistinguishable from the random string x_i^*. $\qquad\square$

5. Secure Query Biased Preview Scheme

The preview scheme contains two steps: (1) storage at which the data owner prepares the previewable document and a searchable index; (2) retrieval at which the user privately retrieves the snippet from the server.

The basic idea of constructing a query-biased previewable document is as follows: divide the document into n snippets with equal size, extract keywords from each piece to form

TABLE 1: Example of a snippet index.

Keyword	s_1	s_2	$\cdots$	s_n
w_1	2	1	$\cdots$	2
w_2	1	2	$\cdots$	1
$\cdots$	$\cdots$	$\cdots$	$\cdots$	$\cdots$
w_i	2	5	$\cdots$	3
$\cdots$	$\cdots$	$\cdots$	$\cdots$	$\cdots$
w_m	3	2	$\cdots$	2

a keyword set which records the snippet information as (keyword, frequency) pairs, and build an index to address the snippets according to the distinct keywords. The index R is a $m \times n$ two-dimensional matrix of the form R(keyword, snippet index), and the value is the keyword frequency in the corresponding snippet. An example is shown in Table 1. The keyword is represented by w_i, and the snippet index is represented by s_i.

The main process of retrieving the best snippet by multi keywords follows the following steps. The user submits mul-tikeywords to the server. The server retrieves the multirows in the index according to the submitted keywords and adds the rows together. The result is a single entry that contains the information about the best matched snippet. The user decrypts the entry, selects the snippet identifier (index number) with the highest score (for simplicity, the score equals the frequency), and privately retrieves the snippet from the server by running a PBR protocol. In order for the server to perform the "addition" operation over the encrypted data, a homomorphic encryption scheme could be used to encrypt the index. We adopt Matrix-AC as the encryption scheme instead of a standard homomorphic encryption scheme as discussed previously.

Now we begin to introduce the definition and the security model of the preview scheme. Note that we assume the server is honest but curious. Additional methods could be added to make those solutions robust against malicious attack; however, we restrict our discussion on honest-but-curious fashion. We also note that all documents are treated as text files the same way as search engine does. For example, if a document is a web page, the style tags will be pruned.

5.1. Scheme Definition. The secure-query biased preview (SecQBP) scheme contains two parties: a user U and a remote server S. U encrypts his private document d to D, generates a secure additive ranking index (SecARI) H, and then outsources them to S. S stores the document, performs the computation for the scores when queried by multiple keywords, and returns the result to U. U then selects the best snippet indexed by i and privately retrieves it from S.

Without loss of generality, we consider the construction for a single document. The scheme could be extended to a document collection with ease. Now we define the SecQBP scheme as follows.

Definition 3 (secure query-biased preview scheme). SecQBP scheme is a collection of six polynomial-time algorithms SecQBP = (Gen, Setup, Query, ComputeScore, DecScore, DecSnip) as follows.

$K \leftarrow \mathtt{Gen}(1^k)$ is a probabilistic algorithm that takes as input a security parameter k and outputs the secret key collection K. It is run by the user, and the keys are kept secret.

$(D, H) \leftarrow \mathtt{Setup}_K(d)$ is a probabilistic algorithm that takes as input a document d and outputs a encrypted document D (using any cryptosystem) and an index H. It is run by the user, and D, H are outsourced to the server.

$q \leftarrow \mathtt{Query}_K(\mathbf{w})$ is a deterministic algorithm that takes as input the queried multiple keywords $\mathbf{w} = (w_1, \ldots, w_n)$ and outputs a secret query token q. It is run by the user, and q is sent to the server.

$r \leftarrow \mathtt{ComputeScore}(q, H)$ is a deterministic algorithm that takes as input the secret query q and the index H and outputs the result r that contains the final score information about each snippet. It is run by the server.

$i \leftarrow \mathtt{DecScore}_K(\mathbf{w}, \overline{d}, r)$ is a deterministic algorithm that takes as input the queried keywords $\mathbf{w}$, the document identifier $\overline{d}$, and the query result r and outputs the snippet index number i. It is run by the user.

$s_i \leftarrow \mathtt{DecSnip}_K(D_i)$ is a deterministic algorithm that takes as input the ciphertext D_i and outputs the recovered plaintext snippet s_i. It is run by the user. Note that, if the user retrieves the entire encrypted document, he could decrypt the document by decrypting each snippet.

5.2. Security Model. Informally speaking, SecQBP must guarantee that, first, given the encrypted document c and the index H, the adversary cannot learn any partial information about the document; second, given a sequence of queries $q = (q_1, \ldots, q_n)$, the adversary cannot learn any partial information about the queried keywords and the matched snippet (including the index number and the content). We now present the security definition for adaptive adversaries.

Definition 4 (semantic security against adaptive chosen keyword attack, CKA2-security). Let $\sum = $ (SecQBP algorithm + SecQBP protocol) be the preview scheme. Let $k \in \mathbb{N}$ be the security parameter. one considers the following probabilistic experiments, where $\mathscr{A}$ is an adversary and $\mathscr{S}$ is a simulator.

$\mathrm{Real}_{\Sigma,\mathscr{A}}(k)$: the challenger runs $\mathtt{Gen}(1^k)$ to generate the key K. $\mathscr{A}$ generates a document d and receives $(D, H) \leftarrow \mathtt{Setup}_K(d)$ from the challenger. $\mathscr{A}$ makes a polynomial number of adaptive queries $\mathbf{w}_1, \ldots, \mathbf{w}_n$ (each set $\mathbf{w}_i$ contains multiple keywords in d), and for each queried keyword set $\mathbf{w}_i$, $\mathscr{A}$ receives a query token $q_i \leftarrow \mathtt{Query}_K(\mathbf{w}_i)$ from the challenger. Finally, $\mathscr{A}$ returns a bit b that is output by the experiment.

$\mathrm{Sim}_{\Sigma,\mathscr{A},\mathscr{S}}(k)$: $\mathscr{A}$ generates a document d. Given only the size $|d|$, $\mathscr{S}$ generates and sends (D^*, H^*) to $\mathscr{A}$. $\mathscr{A}$ makes a polynomial number of adaptive queries $\mathbf{w}_1, \ldots, \mathbf{w}_n$ (each set $\mathbf{w}_i$ contains multiple keywords in d), and for each queried keyword set $\mathbf{w}_i$, $\mathscr{A}$ receives a query token q_i^* from $\mathscr{S}$. Finally, $\mathscr{A}$ returns a bit b that is output by the experiment.

We say that SecQBP is semantic secure against adaptive chosen keyword attack if, for all PPT adversaries $\mathscr{A}$, there exists a PPT simulator $\mathscr{S}$ such that

$$\left| \Pr\left[\mathrm{Real}_{\Sigma,\mathscr{A}}(k) = 1 \right] - \Pr\left[\mathrm{Sim}_{\Sigma,\mathscr{A},\mathscr{S}}(k) = 1 \right] \right| \leq \mathrm{negl}(k),$$
$$(3)$$

where the probabilities are over the coins of $\mathtt{Gen}$ and $\mathtt{Setup}$ (related to the underlying cryptosystem).

Note that, with q_i or q_i^*, $\mathscr{A}$ could run $\mathtt{ComputeScore}(q, H)$ to get the result r, and any internal state is also captured by $\mathscr{A}$. $\mathscr{A}$ could also send query according to the previous result.

5.3. Concrete Construction. Now we describe the concrete construction for SecQBP. We describe the constructions for some core components, and then represent the complete construction.

5.3.1. Encrypting a Document. We consider the problem of extracting keywords from a document. In general, a keyword is followed by a separator. Thus, in a general snippet of 50 characters, no more that 25 keywords are contained. Another problem is that not all words are keywords, and such words do not need indexing, for instance, the words "a," "the," and "and." This kind of words can be found in most of the sentences such that it is useless as a key to index a file. They

---

Input: a document d, the encryption key K
Output: the encrypted document $D = (D_1, \ldots, D_n)$, a keyword-frequency
set collection $e = (e_1, \ldots, e_n)$
Method:
   (1) padding d according to snippet length $|s|$ as discussed
   (2) treat d as $n = |d|/|s|$ pieces $s_1, \ldots, s_n$
   (3) **for** $(i = 1; i \leq n; i + +)$ **do**
   (4)   create a keyword-frequency set e_i for s_i
   (5)   scan s_i for distinct valid keywords. For each keyword, count the
       keyword frequency, and add the vector (keyword, frequency) to
       e_i as set element
   (6)   encrypting the snippet as $D_i \leftarrow \text{ES.Enc}_K(s_i)$
   (7) **end for**

ALGORITHM 2: Encrypting a document: $\text{ED}_K(d)$.

are called stop-word and firstly researched in [37]. The most classical stop word list used abroad is a list of 425 words suggested in [38].

There is a problem that the last word in a snippet may be cut off. In other words, the last word of a snippet may be not short enough to fit the space, and it cannot be split into two words because neither of them is a valid keyword. In a general search engine, such overflowed word is omitted. However, in the scenario of precomputing snippets, if the word is omitted, a keyword may be lost. It means that, when querying the omitted keyword, there will be no matched snippet returned, where actually there is a match for the document. Thus, we add the full word to both the keyword sets of the snippets which contain part of the keyword.

The basic idea for encrypting a document is dividing the document with equal size; therefore, a padding scheme is needed when the last piece of the document is not long enough. We modify the CBC plaintext padding scheme introduced in [39] to meet our goal. Let $|s|$ represent the length of the snippet; the snippet is treated as a sequence of bytes. If the last snippet is a bytes, then pad the snippet with $|s| - a$ bytes with value $|s| - a$. After decryption, the padding will be deleted to recover the original plaintext. For instance, suppose $|s| = 50$; if the final snippet has 15 plaintext bytes, then pad the snippet as

$$\text{byte}_1 \parallel \text{byte}_2 \parallel \cdots \parallel \text{byte}_{15} \parallel 35 \parallel 35 \parallel \cdots \parallel 35, \quad (4)$$

where there are 35 bytes that have the number 35. If the snippet is divisible by $|s|$, here is 50, then add a new snippet with all bytes being 50:

$$50 \parallel 50 \parallel \cdots \parallel 50. \quad (5)$$

Let d represent a document, and D is the encrypted form of d. We introduce the scheme for encrypting a document, shown in Algorithm 2. In the algorithm, "a valid keyword" means the token is not a separator, not a stop word, and not a random-looking string. A word dictionary could be used to check its validity.

TABLE 2: Example of a SecARI.

Index	s_1	s_2	$\cdots$	s_n
$\pi_K(w_2)$	c_{21}	c_{22}	$\cdots$	c_{2n}
$\cdots$	$\cdots$	$\cdots$	$\cdots$	$\cdots$
PAD	PAD	PAD	PAD	PAD
$\pi_K(w_1)$	c_{11}	c_{12}	$\cdots$	c_{1n}
$\cdots$	$\cdots$	$\cdots$	$\cdots$	$\cdots$
$\pi_K(w_m)$	c_{m1}	c_{m2}	$\cdots$	c_{mn}
PAD	PAD	PAD	PAD	PAD
$\pi_K(w_3)$	c_{31}	c_{32}	$\cdots$	c_{3n}
$\cdots$	$\cdots$	$\cdots$	$\cdots$	$\cdots$

5.3.2. Constructing the Secure Index. The secure additive ranking index (SecARI) is the encryption form of the snippet index, as shown in Table 1 (PAD denotes the padding with a random string), and each row is an encrypted entry. For security reason, the number of entries of SecARI must be padded to a certain amount which is independent of the actual number of keywords in the content, or it will leak the information about the number of distinct keywords in the document (it equals the number of rows). An example of a SecARI is shown in Table 2. In the table, π is a pseudorandom permutation which randomizes the order of the keywords, and the value c_{ij} is the encrypted score.

Let us consider the secure amount of the entries. If the document d is small, let a keyword occupy only one byte; then the maximum possible number of keywords is $|d|/2$ (as discussed, a valid keyword is at least 2 bytes); thus, the number of entries must be set to $|d|/2$ (the fractional part is ignored). If the document d is large, the maximum possible number of keywords equals the total number of words in the dictionary. Reference [40] made a detailed word statistical analysis based on 450 million words on Corpus of Contemporary American English (1990–2012). The statistics show that the total words used are about 60000. We set the dictionary used as Δ and define the maximum keyword amount as $|\Delta| = 60000$. Thus, we define the number of entries as follows.

Input:
    (1) $\overline{d}$: the document identifier
    (2) $e = (e_1, \ldots, e_n)$: the keyword-frequency set collection
    (3) $K = \left(K_m, K_p \right)$: consists of the master key K_m for row encryption
         and the permutation key K_p for π
Output: A secure additive ranking index H
Method:
    (1) scan e, extract m distinct keywords $(w_1, \ldots, w_m)$
    (2) create an $m \times n$ data matrix $X = (x_{ij})$, the value of each data x_{ij} is
         the frequency of the keyword w_i in the jth snippet
    (3) for each row i, the encryption/decryption key is $k_i \leftarrow f_{K_m} \left(w_i \, || \, \overline{d} \right)$.
         Thus the keys for all rows form a vector $\mathbf{K}_X = (k_1, \ldots, k_m)$
    (4) create an $m \times n$ matrix C, each cell c_{ij} has length N
    (5) compute $C \leftarrow \text{Code }_{\mathbf{K}_X}(X)$ using Matrix-AC
    (6) for all w_i, set $H \left[\pi_{K_p} \left(w_i \right) \right] = c_i$ where c_i is the ith row of the encrypted matrix C
    (7) if $m < N_{\text{ent}}$, set remaining $N_{\text{ent}} - m$ entries of H to random values

ALGORITHM 3: Constructing SecARI: $\text{Index}_K \left(\overline{d}, e \right)$.

Definition 5 (number of entries). To guarantee security, the number of entries N_{ent} for a SecARI is

$$N_{\text{ent}} = \begin{cases} \dfrac{|d|}{2}, & \dfrac{|d|}{2} < |\Delta|, \\[2mm] |\Delta|, & \dfrac{|d|}{2} \geq |\Delta|. \end{cases} \tag{6}$$

SecARI is in fact a sparse look-up table, and we use indirect addressing method to manage it. Indirect addressing method is also called *FKS dictionary* introduced in [41], which is also adopted in symmetric searchable encryption scheme in [11]. It manages sparse table of the form (address, value). The address is a *virtual address* that could locate the value field. Given the address, the algorithm will return the associated value in constant look-up time and return $\emptyset$ otherwise.

In addition, we make use of a pseudorandom permutation π to index an entry and a pseudorandom function to generate the one-time-pad keys for Matrix-AC:

$$\begin{aligned} \pi &: \{0, 1\}^k \times \{0, 1\}^{|w|} \longrightarrow \{0, 1\}^{|w|}, \\ f &: \{0, 1\}^k \times \{0, 1\}^{|w|+|\overline{d}|} \longrightarrow \{0, 1\}^{N \cdot n}, \end{aligned} \tag{7}$$

where $|w|$ is the keyword length and $|\overline{d}|$ is the length of the document identifier. N is the upper bound discussed in Matrix-AC and n is the number of snippets that is calculated from the document size. The submitted keyword is encrypted by π such that the server cannot figure out what the keyword the user queries.

Let H be a $\{0, 1\}^{|w|} \times \{0, 1\}^{N \cdot n} \times N_{\text{ent}}$ data matrix managed by indirect addressing technique as discussed previously. Now we describe SecARI in Algorithm 3.

5.3.3. The Complete Scheme. In order to hide the information about the number of queried keywords, a SecARI is not enough. When the user submits the queried multiple keywords, each query should be of the same length so that an eavesdropper cannot learn the information about the number of keywords in a query. Let the maximum number of keywords allowed in a single query be W_{max}; the remaining space must be padded. The user and the server should initiate a secure channel such as SSL to transport such message, or the padding may be discovered by an eavesdropper. Since the size of a keyword is small, the bandwidth waste of the padding is rather negligible.

We also determine the upper bound N for Matrix-AC. As discussed, a general snippet contains at most 25 keywords; thus we set $N = 32$ (stored as a standard integer).

Let f be the pseudorandom function, and π is the pseudorandom permutation as described previously. Now we describe the complete scheme in Algorithm 4, and describe the storage and retrieval protocol in Protocol 1. The retrieval protocol describes the retrieval of a query-biased snippet from document d by submitting a multikeyword query $\mathbf{w} = (w_1, \ldots, w_n)$.

Note that it is a scenario for a single document. The protocol also works for a document collection. Thus, the user could retrieve multiple snippets for multiple documents in the same round.

5.4. Proof of Security. The server stores the SecARI, performs homomorphic computation for a query, and returns to the user the score information as a single entry. We prove the security by introducing a theorem as follows.

Theorem 6. *If f is a pseudorandom function, if π is a pseudorandom permutation, and if ES is CPA and CCA secure, then SecQBP is CKA2 secure.*

Proof. We describe a polynomial-size simulator $\mathcal{S}$, for all polynomial-size adversaries $\mathcal{A}$, $\text{Real}_{\Sigma, \mathcal{A}}(k)$ and $\text{Sim}_{\Sigma, \mathcal{A}, \mathcal{S}}(k)$

$\texttt{Gen}\left(1^k\right)$:

   (1) sample index keys $\left(K_m, K_p\right) \leftarrow_U \{0,1\}^k$, generate document
       encryption key $K_d \leftarrow \texttt{ES.Gen}\left(1^k\right)$

   (2) output $K = \left(K_m, K_p, K_d\right)$

$\texttt{Setup}_K(d)$:

   (1) invoke $\texttt{ED}_{K_d}(d)$ to get e and the encrypted document D

   (2) invoke $\texttt{Index}_{(K_m,\ K_p)}(\overline{d}, e)$ to get the secure index H

   (3) output D, H

$\texttt{Query}_K(\mathbf{w})$:

   (1) for each keyword w_i in $\mathbf{w} = (w_1, \dots, w_n)$, compute $t_i \leftarrow \pi_{K_p}(w_i)$

   (2) put $(t_1, \dots, t_n)$ into query q and pad it to length $W_{\max}$

   (3) output the query q

$\texttt{ComputeScore}(q, H)$:

   (1) let k represent the snippet amount, unpack q to get the queried
       tokens $t = (t_1, \dots, t_n)$, set a flag $F = 1$

   (2) select a subset of $t : t' = (t'_1, \dots, t'_m)$ where t'_i is in H. If no element
       is in H, then set $F = 0$

   (3) create the result $h = H\left[t'_1\right] \oplus \cdots \oplus H\left[t'_m\right]$ if $F == 1$, or else randomly
       select an index i and set $h = H[i]$

   (4) put t' into query q' and pad it to length $W_{\max}$

   (5) output $r = \left(h, q', F, k\right)$

$\texttt{DecScore}_K\left(\mathbf{w}, \overline{d}, r\right)$:

   (1) unpack $r = (h, q', F, k)$ and get $t' = (t'_1, \dots, t'_m)$

   (2) **if** the flag $F == 0$ **then**

   (3)   randomly select an index $i \in [1, k]$

   (4) **else**

   (5)   according to t', generate the decryption key $k_j \leftarrow f_{K_m}(w_j \parallel \overline{d})$
          for each matched keyword w_j in $\mathbf{w}$

   (6)   compute the decryption key $k_r = k_1 \oplus k_2 \oplus \cdots \oplus k_m$

   (7)   invoke $a \leftarrow \texttt{Decode}_{k_r}(h)$ using Matrix-AC

   (8)   choose a snippet number i in a with the highest score

   (9) **end if**

   (10) output the snippet index i

$\texttt{DecSnip}_{K_d}(D_i)$: output the plaintext snippet $D_i \leftarrow \texttt{ES.Dec}_{K_d}(D_i)$

ALGORITHM 4: SecQBP algorithm.

Storage:

   (1) the user U runs $\texttt{Gen}\left(1^k\right)$ to generate the key K

   (2) U runs $\texttt{Setup}_K(d)$ to get the encrypted document D and the index H,
       and sends (D, H) to the server S

Query:

   (1) U runs $\texttt{Query}_K(\mathbf{w})$ to get a token q and sends it to S

   (2) S runs $\texttt{ComputeScore}(q, H)$ to produce the score result r, and
       sends it to U along with document identifier $\overline{d}$

   (3) U runs $\texttt{DecScore}_K\left(\mathbf{w}, \overline{d}, r\right)$ to get the index number i (best matched snippet)

   (4) U runs a CPBR protocol as discussed, generates a query token t
       from $\texttt{CPBR.Query}(i)$ and sends t to S

   (5) S responses with o from $\texttt{CPBR.Response}(t)$

   (6) U runs $\texttt{CPBR.Decode}(o)$ to get the encrypted snippet D_i

   (7) U runs $\texttt{DecSnip}_{K_d}(D_i)$ to get the plaintext s_i

PROTOCOL 1: SecQBP protocol.

TABLE 3: Comparisons of preview schemes.

	Data type	Preview mode	Round	Communication	Storage	Computation
General search engine [5]	Plaintext	Query biased	1	$O(s)$	d	$O(d)$
Content mask [7]	Plaintext or ciphertext	Static	1	$O(s)$	$O(d)$	$O(1)$
Our scheme	Ciphertext	Query biased	2	$O(\log(d/s) + s + d/s)$	$O(d)$	$O(1)$

are indistinguishable. Consider the simulator that given the size of the document $|d|$, $\mathcal{S}$ generates the data as follows.

(1) (Simulating H^*) $\mathcal{S}$ computes $m = N_{\text{ent}}$, $n = \lceil |d|/|s| \rceil$. For $1 \leq i \leq m$, $\mathcal{S}$ generates a string $a_i^* \parallel c_i^*$ such that each a_i^* is a distinct string of length $|w|$ chosen uniformly at random, and each c_i^* is a string of length $N \cdot n$ bits chosen uniformly at random. All strings form H^*.

(2) (Simulating q_i^*) $\mathcal{S}$ prepares a query list L that stores the query history. The value in L is of the form (w, a^*). When queried by a keyword set $\mathbf{w}_i$, for each keyword w_k in $\mathbf{w}_i$, $\mathcal{S}$ first scans L to see if there is a match. If not, $\mathcal{S}$ randomly chooses a distinct a_k^* which is not in L and stores the pair (w_k, a_k^*) into L. $\mathcal{S}$ gets $(a_1^*, \ldots, a_{|\mathbf{w}_i|}^*)$ according to $\mathbf{w}_i$ and sets $q_i^* = (a_1^*, \ldots, a_{|\mathbf{w}_i|}^*)$.

(3) (Simulating D_i^*) $\mathcal{S}$ sets D_i^* to a $|D_i|$-bit string chosen uniformly at random. Note that $|D_i|$ is a global parameter known by the user and the server.

We claim that no polynomial-size distinguisher $\mathcal{D}$ could distinguish the following pairs.

(1) (H and H^*) recall that H consists of N_{ent} values. Each value consists of either a string of the form $(\pi_{K_p}(w_i) \parallel c_i)$ or a random string. In any case, with all but negligible probability, the PRP key K_p is not included; therefore the pseudorandomness of π guarantees that $\pi_{K_p}(w_i)$ is indistinguishable from random. The PRF key K_m is also not included; therefore the pseudorandomness of f guarantees that the derived key k_i for each data row is indistinguishable from random, and then the underlying Matrix-AC is CPA-secure, which means that c_i is indistinguishable from random. H^* contains N_{ent} random values. Therefore, as discussed, H and H^* are indistinguishable.

(2) (q_i and q_i^*) recall that q_i is the evaluation of the PRP π. In any case, with all but negligible probability, the PRP key K_p is not included; therefore the pseudo-randomness of π guarantees that all $\pi_{K_p}(w_i)$ in q_i are indistinguishable from random, and q_i^* is a random string of the same length of q_i.

(3) (D_i and D_i^*) recall that D_i is encrypted by a CPA and CCA secure encryption scheme. Since the encryption key K_d is not known by the adversary, the security of the encryption scheme guarantees that D_i and D_i^* are indistinguishable. $\square$

6. Comparison, Application, and Performance Analysis

First, we compare the functionalities and performance of our work with previous works. Then, as a significant example, we discuss how to combine the preview scheme with symmetric searchable encryption to improve the user experience. We also discuss the performance of the preview scheme in the concrete application example.

6.1. Scheme Comparison. Let s denote the snippet length and d the document size; the comparisons of our work with other representative works are shown in Table 3.

The query-biased preview mode is widely used in general search engine, as introduced in [5]. In the scheme, the search engine dynamically scans the document line by line to find the top-ranking snippet. Therefore, the computation complexity is $O(d)$. In [7], Mithal and Tayebi proposed a static preview scheme over encrypted data based on content mask technique. In the scheme, some segments of the plaintext are extracted in advance and are masked with noise in such a way that the so called "masked preview content" could be sent to the user as a preview when queried. The static scheme is fast and informative but does not explain why a document is matched by a query. Note that our scheme costs one extra round of communication since the score results have to be returned to the user in the first round.

6.2. Symmetric Searchable Encryption Extension. We review the generalized definition of symmetric searchable encryption (SSE) introduced in [12]. We assume that the searchable encryption scheme is in guided mode. In other words, the server will first return to the user the identifiers of the matched documents, and the user makes a final choice to select some document identifiers and sends them to the server to retrieve the selected ones.

Definition 7 (extended symmetric searchable encryption). In guided mode, a symmetric searchable encryption scheme is a collection of six polynomial-time algorithms SSE = (Gen, Enc, Token, Search, Retrieve, Dec) such that we have the following.

$K \leftarrow \text{Gen}(1^k)$ is a probabilistic algorithm that takes as input a security parameter k and outputs a secret key K. It is run by the user, and the output key is kept secret by the user.

$(\gamma, C) \leftarrow \text{Enc}_K(D)$ is an algorithm that takes as input a secret key K and a document collection $D = (D_1, \ldots, D_n)$ and outputs a searchable structure γ and a sequence of encrypted documents $C = (C_1, \ldots, C_n)$.

It enables a user to query some keywords, and the server returns the matched documents. For instance, in an index-based searchable symmetric encryption scheme, γ is the secure index. It is run by the user, and (γ, C) is sent to the storage server.

$t \leftarrow \text{Token}_K(\mathbf{w})$ is a deterministic (possibly probabilistic) algorithm that takes as input a secret K and a set of some keywords $\mathbf{w} = (w_1, \ldots, w_n)$ and outputs a search token t (also named trapdoor or capacity). It is run by the user.

$I \leftarrow \text{Search}(\gamma, t)$ (guided mode) is a deterministic algorithm that takes as input the query token t and the searchable structure γ and outputs the matched document identifiers $I = (I_1, \ldots, I_m)$. It is run by the server, and the result I is sent to the user. Note that, if not in guided mode, this algorithm returns the matched documents directly. It is run by the server.

$C' \leftarrow \text{Retrieve}(C, I')$ is a deterministic algorithm that takes as input the encrypted documents and the selected document identifiers $I' \subseteq I$ and outputs the selected documents corresponding to the identifiers. It is run by the server.

$D_i \leftarrow \text{Dec}_K(C_i)$ is a deterministic algorithm that takes as input a secret key K and the returned encrypted document C_i and outputs the recovered plaintext D_i. It is run by the user.

The preview scheme is applied in SSE as follows. The user runs `SSE.Gen`, `SecQBP.Gen`, `SSE.Enc`, and `SecQBP.Setup`, respectively. The server stores the outsourced structure generated by SSE and the encrypted documents generated by SecQBP scheme. To search for some documents, the user runs `SSE.Token` and `SecQBP.Query`, respectively, and sends them to the server. The server produces the identifiers of the matched documents, runs `SecQBP.ComputeScore` for the corresponding documents one by one, and returns the document identifiers and the score results together. The user decodes the score, retrieves the preview snippets from the server, then makes the choice, and sends the selected document identifiers to the server to retrieve the interested documents.

6.3. Performance Analysis.

We adopt SSE-2 introduced in [11] as an instance of a SSE scheme. Table 4 shows the time complexity and storage complexity for single SSE-2 scheme and SSE-2 plus SecQBP in detail.

Let C represent the encrypted document collection, so the total size is $|C|$ bytes. Other than the returned encrypted documents, the extrastorage cost for SSE-2 is $|C|/8$ bytes; thus the storage cost is $O(n)$. The extrastorage cost for SecQBP is H for each document. By definition, the storage cost is $O(n)$. For SSE, the server searches the matched documents and decrypts the identifier list. For SecQBP, the server searches the indices for all matched documents, returns score results for all matched documents, and finally returns the snippets. They are both in time complexity of $O(1)$. The number of rounds for SSE is two (guided mode). First, the server returns

TABLE 4: Properties of SSE-2 + SecQBP.

Properties	SSE-2	SSE-2 + SecQBP
Adaptive adversaries	Y	Y
Number of servers	1	1
Server storage	$O(n)$	$O(n)$
Server computation	$O(1)$	$O(1)$
Number of rounds	2	3
Extracommunication	$O(1)$	$O(\log(d/s) + s + d/s)$

the identifiers of the matched documents and next returns the selected documents. SecQBP adds extra round for retrieving snippets from the snippet server. Moreover, for each matched document, the size of the messages for SEE is $O(1)$. SecQBP is $O(\log(d/s) + s + d/s)$, where d is the document length, and s is the snippet length, since the user will receive a score result of size d/s and a snippet of size s.

The detailed performance of SSE is analyzed in [42]; therefore we just analyze the performance of the SecQBP part. The content of a document d is varied in the real world. By observation in [40], the number of keywords in a document increases along with the document size which satisfies log model, and the worst case satisfies linear model (each word in the document is keyword, such as a dictionary). However, the design for security in our scheme guarantees that the encrypted indices generated from any document are indistinguishable. Therefore, the computation for the server is independent from the models (i.e., the computations for all documents are the same). To simulate the reality, we design the data generator that simulates documents using log model.

In order to demonstrate the optimization for the server, we compare our suggested Matrix-AC scheme with the simplest and, as far as we know, the fastest symmetric homomorphic encryption scheme [30] denoted by SHE and a well-known homomorphic cryptosystem [29] denoted by Paillier cryptosystem. We consider that 100 users submit queries simultaneously. Each query contains 5 keywords, and the score computation is over 100 matched documents (SSE generates the identifiers of the matched documents). The size of each document increases from 50 KB to 1 MB (the sizes for all stored documents are the same), and the computation cost is described by millisecond.

The algorithms are coded in C++ programming language and the server is a Pentium Dual-Core E5300 PC with 2.6 GHz CPU. The result is shown in Figure 2. It demonstrates that:the following. (1) The scheme is secure. The figure shows a linear computation cost, which means the computation is independent of the document content. In other words, the server does not see any differences for all documents while performing the search. (2) In cloud environment, computation for 100 users simultaneously on a single server becomes a burden as the size of the document increases. In other words, the number of servers run as services is determined by the size of the stored documents and the accepted queries. (3) The performance is improved as we adopt Matrix-AC to substitute the homomorphic encryption schemes. From the data, Matrix-AC is about 30% faster than

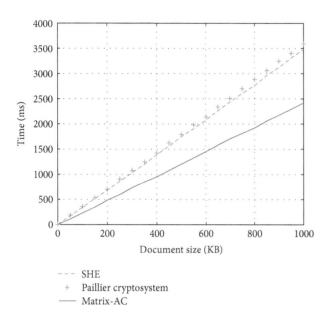

FIGURE 2: Time cost for computing scores (single server, 100 users).

using SHE or Paillier cryptosystem. We assume that the user does not modify the document frequently, and the main operation is just searching for some documents. Therefore, the performance improvement is significant since it could save about 30% virtual machines in the cloud.

7. Conclusions

In this paper, we propose a generalized method of securely retrieving query-biased snippet over outsourced and encrypted data, which allows the users to take a sneak preview over their encrypted data. The preview scheme has strong security and privacy guarantees with relatively low overhead, and it greatly improves the user experience.

Acknowledgments

Part of this work is supported by the Fundamental Research Funds for New Century Excellent Talents in Chinese Universities (Grant no. NCET-10-0298) and Ministry of Science and Technology of Sichuan province (no. 2012HH0003).

References

[1] A. Tombros and M. Sanderson, "Advantages of query biased summaries in information retrieval," in *Proceedings of the 21st annual international ACM SIGIR conference on Research and development in information retrieval*, pp. 2–10, ACM, 1998.

[2] D. Christopher and P. R. H. S. Manning, *Introduction To Information Retrieval*, Cambridge University Press, 2008.

[3] J. Goldstein, M. Kantrowitz, V. Mittal, and J. Carbonell, "Summarizing text documents: sentence selection and evaluation metrics," in *Proceedings of 22nd International ACM SIGIR Conference on Research and Development in Information Retrieval*, pp. 121–128, 2013.

[4] T. Sakai and K. Sparck-Jones, "Generic summaries for indexing in information retrieval," in *Proceedings of the 24th Annual International ACM SIGIR Conference on Research and Development in Information Retrieval*, pp. 190–198, Association for Computing Machinery, 2001.

[5] A. Turpin, Y. Tsegay, D. Hawking, and H. E. Williams, "Fast generation of result snippets in web search," in *Proceedings of the 30th Annual International ACM SIGIR Conference on Research and Development in Information Retrieval (SIGIR '07)*, pp. 127–134, July 2007.

[6] R. W. White, I. Ruthven, and J. M. Jose, "Finding relevant documents using top ranking sentences: an evaluation of two alternative schemes," in *Proceedings of the 25th Annual International Conference on Research and Development in Information Retrieval (ACM SIGIR '02)*, pp. 57–64, Association for Computing Machinery, 2002.

[7] A. K. Mithal and A. Tayebi, Method and System For Facilitating Search, Selection, Preview, Purchase Evaluation, Offering For Sale, Distribution, and/or Sale of Digital Content and Enhancing the Security Thereof, 2009.

[8] A. Nenkova and K. McKeown, "A survey of text summarization techniques," in *Mining Text Data*, pp. 43–76, Springer, 2012.

[9] D. X. Song, D. Wagner, and A. Perrig, "Practical techniques for searches on encrypted data," in *Proceedings of the IEEE Symposium on Security and Privacy*, pp. 44–55, May 2000.

[10] E. J. Goh, "Secure indexes," Tech. Rep., 2003, IACR ePrint Cryptography Archive, http://eprint.iacr.org/2003/216.

[11] R. Curtmola, J. Garay, S. Kamara, and R. Ostrovsky, "Searchable symmetric encryption: Improved definitions and efficient constructions," in *Proceedings of the 13th ACM Conference on Computer and Communications Security*, pp. 79–88, ACM Press, November 2006.

[12] M. Chase and S. Kamara, "Structured encryption and controlled disclosure," in *Proceedings of the 16th International Conference on the Theory and Application of Cryptology and Information Security (ASIACRYPT '10)*, pp. 577–594, Springer, 2010.

[13] D. Boneh, G. D. Crescenzo, R. Ostrovsky, and G. Persiano, "Public key encryption with keyword search," in *International Conference on the Theory and Applications of Cryptographic Techniques (EUROCRYPT '04)*, pp. 506–522, Springer, 2004.

[14] M. Abdalla, M. Bellare, D. Catalano et al., "Searchable encryption revisited: consistency properties, relation to anonymous ibe, and extensions," in *Proceedings of the 25th Annual International Cryptology Conference (CRYPTO '05)*, pp. 205–222, Springer, 2006.

[15] D. Boneh, E. Kushilevitz, R. Ostrovsky, and W. E. Skeith III, "Public key encryption that allows pir queries," in *Proceedings of the 27th Annual International Cryptology Conference (CRYPTO '07)*, pp. 50–67, Springer, 2007.

[16] P. Golle, J. Staddon, and B. Waters, "Secure conjunctive keyword search over encrypted data," in *Proceedings of the 2nd International Conference (ACNS '04)*, pp. 31–45, Springer, 2004.

[17] N. Cao, C. Wang, M. Li, K. Ren, and W. Lou, "Privacy-preserving multi-keyword ranked search over encrypted cloud data," in *IEEE International Conference on Computer Communications (INFOCOM '11)*, pp. 829–837, April 2011.

[18] C. Wang, N. Cao, J. Li, K. Ren, and W. Lou, "Secure ranked keyword search over encrypted cloud data," in *Proceedings of the 30th IEEE International Conference on Distributed Computing Systems (ICDCS '10)*, pp. 253–262, June 2010.

[19] A. Swaminathan, Y. Mao, G.-M. Su et al., "Confidentiality-preserving rank-ordered search," in *Proceedings of the ACM*

Workshop on Storage Security and Survivability (StorageSS '07), pp. 7–12, October 2007.

[20] C. Bosch, R. Brinkman, P. Hartel, and W. Jonker, "Conjunctive wildcard search over encrypted data," in *Proceedings of the 8th VLDB Workshop on Secure Data Management,* pp. 114–127, Springer, 2011.

[21] J. Bringer and H. Chabanne, "Embedding edit distance to allow private keyword search in cloud computing," in *Proceedings of the 8th FTRA International Conference on Secure and Trust Computing, Data Management, and Application,* pp. 105–113, Springer, 2011.

[22] J. Li, Q. Wang, C. Wang, N. Cao, K. Ren, and W. Lou, "Fuzzy keyword search over encrypted data in cloud computing," in *IEEE Conference on Computer Communications (INFOCOM '10),* March 2010.

[23] W. Cong, R. Kui, Y. Shucheng, and K. M. R. Urs, "Achieving usable and privacy-assured similarity search over outsourced cloud data," in *IEEE Conference on Computer Communications (INFOCOM ' 12),* pp. 451–459, IEEE, 2012.

[24] M. Kuzu, M. S. Islam, and M. Kantarcioglu, "Efficient similarity search over encrypted data," in *IEEE 28th International Conference on Data Engineering (ICDE '12),* pp. 1156–1167.

[25] R. L. Rivest, A. Shamir, and L. Adleman, "A method for obtaining digital signatures and public-key cryptosystems," *Communications of the ACM,* vol. 26, no. 1, pp. 96–99, 1983.

[26] A. K. Singh and P. Chandran, "A secure and efficient multi-authority proactive election scheme," in *Proceedings of the 3rd International Conference Information Systems Security (ICISS '07),* pp. 208–218, 2007.

[27] S. Goldwasser and S. Micali, "Probabilistic encryption & how to play mental poker keeping secret all partial information," in *Annual ACM Symposium on Theory of Computing,* pp. 365–377, ACM, 1982.

[28] S. Goldwasser and S. Micali, "Probabilistic encryption," *Journal of Computer and System Sciences,* vol. 28, no. 2, pp. 270–299, 1984.

[29] P. Paillier, "Public-key cryptosystems based on composite degree residuosity classes," in *Proceedings of the International Conference on the Theory and Applications of Cryptographic Techniques (EUROCRYPT '99),* pp. 223–238, 1999.

[30] C. Castelluccia, E. Mykletun, and G. Tsudik, "Efficient aggregation of encrypted data in wireless sensor networks," in *Proceedings of the 2nd Annual International Conference on Mobile and Ubiquitous Systems-Networking and Services,* pp. 109–117, July 2005.

[31] C. Gentry, "Fully homomorphic encryption using ideal lattices," in *Proceedings of the 41st Annual ACM Symposium on Theory of Computing (STOC '09),* pp. 169–178, June 2009.

[32] M. Van Dijk, C. Gentry, S. Halevi, and V. Vaikuntanathan, "Fully homomorphic encryption over the integers," in *Lecture Notes in Computer Science,* pp. 24–43, 2010.

[33] B. Chor, O. Goldreich, E. Kushilevitz, and M. Sudan, "Private information retrieval," *Journal of the ACM,* vol. 45, no. 6, pp. 965–982, 1998.

[34] E. Kushilevitz and R. Ostrovsky, "Replication is not needed: single database, computationally-private information retrieval," in *Proceedings of the 38th IEEE Annual Symposium on Foundations of Computer Science,* pp. 364–373, October 1997.

[35] C. Cashin, S. Micali, and M. Stadler, "Computationally private information retrieval with polylogarithmic communication," in *International Conference on the Theory and Applications of Cryptographic Techniques (EUROCRYPT '99),* pp. 402–414, Springer, 1999.

[36] C. Gentry and Z. Ramzan, "Single-database private information retrieval with constant communication rate," in *Proceedings of the 32nd International Colloquium on Automata, Languages and Programming (ICALP '05),* pp. 803–815, July 2005.

[37] H. P. Luhn, "A statistical approach to mechanized encoding and searching of literary information," in *Pioneer of Information Science, Selected Works,* pp. 94–104, 1969.

[38] C. Fox, "Lexical analysis and stop-lists," in *Information Retrieval: Data Structures and Algorithms,* 1992.

[39] R. L. Rivest and R. W. Baldwin, "The rc5, rc5-cbc, rc5-cbc-pad, and rc5-cts algorithms," in *The Internet Engineering Task Force Request For Comments,* 1996.

[40] M. Davies, Word frequency data, 2012, http://www.wordfrequency.info/.

[41] M. L. Fredman, E. Szemeredi, and J. Komlos, "Storing a sparse table with o(1) worst case access time," *Journal of the ACM,* vol. 31, no. 3, pp. 538–544, 1984.

[42] S. Kamara, C. Papamanthou, and T. Roeder, "Cs2: a searchable cryptographic cloud storage system," Tech. Rep. MSR-TR-2011-58, Microsoft Research, 2011.

17

Selective Segmentation for Global Optimization of Depth Estimation in Complex Scenes

Sheng Liu,[1,2] **Haiqiang Jin,**[1] **Xiaojun Mao,**[1] **Binbin Zhai,**[1] **Ye Zhan,**[3] **and Xiaofei Feng**[4]

[1] *College of Computer Science & Technology, Zhejiang University of Technology, Hangzhou 310023, China*
[2] *Key Laboratory of Visual Media Intelligent Processing Technology of Zhejiang Province, Hangzhou 310023, China*
[3] *School of Accounting, Zhejiang University of Finance and Economics, Hangzhou 310018, China*
[4] *College of Computer and Information Engineering, Zhejiang Gongshang University, Hangzhou 310018, China*

Correspondence should be addressed to Sheng Liu; edliu@zjut.edu.cn

Academic Editors: C. W. Ahn and C. Cattani

This paper proposes a segmentation-based global optimization method for depth estimation. Firstly, for obtaining accurate matching cost, the original local stereo matching approach based on self-adapting matching window is integrated with two matching cost optimization strategies aiming at handling both borders and occlusion regions. Secondly, we employ a comprehensive smooth term to satisfy diverse smoothness request in real scene. Thirdly, a selective segmentation term is used for enforcing the plane trend constraints selectively on the corresponding segments to further improve the accuracy of depth results from object level. Experiments on the Middlebury image pairs show that the proposed global optimization approach is considerably competitive with other state-of-the-art matching approaches.

1. Introduction

Depth estimation from a pair of rectified stereo images is always a challenging research field in vision analysis [1, 2]. The local stereo matching methods often generate outliers in weakly textured areas, discontinuous boundaries, and occlusion areas. Consequently, the global optimization methods [3–7] are designed for more accurate depth estimating in comparison with local ones. Nevertheless, all of these above-mentioned methods neglected the segmentation information in the optimization framework.

The later global optimization methods only partially incorporated the segmentation information into a pixel-level *MRF* model [8–14]. The segmentation information was merely integrated into unary terms or pairwise terms rather than higher order terms. For instance, Wang and Lim [10] proposed a new segment-based stereo matching approach, which takes segments as graph nodes for constructing an irregular segmentation-based graph. In spite of decreasing the computation complexity immensely and showing object-level feature information clearly, it neglected the depth detail

and structure detail within the segment and accordingly resulted in the "Mosaic Effect."

For taking full advantage of segmentation information, Kohli et al. [15] proposed a higher order term including complete detail of each segment. The *Robust P*[n] *Potts model* presented by Kohli was originally designed for segmentation applications, which is based on an assumption that the pixels inside the same segment should be label consistency. The labels are used to identify different objects for image segmentation, other than different disparities for depth estimation. So, the energy function for depth estimation cannot penalize the segment with a linear penalty which takes inconsistency pixel ratio into account. Therefore, Kohli's approach is unable to be applied in depth estimation directly. Xie et al. [16] improved the higher order term proposed by Kohli et al. and applied it to the depth estimation successfully. The improved higher order term enforces impliedly the assumption that all the segments of the input image are regarded as various planes. Nevertheless, this assumption is unreasonable because the surfaces of objects are more likely to be irregular surfaces rather than planes in real scene.

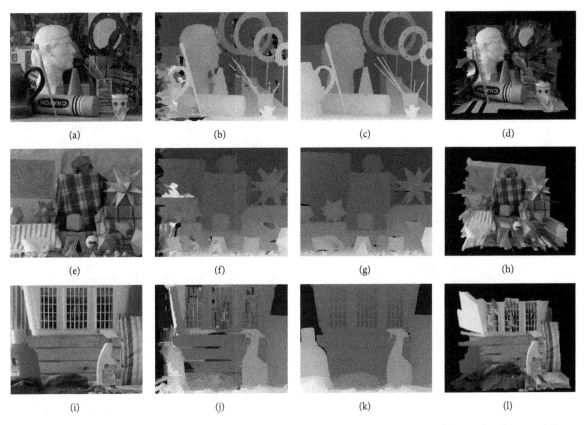

FIGURE 1: Dense depth maps for the Art, Moebius, and Laundry test sets (from top to bottom). From left to right: the input left images, our final depth maps, ground truth, and three-dimensional reconstructed results. Compared with the ground truth, our results obviously acquire most details of the scene with relatively high accuracy.

This paper proposes a segmentation-based global optimization method for the depth estimation. Our approach composed of four energy terms makes the following contributions: unlike those familiar data terms converted from local stereo matching methods directly, our data term combines a self-adapting stereo matching approach and two matching cost optimization strategies aiming at occlusion regions and border of image. Most smoothness terms only enforce a simple smoothness strategy over the whole image, which is obviously unable to satisfy the fact that different regions have varying smoothness requirements in a disparity map. Hence, our smoothness term employs a comprehensive smoothness strategy. We incorporate segmentation information in the form of higher order term and perform a selective planarity operation by enforcing a plane trend or not when facing diverse segments.

Experiment results on the stereo images in Middlebury datasets (Figure 1) have shown that our global optimization method obtains satisfactory depth results and is competitive with the state-of-the-art algorithms.

2. Global Optimization Method for Depth Estimation

2.1. Algorithm Overview. The input of our algorithm is a pair of rectified stereo images, which are used in improved local stereo matching method based on self-adapting matching windows, color segmentation, and process of constructing smooth term. With the handling of two proposed matching cost optimization strategies, the final matching costs for the pixels are used to not only construct data term but also computer refine map. Both smooth term and segmentation term require the segmentation information produced by [17]. The proposed energy function composed of four energy terms is optimized using *α-expansion* move algorithm [18]. The whole procedure of our algorithm is illustrated in Figure 2.

2.2. Energy Function. In this paper, we presented a segmentation-based global optimization approach composed of *integrated data term, comprehensive smoothness term,* and *selective segmentation term.* To make use of the pixel-level information more adequately, the proposed data term is not only decided by the matching costs from the local stereo matching method based on the improved self-adapting window but also mended the replacement for occlusion regions and evaluation for border of image according to two proposed optimization strategies. Due to comprehensive smoothness strategy, our smooth term is able to satisfy the smoothness requirement more fully. By fusing object-level over-segment information in our global optimization framework, we can richly utilize homogeneous information in the same segment. In addition, the selective planarity operation for segments

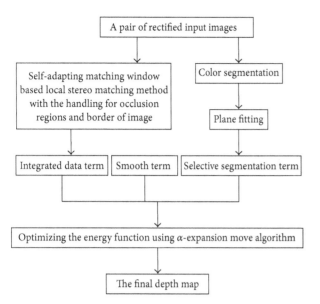

FIGURE 2: Flow chart of the proposed algorithm.

makes our segmentation term more robust. The global energy function for a unique configuration f is as follows:

$$E(f) = E_{\text{data}}(f) + E_{\text{smooth}}(f) + E_{\text{seg}}(f). \quad (1)$$

2.3. Data Term Based on Self-Adapting Window. In most local stereo matching methods, the fixed matching window is employed for depth estimation. Nevertheless, it is difficult to guarantee that all the pixels in a fixed window are of the same depth. Therefore, there exist amounts of outliers in weak-textured areas, discontinuous boundaries, and occlusion regions shown in Figure 3. In order to improve the accuracy of matching costs for the corresponding depths, the local stereo matching approach based on the self-adapting matching window is adopted for computing the matching costs.

The local stereo matching approaches with self-adapting matching window are based on the assumption that when pixels with similar intensity within a constrained window have similar disparity, it is necessary to produce an appropriate matching window for each pixel adaptively. In this paper, we mainly refer to the local stereo matching method proposed by Zhang et al. [22] based on self-adapting matching window. Two aspects of improvement are made on the basis of original approach: firstly, a dynamical argument mechanism of minimum window is proposed for more robust correspondence matching. Secondly, we enforce a replacement strategy for occlusion regions and a suboptimum strategy for borders of image.

Being inspired by five major approaches introduced by Egnal and Wildes [23], we present a replacement strategy to deal with the occlusion regions. Owing to the common assumption that pixels with similar intensity within a neighboring area have similar disparity, the matching costs for occlusion pixels are capable of being replaced with ones for "corresponding" pixels.

For instance, $d(p)$ is the disparity for pixel $p = (x_p, y_p)$ in the left input image, and $d'(p')$ is the disparity for pixel

$p' = (x_p - d(p), y_p)$ in the right image. If $d(p)$, $d'(p')$ and $d(p'')$ satisfy simultaneously the condition that $d(p) > d'(p')$ and $d'(p') \leq d(p'')$ where $p'' = (x_p - d(p) + d'(p'), y_p)$, we would employ a displacement strategy that the matching costs for the pixel p in left image are replaced with the one for the pixel p' in right image.

Neither estimating two disparity maps for left-right consistency check [24, 25] nor applying a simple border extrapolation step, we adopt a suboptimum strategy for the border of image. The corresponding pixel p' will locate outside the right image when $(x_p - d(p)) < 1$, which means that the matching cost $C_d(p)$ cannot be achieved by making use of the corresponding pixels. In this paper, we need the suboptimum label $d^{\wedge}$,

$$d^{\wedge} = \underset{d \in [d_{\min}, d_{\max}], (x_p - d) > 0, d \neq d^*}{\arg \min} C_d(p), \quad (2)$$

where d^* is the optimal label computed as follows:

$$d^* = \underset{d \in [d_{\min}, d_{\max}], (x_p - d) > 0}{\arg \min} C_d(p). \quad (3)$$

At last, we use $C_{d^{\wedge}}(p)$ as the matching cost for pixel p when $(x_p - d(p)) < 1$. The improved local results are shown in Figure 4.

2.4. Smooth Term Based on Comprehensive Management. All kinds of smooth terms are presented for smoothing the coarse local results. In this paper, a new comprehensive smooth term is defined based on the similarity of color for dealing with different smoothing requirements on neighborhoods. The proposed smooth term combines the following two smooth terms.

Assume that there is a neighborhood system N on the pixel set P, $N \subset \{(p_1, p_2) \mid p_1, p_2 \in P\}$, Yu et al. [7] performed the consistency of corresponding pixels and their neighbors in their smooth term as follows:

$$E_{\text{smooth}}(f) = \sum_{(p_1, p_2) \in N} \min((f(p_1) - f(p_2)), k), \quad (4)$$

where k is a constant.

Kolmogorov and Zabih [3] presented a different smooth term, which considers the color information of corresponding pixels and their neighbors. The smooth term is formulated as follows:

$$E_{\text{smooth}}(f) = \sum_{(p_1, p_2) \in N} V_{p_1, p_2} * T(f(p_1) \neq f(p_2)), \quad (5)$$

where V_{p_1, p_2} denotes a positive penalty function which imposes disparate penalties according to color differences between pixels. Suppose $R(p)$, $G(p)$, and $B(p)$ are the respective color components of pixel p in RGB space,

$$V_{p_1, p_2}$$
$$= \begin{cases} 3\lambda, & \text{if } \max(|R(p_1) - R(p_2)|, |G(p_1) - G(p_2)|, \\ & \qquad |B(p_1) - B(p_2)|) < \varepsilon, \\ \lambda, & \text{otherwise,} \end{cases}$$
$$(6)$$

where λ is a penalty constant, ε manages a least color diversity.

(a)   (b)

(c)   (d)

FIGURE 3: Comparison of local stereo matching methods with fixed matching window and self-adapting matching window for the Teddy (from left to right). Top row: the fixed matching window is marked by red, and the self-adapting matching window is marked by green (from left to right). Bottom row (from left to right): the results by NCC with the fixed matching window, and the results by proposed local stereo matching method with self-adapting matching window. In the NCC case, a mass of obvious outliers occurred in weak-textured regions, discontinuous boundaries, and occlusion areas. The proposed local method has achieved much better results.

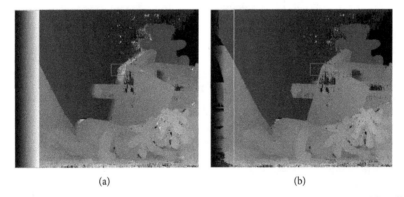

(a)   (b)

FIGURE 4: Comparison between the local depth result without occlusion region and border of image (ORBI) handling and the one with ORBI handling for the Teddy (from left to right). Left column: the local depth results without ORBI handling. Right column: the local depth results with ORBI handling. The red frame demonstrates the comparison in occlusion region, while the green frames denote the comparison in border of image. The results show that ORBI handling makes the matching costs for the corresponding depths more reliable.

Nevertheless, the smoothness on the boundaries between two adjacent objects will influence the accuracy of the final disparity map. So, we only need to perform the smooth operation in the segments. Compositing the above two kinds of smoothness terms, we propose a new hierarchical smoothness strategy in the identical segment. The new smoothness term is as follows:

$$
E_{\text{smooth}}
= \sum_{(p_1, p_2) \in N, S(p_1) = S(p_2)} V'_{p_1, p_2} * \min \left((f(p_1) - f(p_2)), k \right),
$$
(7)

where $S(p)$ is the identification of segment to which the pixel p belongs, V'_{p_1, p_2} denotes a new penalty function which enforces a different penalty on the basis of color differences:

$$
V'_{p_1, p_2}
= \begin{cases}
8\lambda & \text{if } \max \left(|R(p_1) - R(p_2)|, |G(p_1) - G(p_2)|, \right. \\
& \left. |B(p_1) - B(p_2)| < \varepsilon_1 \right), \\
2\lambda & \text{if } \max \left(|R(p_1) - R(p_2)|, |G(p_1) - G(p_2)|, \right. \\
& \left. |B(p_1) - B(p_2)| < \varepsilon_2 \right), \\
\lambda & \text{if } \max \left(|R(p_1) - R(p_2)|, |G(p_1) - G(p_2)|, \right. \\
& \left. |B(p_1) - B(p_2)| < \varepsilon_3 \right), \\
\sigma & \text{otherwise,}
\end{cases}
$$
(8)

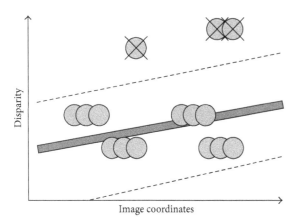

⊗ Deflected pixel

FIGURE 5: Sketch map for deflected pixels.

where σ is a penalty constant, ε_1, ε_2, and ε_3 are several color diversities and $\varepsilon_1 < \varepsilon_2 < \varepsilon_3$.

The smooth terms perform different smoothness strategies inside the segments according to the diverse color differences of neighborhoods.

2.5. Segmentation Term of Selective Planarity. In this paper, we use the segmentation information to construct the segmentation term for further improving the accuracy of depth estimation. Our segmentation term is different from the higher order term presented by Kohli et al. The higher order term in [15] was originally designed for image segmentation, according to the assumption that the pixels in the same segment should share the same label. However, depth estimation is more likely to satisfy the assumption that the pixels in the same region follow the same distribution such as plane distribution or surface distribution; in other words, the pixels in the same segment could have multiple labels other than only a single label. So, directly making use of Kohli's higher order term for depth estimation is unreasonable.

Obviously, the surface distribution is more representative than the plane distribution because the objects in real scene are more likely composed of irregular surfaces rather than planes. Nevertheless, in this paper the plane distribution is adopted with considering its lower computation complexity and more commonly approximate representativeness. The segments obtained by [17] are further divided into many more subsegments using certain plane distribution. The plane distribution is achieved by plane fitting for the local results. And all the pixels in each subsegment are more likely to share the same label.

Not all the segments are appropriate to enforce the plane distributions. If the plane distribution is employed roughly in those segments which are unable to be represented by plane, the worse influences on resulting depth map would occur.

In this paper, before performing the plane distributions in the segments, we employ a segment classify procedure for every segment using a proposed plane-judge approach as shown in Figure 5.

For instance, the pixel p is judged as deflected when it meets the condition that $|f(p) - d^*(p)| > \Phi$, where $d^*(p)$ is the disparity value for the pixel p after plane fitting using the local depths, and Φ is a constant that controls the planarity quality of segments. p_S is a pixel set for all pixels in the segment S, $N_d(f(p_S))$ denotes the number of deflected pixels in the segment S, $N(p_S)$ denotes the number of pixels in the segment S, and $\mu \in (0,1)$ controls the planarity level of the "planar" segment. If $N_d(f(p_S)) > N(p_S) * \mu$, we would not construct a homologous segmentation term for the segment S. Otherwise, the segmentation term would be constructed using the *Robust P^n Potts model*.

The segmentation function $E_{\text{seg}}(f)$ using the *Robust P^n Potts model* is defined as

$$E_{\text{seg}}(f) = \begin{cases} N_i\left(f\left(p_S\right)\right) \dfrac{1}{Q} \gamma_{\max} & \text{if } N_i\left(f\left(p_S\right)\right) \leq Q, \\ \gamma_{\max} & \text{otherwise,} \end{cases} \quad (9)$$

where $N_i(f(p_S))$ denotes the number of pixels in the segment S not taking the dominant label, $\gamma_{\max}$ is the maximum value of label inconsistency cost, and Q is the truncation parameter controlling the rigidity of segmentation function. The *Robust P^n Potts model* proposed by Kohli et al. [15] is shown in Figure 6.

Concrete constructing procedure of segmentation term for each segment is shown in Algorithm 1.

The segmentation terms enforce the plane trends into the segments which can be represented by plane approximately.

2.6. Energy Minimization Process Based on Graph Cuts. In order to minimize the global energy function by graph cut, all energy terms of this energy function must be submodular according to [26]. In the light of additive principle, if every term in energy function is submodular, the whole global energy function will be submodular. The unary term, such as data term, is always submodular. The pairwise term, namely, smooth term, also is submodular since it satisfies the inequality $E^{i,j}(0,0) + E^{i,j}(1,1) \leq E^{i,j}(0,1) + E^{i,j}(1,0)$. And from the definition of *Robust p^n Potts model*, the segmentation term does satisfy the definition of the submodularity on F^N ($N \geq 3$) [27], if and only if all its projections on two variables are submodular.

According to [26], the segmentation terms can be transformed into sum of pairwise terms:

$$E_{\text{seg}} = \min_{m_0,m_1} \left(r_0\left(1-m_0\right) + \theta_d m_0 \sum_{i \in c_d} w_i\left(1-t_i\right) + r_1 m_1 \right.$$

$$\left. + \theta_\alpha \left(1-m_1\right) \sum_{i \in c} w_i t_i - \delta \right). \quad (10)$$

Finally, the global energy function is minimized by utilizing the minimum cut on the graph as shown in Figure 7. The minimum cut can be calculated very efficiently using the *α-expansion* move algorithm [18].

The detailed minimization process is as shown in Algorithm 2.

Input: segment S, constant Φ, ratio μ
Initialize $c \to c = 0$
Do
    If $(|f(p) - d^*(p)| > \Phi)$
        $c \to c = c + 1$
    end If
While $p \in S$
$N_d(f(p_S)) \to N_d(f(p_S)) = c$
If $(N_d(f(p_S)) > N(S)^* \mu)$
    Reject Constructing Segmentation Term
Else
    Constructing Segmentation Term using the *Robust P^n Potts Model.*

ALGORITHM 1: Constructing procedure of segmentation term.

Input: Labeling f, label sets L
Initialize *finish* $\to$ *finish* $= 1$
Repeat
    For $(\alpha \in L)$
        Using one α-*expansion* of f, find $f^* = \arg\min E(f')$ among f'
        If $(E(f^*) < E(f))$
            $f \to f = f^*$
            finish $\to$ *finish* $= 0$
        end If
    end For
Until *finish* $= 1$
Return f

ALGORITHM 2: Energy minimization process by graph cut.

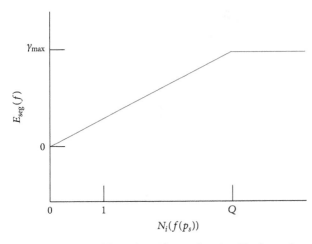

FIGURE 6: Behavior of the *Robust P^n Potts function.* The figure shows how the higher order cost of the *Robust p^n Potts function* changes with the number of pixels in the segment not taking the dominant label.

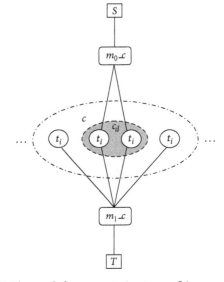

FIGURE 7: The graph for segmentation terms. S is source, T is the sink, and c represents clique; only two auxiliary nodes, namely, m_0 and m_1 are needed for each clique.

3. Experiment

Our program is tested by a personal computer with a 2.20 GHz AMD Dual-Core CPU. All data sets are from [28–31].

For the Middlebury stereo datasets with four stereo test pairs, that is, Tsukuba, Venus, Teddy, and Cones, Table 1 summarizes the quantitative performance of our method and

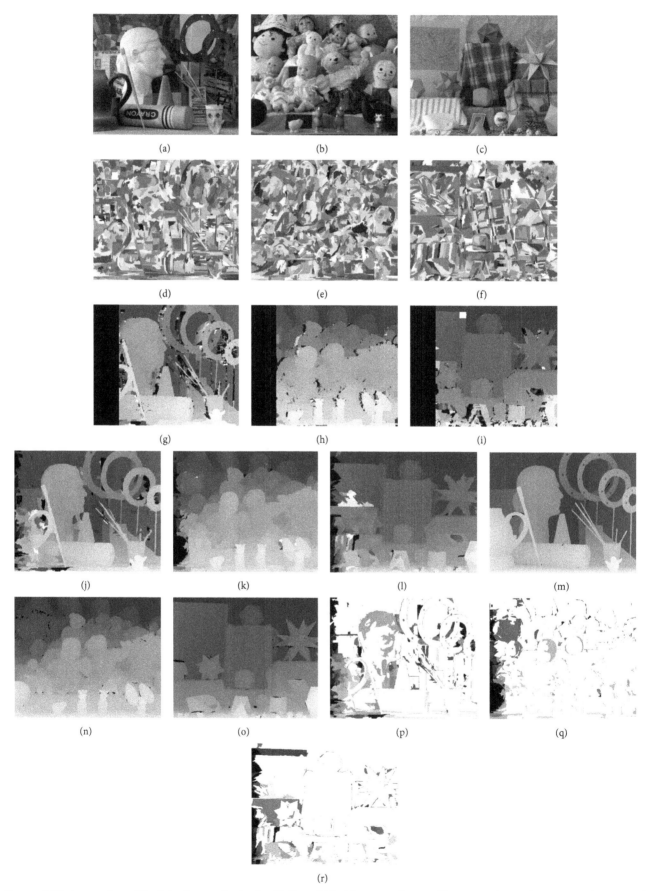

FIGURE 8: The comparison of final depth maps for the Art, Dolls, and Moebius stereo datasets (from top to bottom). First row: the input left images. Second row: the color segmentation results. Third row: the depth results of regular graph cut. Fourth row: the final depth map of our global optimization method. Fifth row: ground truth. Sixth row: "bad pixel" map of matching results.

TABLE 1: Quantitative evaluation results (bad pixels percentage) of different stereo matching methods for the Tsukuba, Venus, Teddy, and Cones stereo test pairs.

Algorithm	Tsukuba	Venus	Teddy	Cones	Average percent of bad pixels
DCBGrid [19]	5.16	1.23	10.8	9.48	6.67
Our method	2.04	1.58	12.60	12.70	7.23
BioPsyASW [20]	4.91	3.41	14.10	11.30	8.43
CSBP [21]	3.84	2.52	17.30	14.20	9.47
Regular GC	4.43	6.56	39.80	59.00	27.45

those of other stereo matching methods, roughly in descending order of overall performance. The comparisons with other approaches show that our global optimization method is fairly competitive with those state-of-the-art approaches.

For sake of declaring the generality of our global optimization method, abundant other stereo image pairs from Middlebury datasets are adopted for depth estimation. Figure 8 illustrates that our global optimization method still achieves satisfactory performance on other stereo images.

4. Conclusion and Discussion

Obviously, the local stereo matching methods based on self-adapting matching window have obtained more outstanding results than fixed matching window based ones. After applying the two proposed matching cost optimization strategies, the local depth results are more accurate in occlusion areas and borders of image. The smooth term makes the surface of segments more close to the real objects. The higher order term, namely, the proposed selective segmentation term, which introduces the plane trend constraint selectively, further enhances the accuracy at object level. In a word, our global optimization method has achieved good performance on Middlebury stereo datasets.

Acknowledgments

This work was supported by the National Natural Science Foundation of China (61173096, 61103140, and 60605013), MOE (Ministry of Education in China) Project of Humanities and Social Sciences (12YJC630281), and the Science and Technology Department of Zhejiang Province (2012R10052, R1110679, Y1090592, Y1110688, Y1100824, and Y1110882).

References

[1] C. Cattani, R. Badea, S. Chen, and M. Crisan, "Biomedical signal processing and modeling complexity of living systems," *Computational and Mathematical Methods in Medicine*, vol. 2012, Article ID 298634, 2 pages, 2012.

[2] Q. Guan, B. Du, Z. Teng et al., "Bayes clustering and structural support vector machines for segmentation of carotid artery plaques in multicontrast MRI," *Computational and Mathematical Methods in Medicine*, vol. 2012, Article ID 549102, 6 pages, 2012.

[3] V. Kolmogorov and R. Zabih, "Computing visual correspondence with occlusions using graph cuts," in *Proceedings of the 8th IEEE International Conference on Computer Vision*, vol. 2, pp. 508–515, July 2001.

[4] P. Zhang, Y. Xu, X. Yang, and L. Traversons, "Multi-scale Gabor phase-based stereo matching using graph cuts," in *Proceedings of the IEEE International Conference onMultimedia and Expo (ICME '07)*, pp. 1934–1937, July 2007.

[5] A. Zureiki, M. Devy, and R. Chatila, "Stereo matching using reduced-graph cuts," in *Proceedings of the 14th IEEE International Conference on Image Processing (ICIP '07)*, vol. 1, pp. 1237–1240, September 2007.

[6] Y. Liu, X. Lin, X. Chen, and L. Hu, "Different labels in energy minimized via graph cuts for stereo matching," in *Proceedings of the IEEE International Conference on Automation and Logistics (ICAL '08)*, pp. 455–459, Qingdao, China, September 2008.

[7] L. Yu, Q. Liao, and Z. Lu, "A novel method using kde and graph cut in stereo matching," in *Proceedings of the IEEE International Workshop on Imaging Systems and Techniques (IST '09)*, pp. 151–154, May 2009.

[8] M. Bleyer, C. Rother, and P. Kohli, "Surface stereo with soft segmentation," in *Proceedings of the IEEE Computer Society Conference on Computer Vision and Pattern Recognition (CVPR '10)*, pp. 1570–1577, June 2010.

[9] M. Bleyer, C. Rother, P. Kohli, D. Scharstein, and S. Sinha, "Object stereo—joint stereo matching and object segmentation," in *Proceedings of IEEE Conference on Computer Vision and Pattern Recognition (CVPR '11)*, pp. 3081–3088, June 2011.

[10] D. Wang and K. B. Lim, "A new segment-based stereo matching using graph cuts," in *Proceedings of the 3rd IEEE International Conference on Computer Science and Information Technology (ICCSIT '10)*, vol. 5, pp. 410–416, Chengdu, China, July 2010.

[11] L. Hong and G. Chen, "Segment-based stereo matching using graph cuts," in *Proceedings of the IEEE Computer Society Conference on Computer Vision and Pattern Recognition (CVPR '04)*, vol. 1, pp. 74–81, July 2004.

[12] S. Chen, H. Tong, and C. Cattani, "Markov models for image labeling," *Mathematical Problems in Engineering*, vol. 2012, Article ID 814356, 18 pages, 2012.

[13] S. Chen, H. Tong, Z. Wang et al., "Improved generalized belief propagation for vision processing," *Mathematical Problems in Engineering*, vol. 2011, Article ID 416963, 12 pages, 2011.

[14] S. Chen, Y. Wang, and C. Cattani, "Key issues in modeling of complex 3D structures from video sequences," *Mathematical Problems in Engineering*, vol. 2012, Article ID 856523, 17 pages, 2012.

[15] P. Kohli, L. U. Ladický, and P. H. S. Torr, "Robust higher order potentials for enforcing label consistency," in *Proceedings of the 26th IEEE Conference on Computer Vision and Pattern Recognition (CVPR '08)*, pp. 1–8, Anchorage, Alaska, USA, June 2008.

[16] Y. Xie, N. Liu, and S. Liu, "Stereo matching using sub-segmentation and robust higher-order graph cut," in *Proceedings of the International Conference on Digital Image Computing Techniques and Applications (DICTA '11)*, Noosa, Australia, December 2011.

[17] P. F. Felzenszwalb and D. P. Huttenlocher, "Efficient graph-based image segmentation," *International Journal of Computer Vision*, vol. 59, no. 2, pp. 167–181, 2004.

[18] Y. Boykov, O. Veksler, and R. Zabih, "Fast approximate energy minimization via graph cuts," *IEEE Transactions on Pattern*

Analysis and Machine Intelligence, vol. 23, no. 11, pp. 1222–1239, 2001.

[19] C. Richardt, D. Orr, I. Davies, A. Criminisi, and N. Dodgson, "Real-time spatiotemporal stereo matching using the dual-cross-bilateral grid," in *Computer Vision—ECCV 2010*, pp. 510–523, 2010.

[20] L. Nalpantidis and A. Gasteratos, "Biologically and psychophysically inspired adaptive support weights algorithm for stereo correspondence," *Robotics and Autonomous Systems*, vol. 58, no. 5, pp. 457–464, 2010.

[21] Q. Yang, L. Wang, and N. Ahuja, "A constant-space belief propagation algorithm for stereo matching," in *Proceedings of the IEEE Computer Society Conference on Computer Vision and Pattern Recognition (CVPR '10)*, pp. 1458–1465, Urbana, Ill, USA, June 2010.

[22] K. Zhang, J. Lu, and G. Lafruit, "Cross-based local stereo matching using orthogonal integral images," *IEEE Transactions on Circuits and Systems for Video Technology*, vol. 19, no. 7, pp. 1073–1079, 2009.

[23] G. Egnal and R. P. Wildes, "Detecting binocular half-occlusions: empirical comparisons of five approaches," *IEEE Transactions on Pattern Analysis and Machine Intelligence*, vol. 24, no. 8, pp. 1127–1133, 2002.

[24] K. J. Yoon and I. S. Kweon, "Adaptive support-weight approach for correspondence search," *IEEE Transactions on Pattern Analysis and Machine Intelligence*, vol. 28, no. 4, pp. 650–656, 2006.

[25] F. Tombari, S. Mattoccia, and L. D. Stefano, "Segmentation based adaptive support for accurate stereo correspondence," *Advances in Image and Video Technology*, vol. 4872, pp. 427–438, 2007.

[26] V. Kolmogorov and R. Zabih, "What energy functions can be minimized via graph cuts?" *IEEE Transactions on Pattern Analysis and Machine Intelligence*, vol. 26, no. 2, pp. 147–159, 2004.

[27] D. Freedman and P. Drineas, "Energy minimization via graph cuts: settling what is possible," in *Proceedings of the IEEE Computer Society Conference on Computer Vision and Pattern Recognition (CVPR '05)*, vol. 2, pp. 939–946, San Diego, Calif, USA, June 2005.

[28] D. Scharstein and R. Szeliski, "High-accuracy stereo depth maps using structured light," in *Proceedings of the 2003 IEEE Computer Society Conference on Computer Vision and Pattern Recognition*, vol. 1, pp. 195–202, June 2003.

[29] D. Scharstein and C. Pal, "Learning conditional random fields for stereo," in *Proceedings of the IEEE Computer Society Conference on Computer Vision and Pattern Recognition (CVPR '07)*, pp. 1–8, Minneapolis, Minn, USA, June 2007.

[30] H. Hirschmller and D. Scharstein, "Evaluation of cost functions for stereo matching," in *Proceedings of the IEEE Conference on Computer Vision and Pattern Recognition (CVPR '07)*, pp. 1–8, June 2007.

[31] D. Scharstein and R. Szeliski, "A taxonomy and evaluation of dense two-frame stereo correspondence algorithms," *International Journal of Computer Vision*, vol. 47, no. 1–3, pp. 7–42, 2001.

18

Iterative Nearest Neighborhood Oversampling in Semisupervised Learning from Imbalanced Data

Fengqi Li, Chuang Yu, Nanhai Yang, Feng Xia, Guangming Li, and Fatemeh Kaveh-Yazdy

School of Software, Dalian University of Technology, Dalian 116620, China

Correspondence should be addressed to Feng Xia; f.xia@ieee.org

Academic Editors: P. Melin and J. Pavón

Transductive graph-based semisupervised learning methods usually build an undirected graph utilizing both labeled and unlabeled samples as vertices. Those methods propagate label information of labeled samples to neighbors through their edges in order to get the predicted labels of unlabeled samples. Most popular semi-supervised learning approaches are sensitive to initial label distribution which happened in imbalanced labeled datasets. The class boundary will be severely skewed by the majority classes in an imbalanced classification. In this paper, we proposed a simple and effective approach to alleviate the unfavorable influence of imbalance problem by iteratively selecting a few unlabeled samples and adding them into the minority classes to form a balanced labeled dataset for the learning methods afterwards. The experiments on UCI datasets and MNIST handwritten digits dataset showed that the proposed approach outperforms other existing state-of-art methods.

1. Introduction

In recent years, the booming information technology leads to databases included a massive amount of data in different fields. Subsequently, the need for mining useful potential is inevitable. The target classes of most of these data records, called unlabeled records, are unknown, and the records with specified target classes are called labeled records. Only a small ration of records are labeled because it is very time consuming and labor intensive to obtain annotates (labels) by domain experts. In machine learning, semisupervised learning (SSL) methods [1] train a classifier by combining labeled and unlabeled samples together, which has attracted attentions due to their advantage of reducing the need for labeled samples and improving accuracy in comparison with most of supervised learning methods. However, although most existing methods have shown encouraging success in many applications, they assume that the distribution between classes in both labeled and unlabeled datasets is balanced, which may not satisfy the reality [2].

If the dataset only contains two classes, a binary classification, the class that has more samples is called the majority class, and the other one is called the minority class. Many popular SSL methods are sensitive to the initial labeled dataset and are suffered from a severe skew of data to the majority classes. In many real-world applications such as text classification [3], credit card fraud detection [4], intrusion detection [5], and classification of protein databases [6], datasets are imbalanced and skewed.

The imbalance learning problem [7] puzzles many machine learning methods established on the assumption that every class has the same or approximate same quantity of samples in raw data. There are various methods proposed to deal with the imbalance classification problems. These methods can be classified into resampling [8], cost-sensitive learning [9], kernel-based learning [10], and active learning methods [11, 12].

Resampling methods include oversampling [13, 14] and undersampling [15] approaches, in which the class distribution is balanced by adding a few samples to the minority class or removing a few samples from the majority class, respectively.

Most existing studies on imbalanced classification focus on supervised imbalanced classification instances [8, 9, 13, 15], and there are few studies on semisupervised methods for imbalanced classification [4]. The bias caused by differing class balances can be systematically adjusted by reweighting [16, 17] or resampling [18].

Focused on the bad performance of SSL algorithm to the imbalanced learning problem, we propose a novel approach based on oversampling in consideration of the SSL's characteristic that there are abounds of unlabeled samples. Li et al. combined active learning with SSL methods that sample a few of most helpful modules for learning a prediction model in [11]. Based on above considerations, Iterative Nearest Neighborhood Oversampling (INNO) algorithm we propose in this paper tries to convert a few unlabeled samples to labeled samples for minority classes, consequently constructing a balanced or approximately balanced labeled dataset for standard graph-based SSL methods afterwards. Therefore, we aim to alleviate the unfavorable impact of typical classifiers in dealing with imbalanced dataset in SSL domain.

In this paper, we provide an effective and efficient heuristic method to eliminate the "injustice" brought by imbalanced labeled dataset. As the samples with a close affinity in a low-dimensional feature space will probably have the same label, we propose an iterative search approach to simply oversample a few unlabeled samples around known labeled samples in order to form a balanced labeled dataset. Extensive experiments on synthetic and real datasets confirm the effectiveness and efficiency of our proposed algorithms.

The remainder of this paper is organized as follows. In Section 2, we provide a brief review of existing studies of semisupervised learning and their applications on imbalanced problem. We give the motivation behind the proposed INNO in Section 3. In Section 4, we revisit some popular algorithms by giving a graph transduction regularization framework, and then we introduce our proposed algorithm INNO in details. The experimental results on some imbalanced dataset are presented in Section 5. Finally, we conclude the paper in Section 6.

2. Related Work

As SSL accomplishes an inspiring performance in combining a small scale of labeled samples and a large number of unlabeled samples effectively, it has been utilized in many real-world applications such as topic detection, multimedia information identification, and object recognition. For the past few years, graph-based SSL approaches have attracted increasing attention due to their good performance and ease of implementation. Graph-based SSL regards both labeled and unlabeled samples as vertices in a graph and builds edges between pairwise vertices, and the weight of edge represents the similarity between the corresponding vertices. Transductive graph-based SSL methods predict the label for unlabeled samples via graph partition or label propagation using a small portion of seed labels provided by initial labeled dataset [19]. Popular transductive algorithms include the Gaussian fields and harmonic function based method (GFHF) [20], the local and global consistency method (LGC) [21], and the graph transduction via alternating minimization (GTAM) [16]; popular inductive methods consist of transductive support vector machines (TSVM) and manifold regularization [22]. Recent researches on graph-based SSL include ensemble manifold regularization [23] and relevance feedback [24]. However, these graph-based SSL methods developed with

smoothness, clustering assumption, and manifold assumption [1] frequently perform a bad classification if provided an imbalanced dataset.

Wang et al. [16] proposed a node regularizer to balance the inequitable influence of labels from different classes, which can be regarded as a reweighting method. They developed an alternating minimization procedure to optimize the node regularizer and classification function, and they greedily searched the largest negative gradient of cost function to determine the label of an unlabeled sample during each minimization step until acquiring all predicted labels of unlabeled samples. Nevertheless, the time complexity of the algorithm is $O(n^3)$, and also it would be suffered from the error that occurred in classification progress, during iteration. Its modified algorithm LDST [17] revises the unilateral greedy search strategy into a bidirectional manner, which can drive wrong label correction in addition to eliminating imbalance problem.

Other graph-based SSL algorithms solve the imbalance problem mainly by resampling methods. Li et al. [2] proposed semisupervised learning with dynamic subspace generation algorithm based on undersampling to handle imbalanced classification. They constructed several subspace classifiers on the corresponding balanced subset by iteratively performing undersampling without duplication on the majority class to form a balanced subnet. However, the algorithm features high complexity in computational time.

3. Motivation

Transductive graph-based SSL methods propagate label information of labeled samples to their neighbors through edges to get the predicted labels of unlabeled samples. Once there is an imbalanced distribution of classes in labeled dataset, the class boundary will severely skew to the majority classes, which have a more possibility to influence the predicted labels of unlabeled samples. We draw the influence of imbalance classification result to three popular transductive GSSL methods on the two-moon toy dataset in Figure 1. The symbols "□" and "▽" stand for classes "+1" and "−1," respectively, in raw data, and we use solid symbol to depict labeled data. Originally, class "+1" contains one labeled samples and class "−1" contains ten labeled data. In Figure 1, the impact of imbalance label distribution to aforementioned algorithms can be seen even on a well-separated dataset. The conventional transductive graph-based SSL algorithms, such as GFHF [20], LGC [21], and GTAM [16], fail to give the acceptable classification result.

Oversampling methods have been shown to be very successful in handling with imbalanced problem. However, Barua et al. [13] reported some cases of insufficiencies and inappropriateness in existing methods. They proposed MWMOTE that generated synthetic minority samples by using clustering approach to select samples according to data importance around a subnet of the minority class; however, it achieves to select minority samples around the class boundary under a large number of training sets. Plessis and Sugiyama [18] proposed a semisupervised learning method to estimate the class ratio for test dataset by combining train and

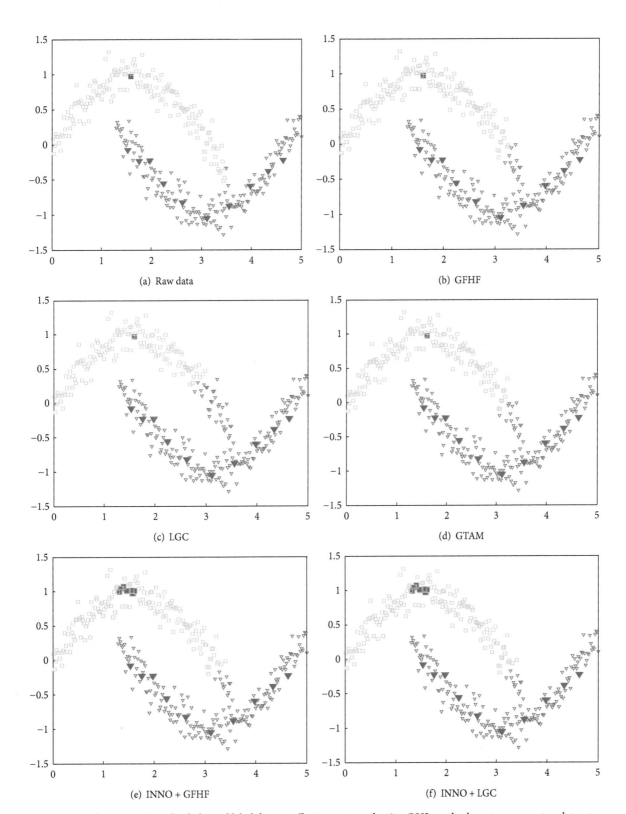

(a) Raw data

(b) GFHF

(c) LGC

(d) GTAM

(e) INNO + GFHF

(f) INNO + LGC

FIGURE 1: A demonstration of imbalanced label dataset affection to transductive GSSL methods on two-moon toy dataset.

test datasets in supervised learning. However, these methods are inapplicable in SSL scenario.

In order to handle with the imbalance problem of labeled dataset in SSL scenario, considering the problem of abundant unlabeled samples in SSL domain, we proposed a simple and effective method, called Iterative Nearest Neighborhood Oversampling, to convert a few of unlabeled samples to labeled samples for minority class, which can construct

FIGURE 2: Workflow of graph-based SSL integrating with INNO.

a balanced labeled dataset for learning methods. We integrate the proposed algorithm with two popular transductive graph-based SSL methods to perform a robust classification to imbalanced problem, and the processing flow can be described as Figure 2.

4. Iterative Nearest Neighborhood Oversampling

4.1. Graph-Based SSL Formulation. Assume a raw dataset $X = \{X_L \cup X_U\}$ contains n samples, where $X_L = \{(x_1, y_1), (x_2, y_2), \ldots, (x_l, y_l)\}$ is the labeled dataset with cardinality $|X_L| = l$ and $X_U = \{x_{l+1}, x_{l+2}, \ldots, x_{l+u}\}$ is the unlabeled dataset with cardinality $|X_U| = u$, where $l + u = n$ and typically $l \ll u$. Define the labels correlation to labeled dataset by $Y_L = \{y_1, y_2, \ldots, y_l\}$, where $y_i \in \{1, 2, \ldots, c\}$ $(i = 1, \ldots, l)$ and c is the count of different classes. The goal of SSL is to infer $Y_U = \{y_{l+1}, y_{l+2}, \ldots, y_{l+u}\}$ of unlabeled samples by combining X_L and X_U.

Graph-based SSL formulates an undirected graph $G = \{X, E, W\}$ in which the vertex set is $X = \{x_i \in R^d\}$ $(i = 1, \ldots, n, d$ is the number of features) and the edge set between vertex is $E = \{e_{ij}\}$. The samples are treated as vertex, and the edges e_{ij} can be weighted by $W_{ij} = k(x_i, x_j)$, where $k(x_i, x_j)$ could be a similarity measure such as Euclidean distance, RBF distance, or cosine distance; thus, the weight matrix can be represented as $W = \{W_{ij}\}$.

Define the graph Laplacian $\Delta = D - W$ and the normalized graph Laplacian by $L = D^{-1/2} \Delta D^{-1/2} = I - D^{-1/2} W D^{-1/2}$, where $D = \text{diag}\{D_{11}, D_{22}, \ldots, D_{nn}\}$ is the node degree matrix with diagonal element $D_{ii} = \sum_j W_{ij}$. The binary label matrix $Y = \{Y_{ij} \in B^{n \times c}\}$ is set as $Y_{ij} = 1$ if x_i is labeled as class j and $Y_{ij} = 0$ otherwise.

Most graph-based SSL methods perform label propagation procedure based on manifold assumption; that is, the labels are smooth on the graph. Therefore, they essentially estimate a classification function $\{F : X \rightarrow R^{n \times c}\}$ constrained to give the true label for labeled samples and give smooth labels over the whole graph. Mathematically, graph-based SSL methods formulate a regularization framework by a cost function as follows:

$$Q\{F\} = Q_l(F) + Q_s(F), \tag{1}$$

where $Q_l(F)$ is a loss function to penalize the deviation from the given labels and $Q_s(F)$ is regarded as the smooth regularizer to prefer the label smoothness. The optimal $F^* = \arg \min_{F \in \mathbb{F}} Q(F)$ can be calculated by minimization of the cost function $Q\{F\}$. Therefore, different graph-based SSL methods can be obtained by assigning different loss functions and regularizers to $Q_l(F)$ and $Q_s(F)$.

4.2. Methodology. In real-world applications, labeled samples are always sampled according to normalization distribution. Labels of samples in some classes are easy to obtain, and in others they are not, even if they are of the same important level. To deal with the imbalance classification problem in semisupervised learning scenarios, we assume that there are lots of unlabeled samples around a labeled sample in a low-dimensional feature space. Therefore, we can select a few unlabeled samples for the minority class to form a balanced dataset. We describe our oversampling model as follows.

Consider the multiclass classification scenarios; let $r = \{r_1, r_2, \ldots, r_c\}$ denote the size set of labeled samples in labeled dataset, where r_j $(j = 1, \ldots, c)$ is the number of labeled samples in class j. We use standard variance var (r) to represent the dispersion degree of the quantity of labeled samples in each class, and the imbalance ratio var (r) can be described as follows:

$$\text{var}(r) = \left(\frac{1}{c} \sum_{j=1}^{c} (r_j - \bar{r})^2 \right)^{1/2}, \tag{2}$$

where $\bar{r} = (1/c) r_{\text{sum}}$, $r_{\text{sum}} = \sum_{j=1}^{c} r_j$.

We propose a novel approach to iteratively increase the labeled samples of the minority class, named Iterative Nearest Neighborhood Oversampling (INNO), in order to eliminate the adverse influence of imbalanced labeled dataset. During iteration, we obtain the class j containing the smallest number of labeled data and traverse k neighbors of each labeled samples in class j to select the most similar sample to all labeled samples of class j in the unlabeled dataset. The most similar sample can be defined as

$$x_{\text{max } k} = \arg \max_{x_k \in X_u} k(x_k, x_j), \tag{3}$$

where x_j is the labeled samples in class j.

To avoid $x_{\text{max } k}$ deriving from classification boundary, we skip the samples which are connected to labeled samples of remainder classes. Then, we simply label the sample $x_{\text{max } k}$ with class j, remove it from unlabeled dataset X_U, and add it to the labeled dataset X_L. We formalize the INNO approach as Algorithm 1.

As labeled dataset is a very scarce scale compared with unlabeled samples set in the background of semisupervised learning, it is difficult to infer the class boundary by a small number of labeled data, caused by intrinsic sample selection bias or inevitable nonstationarity. Therefore, classic oversampling methods [9, 13] are not capable in this situation, because they need to judge the informative data close to class boundary, in order to synthetically generate new samples for the minority class. On the contrary, we try to skip the unlabeled samples close to class boundary to reduce the risk of introducing reckless mistakes in SSL scenarios. So, we simply set $r_j = r_{\text{max}}$ if the iteration finds that all the neighbors of labeled samples in class j have edges with labeled samples in other classes; that is, no more samples will be introduced for class j. Moreover, our method is capable of multiclass classification, though most sampling methods are used to diagnose between-class imbalance problem.

Input: kNN graph, affinity matrix W, stop parameter s, imbalanced labeled dataset X_L and
unlabeled dataset X_U;
Output: balanced or approximate balanced labeled dataset.
Procedure:
1 while $\mathrm{var}(r) > s$
2   Initialization $r_j = \min_{j \in 1 \ldots c} r$, max $= -\infty$, max $k = 0$;
3   for each labeled sample x_j in class j
4   for each neighbors x_k of x_j
5   skip the x_k if it is in X_L or x_k has edges between labeled samples in other class;
6   if $W_{ij} > $ max, then update max, max k
7   end for
8   end for
9   if max $k = 0$ // all the neighbors of labeled samples in class j have edges with labeled samples
in other classes, then $r_j = r_{\max}$, continue;
10   label $x_{\max k}$ with class j, remove it from X_U, add it to X_L, $r_j = r_j + 1$;
11 end while

ALGORITHM 1: Iterative Nearest Neighborhood Oversampling (INNO).

Here we consider a binary classification demonstration in Figure 3, where the stars and circles represent the samples of majority and minority classes, respectively, and the yellow points are unlabeled samples. The imbalance ratio of labeled dataset between classes "+1" and "−1" is $r_{+1} : r_{-1} = 2 : 4$. We employ a k-nearest neighbor (kNN) classifier on the graph (assuming $k = 2$) and only consider the neighborhood connections in class "+1". We set the stop parameter $s = 0$; that is, the iteration will stop when all classes have the same quantity of samples. As we can see, samples A and B are the initial labeled samples in minority class "+1," and then we show the process of INNO algorithm to balance the labeled dataset. The algorithm searches all neighbor unlabeled samples of A and B, finding the closest sample C which is not in labeled dataset and has no connections to labeled samples of class "−1"; therefore, label C with "+1" remove it from unlabeled dataset, and add it into labeled dataset. The algorithm continues to search the neighbors of A, B, and C to find the sample D, but the D is connected to labeled sample of class "−1", so it skips D and E as well. Thereby it finds sample F which satisfies all search conditions. At this moment, a balanced labeled dataset is obtained, and the algorithm ends with $s = 0$.

4.3. Complexity Analysis. Our method queries k neighbors for every labeled sample in each iteration. The time of query is $(r_{\mathrm{sum}} + r_{\mathrm{sum}} \times k) \times k$, and the time of iteration in the worst situation is $r_{\max} \times c - r_{\min} \times (c - 1)$, where $r_{\max}$ and $r_{\min}$ are the largest and smallest number of labels. The time complexity of the proposed algorithm is $O(c \times r_{\max} \times k^2 \times (r_{\max}(r_{\max} - 1)/2) \times k) = O(ck^3 r_{\max}^3)$. As the scale of labeled samples is small, the $r_{\max} < l \ll n$ inequality is held. Clearly, class numbers c and neighbor number k are very small, thus resulting in low computational complexity for our algorithm.

5. Experiments

There are many accuracy measures for evaluating the two-class classification problems, such as precision, recall,

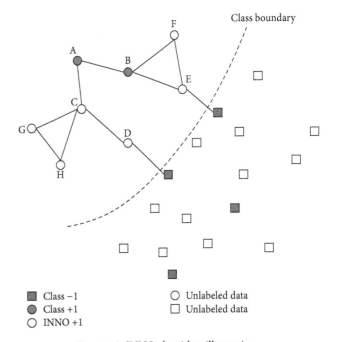

FIGURE 3: INNO algorithm illustration.

geometric-mean (G-mean), and F-measure [24]. To evaluate the classifier performance, we calculate the accuracy by a confusion matrix as illustrated in Table 1.

According to Table 1, many performance measures can be derived and domain classes are regarded as positive and negative classes. One of the most common criteria is overall accuracy which is used for two-class classification problems in this paper.

It can be defined as

$$\mathrm{accuracy} = \frac{\mathrm{TP} + \mathrm{TN}}{p + n}. \tag{4}$$

This measure provides a simple way of describing a classifier's performance on a given dataset. Meanwhile, we

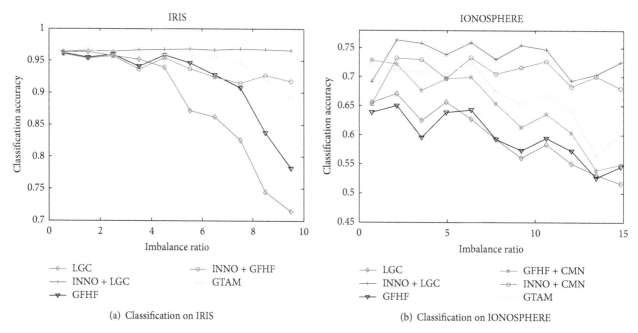

(a) Classification on IRIS   (b) Classification on IONOSPHERE

FIGURE 4: Influence of imbalanced ratio in labeled dataset to the classification accuracy.

TABLE 1: Confusion matrix.

	True class	
Y	TP (true positives)	FP (false positives)
N	FN (false negatives)	TN (true negatives)
Row sum	p	n

apply RBF kernel function $W_{ij} = \exp(\Sigma_d |x_{id} - x_{jd}|^2 / \sigma^2)$ to calculate the similarity measure between samples and set parameter $\alpha = 0.99$ in LGC [22] and $\mu = 99$ in GTAM [15] during the experiments, and the results are the average results of 50 runs. All the experiments are run on a Dell Optiplex-380 PC with Intel Pentium dual-core processors 2.93 GHz and main memory of 3GB.

5.1. UCI Datasets. Firstly we evaluate the effectiveness of our proposed INNO algorithm combined with SSL methods on IRIS and Ionosphere datasets from UCI repository. Iris dataset consists of three different categories of flower, "setosa," "versicolor," and "virginica." Each category contains 50 samples, and the feature dimension of a sample is 4. We fix the number of labeled samples in category "setosa" at 10 but range the number of labeled samples in category "versicolor" from 1 to 10 and also range the number of labeled samples in category "virginica" from 10 to 20. Stop parameter *s* is set to zero on this dataset; namely, the balance algorithm stops when the labeled dataset is completely balanced. Set $\sigma = 0.26$ in RBF kernel function and the neighbors $k = 5$ in k-NN. Figure 5(a) shows the classification result on IRIS.

IONOSPHERE dataset has 351 samples of "g" and "b" categories. Categories "g" and "b" contain 225 and 126, respectively, and each sample has 34 dimensions. We set the stop parameter $s = 0$ in INNO algorithm. As the class

distribution in the original data set is not balanced, the label balance algorithm can stop at the right point where the imbalance ratio of labeled dataset is consistent with that of the original dataset. Zhu et al. proposed the CMN method in [20] to solve the negative influence to the classification result caused by imbalanced labeled dataset. We compared it with our algorithm in this paper. In this experiment, we set the size of labeled samples in category "g" to the range 12 to 21 and set the size of labeled samples in category "b" to 2–11. We set $\sigma = 1$ in RBF kernel function and $k = 10$ in k-NN. Figure 5(b) shows the classification accuracy on IONOSPHERE.

It can be seen in Figure 4(a) that all algorithms have high classification accuracy when each class has the same number of labeled data. As the imbalanced ratio increases between different classes in labeled dataset, classification accuracy drops gradually in GFHF, LGC, and GTAM algorithms around 70% when imbalance ratio is about 9, while the proposed INNO + GFHF and INNO + LGC algorithms remain stable, basically maintained at about 95%. Therefore, INNO algorithm shows a better robustness when dealing with imbalanced labeled dataset. We can get similar results from Figure 4(b), although GRF + CMN method can reduce the influence of imbalanced labeled dataset to classification results to some extent; it is under the assumption that the labeled dataset has the same distribution with the original data from the class definitely. Therefore, the classification accuracy drops when the class distribution in the original data is different from the class distribution in labeled dataset.

5.2. Handwritten Digit Dataset. In this section, we conduct two classification experiments on MNIST handwritten digit dataset. MNIST handwritten dataset has a training set of 60000 samples and a test set of 10000 samples, each sample has a pixel of 28×28, and each pixel is a grayscale range

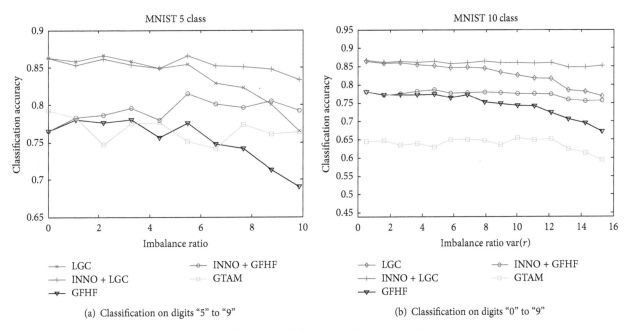

FIGURE 5: Influence of unbalanced labeled samples to the classification accuracy.

from 0 to 255. In these experiments, we combined the training and test sets together, and the pixel values of the image were used directly as features; that is, each sample has a feature number of 784. We randomly selected 200 samples of the numbers "0" to "9" from the entire data set, so the sample set has 2000 samples. We used the parameter $\sigma = 380$ that Zhu et al. [20] set in MNIST and set the stop parameter $s = 0$ in INNO. We selected digits "5" to "9" to conduct a 5-class experiment and digits "0" to "9" to conduct a 10-class experiment. Figure 5 shows that the classification accuracy of each algorithm curves as we continue increasing the imbalanced ratio of labeled dataset.

Figure 5 illustrates that the label balance algorithm is not necessary when the imbalanced ratio approximates to 0; therefore, LGC, INNO + LGC, GFHF, and INNO + GFHF algorithms have the same classification accuracy; namely, the algorithm we propose will not affect the accuracy of the original algorithm when the labeled dataset is balanced at the beginning. While the classification accuracy of GFHF, LGC, and GTAM is decreased significantly when the imbalance ratio increases gradually, INNO + GFHF and INNO + LGC raised in the figure show a stable performance. It also can be seen that the experiments on digits "5" to "9" and digits "0" to "9" show that the accuracy of GTAM algorithm decreases along with the class numbers increasing obviously, while others do not.

5.3. *Parameter Discussion.* Intuitively, the number of neighbors, k, will affect the result of INNO algorithm. To validate this conjecture, we perform an experiment on the UCI datasets. We fix the imbalanced ratio of labeled dataset at $10:1:20$ with categories "setosa", "versicolor," and "virginica" on IRIS dataset, so var $(r) = 9.50$, and fix the imbalanced ratio of labeled dataset at $23:2$ between classes "g" and "b"

on IONOSPHERE dataset, so var $(r) = 14.85$. Set the stop parameter s to zero; the classification accuracy trends are shown in Figure 6.

The classification accuracy is not high when k value is too small, so by increasing k, the classification accuracy increases drastically, and then the classification accuracy on IRIS fluctuates lenitively around 90%~95% when k remains in a certain region. However, if k continues to increase, the classification accuracy begins to drop severely down to 75%. It is because, when k is too large, the number of nearest neighbors is excessive, so INNO algorithm will find that all the neighbors are connected to other categories. Then INNO algorithm is unable to balance the labeled samples, resulting in lower classification accuracy.

Moreover, we consider the influence of stop parameter s to classification accuracy. We perform another experiment on IRIS and IONOSPHERE with k to 5 and 10, respectively and fix the imbalanced ratio like the above. We change the stop parameter s to observe the oscillation on classification accuracy in Figure 7. As we can see from Figure 7(a), it shows little improvement of the classification accuracy when the stop parameter and the original imbalanced ratio are nearly the same. At this point, INNO algorithm does not convert enough unlabeled samples into labeled data. The labeled dataset tends to become more and more balanced and the classification accuracy increases quickly and falls in a certain range, when the stop parameter is decreased.

Improved classification accuracy could be achieved by choosing smaller stop condition values. But the results are not as supposed and oscillate in a certain range, as shown in Figure 7(b). One possible reason is that the INNO algorithm skips the classification boundary of unlabeled samples at algorithm step 5 if all the neighbors of labeled samples in the minority class have edges with labeled samples in other

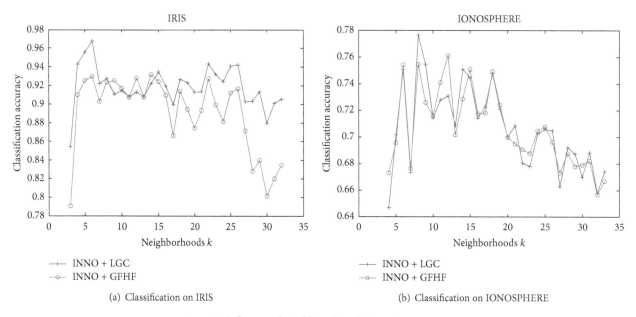

(a) Classification on IRIS

(b) Classification on IONOSPHERE

FIGURE 6: Influence of neighbors k to classification accuracy.

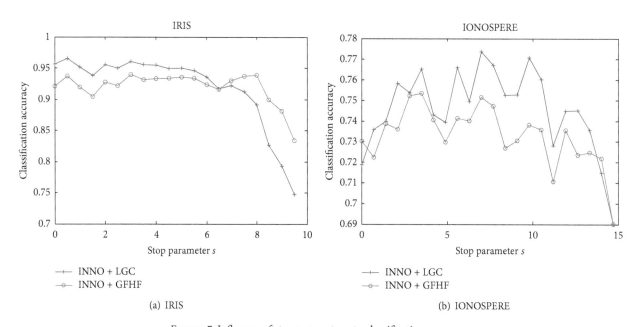

(a) IRIS

(b) IONOSPERE

FIGURE 7: Influence of stop parameter s to classification accuracy.

classes. When the stop parameter becomes smaller, more unlabeled samples will be selected and the probability of the unlabeled samples close to classification boundary is higher. As the algorithm searched the neighbors of labeled samples in the minority class, the labeled number of the current class will be simply set to r_{max} at the algorithm step 9; therefore, it will not introduce new labeled samples in this class. Taking into account the randomness of labeled samples selected from raw data by algorithm, we cannot foresee the occurrence of such a situation [18]; namely, the imbalanced output may also occur even if the stop condition s is 0, so the classification accuracy ranges in a certain scope.

6. Conclusion

In classification scenarios, state-of-art semisupervised learning methods estimate a classification function on the assumption that there is a balanced distribution in labeled and unlabeled datasets. However, the class boundary will be severely skewed by the majority class in an imbalance between-class classification, which is proved by the experiments on UCI datasets and MNIST digit recognition.

As the bias caused by disproportionately imbalanced dataset adjusted by resampling or reweighting, we proposed the INNO algorithm to settle down this imbalance problem simply and effectively, which eliminates the "injustice" brought by imbalanced labeled dataset to popular transductive graph-based SSL methods. Our method iteratively searches the neighbors of labeled samples in the minority class to seek out the nearest neighbor to all labeled samples of the minority class and try to skip the unlabeled samples close to the class boundary. Therefore, we can construct a balanced or approximately balanced labeled dataset for the learning methods. The experiments show a better classification result of SSL methods combined with INNO.

References

[1] O. Chapelle, B. Schökopf, and A. Zien, Eds., *Semi-Supervised Learning*, MIT Press, Cambridge, Mass, USA, 2006.

[2] S. Li, Z. Wang, G. Zhou, and S. Y. M. Lee, "Semi-supervised learning for imbalanced sentiment classification," in *Proceedings of the 22nd International Joint Conference on Artificial Intelligence*, vol. 3, pp. 1826–1831, AAAI Press, Barcelona, Spain, 2011.

[3] L. Zhuang and H. Dai, "Parameter estimation of one-class SVM on imbalance text classification," *Advances in Artificial Intelligence*, vol. 4013, pp. 538–549, 2006.

[4] C. Phua, V. Lee, K. Smith, and R. Gayler, "A comprehensive survey of data mining-based fraud detection research," *Artificial Intelligence Review*, 2005.

[5] R. Sommer and V. Paxson, "Outside the closed world: on using machine learning for network intrusion detection," in *Proceedings of the 31st IEEE Symposium on Security and Privacy (SP '10)*, pp. 305–316, IEEE CS Press, May 2010.

[6] P. Radivojac, N. V. Chawla, A. K. Dunker, and Z. Obradovic, "Classification and knowledge discovery in protein databases," *Journal of Biomedical Informatics*, vol. 37, no. 4, pp. 224–239, 2004.

[7] P. Chan and S. Stolfo, "Toward scalable learning with non-uniform class and cost distributions," in *Proceedings of the International Conference on Knowledge Discovery and Data Mining*, pp. 164–168, 1998.

[8] A. Estabrooks, T. Jo, and N. Japkowicz, "A multiple resampling method for learning from imbalanced data sets," *Computational Intelligence*, vol. 20, no. 1, pp. 18–36, 2004.

[9] K. M. Ting, "An instance-weighting method to induce cost-sensitive trees," *IEEE Transactions on Knowledge and Data Engineering*, vol. 14, no. 3, pp. 659–665, 2002.

[10] X. Hong, S. Chen, and C. J. Harris, "A kernel-based two-class classifier for imbalanced data sets," *IEEE Transactions on Neural Networks*, vol. 18, no. 1, pp. 28–41, 2007.

[11] M. Li, H. Zhang, R. Wu, and Z.-H. Zhou, "Sample-based software defect prediction with active and semi-supervised learning," *Automated Software Engineering*, vol. 19, no. 2, pp. 201–230, 2012.

[12] S. Ertekin, J. Huang, L. Bottou, and C. Lee Giles, "Learning on the border: active learning in imbalanced data classification," in *Proceedings of the 16th ACM Conference on Information and Knowledge Management (CIKM '07)*, pp. 127–136, November 2007.

[13] S. Barua, M. Isam, X. Yao, and K. Murase, "MWMOTE—majority weighted minority oversampling technique for imbalaced data set learning," *IEEE Transactions on Knowledge and Data Engineering*, 2012.

[14] N. V. Chawla, K. W. Bowyer, L. O. Hall, and W. P. Kegelmeyer, "SMOTE: synthetic minority over-sampling technique," *Journal of Artificial Intelligence Research*, vol. 16, pp. 321–357, 2002.

[15] X.-Y. Liu, J. Wu, and Z.-H. Zhou, "Exploratory under-sampling for class-imbalance learning," in *Proceedings of the 6th International Conference on Data Mining (ICDM '06)*, pp. 965–969, December 2006.

[16] J. Wang, T. Jebara, and S.-F. Chang, "Graph transduction via alternating minimization," in *Proceedings of the 25th International Conference on Machine Learning*, pp. 1144–1151, July 2008.

[17] J. Wang, Y.-G. Jiang, and S.-F. Chang, "Label diagnosis through self tuning for web image search," in *Proceedings of the IEEE Computer Society Conference on Computer Vision and Pattern Recognition Workshops (CVPR '09)*, pp. 1390–1397, June 2009.

[18] M. Plessis and M. Sugiyama, "Semi-supervised learning of class balance under class-prior change by distribution matching," in *Proceedings of the International Conference on Machine Learning*, pp. 823–830, 2012.

[19] W. Liu, J. Wang, and S.-F. Chang, "Robust and scalable graph-based semisupervised learning," *Proceedings of the IEEE*, vol. 100, no. 9, pp. 2624–2638, 2012.

[20] X. Zhu, Z. Ghahramani, and J. Lafferty, "Semi-supervised learning using Gaussian fields and harmonic functions," in *Proceedings of the 20th International Conference on Machine Learning*, pp. 912–919, August 2003.

[21] D. Zhou, O. Bousquet, T. N. Lal, J. Weston, and B. Schölkopf, "Learning with local and global consistency," in *Advances in Neural Information Processing Systems*, vol. 16, pp. 321–328, MIT Press, Cambridge, Mass, USA, 2004.

[22] M. Belkin, P. Niyogi, and V. Sindhwani, "Manifold regularization: a geometric framework for learning from labeled and unlabeled examples," *Journal of Machine Learning Research*, vol. 7, pp. 2399–2434, 2006.

[23] D. Tao, C. Xu, L. Yang, and X. S. Hua, "Ensemble manifold regularization," *IEEE Transactions on Pattern Analysis and Machine Intelligence*, vol. 34, pp. 1227–1223, 2012.

[24] Y. Yang, F. Nie, D. Xu, J. Luo, Y. Zhuang, and Y. Pan, "A multimedia retrieval framework based on semi-supervised ranking and relevance feedback," *IEEE Transactions on Pattern Analysis and Machine Intelligence*, vol. 34, no. 4, pp. 723–742, 2012.

19

Optimizing Instruction Scheduling and Register Allocation for Register-File-Connected Clustered VLIW Architectures

Haijing Tang,[1] **Xu Yang,**[1] **Siye Wang,**[2] **and Yanjun Zhang**[2]

[1] *School of Software, Beijing Institute of Technology, Beijing, China*
[2] *School of Information and Electronics, Beijing Institute of Technology, Beijing, China*

Correspondence should be addressed to Xu Yang; yangxu@tsinghua.edu.cn

Academic Editors: E. Denti, J. Montero, and G. Wei

Clustering has become a common trend in very long instruction words (VLIW) architecture to solve the problem of area, energy consumption, and design complexity. Register-file-connected clustered (RFCC) VLIW architecture uses the mechanism of global register file to accomplish the inter-cluster data communications, thus eliminating the performance and energy consumption penalty caused by explicit inter-cluster data move operations in traditional bus-connected clustered (BCC) VLIW architecture. However, the limit number of access ports to the global register file has become an issue which must be well addressed; otherwise the performance and energy consumption would be harmed. In this paper, we presented compiler optimization techniques for an RFCC VLIW architecture called Lily, which is designed for encryption systems. These techniques aim at optimizing performance and energy consumption for Lily architecture, through appropriate manipulation of the code generation process to maintain a better management of the accesses to the global register file. All the techniques have been implemented and evaluated. The result shows that our techniques can significantly reduce the penalty of performance and energy consumption due to access port limitation of global register file.

1. Introduction

very long instruction words (VLIW) architecture [1] typically has multiple functional units (FUs), which allows multiple instructions to be executed in parallel. This feature offers a significant opportunity to enhance the instruction level parallelism (ILP), also largely enhancing the processing ability, which is very desirable in encryption application domain. However, if centralized register file is used, when the number of FUs in the VLIW architecture grows large, there will be a strong pressure on the register file.

First, the number of needed registers becomes huge, when the number of FUs grows large. Typically, large register file is area consuming and will lead to more energy consumption.

Second, the number of accesses to the register file becomes huge, when the number of FUs grows large, either read or write. This will unavoidably lead to access conflicts when there are no sufficient access ports to the register file. Some of the FUs might need to wait until others finish accessing the register file. This will lead to performance degradation

and more energy consumption. The problem is that we cannot solve it by simply increasing the number of access ports to the register file because that will both increase the design complexity of the register file, and lead to significant growth in area and energy consumption of the register file.

So, clustering becomes a common trend in the design of VLIW architecture due to its ability to alleviate power-, thermal-, and complexity-related problems of unclustered VLIW architecture.

In a clustered VLIW architecture, the FUs and register files are divided into several smaller groups. Each group is called a cluster. FUs can directly access data stored in registers of its own cluster. However, inter-cluster data access needs some specific mechanism.

Traditional clustered VLIW architectures use buses to connect different clusters. In the bus-connected clustered VLIW (BCC VLIW) architecture, when an inter-cluster data communication occurs, an explicit data moving instruction is inserted in the original instruction queue. The data moving instruction accesses data stored in the remote cluster and moves it to one of the registers in the local register file. The execution of this additional data moving instruction needs resources, consumes additional energy, and has nonzero latency. The insertion of these additional data moving instructions might lead to extension of total execution time, which in turn might cause performance degradation, and an increase of energy consumption.

Register-file connected clustered VLIW (RFCC VLIW) architecture has been developed to overcome this performance and energy consumption penalty related to BCC VLIW architecture [2]. In RFCC VLIW architecture, local register file of each cluster can only be accessed by the FUs in that cluster, same mechanism as in BCC VLIW architecture. The difference is that there is also a global register file in RFCC VLIW, which can be accessed by all the FUs through the access ports of its own cluster, either read or write. So, when an inter-cluster data communication is needed, the FU which generates the data writes it in the global register file, and the FU needing that data reads the data from the global register file.

Compared to the BCC VLIW architecture, the advantages of RFCC VLIW architecture are (1) zero latency for inter-cluster data communications; (2) no need for additional inter-cluster data moving instruction. Thus, using RFCC VLIW architecture can avoid performance degradation and energy penalty due to inter-cluster data moving instruction as in BCC VLIW.

However, for the consideration of design complexity, area, and energy efficiency of the global register file, the number of access ports to the global register file from each cluster should be limited. Thus, the accesses to the global register file must be well managed; otherwise, there will be conflicts when the number of simultaneously accesses to the global register file exceeds the number of access ports. The conflicts lead to delay of some accesses to the global register file, which means the delay of execution of some instructions. This may lead to the extension of the whole execution time, which means performance degradation and more energy consumption.

So, we need to minimize the situation where access conflicts to the global register file happen for RFCC VLIW architecture, for the sake of performance enhancement and energy consumption reduction.

The problem can be solved by (1) minimizing the number of accesses to global register file or (2) balancing the distribution of the access to global register file among the whole execution time so as to minimize the situation where the number of simultaneously accesses exceeds the port limitation. And, in order to minimize the number of accesses to global register file, we could (1) minimize unnecessary inter-cluster data communications and (2) minimize unnecessary global register allocation.

The main contributions of this work are (1) force-balanced-two-phase (FBTP) instruction scheduling algorithm to minimize unnecessary inter-cluster data communications and balance the distribution of the access to global register file among the whole execution time; (2) localization-enhanced (LE) register allocation mechanism to minimize unnecessary global register allocation.

The Lily architecture is of RFCC VLIW architecture. It is designed for real-time video encryption system, which demands high performance and low energy consumption at the same time. We have implemented the presented techniques in LilyCC compiler designed for Lily architecture.

This paper is organized as follows: Section 2 will discuss the Lily architecture; in Section 3, we will give an introduction to LilyCC compiler; the FBTP instruction scheduling algorithm is presented in Section 4; Section 5 describes LE register allocation mechanism for RFCC VLIW architecture; related works will be discussed in Section 6; we will discuss the experimental framework and results in Section 7; and finally we give conclusions in Section 8.

2. Architecture of Lily

The details of the Lily architecture can be found in [3], so we only give a brief description here. The Lily architecture is a scalable RFCC VLIW architecture. The scalability includes the number of cluster, the number and type of FUs in each cluster, the number and width of registers in the local register file, the number and width of registers in the global register file, the number of read and write access ports to the global register file of each cluster, and the instruction set.

The Lily architecture is dedicated for fixed-point processing, and does not support float-point processing. There are three different types of FUs presented in current design, which are Unit A, Unit M, and Unit D, respectively. Unit A can execute arithmetic instructions, logical instructions, and shift instructions. Unit M can execute multiplication instructions, as well as some arithmetic and logical instructions. Unit D is in charge of memory access and process controlling and can execute some arithmetic and logical instructions.

The Lily architecture has a combined instruction set of both 16-bit instructions and 32-bit instructions, to provide better flexibility. They can be distinguished by the second and third least significant bits of the instruction code. Designer using Lily architecture can customize their own instruction set by choosing instructions from the default instruction set. Lily instruction set includes specific instructions for speeding up the multimedia signal processing, instruction dedicated for encryption operation, and SIMD instructions.

An example of Lily architecture is shown in Figure 1. It has two clusters, and there are three FUs in each cluster, one of each type. Each cluster has its own local register file, composed of 24 registers of 32 bits. The global register file consists of 8 registers of 32 bits. There are two read access ports and one write access port to the global register file from each cluster.

There are 4 bits in the instruction code of the 16-bit instruction dedicated to register access, so they can access only 16 registers. So, in this example, 16-bit instruction can access only 4 of 8 global registers, and 12 of 24 local registers 32-bit instruction has 5 bits for register access, so they can access all the 8 global registers and the 24 local registers in this case.

3. LilyCC Compiler

LilyCC [3] is designed based on Open64 compiler. The architecture of LilyCC is illustrated in Figure 2. In LilyCC, we have

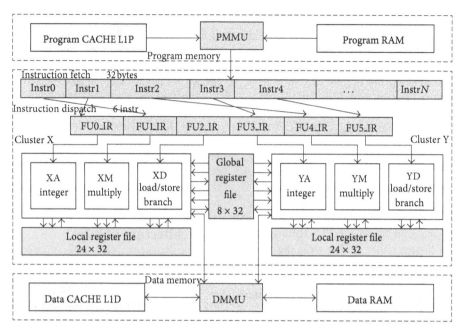

FIGURE 1: An example of the Lily architecture.

implemented four different optimization levels, which are O0, O1, O2, and O3, respectively.

LilyCC is composed of three parts. The front end takes application programs written in C/C++/Fortran languages as input, performs syntax and semantics checking and analysis, and translates the application programs into intermediate representation (IR) structures. The middle end contains optimization phases like loop nest optimization, global optimization, and so on. The back end, or the code generator, translates the IR structure into final assembly code and emits them. Many target-dependent optimization phases, including control flow optimization, extended block optimization, and software pipelining, are performed in the back end.

LilyCC compiler is retargetable. The information of hardware architecture is stored in the machine description files. To retarget to a new architecture, the machine description files must be implemented first. The machine description files contain information of the instruction set architecture (ISA), the application binary interface (ABI), and the processor model of the target architecture.

The code generator of LilyCC can be divided into five major phases: code expansion, global register allocation, instruction scheduling, local register allocation, and code emission.

LilyCC compiler supports automatic vectorization. A lot of existing approaches in research perform automatic vectorization at a late stage of the compilation process, that is, in the back end, because more information is available at the back end, such as a more precise data flow of the input program and the info about the underling target hardware. However, the disadvantage is that the data parallelism in loops cannot be effectively exploited by these techniques, so the code quality can be less optimal.

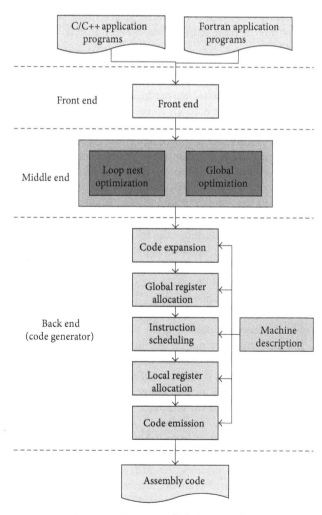

FIGURE 2: Structure of LilyCC compiler.

The automatic vectorization technique used in LilyCC is similar as the one used in [4], which is a high-level automatic vectorization technique to generate vectorized code by examining the loop code. It runs in the early stage of the compilation process, just after the input source code program has been transformed into the IR structure. As this approach only needs simple knowledge of the target machine's instruction set architecture, it is easily retargetable.

4. FBTP Instruction Scheduling Algorithm

In order to enhance performance and energy efficiency, instruction scheduling process for RFCC VLIW architecture has three tasks: (1) minimizing the number of inter-cluster data communications; (2) balancing the distribution of inter-cluster data communications to minimize the situation where the number of concurrent inter-cluster data communications exceeds the number of registers in the global register file or the number of read or write ports to the global register file from one cluster at a single clock cycle; (3) minimizing the number of execution cycles.

In FBTP instruction scheduling algorithm, the three tasks are achieved by the following.

(1) Dividing the instruction scheduling process into two phases: Predecision phase and main scheduling phase. The first phase outputs a preliminary cluster assignment decision for all the instructions. The second phase performs cycle scheduling according to the cluster assignment decisions from the first phase. Although the decisions of cycle scheduling and cluster assignment are made in separate phases, the main interactions between cluster assignment and cycle scheduling are actually estimated and considered.

(2) Using gravitation force (GF) Array to describe the data dependence relations between instructions, and using repulsion force (RF) Array to describe the resource availability. The two forces are balanced to conduct the cycle scheduling and cluster assignment, so as to minimize the number of inter-cluster data communications and the number of execution cycles.

(3) Transforming the distribution of inter-cluster data communications into data dependence relations between instructions and resource availability, when calculating GF array and RF array, in order to minimize the number of concurrent inter-cluster data communications.

4.1. The Predecision Phase. The procedure of Predecision phase is shown in Algorithm 1. The input of the Predecision phase is the Data Dependence Graph (DDG). DDG can be denoted as $DDG = \{N, E\}$, where N is the set of instructions in DDG and E is the set of edges in DDG. In Predecision phase, all the instructions will be prescheduled to a *Schedule-Point* (p, q), where p denotes the cluster, and q denotes the clock cycle. The cluster assignment decision for all the instructions is the output of the Pre-Decision phase, while the clock cycle pre-scheduled for each instruction is used only

in this phase for estimating and considering the interactions between cluster assign and cycle schedule.

As soon as Possible (ASAP) scheduling and as late as possible (ALAP) scheduling are performed to get the earliest possible execution cycle T_e and the latest possible Execution Cycle T_l for each instruction in the ready list. Then an instruction is selected from the ready list according to predefined rules.

Gravitation force (GF) values and repulsion force (RF) values are calculated for that instruction at every possible schedule point. Then the GF values and RF values are normalized to calculate the Balance Force (BF) values. The algorithm finds out the schedule point with the maximize BF value, and schedules the instruction to it.

The process is repeated until all the instructions are successfully pre-scheduled. The details of this algorithm will be discussed in the following.

4.1.1. Calculation of GF Value. Gravitation force value $GF(i, x, y)$ indicates the tightness of data dependence relation between *Instruction i* and *Schedule-Point* (x, y). The calculation of GF values only applies to the possible schedule point of *Instruction i*.

There are three factors that will influence the GF value.

(i) The number of data dependence relations from each cluster. For the purpose of minimizing the number of inter-cluster data communications, we would like instructions having data dependence relations to be placed in the same cluster. For example, when *Instruction i* is to be prescheduled, if there are three data dependence relations from *Cluster A* and only one data dependence relation from *Cluster B*, then, assigning *Instruction i* to *Cluster A* would be a better choice, because we only have one inter-cluster data communications.

(ii) The span of the data dependence relations. If the number of active inter-cluster data communications exceeds the number of registers in the global register file, then some instructions must delay their write access to the global register file. So, if an inter-cluster data communication is unavoidable, then we would like it to be a short one. For example, if both *Instruction j* from *Cluster A* and *Instruction k* from *Cluster B* have data dependence relations with *Instruction i* and *Instruction j* is scheduled two clock cycles before *Instruction k*, then when *Instruction i* is to be prescheduled, it is preferred to pre-schedule *Instruction i* to *Cluster A*, because in that case, we will get a shorter inter-cluster data communications.

(iii) The number of active inter-cluster data communications at *Schedule-Point* (x, y) of instructions from the neighborhood of *Instruction i*. the neighborhood of *Instruction i*, $B(i)$ is defined as the set of instructions that have data dependence relations with *Instruction i*. And an active inter-cluster data communication from *Instruction j* means that (1) *Instruction j* is not in *Cluster x* (2) the inter-cluster data communication from

Input:
Data Dependence Graph, $G = \{N, E\}$;
Ready list, $R = N$;

Output:
Preliminary cluster assignment decision for each instruction;

(1) **while** $(R \neq \phi)$ **do**
(2)   Perform ASAP scheduling and ALAP scheduling
(3)   Select *Instruction i* from R
(4)   Find the neighborhood of *Instruction i*,
      $B(i) = \{j | j \neq i, j \in N, \text{and edge} < i, j > or < j, i > \in E\}$
(5)   Calculate GF Array for *Instruction i*

$$\delta(j, x) = \begin{cases} 1, & \text{if } j \text{ is scheduled in cluster } x \\ \dfrac{1}{N_c(j)}, & \text{if } j \text{ is not scheduled} \\ 0, & \text{otherwise} \end{cases}$$

$$\lambda(j, x, y) = \begin{cases} n, & \text{if } j \text{ has n active inter-cluster data communication at } Schedule\text{-}Point\ (x, y) \\ \dfrac{1}{N_c(j)}, & \text{if } j \text{ is not scheduled} \\ 0, & \text{otherwise} \end{cases}$$

$$t(j) = \begin{cases} k, & \text{if } j \text{ is scheduled in clock cycle } k \\ T_e(j), & \text{if } j \text{ is not scheduled} \end{cases}$$

$$W(i, j, x, y) = |t(j) - y|$$

$$\text{GF}(i, x, y) = \sum_j [\delta(j, x) - \lambda(j, x, y)]\, W(i, j, x, y),$$

$$j \in B(i),\ T_e(i) \leq y \leq T_l(i)$$

(6)   Calculate RF Array for *Instruction i*
      $$M(j) = [T_l(j) - T_e(j) + 1]$$

$$\gamma(j, x, y) = \begin{cases} 1, & \text{if } j \text{ is scheduled in cluster } x \text{ cycle y} \\ \dfrac{1}{M(j)\, N_c(j)}, & \text{if } j \text{ is not scheduled} \\ 0, & \text{otherwise} \end{cases}$$

$$\text{RF}(i, x, y) = \sum_j \gamma(j, x, y) + \beta(x, y),$$

$$j \neq i, j \in N,\ T_e(j) \leq y \leq T_l(j),\ T_e(i) \leq y \leq T_l(i)$$

(7)   Normalize GF Array and RF Array
(8)   Calculate the BF Array for *Instruction i*
      $$\text{BF}(i, x, y) = \text{GF}(i, x, y) - \text{RF}(i, x, y)$$
(9)   Pre-schedule *Instruction i* to *Schedule-Point* (p, q) with the maximize value of BF Array
(10) Delete *Instruction i* from R.
(11) **end while**

ALGORITHM 1: Predecision phase.

Instruction j goes to *Cluster x*, and (3) the inter-cluster data communication is not finished at *Cycle y*.

When calculating gravitation force, these three factors must all be taken into consideration.

In Step 5 of Algorithm 1, $\delta(j, x)$ denotes the possibility that *Instruction j* from the neighborhood of *Instruction i* is in *Cluster x*. It is mainly used to estimate the influence of the number of data dependence relations from each cluster on GF value. $W(i, j, x, y)$ denotes the weight of the edge between *Instruction i* and *Instruction j*, which is defined as the span of that edge. It is used to estimate the influence of the second factor on GF value. $t(j)$ is the execution time of *Instruction j*. $N_c(j)$ denotes the number of clusters that *Instruction j* can be

scheduled in. $\lambda(j, x, y)$ is the number of active inter-cluster data communications from *Instruction j*, which is a member of the neighborhood of *Instruction i*, to *Cluster x* at *Cycle y*. It is mainly used to estimate the influence of the third factor on GF value.

4.1.2. Calculation of RF Value. Repulsion force value $\text{RF}(i, x, y)$ represents the resource availability when *Instruction i* is to be prescheduled to *Schedule-Point* (x, y). There are two factors that will influence the RF value.

(i) The available resources in each cluster. For the purpose of minimizing the number of execution cycles, we need to distribute instructions evenly in each cluster, which means we would like to pre-schedule instructions to cluster which has more available resources.

(ii) The existed inter-cluster data communications in each cluster. As we know, for the purpose of balance the distribution of inter-cluster data communications, it is beneficial to pre-schedule instructions to cluster which has smaller number of existed inter-cluster data communications.

In step 6 of Algorithm 1, $M(j)$ is the mobility of *Instruction j*, which indicates the possibility of *Instruction i* to move between different cycles. $\gamma(j, x, y)$ denotes the possibility that *Instruction j* is in *Schedule-Point* (x, y). $\sum_j \gamma(j, x, y)$ represents current resource occupation at *Schedule-Point* (x, y). It is used to calculate the influence of the first factor on RF value. $\beta(x, y)$ is the number of existed active inter-cluster data communications from other clusters to *Cluster x* at *Cycle y*. It is used to calculate the influence of the second factor on RF value.

4.1.3. Calculation of BF Value. As discussed before, instruction scheduling process for RFCC VLIW architecture has three tasks: (1) minimizing the number of inter-cluster data communications; (2) balancing the distribution of inter-cluster data communications to minimize the situation where the number of concurrent inter-cluster data communications exceeds the number of registers in the global register file or the number of read or write ports to the global register file from one cluster at a single clock cycle; (3) minimizing the number of execution cycle.

In order to fulfill the first task, the instruction should be prescheduled to the schedule point that has the largest GF value. For the third task, the instruction should be prescheduled to the schedule point with the least RF value. And for the second task, we would like to schedule instruction to the schedule point with the largest GF value and the least RF value. So, we should take into account both GF and RF values.

Thus, we have introduced balance force (BF) to comprehensively consider the influence of both GF values and RF values. In order to calculate BF values, both GF values and RF values of all the possible schedule points must be normalized first. Then the BF values is calculated as indicated in step 8 of Algorithm 1.

4.2. Main Scheduling Phase. After the Predecision phase, the preliminary decision of cluster assignment of all the instructions is delivered to the second phase. The main scheduling phase is a modified version of the list-scheduling algorithm [5]. The commonly used heuristics—scheduling those instructions on the critical path first—is used to guide the selection order of instructions from the ready list. Here, instruction with mobility of zero is defined as on the critical path.

As the set of instructions with mobility of 0 would change dynamically during the schedule process, thus in order to greedily ensure that instructions with mobility of 0 always be selected first, after scheduling of each instruction, the algorithm must update the earliest possible execution cycle and

the latest possible execution cycle for all the unprocessed instructions. This could guarantee that the stretching of critical paths is minimal and subject to the finite resource constraints of target machine.

4.3. Complexity of the FBTP Algorithm. In FBTP algorithm, let n be the number of instructions. For each instruction, it will take at most $O(n)$ effort to calculate the GF value and at most $O(n)$ effort to calculate the RF value. Thus, it will take at most $O(2n^2)$ effort to finish the Predecision stage. In the main scheduling, it will take at most $O(n)$ effort to finish the cycle scheduling procedure.

Thus the worst-case complexity of FBTP algorithm is $O(n^2)$, whereas the worst-case complexity of list schedule is $O(n^2 \log n)$.

5. Localization-Enhanced Register Allocation Mechanism

The localization-enhanced (LE) register allocation mechanism for RFCC VLIW architecture is presented in Algorithm 2. It is used as an enhancement engine for register allocation in basic block (BB). The main purpose of this mechanism is to guide the register allocation process so as to avoid unnecessary allocation of global register. In this mechanism, we guarantee that only two kinds of variables have the privilege to be allocated to the global register: (1) the variables active at the exit of a BB, to provide generality; (2) the variables of which their def and uses have different clusters.

Let n be the number of instructions. Then the worst-case complexity of LE mechanism is $O(n)$.

6. Related Work

Since the introduction of VLIW [1] in 1983, there have been many researches reported. Payá-Vayá et al. [6] have presented a forwarding-based approach to increase the code compaction of VLIW media processors, so as to enhance the performance and to reduce the number of needed read/write ports to the register file. Wang and Chen [7] have introduced an architecture-dependent register allocation and instruction scheduling algorithm for VLIW architecture. Uchida et al. [8] have present an energy-aware SA-based instruction scheduling for fine-gained power-gated VLIW processors.

As clustering has become a common trend, there emerged a lot of works concerning either the instruction scheduling or the register allocation of clustered architectures.

Zalamea et al. [9] have presented an instruction scheduling, algorithm for clustered VLIW architecture, which uses limited backtracking to reconsider previously taken decisions, thus providing the algorithm with additional possibilities for obtaining high throughput schedules with low spill code requirements. Codina et al. [10] have introduced a modulo scheduling framework for clustered ILP processors that integrates the cluster assignment, instruction scheduling, and register allocation steps in a single phase. The proposed framework includes a mechanism to insert spill code on

Input:
    The variable needs to be allocated, v;
    Living range of that variable;
Output:
    Register allocation of variables v;
(1) **if** v is active at the exit of BB, and global register g is available at that time **then**
(2)   Allocate v to g
(3)   Update preferred register for related variables
(4) **end if**
(5) **if** v has preferred register p_r **then**
(6)   **if** p_r is a global register **then**
(7)   **if** p_r is available, and one of the uses has different cluster from the def of v **then**
(8)   Allocate v to p_r
(9)   Update preferred register for related variables
(10)   **end if**
(11)   **else**
(12)   **if** p_r is available, and all the uses has same cluster as the def of v **then**
(13)   Allocate v to p_r
(14)   Update preferred register for related variables
(15)   **end if**
(16)   **end if**
(17) **else**
(18)   **if** One of the uses has different cluster from the def of v **then**
(19)   **if** Global register g is available **then**
(20)   Allocate v to g
(21)   Update preferred register for related variables
(22)   **else**
(23)   Insert spill and restore instructions
(24)   **end if**
(25)   **else**
(26)   **if** Local register l is available **then**
(27)   Allocate v to l
(28)   Update preferred register for related variables
(29)   **else**
(30)   Insert spill and restore instructions
(31)   **end if**
(32)   **end if**
(33) **end if**

ALGORITHM 2: Localization-enhanced register allocation mechanism.

the fly and heuristics to evaluate the quality of partial schedules considering simultaneously inter-cluster communications, memory pressure, and register pressure. Later, they have exploited a concept of virtual cluster to assist the instruction scheduling for clustered architecture [11].

In 2001, Aleta et al. [12] have presented a graph-partitioning-based instruction scheduling for clustered architecture. In 2009, they [13] have presented another graph-based approach, called AGAMOS, to modulo-schedule loops on clustered architectures, which uses a multilevel graph partitioning strategy to distribute the workload among clusters and reduces the number of inter-cluster communications at the same time. Arafath and Ajayan [14] have implemented an integrated instruction partitioning and scheduling technique for clustered VLIW architectures, which is a modified list scheduling algorithm using the amount of clock cycles followed by each instruction and the number of successors of an instruction to prioritize the instructions. Zhang et al. [15]

presented a phase coupled priority-based heuristic scheduling algorithm, which converts the instruction scheduling problem into the problem of scheduling a set of instructions with a common deadline.

Xu et al. [16] have presented their study on the design of inter-cluster connection network in clustered DSP processors. The approach starts with determining the minimum number of buses required in polynomial time for any given schedules and then further determines an underlying inter-cluster connection scheme with the number of buses determined in the previous step. They have also given a computation and communication coscheduling algorithm to generate schedules which lead to fewer minimum buses required for the inter-cluster connection network. Nagpal and Srikant [17] have presented their instruction scheduling algorithm which exploits the limited snooping capability of snooping-based clustered VLIW architectures to reduce the register file energy consumption.

Huang et al. [18] have introduced a worst-case-execution-time-aware re-scheduling register allocation (WRRA) approach, which is used to achieve worst-case-execution-time (WCET) minimization for real-time embedded systems with clustered VLIW architecture. In this approach, the effects of register allocation, instruction scheduling, and cluster assignment on the quality of generated code are all taken into account for WCET minimization. Yang et al. [19] have presented a triple-step data-dependence-graph-based (TDB) scheme for clustered VLIW architecture, which performed a backtracking optimization after instruction schedule to bring further improvement.

However, these researches are all focused on BCC VLIW architecture. The efforts focusing on the optimization for RFCC VLIW architecture are not much.

Zhou et al. [20] have presented a two-dimension force-directed (TDFD) scheduling algorithm for RFCC VLIW architecture. It is used as the default instruction scheduling algorithm in LilyCC compiler. However, TDFD simply considered the balancing of influences of data dependence relations and available resources on instruction scheduling, but has not actually taken into account the influence of limitation on access ports to the global register file on the instruction scheduling.

7. Results and Discussions

7.1. Experimental Framework. To evaluate the effectiveness of our algorithm, we used a suite of 20 applications from different benchmark sets. The characteristics of these application codes can be found in [21, 22]. The domain we focused on is the multimedia processing, which depends heavily on the capability to perform DSP applications. We chose these applications for their qualified representative in the DSP scope.

All analyzed benchmarks were validated against precompiled binaries in the original benchmark suite. We have built a simulator for Lily architecture, based on Gem5 [23] simulator. This simulator is used to run the compiled benchmarks and to collect data. The energy model used in our simulator is based on [24]. We have conducted a series of RTL simulations, using Cadence EDA tool chain to extract the parameters needed for construction of the energy model.

The effectiveness of our proposed techniques are compared with several state-of-the-art techniques, including TDFD [20] (LilyCC's default instruction scheduling algorithm), AGAMOS [13], and TDB [19] algorithms.

7.2. Results and Discussions

7.2.1. Evaluation of the Influence of the Number of Global Registers on Performance and Energy Consumption. In order to evaluate the influence of the number of global registers, we have defined three configurations. All the three configurations have two clusters. Each cluster has one Unit A, one Unit M, and one Unit D. And there are 2 read ports and 1 write port to the global register file for each cluster. The first configuration has 4 global registers in the global register file, the second one has 8 global registers, and the third one has 16 global

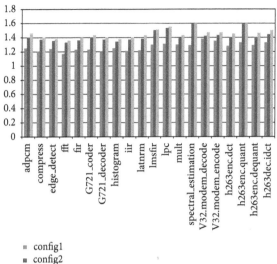

config1
config2
config3

FIGURE 3: Evaluation of performance with different scales of global register file.

registers. Figure 3 shows the evaluation of performance when the scale of global register file varies. The result shown in the figure is the performance enhancement with respect to the default LilyCC scheduler TDFD.

In all the situations, FBTP outperforms TDFD. The performance enhancement for the first configuration is in general less than the other two configurations. The reason is that, in the first configuration, the number of global registers is too small. So the chance that global register access conflicts happen is high, and there is not much space for optimization.

And it can also be noticed that the differences between the performance enhancement for configuration 2 and for configuration 3 are not much. Actually, if the number of global registers is larger than the maximum number of possible concurrent inter-cluster data communications, there will be no extra gain. The results of comparison of energy consumption shown in Figure 4 also indicate this.

7.2.2. Evaluation of the Influence of the Number of Access Ports to the Global Register File on Performance and Energy Consumption. When evaluating the influence of the number of access ports to the global register file on performance and energy consumption, we choose 4 configurations. All the configurations have 2 clusters. Each cluster is composed of one Unit A, one Unit M, and one Unit D. There are 8 registers in the global register file. The first configuration has 1 read port and 1 write port in each cluster. The second configuration has 2 read ports and 1 write port in each cluster. The third configuration has 3 read ports and 2 write ports in each cluster. The fourth configuration has 4 read ports and 2 write ports in each cluster.

The comparison of performance enhancement with respect to TDFD is shown in Figure 5. From the picture, we can see that when the number of access ports to the global register file grows, the performance enhancement improves.

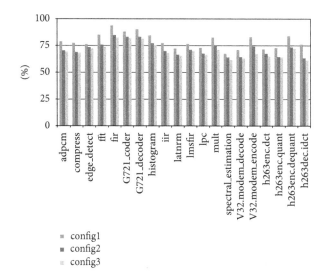

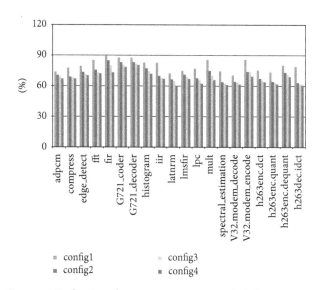

FIGURE 4: Evaluation of energy consumption with different scales of global register file.

FIGURE 6: Evaluation of energy consumption with different configurations of access ports.

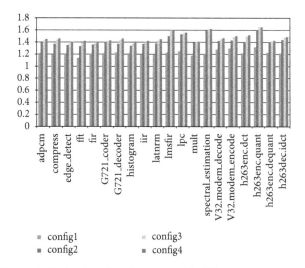

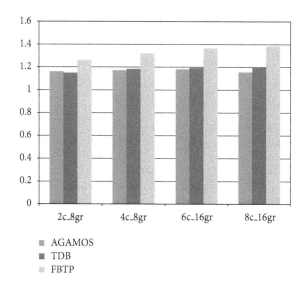

FIGURE 5: Evaluation of performance with different configurations of access ports.

FIGURE 7: Evaluation of performance with different numbers of clusters.

However, the area, design complexity, and energy consumption cost related to the access ports must also be taken into consideration when designing the processor. The differences of performance enhancement between configuration 3 and 4 are much smaller compared to the differences between configuration 1 and 2. So, configuring each cluster of 2 read ports and 1 write port might be a reasonable choice.

The energy consumption of FBTP compared with TDFD is shown in Figure 6.

7.2.3. Evaluation of the Influence of the Number of Clusters on Performance and Energy Consumption. We differ the number of clusters, to verify the effectiveness of our technique. We have chosen 4 configurations.

The first configuration has 2 clusters, and each cluster is composed of one Unit A, one Unit M, and one Unit D. And there are 8 registers in the global register file. Each cluster has 2 read and 1 write access ports to the global register file.

The second configuration has 4 clusters, and each cluster is composed of one Unit A, one Unit M, and one Unit D. And there are 8 registers in the global register file. Each cluster has 2 read and 1 write access ports to the global register file.

The third configuration has 6 clusters, and each cluster is composed of one Unit A, one Unit M, and one Unit D. And there are 16 registers in the global register file. Each cluster has 2 read and 1 write access ports to the global register file.

The fourth configuration has 8 clusters, and each cluster is composed of one Unit A, one Unit M, and one Unit D. And there are 16 registers in the global register file. Each cluster has 2 read and 1 write access ports to the global register file.

The result shown in Figure 7 is the performance enhancement compared to the default LilyCC scheduler TDFD. The blue bar represents the performance enhancement of AGAMOS compared to TDFD. The red bar represents the performance enhancement of TDB compared to TDFD.

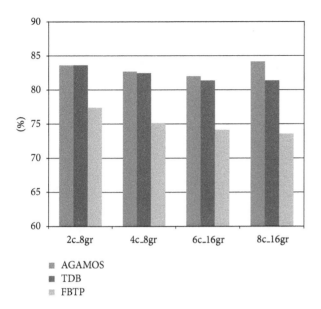

FIGURE 8: Evaluation of energy consumption with different numbers of clusters.

The green bar represents the performance enhancement of FBTP compared to TDFD.

In all the situations, FBTP outperforms other schedulers. Although AGAMOS and TDB are schedule algorithms optimized for clustered architecture, they are not quite suit for RFCC VLIW. TDFD is designed for RFCC VLIW; however, it simply considered the balancing of influences of data dependence relations and available resources on instruction scheduling but has not actually taken into account the influence of limitation on access ports to the global register file on the instruction scheduling. So, the effectiveness of TDFD on RFCC VLIW is limited. It can be concluded from the figures that the effectiveness of FBTP is not affected by the varying of the number of clusters. The results of energy reduction compared to TDFD are shown in Figure 8.

8. Conclusions

In this paper, we have presented an instruction scheduling algorithm for RFCC VLIW architecture which is called FBTP algorithm. FBTP tries to ease the penalty of performance and energy consumption of RFCC VLIW architecture due to limitation of access ports to the global register file. The goal is achieved through (1) dividing the instruction scheduling into two phases, to make decisions of cycle scheduling and cluster assignment in separate phases, but considering the main interactions between cluster assign and cycle scheduling in the process; (2) using gravitation force (GF) value to describe the data dependence relations between instructions, and using repulsion force (RF) value to describe the resource availability; (3) balancing those two forces to conduct the cycle scheduling and cluster assignment, so as to minimize the number of inter-cluster data communications and the number of execution cycles; (4) transforming the distribution of inter-cluster data communications into data dependence

relations between instructions and resource availability, when calculating GF value and RF value, in order to minimize the number and scale of concurrent inter-cluster data communications.

We have also presented an LE register allocation mechanism for RFCC VLIW architecture. The LE mechanism is used as an enhancement engine for register allocation in BB, to avoid unnecessary use of global registers, thus to ease the pressure of global register file.

The result shows that our algorithms can largely enhance the performance and reduce the energy consumption. The influence of different types of configure parameters on the effectiveness of the algorithms is evaluated. The performance enhancement compared to default LilyCC scheduler TDFD can up to 38.65%, while the energy consumption reduction compared to default LilyCC scheduler TDFD can up to 26.43%.

Acknowledgment

This paper is supported by the National Natural Science Foundation of China (no. 61201182).

References

[1] J. A. Fisher, "Very long instruction word architectures and the ELI-512," in *Proceedings of the 10th Annual International Symposium on Computer Architecture (ISCA '83)*, pp. 140–150, June 1983.

[2] Y. J. Zhang, H. He, and Y. H. Sun, "A new register file access architecture for software pipelining in VLIW processors," in *Proceedings of the Asia and South Pacific Design Automation Conference (ASP-DAC '05)*, vol. 1, pp. 627–630, January 2005.

[3] Z. Shen, H. He, X. Yang, D. Jia, and Y. H. Sun, "Architecture design of a variable length instruction set VLIW DSP," *Tsinghua Science and Technology*, vol. 14, no. 5, pp. 561–569, 2009.

[4] X. Yang and H. He, "An advanced compiler designed for a VLIW DSP for sensors-based systems," *Sensors*, vol. 12, no. 4, pp. 4466–4478, 2012.

[5] R. Sethi, *Algorithms for Minimal-Length Schedules*, John Wiley & Sons, New York, NY, USA, 1976.

[6] G. Payá-Vayá, J. Martín-Langerwerf, H. Blume, and P. Pirsch, "A forwarding-sensitive instruction scheduling approach to reduce register file constraints in VLIW architectures," in *Proceedings of the 21st IEEE International Conference on Application-Specific Systems, Architectures and Processors (ASAP '10)*, pp. 151–158, Rennes, France, July 2010.

[7] L. Wang and G. Chen, "Architecture-dependent register allocation and instruction scheduling on VLIW," in *Proceedings of the 2nd International Conference on Computer Engineering and Technology (ICCET '10)*, vol. 2, pp. 292–296, Chengdu, China, April 2010.

[8] M. Uchida, I. Taniguchi, H. Tomiyama, and M. Fukui, "Energy-aware SA-based instruction scheduling for fine-grained power-gated VLIW processors," in *Proceedings of the International SoC Design Conference (ISOCC '12)*, pp. 139–142, Jeju Island, Republic of Korea, November 2012.

[9] J. Zalamea, J. Llosa, E. Ayguadé, and M. Valero, "Modulo scheduling with integrated register spilling for clustered VLIW architectures," in *Proceedings of the 34th Annual International*

Symposium on Microarchitecture (ACM/IEEE '01), pp. 160–169, December 2001.

[10] J. M. Codina, J. Sánchez, and A. González, "A unified modulo scheduling and register allocation technique for clustered processors," in *Proceedings of the Internatinal Conference on Parallel Architectures and Compilation Techniques (PACT '01)*, pp. 175–184, September 2001.

[11] J. M. Codina, J. Sánchez, and A. González, "Virtual cluster scheduling through the scheduling graph," in *Proceedings of the International Symposium on Code Generation and Optimization (CGO '07)*, pp. 99–101, San Jose, Calif, USA, March 2007.

[12] A. Aleta, J. M. Codina, J. Sanchez, and A. Gonzalez, "Graph-partitioning based instruction scheduling for clustered processors," in *Proceedings of the 34th ACM/IEEE International Symposium on Microarchitecture (MICRO '01)*, pp. 150–159, December 2001.

[13] A. Aletè, J. M. Codina, J. Sánchez, A. González, and D. Kaeli, "AGAMOS: a graph-based approach to modulo scheduling for clustered microarchitectures," *IEEE Transactions on Computers*, vol. 58, no. 6, pp. 770–783, 2009.

[14] K. M. I. Y. Arafath and K. K. Ajayan, "A novel instruction scheduling scheme for clustered VLIW architecture," in *Proceedings of the IEEE Recent Advances in Intelligent Computational Systems (RAICS '11)*, pp. 783–787, Trivandrum, India, September 2011.

[15] X. M. Zhang, H. Wu, and J. L. Xue, "An efficient heuristic for instruction scheduling on clustered VLIW processors," in *Proceedings of the 14th International Conference on Compilers, Architectures and Synthesis for Embedded Systems (CASES '11)*, pp. 35–44, October 2011.

[16] C. Q. Xu, C. J. Xue, J. T. Hu, and E. H. M. Sha, "Optimizing scheduling and intercluster connection for application-specific DSP processors," *IEEE Transactions on Signal Processing*, vol. 57, no. 11, pp. 4538–4547, 2009.

[17] R. Nagpal and Y. N. Srikant, "Register file energy optimization for snooping based clustered VLIW architectures," in *Proceedings of the 19th International Symposium on Computer Architecture and High Performance Computing (SBAC-PAD 07)*, pp. 161–168, Rio Grande do Sul, Brazil, October 2007.

[18] Y. Z. Huang, M. Y. Zhao, and C. J. Xue, "WCET-aware rescheduling register allocation for real-time embedded systems with clustered VLIW architecture," in *Proceedings of the 13th ACM SIGPLAN/SIGBED International Conference on Languages, Compilers, Tools and Theory for Embedded Systems (LCTES '12)*, pp. 31–40, May 2012.

[19] X. Yang, H. He, and Z. Z. Tang, "Energy consumption optimized scheduling algorithm for clustered VLIW architecture," *Journal of Low Power Electronics*, vol. 8, no. 2, pp. 146–157, 2012.

[20] Z. X. Zhou, H. He, Y. J. Zhang, Y. H. Sun, and A. Chen, "A 2-dimension force-directed scheduling algorithm for register-file-connectivity clustered VLIW architecture," in *Proceedings of the IEEE International Conference on Application-Specific Systems, Architectures and Processors (ASAP '07)*, pp. 371–376, Montreal, Canada, July 2007.

[21] C. Lee and M. Stoodley, "UTDSP BenchMark Suite," 2012, http://www.eecg.toronto.edu/~corinna/DSP/infrastructure/UTDSP.html.

[22] 2012, http://euler.slu.edu/~fritts/mediabench/.

[23] "The gem5 simulator system: a modular platform for computer system architecture research," 2012, http://www.m5sim.org/Main_Page.

[24] A. Bona, M. Sami, D. Sciuto, C. Silvano, V. Zaccaria, and R. Zafalon, "Reducing the complexity of instruction-level power models for VLIW processors," *Design Automation for Embedded Systems*, vol. 10, no. 1, pp. 49–67, 2005.

Permissions

The contributors of this book come from diverse backgrounds, making this book a truly international effort. This book will bring forth new frontiers with its revolutionizing research information and detailed analysis of the nascent developments around the world.

We would like to thank all the contributing authors for lending their expertise to make the book truly unique. They have played a crucial role in the development of this book. Without their invaluable contributions this book wouldn't have been possible. They have made vital efforts to compile up to date information on the varied aspects of this subject to make this book a valuable addition to the collection of many professionals and students.

This book was conceptualized with the vision of imparting up-to-date information and advanced data in this field. To ensure the same, a matchless editorial board was set up. Every individual on the board went through rigorous rounds of assessment to prove their worth. After which they invested a large part of their time researching and compiling the most relevant data for our readers. Conferences and sessions were held from time to time between the editorial board and the contributing authors to present the data in the most comprehensible form. The editorial team has worked tirelessly to provide valuable and valid information to help people across the globe.

Every chapter published in this book has been scrutinized by our experts. Their significance has been extensively debated. The topics covered herein carry significant findings which will fuel the growth of the discipline. They may even be implemented as practical applications or may be referred to as a beginning point for another development. Chapters in this book were first published by Hindawi Publishing Corporation; hereby published with permission under the Creative Commons Attribution License or equivalent.

The editorial board has been involved in producing this book since its inception. They have spent rigorous hours researching and exploring the diverse topics which have resulted in the successful publishing of this book. They have passed on their knowledge of decades through this book. To expedite this challenging task, the publisher supported the team at every step. A small team of assistant editors was also appointed to further simplify the editing procedure and attain best results for the readers.

Our editorial team has been hand-picked from every corner of the world. Their multi-ethnicity adds dynamic inputs to the discussions which result in innovative outcomes. These outcomes are then further discussed with the researchers and contributors who give their valuable feedback and opinion regarding the same. The feedback is then collaborated with the researches and they are edited in a comprehensive manner to aid the understanding of the subject.

Apart from the editorial board, the designing team has also invested a significant amount of their time in understanding the subject and creating the most relevant covers. They scrutinized every image to scout for the most suitable representation of the subject and create an appropriate cover for the book.

The publishing team has been involved in this book since its early stages. They were actively engaged in every process, be it collecting the data, connecting with the contributors or procuring relevant information. The team has been an ardent support to the editorial, designing and production team. Their endless efforts to recruit the best for this project, has resulted in the accomplishment of this book. They are a veteran in the field of academics and their pool of knowledge is as vast as their experience in printing. Their expertise and guidance has proved useful at every step. Their uncompromising quality standards have made this book an exceptional effort. Their encouragement from time to time has been an inspiration for everyone.

The publisher and the editorial board hope that this book will prove to be a valuable piece of knowledge for researchers, students, practitioners and scholars across the globe.

List of Contributors

Jong-Hyun Lee and Chang Wook Ahn
Department of Computer Engineering, Sungkyunkwan University (SKKU), Suwon 440-746, Republic of Korea

Jinung An
Robot Research Division, Daegu Gyeongbuk Institute of Science & Technology (DGIST), Daegu 711-873, Republic of Korea

Yongquan Zhou
College of Information Science and Engineering, Guangxi University for Nationalities, Nanning 530006, China
Guangxi Key Laboratory of Hybrid Computation and IC Design Analysis, Nanning 530006, China

Hongqing Zheng
College of Information Science and Engineering, Guangxi University for Nationalities, Nanning 530006, China

Simona Bernardi
Centro Universitario de la Defensa, Academia General Militar, Zaragoza, Spain

Jose Merseguer
Departamento de Informatica e Ingenieria de Sistemas, Universidad de Zaragoza, 50018 Zaragoza, Spain

Dorina C. Petriu
Department of Systems and Computer Engineering, Carleton University, Ottawa, ON, Canada

Lihong Guo
Changchun Institute of Optics, Fine Mechanics and Physics, Chinese Academy of Sciences, Changchun 130033, China

Gaige Wang
Changchun Institute of Optics, Fine Mechanics and Physics, Chinese Academy of Sciences, Changchun 130033, China
Graduate School of Chinese Academy of Sciences, Beijing 100039, China

Hong Duan
School of Computer Science and Information Technology, Northeast Normal University, Changchun 130117, China

Yi-Ling Wu and Bertrand M. T. Lin
Institute of Information Management, National Chiao Tung University, Hsinchu 30010, Taiwan

Tsu-Feng Ho and Shyong Jian Shyu
Department of Computer Science and Information Engineering, Ming Chuan University, Taoyuan 33348, Taiwan

Ajit Narayanan and Yi Chen
School of Computing and Mathematical Sciences, Auckland University of Technology, Auckland 1010, New Zealand

Shaoning Pang
Department of Computing, Unitec Institute of Technology, Auckland 1025, New Zealand

Ban Tao
National Institute of Information and Communications Technology, Tokyo 184-8795, Japan

Yang-Cheng Lin
Department of Arts and Design, National Dong Hwa University, Hualien 974, Taiwan

Chung-Hsing Yeh
Faculty of Information Technology, Monash University, Clayton, VIC 3800, Australia

Chen-Cheng Wang
Department of Computer Simulation and Design, Shih Chien University, Kaohsiung 845, Taiwan

Chun-Chun Wei
Department of Industrial Design, National Cheng Kung University, Tainan 701, Taiwan

Jun-Yi Hu
School of Mechanical Engineering, Southwest Jiaotong University, Chengdu 610031, China
CSR Qishuyan Institute Co. Ltd., Changzhou 213011, China

Rong-Jiang Ma and Nan-Yang Yu
School of Mechanical Engineering, Southwest Jiaotong University, Chengdu 610031, China

Jing Tian, Bing Yu, Dan Yu and Shilong Ma
State Key Laboratory of Software Development Environment, Beihang University, No. 37 Xueyuan Road, Haidian District, Beijing 100191, China

Liping Chen and Weitao Ha
College of Mathematics and Information Science, Network Engineering Technology Center, Weinan Normal University, Weinan 714000, China

Guojun Zhang
College of Communication Engineering, Network Engineering Technology Center, Weinan Normal University, Weinan 714000, China

Shingchern D. You and Woei-Kae Chen
Department of Computer Science and Information Engineering, National Taipei University of Technology, Taipei 104, Taiwan

Wei-Hwa Chen
Hon-Hai Precision Industry Co. Ltd, Tucheng District, New Taipei City 236, Taiwan

Yanjiang Wang, Yujuan Qi and Yong ping Li
College of Information and Control Engineering, China University of Petroleum, No. 66, Changjiang West Road, Economic and Technological Development Zone, Qingdao 266580, China

Aihab Khan
Department of Computing & Technology, Iqra University, Islamabad 44000, Pakistan

Syed Afaq Husain
Faculty of Computer Science & IT, King Faisal University, Ahsaa 31982, Saudi Arabia

Mehmet Baygin
Computer Engineering Department, Ardahan University, Ardahan, Turkey

Mehmet Karakose
Computer Engineering Department, Firat University, Elazig, Turkey

Ruirui Zhang, Tao Li and Xin Xiao
College of Computer Science, Sichuan University, Chengdu 610065, China

Yuanquan Shi
College of Computer Science, Huaihua University, Huaihua 418000, China

Ningduo Peng, Guangchun Luo, Ke Qin and Aiguo Chen
School of Computer Science and Engineering, University of Electronic Science and Technology of China, Chengdu, Sichuan 611731, China

Sheng Liu
College of Computer Science & Technology, Zhejiang University of Technology, Hangzhou 310023, China
Key Laboratory of Visual Media Intelligent Processing Technology of Zhejiang Province, Hangzhou 310023, China

Haiqiang Jin, Xiaojun Mao and Binbin Zhai
College of Computer Science & Technology, Zhejiang University of Technology, Hangzhou 310023, China

Ye Zhan
School of Accounting, Zhejiang University of Finance and Economics, Hangzhou 310018, China

Xiaofei Feng
College of Computer and Information Engineering, Zhejiang Gongshang University, Hangzhou 310018, China

Fengqi Li, Chuang Yu, Nanhai Yang, Feng Xia, Guangming Li and Fatemeh Kaveh-Yazdy
School of Software, Dalian University of Technology, Dalian 116620, China

Haijing Tang and Xu Yang
School of Software, Beijing Institute of Technology, Beijing, China

Siye Wang and Yanjun Zhang
School of Information and Electronics, Beijing Institute of Technology, Beijing, China